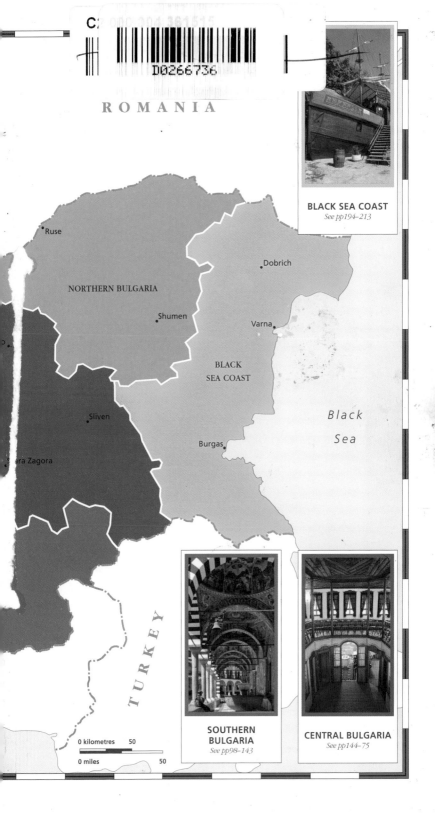

ROMANIA

BLACK SEA COAST
See pp194–213

Ruse

Dobrich

NORTHERN BULGARIA

Shumen

Varna

BLACK
SEA COAST

Sliven

Burgas

Black

Sea

ara Zagora

TURKEY

**SOUTHERN
BULGARIA**
See pp98–143

CENTRAL BULGARIA
See pp144–75

0 kilometres   50

0 miles   50

D0266736

BULGARIA

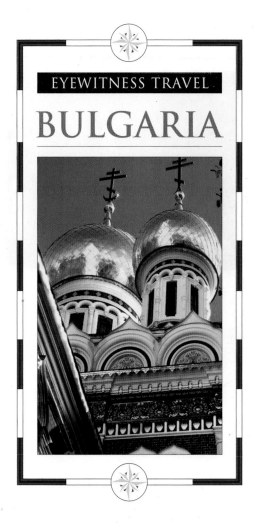

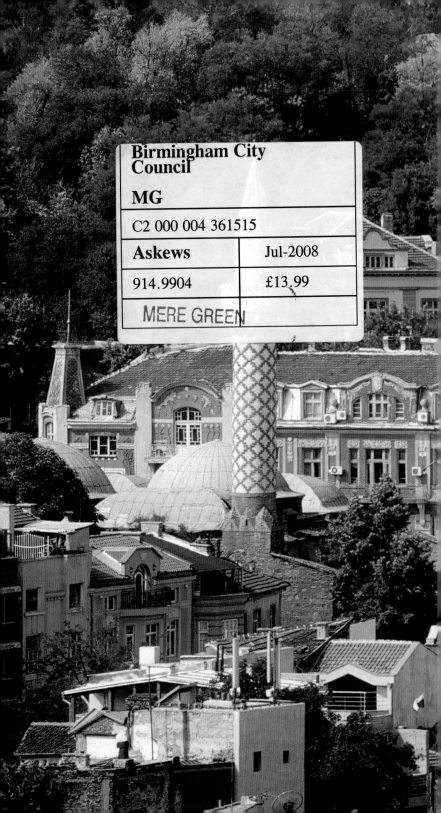

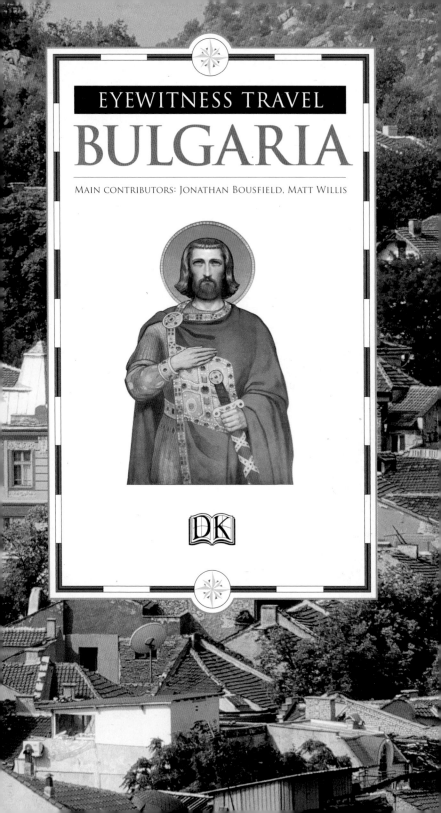

EYEWITNESS TRAVEL

BULGARIA

Main contributors: Jonathan Bousfield, Matt Willis

DK

LONDON, NEW YORK,
MELBOURNE, MUNICH AND DELHI
www.dk.com

Produced by Hachette Livre Polska Sp. z o.o.

MAIN CONTRIBUTORS Jonathan Bousfield, Matt Willis

SENIOR GRAPHIC DESIGNER Paweł Pasternak
GRAPHIC DESIGNER Paweł Kamiński
SENIOR EDITOR Agnieszka Trzebska-Cwalina
EDITOR Anetta Radziszewska

PHOTOGRAPHERS
Dorota and Mariusz Jarymowicz, Mirek Osip, Piotr Ostrowski

ILLUSTRATORS
Michał Burkiewicz, Dorota Jarymowicz, Paweł Marczak, Joanna Sitarek

CARTOGRAPHER
Magda Polak

Dorling Kindersley Limited
LIST MANAGERS Vivien Antwi, Christine Stroyan
MANAGING ART EDITOR Jane Ewart
SENIOR EDITOR Hugh Thompson
DESIGNER Kate Leonard
EDITOR Lucilla Watson
FACTCHECKER Petya Mulkova
DTP Natasha Lu, Jamie McNeill
PRODUCTION Linda Dare

Reproduced in Singapore by Colourscan
Printed and bound by L. Rex Printing Company Limited, China

First published in Great Britain in 2008
by Dorling Kindersley Limited
80 Strand, London WC2R 0RL

ISBN 978 1 40532 938 5

FLOORS ARE REFERRED TO THROUGHOUT IN ACCORDANCE WITH
UK USAGE; IE THE "FIRST FLOOR" IS THE FLOOR ABOVE GROUND LEVEL.

Front cover main image: Bachkovo Monastery

**The information in this
DK Eyewitness Travel Guide is checked regularly.**

Every effort has been made to ensure that this book is as up-to-date
as possible at the time of going to press. Some details, however,
such as telephone numbers, opening hours, prices, gallery hanging
arrangements and travel information are liable to change. The publishers cannot accept responsibility for any consequences arising
from the use of this book, nor for any material on third party web-
sites, and cannot guarantee that any website address in this
book will be a suitable source of travel information. We value the
views and suggestions of our readers very highly. Please write to:
Publisher, DK Eyewitness Travel Guides, Dorling Kindersley,
80 Strand, London WC2R 0RL.

Limestone cliffs near Kamen Briag,
on the Black Sea coast

CONTENTS

HOW TO USE
THIS GUIDE **6**

INTRODUCING
BULGARIA

DISCOVERING
BULGARIA
10

PUTTING BULGARIA
ON THE MAP **12**

A PORTRAIT OF
BULGARIA **14**

BULGARIA THROUGH
THE YEAR
34

Church of the Archangels Michael
and Gabriel at Arbanasi

◁ View over the Old Town, Plovdiv

Raikova Kŭshta, a 19th-century
house-museum in Tryavna

Sculpture of a lion at the Tomb of
the Unknown Soldier in Sofia

Houses on the cliffside at Veliko
Tŭrnovo, on the Yantra River

Aleksandŭr Nevski Memorial Church in
Sofia, the city's finest building

HOW TO USE THIS GUIDE

This travel guide helps you to get the most from your visit to Bulgaria, providing detailed practical information as well as expert recommendations. *Introducing Bulgaria* maps the whole country and sets it in its historical and cultural context. The first section, on *Sofia*, gives an overview of the capital's main attractions. Bulgaria's regions are charted in the *Area by Area* section, which covers all the important towns, cities and places around the country, with photographs, maps and illustrations. Details of hotels, restaurants, shops and markets, entertainment and sports are found in *Travellers' Needs*, while the *Survival Guide* contains advice on everything from medical services and public transport to personal safety.

SOFIA

An individual section is devoted to Sofia. This features all the main sights in the city centre as well as other major attractions in the outskirts.

1 City Map
For easy reference, Sofia's main sights and attractions are numbered and plotted on a map. Sights in the city centre are also shown on the Sofia Street Finder *on pages 92–7.*

A suggested route for a walk is shown in red.

2 Street-by-Street map
This bird's-eye view shows the heart of each sightseeing area. The sights carry the same numbers here as on the city map and the fuller description on subsequent pages.

Stars indicate the sights that no visitor should miss.

3 Detailed information
All the important sights in Sofia are described individually. Practical information includes a map reference, opening hours and telephone numbers. The key to the symbols used can be found on the back flap.

SOUTHERN BULGARIA

1 Introduction
The landscape, history and character of each region are portrayed here, with a description of how the area has developed over the centuries and what it offers to visitors today.

BULGARIA AREA BY AREA
The coloured areas shown on the map on the book's inside front cover show the five main sightseeing regions, into which Bulgaria has been divided. Each is covered in a full chapter in *Bulgaria Area by Area (see pp54–5)*. The most interesting towns and places to visit are numbered on *Regional Maps* throughout the book.

Exploring Central Bulgaria

2 Regional Map
This shows the road network and gives an illustrated overview of the whole area. All interesting places to visit are numbered and there are also useful tips on getting around the region by road or train.

Each area of Bulgaria can be quickly identified by the colour coding on the inside front cover.

Sights at a Glance shows all sights that are covered in the chapter.

3 Major sights
Historic buildings are dissected to reveal their interiors; museums and galleries have colour-coded floorplans to help you find the most important exhibits.

Bachkovo Monastery

The Visitors' Checklist gives all the practical information needed to plan your visit.

4 Detailed information
All the important towns and other places to visit are described individually. They are listed in order, following the numbering on the Exploring map. Each entry has details of the main sights.

Nesebŭr

A town map shows the location of all the sights described in the text.

INTRODUCING BULGARIA

DISCOVERING BULGARIA

With fine beaches and ski resorts, Bulgaria is well known both as a summer holiday destination and as a mecca for winter sports enthusiasts. But the country offers much more than this. Away from the bustling and sophisticated capital, Sofia, are the fascinating highland villages of the central Balkans

Bulgarian farmer on a donkey

and picturesque small towns with icon-filled churches, the dramatic cliffscapes of the Black Sea coast and several nature reserves. Medieval monasteries nestle in the folds of the Rila, Pirin and Rhodope mountains and, all over the country, medieval fortresses stand as reminders of Bulgaria's illustrious history.

Banya Bashi Mosque in central Sofia, built in the 16th century

SOFIA

- National Archaeological Museum
- Aleksandûr Nevski Memorial Church
- Open spaces of Mt Vitosha

Few capitals bear the imprint of history as clearly as Sofia, Bulgaria's largest city and home to up to one fifth of its inhabitants. Roman masonry still juts from the walls of city-centre churches such as Sveta Sofia and the Rotunda of St George, while fragments of Byzantine fortifications survive in pedestrian subways.

The Ottomans left Sofia with some fine 15th-century architecture, such as the Banya Bashi Mosque and the Buyuk Mosque. The latter is now home to the **National Archaeological Museum** *(see pp68–9)*, with an impressive collection of ancient Thracian, Roman and medieval exhibits.

The end of Ottoman rule in 1878 was followed by a building boom that brought western European architectural styles to Sofia's central streets. However, the most imposing edifice of the post-Liberation era is the many-domed **Aleksandûr Nevski Memorial Church** *(see pp72–3)*, raised to commemorate Russia's role in the Liberation and built in a Russian architectural style.

On the outskirts of Sofia, the hillside-hugging suburb of Boyana contains the National History Museum, in a residence formerly used by the country's Communist elite, and Boyana Church, a masterpiece of medieval Bulgarian art whose interior

is covered in dazzling 13th-century frescoes. Above Boyana looms **Mount Vitosha** *(see pp88–9)*, whose forested slopes are ideal for some gentle hiking and fresh air.

Apart from its cultural and historical attractions, Sofia is a brash, fast-moving city buzzing with activity day and night. Theatres, cinemas and nightclubs make for a vibrant nightlife. There is also a wider variety of restaurants here than anywhere else in Bulgaria, and a great choice of lively cafés and bars.

SOUTHERN BULGARIA

- Cobbled streets of Plovdiv
- Stunning natural wonders of the Rhodope Mountains
- Unmissable Rila Monastery

Any exploration of southern Bulgaria usually starts in **Plovdiv** *(see pp134–9)*, where Roman, Ottoman and restored 19th-century Bulgarian monuments are crowded together in a tight maze of delightful cobbled alleyways. Immediately to the south of

The Seven Lakes region in the Rila Mountains of southwestern Bulgaria

◁ Early 19th-century illustration of a Bulgarian village on the Danube

Plovdiv are the **Rhodope Mountains** *(see pp126–41)*, a culturally mixed area where Muslim and Christian villages nestle in pine-covered valleys. The Rhodopes also have some stunning natural attractions, with the Trigrad Gorge and stalactite-filled Yagodina Cave among the highlights.

To the southwest, the skiing and hiking resort of Bansko is the gateway to the Pirin Mountains, characterized by steep granite peaks and the alluring shapes of the sand pyramids above the vine-growing town of Melnik.

Northwest of the Rhodopes are the Rila Mountains, where Bulgaria's highest peaks tower above glacial lakes and alpine meadows. The region's hub is the unmissable **Rila Monastery** *(see pp108–11)*, a centre of the arts and scholarship in the 19th century, and an enduring symbol of the struggle to keep Bulgarian culture alive during the long period of Ottoman rule.

CENTRAL BULGARIA

- **Medieval Veliko Tŭrnovo**
- **Pretty rural heritage and architecture in Koprivshtitsa**
- **Colourful folk festivals in the Valley of the Roses**

The city of **Veliko Tŭrnovo** *(see pp156–60)*, with hilltop fortress, medieval churches, and cliff-hugging 19th-century houses, was Bulgaria's capital in the Middle Ages, and it is still the symbolic heartland of Bulgarian culture.

Many of the great monastic foundations nestle in nearby valleys. Among them is Troyan Monastery, which is filled with vibrant frescoes and icons. The surrounding hills are dotted with towns and villages where traditional Bulgarian architecture and folk art have been beautifully preserved as museum-towns. **Koprivshtitsa** *(see pp172–5)*, is the most famous of these, although the less visited Bozhentsi, south of Veliko Tŭrnovo, and Zheravna, in the east, are equally delightful.

Courtyard at Troyan Monastery, with frescoes of the Last Judgment

The southern edge of central Bulgaria is marked by the **Valley of the Roses** *(see p166)*. It is lined with historic towns associated with Bulgaria's rose-oil industry, celebrated at the annual Festival of Roses.

NORTHERN BULGARIA

- **Extraordinary geological features**
- **Dramatic Rusenski Lom**
- **Compelling historic sites**

Rolling plateaus and plains make up much of northern Bulgaria. The western part of the region, however, features some extraordinary geological features, such as the dramatic **Vratsa and Iskur Gorges** *(see p183–4)* and the eerie pillars of **Belogradchik** *(see p180)*. To the north the region is bordered by the Danube, whose banks are lined with

historic towns. Other highlights are the riverside fortress at Vidin, in the far northwest, and fine Art Nouveau houses at Ruse, to the northeast. Hidden away in **Rusenski Lom** *(see p188)*, immediately south of Ruse, are dramatic vestiges of Bulgarian medieval culture, notably the cave-hewn rock monasteries of Ivanovo and the hilltop fortress of Cherven.

Near Ruse lie some of the country's most compelling historic sites – the **Sveshtari Thracian Tomb** *(see p189)*, the Roman city of **Nikopolis ad Istrum** *(see p185)*, the enigmatic rock-carved **Madara Horseman** *(see p192)*, and medieval citadels at Preslav and Shumen.

BLACK SEA COAST

- **Gorgeous sandy beaches**
- **Spectacular rocky cliffs**
- **Historic heritage**

With plenty of sunshine and long **sandy beaches**, the Black Sea coast has long been a key summer destination. Part of it consists of resorts with beachfront hotels and bars, but there are also quiet villages and rocky coves to explore, with Strandzha Nature Park to the south and the **rugged cliffs** to the north *(see pp202–3)*.

The region also has a rich historic heritage – Roman ruins in **Varna** *(see pp198–9)*, medieval churches in **Nesebŭr** *(see pp208–9)* and old houses in **Sozopol** *(see p210)*.

Dramatic limestone cliffs at Kamen Briag, on the northern Black Sea coast

Putting Bulgaria on the Map

Located in the southeastern corner of Europe, Bulgaria covers an area of 110,550 sq km (42,685 sq miles). It is bordered by Turkey, Greece, Macedonia, Serbia and Romania, with the Black Sea on its eastern side, and the Danube as much of its northern border. The rugged Stara Planina, or Balkan range, runs across central Bulgaria from west to east, with the higher Rila and Pirin massifs to the southwest, and the Rhodope mountains to the south. Sofia, the capital, is Bulgaria's largest city, and the hub of the country's political, economic and cultural life.

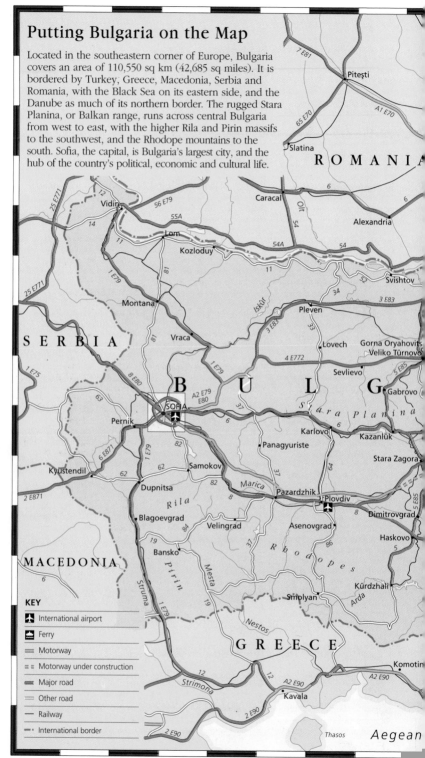

KEY

✈	International airport
⛴	Ferry
═	Motorway
═ ═	Motorway under construction
▬	Major road
═	Other road
—	Railway
–·–	International border

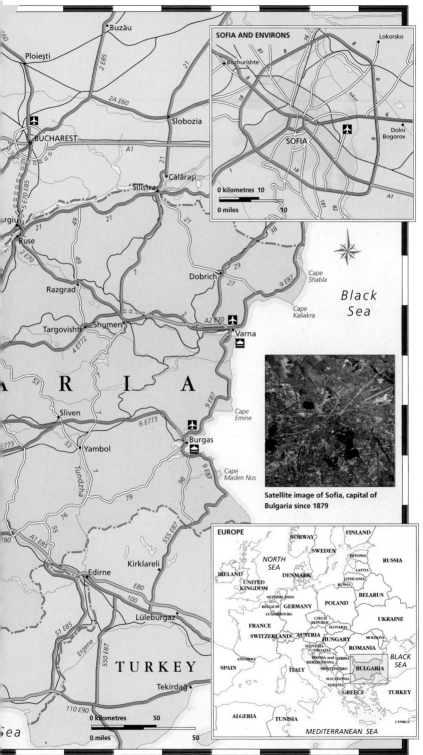

Buzău

Ploieşti

2 E85

21

2A E60

Slobozia

SOFIA AND ENVIRONS

16

81

8

Lokorsko

Bozhurishte

8

18

8

Iskŭr

6

SOFIA

Dolni
Bogorov

18

8

Călăraşi

BUCHAREST

A1

0 kilometres   10

0 miles   10

181

82

A1

21

Silistra

21

21

rgiu

21   69

Ruse   49

2 E70

21

38

Razgrad   1

29

Dobrich

27

9 E87

Cape
Shabla

Black
Sea

Targovishte   Shumen

4 E772

A2 E70

Cape
Kaliakra

2

Varna

A   R   I   A

53

Sliven

1

6 E773

Cape
Emine

E773   53

Yambol

Tundzha   1

Burgas

9 E87

Cape
Maslen Nos

98

Satellite image of Sofia, capital of
Bulgaria since 1879

79

76

55

80

A1 E85

Kirklareli

Edirne

E80

100

Lüleburgaz

Ergene

51 E85

550 E87

EUROPE

NORWAY   FINLAND

NORTH
SEA   SWEDEN   ESTONIA   RUSSIA

IRELAND   DENMARK   LATVIA

UNITED
KINGDOM   LITHUANIA
RUSSIA   BELARUS

NETHERLANDS
BELGIUM   GERMANY   POLAND

LUXEMBOURG   UKRAINE

CZECH
REPUBLIC

FRANCE   SLOVAKIA

SWITZERLAND   AUSTRIA   HUNGARY   MOLDOVA

SLOVENIA
CROATIA   ROMANIA   BLACK
SEA

ANDORRA   BOSNIA and   SERBIA
HERZEGOVINA

SPAIN   ITALY   MONTENEGRO   BULGARIA

MACEDONIA   TURKEY

ALBANIA

GREECE

ALGERIA   TUNISIA   CYPRUS

MEDITERRANEAN SEA

TURKEY

Tekirdağ

110 E90

ea

0 kilometres   50

0 miles   50

A PORTRAIT OF BULGARIA

A combination of stunning scenery and Mediterranean climate have made Bulgaria one of Europe's fastest-growing tourist destinations. Attention has focused on the Black Sea beaches and high-altitude winter resorts, but the sheer diversity of natural beauty spots, archaeological sites and picture-postcard villages ensures that there is much more here to stir the traveller's imagination.

Heritage plays a highly visible role in Bulgarian society, with medieval churches and monasteries drawing a steady stream of pilgrims, and folk festivals retaining an important position in rural life. Such traditions provide a contrast with contemporary Bulgaria's rapid transformation into a modern European society. Recent decades have witnessed the end of Communism, the birth of a market economy, and the country's integration into the European Union. This roller coaster of social change makes today's Bulgaria one of Europe's most vibrant and invigorating destinations.

Thracian gold from Kazanlŭk

Lined with long sandy beaches, Bulgaria's Black Sea coast is the country's most obviously captivating natural attribute – with purpose-built resorts such as Sunny Beach and Golden Sands alternating with historic ports such as Nesebûr and Sozopol.

Inland, some two-thirds of Bulgaria's territory is made up of hills and mountains. This vast area of wilderness provides plenty of scope for active holidays, whether hiking in summer or skiing in winter. The natural beauty and geographical isolation of the highland regions is one reason why so many monasteries were founded here in the Middle Ages.

Golden Sands, a popular purpose-built resort on the Black Sea coast

◁ Characterful 19th-century National Revival houses in the Old Town of Plovdiv

A glacial lake set in the extraordinary wild and remote Rila Mountains of southwestern Bulgaria

Rich in luminous icons and vibrant frescoes, monasteries such as Rila and Bachkovo shelter communities that preserve the spiritual heritage of the Bulgarian Orthodox Church. In many mountain villages, a traditional way of life, often based on sheep- or goat-farming, also survives. Settlements in the Pirin and Rhodope mountains still boast a wealth of 19th-century houses built in wood or stone. Some of these have opened their doors to tourists as rustic bed-and-breakfast establishments, giving these once-isolated communities a new lease of life.

BULGARIA'S BIGGEST CITIES

Bulgaria's key cities have very different personalities. Sofia, the capital, grew out of virtually nothing in the late 19th century, its boulevards laid out in imitation of those of Paris and Vienna. Vastly expanded during the Communist period, when huge housing estates were constructed for a growing population, Sofia is currently undergoing an even more dramatic metamorphosis into a metropolis of shopping malls, multiplex cinemas and glass-and-steel business hotels. Plovdiv, Bulgaria's second city, could not be more different, with a historic centre of cobbled alleys and the Oriental-flavoured mansions of wealthy Balkan trading dynasties. Bulgaria's summer capital is Varna, a brash riviera town boasting a lively nightlife and a prestigious programme of major cultural festivals. The centrally located city of Veliko Tûrnovo, with its dramatic castle ruins set above a

Sofia, Bulgaria's busy but beautiful capital

river gorge, is a lasting monument to the glories of Bulgaria's medieval tsars. Ruse is perhaps Bulgaria's most individual city, a Danube port that grew wealthy in the 19th century and is still full of Austrianate architecture.

MEETING POINT OF CIVILIZATIONS

Wherever you are in the country you will find the remnants of former civilizations. The Thracians ruled the country until they were conquered by the Romans in the 1st century BC. Thracian burial sites at Sveshtari, Kazanlûk and Starosel feature exquisite stone tombs, and deserve a place on every traveller's itinerary. Intricate Thracian jewellery also constitutes a major attraction of Bulgaria's museums.

The Thracians were superseded by the Romans, whose legacy is still visible in the ruined city of Nikopolis ad Istrum, the bathhouse complex in Varna, and in many other locations. The arrival of the Bulgars in the 7th century led to the construction of huge fortresses at Pliska and Preslav, whose ruins still make a dramatic impression. The medieval Bulgarian fortresses at Veliko Tûrnovo, Shumen and Cherven are more awe-inspiring still.

Roman theatre in Plovdiv, built in the 2nd century AD

Medieval Bulgaria was conquered by the Ottoman Turks, who in their turn left a significant cultural and architectural imprint on the country. Surviving mosques in towns and cities such as Sofia, Shumen and Plovdiv are among the most beautiful in the Balkans. During nearly five centuries of Ottoman rule, Bulgarian culture and traditions were preserved in the monasteries. A 19th-century upsurge in traditional values known as the National Revival led to the renovation of the great monasteries such as Rila, Troyan and Bachkovo, each of which was covered in glorious frescoes. Merchants in prosperous trading towns like Bansko, Koprivshtitsa and Tryavna built beautiful mansions using traditional crafts. Many of these mansions are open to visitors today.

Traditional country house in Melnik

MODERNITY AND TRADITION

One of Bulgaria's immediately visible peculiarities is that, unlike the rest of Europe, locals shake their heads when they say "yes", and nod when they mean "no". Such body language is symbolic of the way in which the country has remained remarkably resilient to outside influences and has preserved much of its folk culture.

Although 21st-century Bulgaria is an urbanized, skilled society, modernity coexists with much that is traditional. Goatherds graze flocks beside highways; donkeys are a viable, efficient alternative to tractors; and traditional foodstuffs play an important part in the Bulgarian lifestyle. Most people still buy their fruit and vegetables from open-air markets, preserving a taste for fresh, local produce. Knowledge of natural medicine is still widespread, and herbal pharmacies a feature of every high street. Folk festivals still mark the social calendar, ensuring that traditional songs, dances and costumes remain firmly rooted in the contemporary cultural mainstream. Even Bulgarian pop music is more in tune with the melodies and rhythms of the Orient than with anything from the West.

Priest at a Bulgarian Orthodox Church service

PEOPLE AND SOCIETY

Bulgaria has a population of just under 7.5 million. The majority of its inhabitants are Christian Orthodox Bulgarians, descended from the Slav tribes who settled in the eastern Balkans in the 6th century. They speak a language related to Serbian, Croatian and Slovene, and more distantly to Czech, Polish and Russian.

Like other Orthodox Slav nations, they use the Cyrillic alphabet – although there are plenty of young Bulgarians who use Latin script for text messages or emails. Just over 12 per cent of the population are Muslim descendants of Turks who settled here in the late Middle Ages, or ethnic Bulgarians who converted to Islam under the Ottoman occupation. Bulgaria's Turks were persecuted in the 1980s, but now enjoy equal rights and representation in parliament.

Bulgaria is also home to between 350,000 and 500,000 Roma, or gypsies, who are split roughly half-and-half between the Christian and Islamic faiths.

Traditional mule carts among vineyards in the Gavrailovo district near Sliven, central Bulgaria

The Roma have been largely excluded from the social mainstream, and the question of how to improve their social position is a recurring theme of Bulgarian politics.

A largely agricultural country, Bulgaria is a major producer of wine, tobacco, fruit, vegetables and grain. It also supplies the world's cosmetics industry with rose oil, from plantations in the aptly-named Valley of Roses in central Bulgaria.

Young rose-petal picker dressed in traditional costume

Recent decades have seen Bulgaria buffeted by social and economic change. Under the Communist regime, the Bulgarian people became accustomed to regular employment, low housing costs, free education and health care. The collapse of the Communist system in 1989 removed many of these certainties. Trade with Soviet Russia, the main export market, disappeared overnight. The conflicts in Yugoslavia disrupted transport routes to central Europe. Profitable industries were driven towards bankruptcy, and people lost their right to job security and adequate state pensions. Provincial towns suffered serious depopulation as young people left to find work in the cities. Between 1990 and 2005, an estimated 800,000 people, mostly young and well-qualified, went abroad in search of better jobs. These are people Bulgaria can ill afford to lose; its birth rate is among the lowest in Europe, and the population will decline further unless current demographic trends are reversed.

PRESENT-DAY BULGARIA

The last few years have witnessed dramatic changes in Bulgaria's political and economic fortunes. Bulgaria's accession to the European Union in January 2007 led to a huge increase in foreign investment. Government corruption, a major issue in the 1990s, was brought under a measure of control. Most importantly, the fruits of economic growth began to trickle down to ordinary Bulgarians, whose standards of living finally began to rise.

One of these success stories has been the tourist industry. The Bulgarian Black Sea coast was a big draw for Eastern European holidaymakers from the 1960s onwards, and the tourist industry has gone from strength to strength with Bulgaria's discovery by the rest of the world. Bulgaria's popularity as a holiday and second-home-owning destination has turned real estate into one of the fastest-growing sectors of the economy. While this has led to the construction of unattractive apartment blocks along the coast, it has also helped regenerate depopulated inland villages, where rustic houses are being restored and returned to life.

Visitors at a seafront restaurant in Nesebŭr

Bulgaria's Folk Heritage

The National Revival *(see pp48–9)* ensured that Bulgaria's folk traditions were kept alive and that local arts became part of a national movement. Further encouragement and organization on a national scale came during the Communist period, as folk arts were seen as suitable for the people. Today, as well as being a major feature of its museums, Bulgaria's folk heritage is very much a living tradition.

Ornately carved chair Many women still practise handicrafts such as embroidery and weaving, and tablecloths, rugs and blouses decorated with traditional folk motifs are a regular feature of outdoor markets.

Agriculture *is still very important to Bulgaria and the country's festivals are usually related to the annual cycles of nature.*

TRADITIONAL FOLK COSTUME

This differs greatly from one region to another in Bulgaria, with even the choice of colours varying from one village to the next. Men's costumes are less bright, although jackets and trousers can be decorated with fine braiding. The *kalpak,* a black sheepskin hat, has always been something of a national trademark, although it is rarely seen on the streets these days.

Traditional women's folk costumes *often feature a sukman (linen dress), a riza or koshulya (blouse with abstract or floral motifs) and a prestilka (patterned apron). Traditionally, married women wore headscarves, and unmarried girls went bare-headed, with flowers or strings of coins in their hair.*

Pafti *are large belt buckles, here of silver with finely wrought natural designs, that secured colourful woollen belts.*

EMBROIDERY AND WEAVING

Embroidery was used to add diversity, individuality and regional styles to folk costumes. Carpet weaving, which came from the East, flourished in the 18th to 19th centuries as Bulgaria supplied the Ottoman lands. The most famous carpet-weaving centres are Chiprovtsi and Kotel. Chiprovtsi carpets have geometric patterns based on birds and trees *(right, top)*. Kilims from Kotel display a wider range of primary colours and more abstract designs *(right, below)*.

Embroidery *stitching involves repetitive, layered geometric and floral designs and usually the colour red. Gabrovo is famous for its embroidery using gold threads.*

Handwoven rugs, *or* kilims, *are still made in a handful of villages in Bulgaria. The women work on wooden hand looms to produce the brightly patterned kilims that are so popular in the West.*

BULGARIAN FOLK MUSIC

Bulgarian singing has a huge repertoire of ritual songs and powerful, haunting laments, usually performed by women without musical accompaniment. Rural merrymaking involves a circle dance *(horo)* accompanied by a four- or five-piece band that often includes instruments such as the *gadulka*, the *tambura* (a long-necked lute) and the *tapan* (a bass drum). Highland shepherds play the *kaval* (wooden flute) and *gaida* (goatskin bagpipes), while the *zurna* is a clarinet-type instrument of the south.

Bulgaria's gypsies traditionally have an important place in village music-making and provide entertainment at rural wedding parties. Gypsy brass bands are a feature of towns in the northwest.

The gadulka *is a stringed instrument played with a bow, perhaps recalling the lyre of Orpheus?*

Musician playing the gaida (bagpipes)

FOLK FESTIVALS

A busy calendar of festivals and religious celebrations ensures that age-old songs and dances remain part of contemporary life. Traditional costumes, while no longer forming part of everyday attire, are still donned on such festive occasions. Some of these folk festivals attract participants and spectators from countries all over the world. Probably the largest folk event is the summer Koprivshtitsa Folk Festival, held every five years (the next one is in 2010). Other important summer festivals include the Apollonia Arts Festival in Sozopol, and international folk fairs in Varna and Nesebûr, on the Black Sea coast.

Baba Marta *is a tradition of giving red and white tassels on 1 March for good luck.*

Festival of the Rose *takes place in the Kazanlûk region from the end of May to mid-June and celebrates the rose-petal harvest. After the harvest has been completed, there is singing, dancing and celebration.*

OTHER FOLK ARTS

Expressions of creativity, folk arts usually develop unaided by any formal education or training, before then becoming characteristic of the culture in which they evolved. In an illiterate Bulgarian society, folk arts were an important means of preserving native culture. This is why they received such a boost during the National Revival. The importance of keeping folk crafts and traditions alive is still highly appreciated in Bulgaria. Together with commercial reasons, this is why Bulgarian folk traditions still flourish.

Woodcarving *flourished during the National Revival, when it was used for iconostases and grand ecclesiastical pieces. Today it embellishes more modest items, like this icon of the Madonna and Child.*

Folk pottery *is typically rustic and practical, with appliqué of floral or natural motifs and a simple glaze.*

Bulgarian Orthodox Church

Under Khan Boris I, Bulgaria was one of the first Eastern European nations to adopt the Christian faith. The religion spread rapidly in the country after the development of the Cyrillic alphabet, and later both Christianity and the Cyrillic script were exported to other Slav countries such as Serbia and Russia. In 1054 the Great Schism split the Christian community into the Roman Catholic Church in Western Europe and the Orthodox Church in the East. During the Ottoman period, the Bulgarian Orthodox Church was crucial in nurturing Bulgarian language and culture and is still an important part of the country's social fabric today.

Khan Boris I *was converted to Christianity by Kliment and Naum, the disciples of Cyril and Methodius, in AD 865.*

EARLY HISTORY

Khan Boris I wanted an autonomous Church for Bulgaria. He negotiated with both seats of Christian power, Constantinople and Rome, until in AD 870 the former granted Bulgaria an auto-nomous bishopric. In 1054, after disagreements mainly over doctrinal issues and jurisdiction, these two centres of Christianity split into what would become the Orthodox and Catholic churches.

Cyril and Methodius *were 9th-century Greek monks who tried to convert the Slavs. Cyrillic script is named after St Cyril, who laid the foundations of the Cyrillic alphabet.*

Candles are symbolic of many things, including the faith of the worshippers and the light of knowledge.

Monasteries, *like this one at Bachkovo (see pp142–3), were built in mountain valleys so as to be near God and far from worldly temptations. In the Ottoman period, the monasteries became important repositories of Bulgarian culture, language and faith.*

ORTHODOX WORSHIP

Orthodox services can be very atmospheric as the church is lit mainly by candles, and the air is heavy with incense. The whole service is sung, as the human voice is believed to be the best instrument for praising the Lord. The service is a sung dialogue between the clergy and the people. Traditionally there are no chairs as everyone, except the infirm, stands during the service as a sign of respect.

Under the Ottomans *the Bulgarian Church was again subordinate to Constantinople. But when Ottoman power waned, the Church re-asserted itself. By 1895 Christianity was the national religion and the Bulgarian Church won its independence in 1945. The seat of the patriarchate is the Aleksandûr Nevski Memorial Church (right).*

The Church struggled *under Communism and did not elect a patriarch until 1953. Maxim of Lovech (right) was elected in 1971. The 1991 Constitution recognizes Eastern Orthodoxy as the national religion.*

The cross *is an important symbol of the Church and has been described as the joining of the heavenly and the earthly. The three-barred cross, popular in Slavic countries, has an upper bar that represents the inscription over Christ's head, while the lower slanting bar represents the foot rest.*

PARTS OF A CHURCH

Orthodox churches are usually oriented on an east–west axis. Worshippers enter the church from the west (associated with Sin) and head up the aisle towards the light of Truth (in the east). The plan of a church is often either rectangular, like a ship (or Ark), or cruciform (like the Cross). Inside, the main space is the nave, with walls usually decorated with icons and frescoes. The altar, in the sanctuary, is hidden from worshippers' sight behind the icon screen, or iconostasis, but is visible during services, when the Royal Doors are opened.

Icons *of Christ and the saints play a major role in the Orthodox Church. Not a mere illustration, the icon is a sanctified object that helps the faithful sense the presence of God. Icons have therefore always been highly stylized, and are not intended to be realistic works of art. Icons were especially useful when literacy was very low.*

The congregation is traditionally separated, with men standing on the right and women on the left.

ICONOSTASIS

The iconostasis is a screen on which icons of saints are displayed. Dividing the faithful from the Sanctuary, it also symbolizes the division between Earth and Heaven. It is usually of dark wood delicately carved with natural motifs. Dragons, symbolizing sinful passions tamed by Christian faith, are a frequent motif in Bulgarian iconostases.

Beautiful frescoes, *like these 16th-century ones at Arbanasi, cover the walls of Bulgarian churches and monasteries. Fresco-painting was introduced from Byzantium in the Middle Ages, and Bulgarian artists developed their own style. A popular subject on west walls of churches is the Apocalypse, reminding the departing faithful of judgment for their actions.*

The order of icons *on an iconostasis is not rigid but usually follows the plan on the right. Rows may not follow the same sequence, and all five are not always featured. An icon of one of the church's patron saints sometimes takes the place of the icon of Christ.*

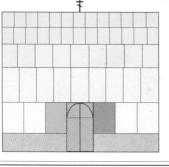

KEY

☐	Icons of the Patriarchs
☐	Icons of the Prophets
☐	Icons of Liturgical Feasts
☐	Deesis (most important)
☐	The Sovereign Row
☐	Icon of the Virgin
☐	Icon of Christ or Church
☐	The Royal Doors

Bulgarian Architecture

From Thracian times to the present day, Bulgaria has been home to several remarkable civilizations. As a result, the country's architectural landscape is rich and varied. While the Thracians left impressive decorated tombs, the Romans, who made Bulgaria part of their Balkan empire, were great builders of theatres, temples and public baths. Their Byzantine and Bulgarian successors built sturdy fortresses and spectacular churches. The Ottomans also had a taste for grand civic projects, erecting mosques, bazaars and elegant stone bridges. The 19th-century National Revival led to a flowering of domestic architecture rich in ornamentation. By contrast, modern architecture is generally far less appealing.

Aleksandûr Nevski Memorial Church in Sofia, built in the Neo-Byzantine style

ANCIENT ARCHITECTURE

Burial mounds built by ancient Thracian rulers are one of the trademarks of the Bulgarian landscape. Many have been excavated, revealing domed burial chambers richly decorated with finely executed paintings and sculpture. The graves were also filled with exquisite gold and silver treasure *(see pp40–41)*. The Thracians were conquered by the Romans, who built set-piece cities such as Nikopolis ad Istrum (now ruined), north of present-day Veliko Tûrnovo, and the first Christian churches such as the beautifully proportioned Rotunda of Sveti Georgi *(see p65)*.

The Roman amphitheatre in Plovdiv was built in the 2nd century AD, and is still used for concerts.

Thracian tomb *built around the 4th century BC for a king or rich nobleman. The design of these tombs vary, being either barrel-vaulted, pyramidal or beehive-shaped (as here).*

The interior of the tombs often features frescoes depicting burial rituals.

MEDIEVAL ARCHITECTURE: 12TH–14TH CENTURIES

The medieval Bulgarian tsars were prolific fortress-builders. Ruins at Pliska, Preslav and Cherven reveal thick walls constructed from impressively sized blocks of stone. The hilltop stronghold of Veliko Tûrnovo has been largely reconstructed to show just how formidable a 14th-century fortress really was. The 13th and 14th centuries were a golden age for Orthodox Church architecture, when both Bulgarian and Byzantine architects experimented with ever more graceful forms. The coastal town of Nesebûr contains several spectacular examples of churches from this period.

Veliko Tûrnovo *was the fortified capital of the 12th-century Second Bulgarian Kingdom. Despite walls 4 m (12 ft) thick, the fortress was captured by the Ottomans in 1393.*

Zemen Monastery Church, *built to a simple cruciform plan with a central cupola, is a wonderful example of 12th-century Bulgarian religious architecture. It is the only surviving building from the whole monastery complex.*

OTTOMAN ARCHITECTURE: 14TH–19TH CENTURIES

Hugely impressed by Balkan churches, Ottoman architects based the design of many of their mosques on the same basic principles. The 16th-century mosques in Sofia and Kyustendil feature graceful domes resting on cube-shaped buildings of brick and stone. The 18th-century Tombul Mosque in Shumen, complete with arcaded courtyard and ornate fountain, marks the high point of Ottoman architecture in Bulgaria. Although the last 100 years have seen the loss of many Ottoman buildings, many fine examples still remain, including caravanserai at Shumen and Yambol, public drinking fountains in Samokov, and beautiful hump-backed bridges in the Rhodope Mountains.

Tombul Mosque (1744), *the largest in Bulgaria, has an interesting structure. The base is square and the middle level octagonal, topped by a circular dome.*

The Devil's Bridge *at Ardino is 56 m (185 ft) wide and was built on an ancient trade route to the northern Aegean coast.*

NATIONAL REVIVAL: 19TH CENTURY

As well as creating great monasteries, the National Revival brought about a distinct domestic architecture. In the 19th century, merchants built lavish houses, mixing ideas imported from Western Europe with home-grown arts and crafts. With ornately painted exteriors, these houses featured fine carpets and carved wooden ceilings displaying local craftsmanship. Bulgaria's most famous 19th-century architect was Nikola Fichev, who used Bulgarian folk motifs in projects such as the Turkish Governor's House in Veliko Tûrnovo, the Church of Sveta Troitsa in Svishtov, and the Covered Bridge in Lovech.

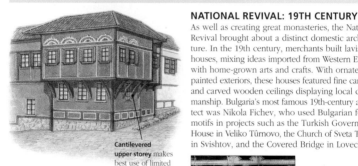

Cantilevered upper storey makes best use of limited ground space.

National Revival houses *mixed practicality with visual appeal. Originally the lower storey was made of stone, with few windows as it was a fortification.*

Oslekov House *(see p175), in the town of Koprivshtitsa, has a vivaciously painted façade held up by cedar pillars.*

MODERN ARCHITECTURE

Modernist currents had little influence in Bulgaria, although the Bulgarian National Bank in Sofia (1938) was an attempt to combine functionalism with Bulgarian style. After World War II the Communist regime built a handful of prestigious buildings, such as the Neo-Classical Party House in Sofia. To provide cheap housing, the Communists also built many concrete apartment blocks, which now look dull and neglected. Since the fall of Communism, sleek glass-walled office blocks have sprung up all over Bulgaria, although few of these are likely to stand the test of time. The Black Sea coast has also seen rapid building development.

National Palace of Culture (NDK), *built in Sofia and opened in 1981, has a muscular functionality. It is the largest conference and arts centre in southeastern Europe.*

Elenite, *a resort on the Black Sea Coast, marks a gradual move away from the ugly developments of the 1970s and 80s. The design recalls Rila Monastery's arcaded interior.*

Landscape and Wildlife of Bulgaria

The Bulgarian landscape offers enormous variety and biodiversity. Known for its long sandy beaches, the Black Sea coast also features dramatic cliffs and swampy river estuaries. Inland, fertile agricultural plains alternate with rugged mountain chains harbouring some of the most unspoiled wilderness areas in Europe. This pristine resource is inhabited by spectacular wildlife, such as wolves, bears, eagles and vultures. However, visitors are more likely to enjoy wildflower meadows flickering with clouds of colourful butterflies, and scenic rivers, lakes and marshes popular with native and migrant birds.

One of the beautiful high-altitude lakes of the Pirin Mountains

THE MOUNTAINS

European lynx

Bulgaria is home to four main mountain ranges: the Rila and Pirin in the south-west, the Rhodopes in the south, and the Balkan range, which runs the length of the country from east to west. The highest peak is Musala Ridge (2,952 m/9,700 ft) in the Rila Mountains. Moufflon and lynx prowl among Rhodope pine forests, where raspberries, bilberries and mushrooms grow. Brown bears, even, can be found in the wilder regions of the Rila, Pirin and Balkan ranges. The area also harbours numerous birds of prey, alongside rare woodpeckers and elusive black storks.

Edelweiss *flourishes at altitudes of more than 2,000m (6,560ft). A symbol of the Pirin Mountains, it is also a protected species.*

The rare black stork *can be found in spring, nesting in the limestone cliffs of the Rhodopes. From late summer, migrating populations can be seen along the Black Sea coast, heading south.*

ROCK FORMATIONS

Swallowtail butterfly

Spectacular rock formations dot the landscape – sheer-walled gorges, deep bat-filled caves, and bizarrely shaped stone columns. These are visitor attractions in their own right and home to many wildlife species. At Belogradchik, in northwestern Bulgaria, a huge area of red-brown rock pillars stands in stunning contrast to the woodland. The stone columns poking up from an arid landscape west of Varna are similarly dramatic, but the most famous rock formations are the so-called sand pyramids of Melnik. Here the brittle sandy hills have been eroded to form an other-worldly landscape of cones and pillars.

Egyptian vultures, *an endangered species, like open, dry and rocky terrain. One of the smaller varieties of vultures, they feed mainly on carrion, especially roadkill.*

The lesser horseshoe bat *is one of many bat species found in Bulgaria. Large colonies roost in caves and emerge together at dusk to hunt for insects.*

VALLEY OF ROSES

Really a lowland trough comprising three neighbouring valleys, the Valley of Roses is framed by the lofty Balkan mountains to the north and the thickly forested Sredna Gora hills to the south. The valley is named after the rose plantations which for centuries have supplied Bulgaria's rose-oil industry. Grown in villages around Karlovo and Kazanlûk, the crop is harvested as soon as the blooms appear in late May – before the oil evaporates, so you won't see the pink flowers unless you're visiting then. The valley also features vineyards, luscious fruit orchards, and meadows covered in wild flowers every spring.

The damask rose, imported for cultivation by Ottoman merchants

THE DANUBIAN PLAIN

North of the Balkan mountains, the area of rolling hills and fertile farmland known as the Danubian Plain stretches towards the Danube. Thanks to a temperate climate, leafy vineyards thrive here, producing some of the country's best wines. Elsewhere, broad fields of sunflowers provide glorious bursts of colour in summer. The easternmost part of the plain is

Pelican

Bulgaria's principal wheat-growing region. The vast Danube river system is home to many ducks, geese and herons, and in spring and autumn all of northern Bulgaria becomes a feeding ground for migrating birds, especially pelicans and white storks. The Danube island of Belene is also home to a colony of spoonbills in May.

Spoonbills *hunt for food by sieving water through their bill, and snapping it shut on insects, crustacea or small fish.*

THE COAST

The Black Sea coast, especially in the south, offers any number of glorious white-sand beaches. The northern part, around the Kaliakra peninsula, features dramatic cliffs, and coastal steppe land covered in

Lesser grey shrike

wild flowers. The estuaries of the Ropotamo and Kamchiya rivers are rich in subtropical vegetation and are a haven for water-snakes and other wildlife. In spring and autumn, the fish and insects of the coastal lagoons and lakes attract migrating birds such as lesser grey shrikes, pied wheateaters and all manner of terns.

Grass snakes *are harmless to humans and feed mainly on amphibians. Fairly common, they are easily identified by their yellow collar.*

Sunflowers *are a very important Bulgarian crop. Oil is extracted from the seeds.*

Wild flowers *are at their most colourful in the steppe between March and mid-July. You can see blue flax, peonies, adonises and every colour of iris. The meadows also attract many birds.*

Wine Growing Areas of Bulgaria

Thracian drinking vessel, or *rhyton*

Wine has been produced in Bulgaria since ancient Thracian times, when it played an important part in religious rituals. In the early 20th century, Western European grape varieties were introduced to the country, but it was not until the 1960s that Bulgaria started producing large quantities of quality wines and becoming one of the world's major wine exporters. Since then, Bulgarian wine has become a byword for high quality at a very affordable price.

Small oak casks *are used to add beneficial phenolic compounds to Bulgarian wines. The result is "Reserve" quality wines – the highest category.*

The Danubian Plain *holds about 30% of the country's vineyards. It is most famous for its red wine, especially Cabernet Sauvignon. The grapes are mostly still harvested by hand.*

Struma Valley's *favourable climate produces an excellent wine – Melnik Red – from a native varietal grape, Shiroka Melnishka, as well as good Merlots, and Cabernet Sauvignons.*

Vidin
Oryahovo
Danube
Svishtov
3 E83
Iskar
Pleven
Suhindol
4 E772
Stara Planina
Stara Planina
Sofia
Karlovo
Kazanluk
6
Marica
Plovdiv
Rila
Blagoevgrad
Brestovica
Asenovgrad
8
Rhodopes
Pirin
Struma
Melnik
Arda

BUYING WINE

Well-known vineyards like Damianitza, near Melnik *(see pp116–17),* and Todoroff, near Plovdiv *(see pp134–9),* are open to tourists, who can sample the wines and buy a bottle or two to take home. Elsewhere in Bulgaria, wine is usually sold direct from wine cellars, or from roadside stalls, and is often decanted straight from the barrel into plastic bottles or other containers. This is a fun way to buy wine cheaply, but the quality can vary. It is often better to wait until you can buy a labelled bottle of wine from a reputable shop. Specialist wine shops include Loza in Sofia, and Bai Gencho, a chain with branches throughout the country.

Wine outlet attached to a local vineyard

The Valley of Roses *contains some of the country's most fertile land. The eastern side of the region is known for its Red Misket – the rosy red grape yields a straw-coloured dry white wine. The western side produces a mix of red and white wines. The Rose Valley winery at Karlovo is known for its sweet white wine, Karlovski Misket.*

Black Sea vineyards, *such as those at the former royal palace of Evksinograd, produce excellent sweet dessert wines thanks to the long mild autumns. Inland, the rolling hills of Preslav are known for their dry white Traminer wine.*

Silistra
Ruse
Dobrich
Gorna Oryahovitsa
Veliko Turnovo
Shumen
Kamčija
Varna
Sliven
Sungurlare
Pomorie
Yambol
Burgas
Stara Zagora
Tundzha
Marica
Haskovo
Black Sea

KEY

	Danubian Plain
	Black Sea
	Valley of Roses
	Thracian Plain
	Struma Valley
	Regional red wine of quality
	Regional white wine of quality

Thracian Plain *enjoys long, dry summers and develops good, robust, red wines – Mavrud from Asenovgrad and Merlot from around Haskovo.*

Typical red wines *include Merlot and Cabernet Sauvignon, but there are native varieties, notably Melnik, Mavrud and Gumza. Rkatziteli was the first grape used for white wine, but today Chardonnay is more popular.*

TRIFON ZAREZAN

One of the most important days in the vintner's calendar, St Tryphon's feast day marks the start of the pruning season. It is celebrated by ritually sprinkling the vineyard with a mix of holy water and last year's wine, ensuring healthy growth and a good harvest in the year to come. Celebrations take place on 1 or 15 February, depending on the area, and the feasting and merrymaking continue well into the night.

Local dignitary celebrating Trifon Zarezan

Ski Resorts in Bulgaria

Offering spectacular scenery, snow from December through to May and excellent value for money, Bulgaria's ski resorts have long attracted foreign visitors. Over the last decade, the resorts' facilities and standard of accommodation have been dramatically modernized. The "Big Three" ski resorts are Bansko, Borovets and Pamporovo, each of which has its own character, ski runs for all levels of skill, and lively après-ski culture. However, do also consider staying at one of the smaller satellite resorts for a quieter, more traditional holiday.

Skiers on a piste on the slopes of Mount Musala, near Borovets

Dragalevtsi has a chair lift, about 30 minutes' walk uphill from the centre, which takes skiers to Aleko.

Mount Musala has some of the best snow cover in Bulgaria. Peaking at 2,925 m (9,600 ft), it is also the highest mountain in the Balkans.

Vitosha

Although it is somewhat overshadowed by the Big Three resorts, Mt Vitosha (see p88–9) has enough runs and is close enough to Sofia to be extremely attractive to many skiers in the capital – it can get very crowded at weekends. However, because of poor hotel facilities at Aleko, visitors are advised to find accommodation at Dragalevtsi or Simeonovo, further down the mountain.

Star attractions: Only 30 minutes from Sofia centre with fantastic city views from the runs

Borovets

The resort sits amid stunning scenery at the forested foot of Mount Musala. A combination of carpet lifts, gondolas and chair lifts whisk skiers to the top of the mountain. It caters for advanced skiers as well as beginners and there's even a ski-jump area. Long considered Bulgaria's top skiing destination, Borovets (see p107) has been eclipsed by Bansko's rampant growth. However, a €400 million "Super Borovets" project will vastly increase the resort's facilities and enhance its status.

Star attractions: Night skiing, great night life

Bansko

The newest of Bulgaria's "Big Three" resorts, Bansko (see pp118–120) has had massive investment in recent years. Hotels and apartment blocks have been built, and ski runs, lifts and cable cars cover the Pirin Mountains that tower majestically over the town. The ski runs are suitable for all abilities and for all types of skiing – boarders, cross-country, extreme and an area for tricks. However, despite intense development, Bansko is still a cozy town, with traditional taverns as well as modern bars and clubs.

Star attractions: Snowboard Park at 2,500 m (8,200 ft), uninterrupted 16-km (10-mile) ski run

The Pirin Mountains in winter, spectacular playground of skiers, snowboarders and snowshoers from Bulgaria and western Europe

Chepelare is a very small skiing resort with four fairly undemanding ski runs and a highest peak of 1,873 m (6,145 ft). However, it has a children's ski centre and would make a good place to stay for beginners. It is also a convenient and inexpensive base from which to ski at the much larger and more developed resort of Pamporovo.

Pamporovo

Bulgaria's southernmost and sunniest ski resort, Pamporovo is a purpose-built resort, with villas and hotels scattered around the base of pine-forested ski runs. Geared to catering for large groups, Pamporovo has long attracted Western European visitors on inexpensive package holidays.

Star attractions:

Beautiful scenery
Excellent for beginner/intermediate skiers

Mount Snezhanka, which is just 1,926 m (6,321 ft) high, has gentle slopes, with short runs suitable for beginners and intermediate skiers.

STATISTICS

BANSKO
Resort at 925 m (3,035 ft)
Highest skiing 2,600 m (8,500 ft)
65 km (40 miles) from Sofia
13 lifts, 14 runs
Longest run 7 km (4 miles)
Total skiing 65 km (40 miles)
Cross country 5 km (3 miles)
Snow December– May

BOROVETS
Resort at 1,350 m (4,430 ft)
Highest skiing 2,560 m (8,400 ft)
73 km (45 miles) from Sofia
14 lifts, 19 runs
Longest run 12 km (7½ miles)
Total skiing 58 km (36 miles)
Cross country 35 km (22 miles)
Snow December–April

PAMPOROVO
Resort at 1,650 m (5,410 ft)
Highest skiing 1,937 m (6,350 ft)
260 km (160 miles) from Sofia
18 lifts, 8 runs
Total skiing 25 km (16 miles)
Cross country 40 km (25 miles)
Snow December–April

VITOSHA
Resort at 1,800 m (5,900 ft)
Highest skiing 2,290 m (7,500 ft)
10 km (6 miles) from Sofia
8 lifts, 6 runs
22 km of runs
Longest run 5 km (3 miles)
Total skiing 40 km (25 miles)
Cross country 10 km (6 miles)
Snow December–May

KEY

═══ Motorway

── Main road

── Other road

△ Peak

✕ Pass

SNOWSHOEING

The sport developed from the necessity of having to get around in deep snow. Tribesmen used sticks and animal skins to create shoes with a large enough surface area to support the wearer's weight on the snow. These days, however, you use lightweight ski poles to help with balance and effective snowshoes, and once you work up a rhythm it comes quite naturally. It's easy but quite tiring. The joy of it is that you can get away into the silent, unspoilt wilderness of the mountains and really have a chance to take it in. And it's great exercise too. Snowshoeing trips can be organized for you by many tour operators (see p251).

Snowshoers enjoying the beautiful winter scenery of the mountains

Bulgaria's Coastline

Bulgaria is deservedly famous for its golden sandy beaches. These make up 30 per cent of the country's Black Sea coastline, which stretches for 378 km (235 miles). At the major resorts of Sunny Beach, Golden Sands and Albena, the beaches have Blue Flag status and life-guards, and offer waterskiing, jet-skiing, para-skiing, and a multitude of other water-related activities. However, swimmers and sunbathers must pay to use these beaches, which also become uncomfortably crowded in the high season. Away from the major resorts, beaches are less crowded and access to them is free, although they may lack facilities and are unlikely to have lifeguards. The beaches further towards the south are windy enough to attract surfers, windsurfers and kite surfers.

Sunny Beach *is an enormous resort that just keeps on growing and has everything the package tourist could ask for. A glut of bars, clubs, restaurants and shops cater for the thousands of European tourists that pass through every season.*

Dyuni is a wonderful windswept strip of beach that separates the sea from a marshy inland lake. A large hotel complex dominates the northern end, but the rest of the beach is free for the public to enjoy.

Obzor is a small seaside town that dates back to ancient times. While Greek and Roman remains ornament its pretty park, large new hotels have recently sprung up along its superb beach.

Lozenets, *once a quiet fishing village, is the current hotspot for well-to-do Bulgarians attracted by wind- and kite-surfing opportunities and some of the liveliest night-life outside the big resorts.*

Arapya, a hugely popular destination with Bulgarians, consists of a number of wooden beachfront restaurants and bars and a sprawling, partially shaded campsite.

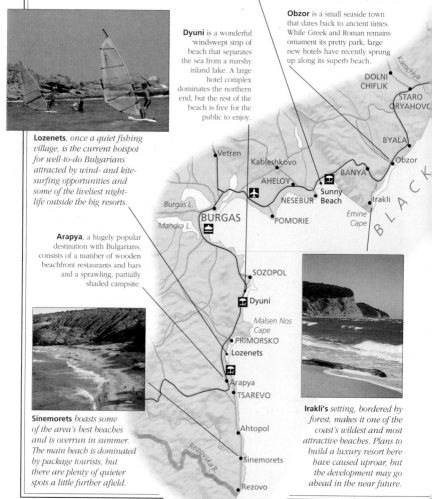

Sinemorets *boasts some of the area's best beaches and is overrun in summer. The main beach is dominated by package tourists, but there are plenty of quieter spots a little further afield.*

Irakli's *setting, bordered by forest, makes it one of the coast's wildest and most attractive beaches. Plans to build a luxury resort here have caused uproar, but the development may go ahead in the near future.*

Map labels:
Kamchiya
DOLNI CHIFLIK
STARO ORYAHOVO
BYALA
Obzor
Vetren
Kableshkovo
BANYA
AHELOY
Sunny Beach
NESEBUR
Irakli
Burgas L.
BURGAS
POMORIE
Emine Cape
Mandra L.
BLACK
SOZOPOL
Dyuni
Malsen Nos Cape
PRIMORSKO
Lozenets
Arapya
TSAREVO
Ahtopol
Rezovska R.
Sinemorets
Rezovo

Kaliakra *is a spectacular 70-m (230-ft) high cape which juts 2 km (over a mile) into the sea and is the site of a once mighty fortress. Occupied by successive conquerors of Bulgaria since ancient times, the fortress is of great historic interest. A nature reserve, the cape is a good place for spotting wild flowers, sea birds and dolphins.*

LOCATOR MAP

— Area Illustrated

Krapets *has by far the best beach on the northern coast, so this sleepy fishing village was unlikely to escape major development for long. As with other quiet spots along the coast, a number of new hotels have appeared in recent years and the trend looks set to continue.*

Albena is a vast resort that is spread out among well-kept parks and forests and borders a superb beach. Its curious 1970s architecture is oddly appealing and, of the big three resorts, Albena is the most peaceful and family-oriented.

KEY

— Major road

— Other road

▬ International border

✈ Airport

⛴ Ferry

🏖 Beach resort

☐ Beach area

▨ Urban area

Varna *is the coast's largest city and its appealing pedestrianized centre bustles with an impressive Byzantine church, attractive fountains and outdoor cafés. The wooded sea gardens offer some welcome respite from the heat, and the bars and clubs lining the beach have some of the Black Sea's best nightlife.*

Golden Sands, *with a fantastic beach and all the customary facilities, is one of Bulgaria's big three resorts. History buffs can also visit the nearby Aladzha Monastery, where monks' cells and chapels are cut into a cliff face.*

0 kilometres   20

0 miles   20

BULGARIA
THROUGH THE YEAR

Bulgaria has four distinct seasons, with a warm spring, a long hot summer, a golden autumn and a crisp, cold winter. Religious holidays, saints' days and folk festivals form the backbone of Bulgaria's festive calendar. Although the Orthodox Church ties the dates of religious festivals to the Gregorian calendar, some

Baba Marta dolls, bringers of luck

rural communities still keep to the Julian calendar. The year is also punctuated by a wealth of arts festivals, ranging from film to jazz and classical music. Some of these events are of international importance. Lastly, Bulgaria fetes its bountiful produce, with festivals celebrating wine and the roses from which fragrant oil is extracted.

SPRING

Spring presents Bulgaria at its most beautiful, with both open countryside and city parks bright with lush green grass and flowers in full bloom. Cultural activity is also at its height at this time. Concert seasons reach their climax in Sofia and Plovdiv. Easter, marked by religious processions as well as joyful family reunions and much feasting, is the high point of the church year.

MARCH

Baba Marta (*1 Mar*). Red and white tassels are worn as bracelets or hung on trees in order to bring good fortune and prosperity in the coming year.

Masked mummers at Shirokolushki peshyatsi in Shiroka Lûka

Easter Sunday procession, with an icon of Christ

Shirokolushki peshyatsi (*1st weekend in Mar*). Mummers parade through the village of Shiroka Lûka, in the Rhodope Mountains.
St Theodore's Day (*Todorovden; 1st Saturday in Lent*). Horse races in Koprivshtitsa, Dobrinishte and Momchilovtsi.
March Music Days (*late Mar*), Ruse. Series of concerts of classical music.

APRIL

St Lazar's Day (*Lazarovden; Saturday before Easter*). In this important coming-of-age ritual, carried out in villages all over Bulgaria, girls perform songs and dances collectively known as *Lazaruvane* to mark their passage from childhood to puberty. *Lazaruvane* bring health, happiness, and the promise of a good marriage partner in the future.
Easter (*variable dates*). Families celebrate Easter by decorating eggs with colourful designs and displaying them in the home. The main church

service takes place late on Easter Saturday. At midnight, the priest emerges from behind the iconostasis, with a candle representing the Resurrection.
Easter Sunday Eleshnitsa and elsewhere in Bulgaria. Processions by *kukeri* (*see p102*).

MAY

St George's Day (*Gergyovden; 6 May*). Military parades throughout Bulgaria. Openair feasting at Ak Yazula Baba Tekke, near Obrochishte, and Demir Baba Tekke, near Sveshtari.
Festival of Humour and Satire (*mid-May*), Gabrovo.
Sofia Music Weeks (*late May–early Jun*). Concerts by Bulgaria's leading orchestras and chamber musicians.

Military parade of uniformed soldiers on St George's Day

AVERAGE DAILY HOURS OF SUNSHINE

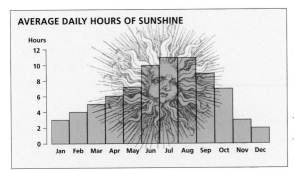

Hours

12
10
8
6
4
2
0

Jan Feb Mar Apr May Jun Jul Aug Sep Oct Nov Dec

Sunshine Chart
Bulgaria's weather is very complex. It has two overlapping climate zones – Continental from the north and Mediterranean from the south. This brings plenty of of sun from June to September, and reasonable levels of sunshine all year round.

Dancers in traditional costume at the Karlovo Rose Festival

SUMMER

Over the long, hot summer, mountain and coastal regions offer a welcome respite from the heat. While folk festivals take place all over the country, cultural activity centres on the Black Sea coast, where many arts festivals are held.

JUNE

Fire Dancing *(Nestinarstvo; 4 Jun or nearest weekend).* Bûlgari. A village event with dancing on hot coals.
Varna Summer *(Varnensko lyato; early Jun).* Bulgaria's foremost festival of international contemporary theatre.
Verdi Festival *(first 2 weeks in Jun),* Plovdiv. Opera in the ancient amphitheatre.
Karlovo Rose Festival *(first Saturday in Jun).* The rose harvest is celebrated with parades, music and dancing.
Kazanlûk Rose Festival *(first Sunday in Jun).* Bulgaria's largest rose festival.

Festival of Chamber Music *(mid-Jun, odd-numbered years),* Plovdiv. Prestigious international event.
St John's Day *(Enyovden; 24 Jun).* People go into the fields to gather medicinal herbs.

JULY

Varna International Music Festival *(early–late Jul).* Classical music.
Varna International Ballet Competition *(mid–late Jul).* Major event for young dancers.
St Elijah's Day *(Ilinden; 20 Jul or 3 Aug, depending on region).* Celebrations in towns and villages with a church dedicated to St Elijah.
International Folk Festival *(late Jul),* Plovdiv. Celebration of folk dance and music.

AUGUST

Varna Jazz Festival *(early Aug).* Major jazz event.
Pirin Sings *(Pirin pee; even-numbered years),* Predel Pass, near Bansko. Folk music.

St Elijah's Day Gathering *(Ilindenski subor; early Aug),* Gela. Folk festival.
International Jazz Festival *(early-mid-Aug),* Bansko.
Rozhen Festival *(early to mid-Aug, even-numbered years),* in a meadow near Smolyan. Major Rhodopean folk festival.
Trigrad Festival *(mid-Aug),* Trigrad Gorge. Folk and pop music.
Feast of the Assumption *(15 Aug).* Parades of icons at Troyan Monastery and Bachkovo Monastery.
Koprivshtitsa Festival *(mid-Aug, every five years, the next in 2010).* Bulgaria's largest folk festival, featuring traditional performers from around the world. A smaller gathering, with local folk groups, is held annually.
Thracian Summer *(Trakiisko lyato; mid–late Aug),* Plovdiv. Chamber music concerts in old-town mansions.
White Brotherhood Gathering *(late Aug),* Seven Lakes, Rila Mountains. Dressed in white robes, followers of Petûr Dunov gather to take part in mass callisthenics and nature-worship.

Performance at the International Jazz Festival in Bansko

AVERAGE MONTHLY RAINFALL

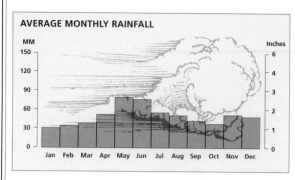

MM / Inches

| | Jan | Feb | Mar | Apr | May | Jun | Jul | Aug | Sep | Oct | Nov | Dec |

150 / 6
120 / 4
90 / 3
60 / 2
30 / 1
0 / 0

Rainfall Chart
Late spring-early summer is surprisingly humid in Bulgaria with high levels of rainfall, especially in the mountains. Winter in the the north sees lots of precipitation in the form of snow over high areas. The Black Sea coast and south has less rainfall generally.

AUTUMN

Autumn is generally a very pleasant season in Bulgaria. The weather usually remains mild well into November with little rainfall, making this a good time for hiking and exploring rural areas. Besides many religious festivals, a wide spectrum of arts festivals fills the autumn months. The season starts with the great Apollonia Arts Festival in Sozopol, the largest event of its kind in Bulgaria.

Participants at celebrations to mark the Day of the National Enlighteners

SEPTEMBER

Apollonia Arts Festival (*early Sep*), Sozopol. Music, theatre and dance of all kinds, at various venues in the town.
Birth of the Virgin (*Malka Bogoroditsa; 6 Sep*), Rozhen Monastery. Parade of icons.

Feast of the Cross (*Krustovden; 14 Sep*). Pilgrimages to Krustova Gora, in the Rhodope Mountains.
Feast of St Sofia (*17 Sep*). Sofia. Day of the city's saint.
Scene at the Crossroads (*mid-Sep*), Plovdiv. This is an international theatre festival.
Chamber Music Days (*mid-Sep*), Gabrovo.

International Puppet Theatre Festival (*late Sep*), Plovdiv.

OCTOBER

Harvest Festivals (*mid-Oct*), Bansko, Blagoevgrad, Gotse Delchev and Melnik. Typical harvest celebrations.
Feast of St John of Rila (*19 Oct*), Rila Monastery. Festival in honour of the monastery's 9th-century founder.
St Demetrius's Day (*Dimitrov den; 26 Oct*). Celebrated where the churches are associated with St Demetrius.

NOVEMBER

Day of the National Enlighteners (*1 Nov*). Concerts and events all over the country.
Feast of the Archangel Michael (*Arhangelovden; 8 Nov*). Orthodox Bulgarians make offerings to St Michael, protector of the dead.
Kurban Bayram (*variable; falls in Dec in 2008, and in Nov in 2009 and 2010*). Muslim areas. Feasting to commemorate the Sacrifice of Abraham.

Band of musicians in concert at the Apollonia Arts Festival

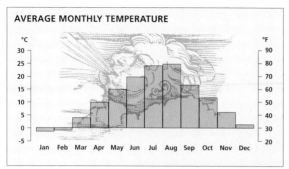

AVERAGE MONTHLY TEMPERATURE

Temperature Chart

Thanks to the Black Sea, the coast avoids extremes of hot and cold. High areas are cooler all year round, but in valleys, such as along the Danube, it can be stifling in summer and icy in winter. For Sofia, mountains stop icy Russian winter winds and its elevation cools it in summer.

WINTER

While the Black Sea coast enjoys mild winters, inland regions can be bitterly cold, and mountains are covered with a thick carpet of snow. This is welcomed by winter sports enthusiasts, with the skiing season starting in mid-December and lasting until March or April. Winter is particularly associated with *kukeri* rituals, when mummers wearing monstrous animal masks perform wild dances, shaking cowbells to drive away the evil spirits that are abroad during the long dark winter nights. Although traditionally associated with Cheese Shrovetide (the first Sunday before Lent), *kukeri* rituals take place at different times. They occur in January across much of southwestern Bulgaria, but are held in March in Shiroka Lûka, and as late as Easter in Eleshnitsa.

DECEMBER

Young Red Wine Festival *(early Dec)*, Sandanski. The new season's wine is feted.
St Nicholas's Day *(Nikulden; 6 Dec)*.
Christmas *(Koleda; 25 Dec)*. *Koledari* (carol singers) tour villages, and are offered specially made bread in return.

JANUARY

New Year's Day Children tour their neighbourhood bearing *survachki*, cornel twigs decorated with dried

Christmas lights, trees and decorations in a Sofia street

fruit, corn and ribbons. Householders are lightly beaten with the twigs to bring them luck in the coming year.
Kukeri processions *(1 Jan)*, Razlog.
Jordan Day *(Yordanovden; 6 Jan)*, Kalofer. People jump into an icy river to retrieve a wooden cross.
St John's Day *(Ivanovden; 7 Jan)*. The greatest name-day of the year, and a time of celebration for everyone called Ivan.
Kukeri processions *(14 Jan)*, Pernik, Radomir and Breznik.

Costumed participants in Trifon Zarezan, the vine-pruning festival

FEBRUARY

Trifon Zarezan *(1 or 15 Feb, depending on region)*. Vine-pruning festival celebrated in wine-growing areas. Vineyards are sprinkled with the previous season's wine so as to ensure a good crop in the coming year.

PUBLIC HOLIDAYS

New Year's Day 1 January

Liberation Day 3 March

Easter Sunday & Easter Monday variable

Labour Day 1 May

St George's Day – Bulgarian Army Day 6 May

Day of Bulgarian Education and Culture 24 May

Unification Day 6 September

Independence Day 22 September

Christmas 25, 26 December

THE HISTORY OF BULGARIA

A
t the crossroads of Europe and the Orient, Bulgaria has come under the influence of many neighbouring cultures, from Greek and Roman to Byzantine and Bulgar. Part of the Ottoman Empire for nearly 500 years, Bulgaria gained independence in 1878, but became a Communist republic in 1946. Today, Bulgaria is a fully democratic state and a member of the European Union.

With a warm climate and fertile soil, the region that is now Bulgaria attracted human settlement from ancient times. Archaeological discoveries at Stara Zagora show that, as early as 5500 BC, Neolithic people were living in the region, where they grew crops, raised animals and made vividly decorated pottery. By 4000 BC, metalworking techniques in the region had developed to become one of the most advanced in Europe, as the exquisite gold jewellery found near Varna shows so vividly.

Neolithic pottery figure from Stara Zagora

THRACIANS AND GREEKS

By 1000 BC, southeastern Europe was falling under the power of a people known as the Thracians. Across a territory consisting of present-day Bulgaria, Romania and northern Greece, the Thracians formed tribal states. These were ruled by warrior-kings who may also have played a priestly role.

It is thought that the Thracians performed ecstatic religious rituals similar to the wine-fuelled Dyonisiac revels of ancient Greece. The Thracians also believed in an after-life, and it is likely that the cult of

Orpheus, who journeyed to the Underworld in search of his wife Eurydice, originated in Thrace before it became established in Greece.

From the 7th century BC, Thracians and Greeks maintained close contact, with Greeks from Asia Minor establishing colonies on Thrace's Black Sea coast. Greek settlements such as Mesembria (present-day Nesebûr) and Apollonia (Sozopol) supplied Athens and other Greek cities with grain, honey and animal hides from the Thracian hinterland.

After the 4th century BC, several Thracian tribes, notably the Odrysae in central Bulgaria and the Getae in the northeast, established powerful states. But, being disunited, the Thracians were unable to resist their more powerful neighbours. Philip II of Macedon invaded southern Thrace in the 4th century BC, founding the city of Philippopolis (present-day Plovdiv). In 335 BC, his son Alexander the Great subdued Thracian tribes as far north as the Danube. As Macedonian influence grew, the Thracian tribes lost their independence, but this brought them into closer contact with Greek culture.

TIMELINE

5500 BC Neolithic farmers in the Stara Zagora region produce richly patterned pottery

700 BC The Black Sea ports of Apollonia (Sozopol) and Mesembria (Nesebûr) are founded by Greek colonists from Asia Minor

342 BC Philip II of Macedon founds Philippopolis (Plovdiv)

6000 BC		4000 BC		2000 BC		0 AD

Neolithic marble fertility goddess

2500 BC Hunter-gatherers in north-western Bulgaria decorate Magura Cave with vibrant paintings

1000–800 BC The Thracians begin to form powerful tribal states in Bulgaria

148 BC Macedonia becomes part of the Roman Empire

73 BC The Thracian-born Spartacus leads a slave revolt against Rome

◁ Fresco of St George and the Dragon at an Orthodox church in Varna, on the Black Sea coast

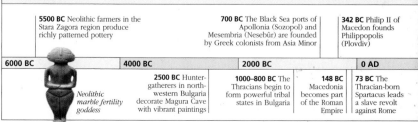

The Ancient Thracians

The Thracians first emerged as a distinct tribal culture in the second millenium BC, but they never developed a written language, so we know relatively little about them. It is not until the 5th century BC that any information appears. According to Herodotus, the Thracians were the most numerous people in Europe. Politically divided, they often fought among themselves.

Archaeological evidence shows that in the 5th to 1st centuries BC, the Thracians established a thriving trading civilization in the Balkans, much influenced by the Greeks of Asia Minor. Despite brief periods of unity under individual warrior-chiefs, the constant warring left them open to the Roman conquest in the 1st century AD.

LOCATOR MAP

☐ *Thracian Tribal Lands c.500 BC*

RELIGION, MYTHS AND LEGENDS

The Thracians' key religious beliefs involved fertility, birth and death. They held a strong belief in life after death, and it is likely that the cult of Orpheus began in Thrace before it won popularity in Greece. It is also thought that the Thracians practised ecstatic religious rites similar to the wine-fuelled Dionysiac revels of ancient Greece. Another important deity was the fierce Thracian Rider or Hero.

Servant offers wine, symbolic of Dionysus who died each winter to be reborn in spring.

The Thracian Rider, *here on a 4th-century BC silver plaque from Letnitsa, was an archetypal hero. Very popular as a cult figure, his image appears in hundreds of tombs of the 3rd century BC. His cult lived on in the image of dragon-slaying Christian saints such as St George.*

Two musicians play the trumpet. Music was linked to death and rebirth, as in the Orpheus myth.

The Great Mother Goddess *was a central figure in Thracian religion. She guaranteed fertility in spring and the harvests in autumn, and presided over the mysteries of life and death. As on this pitcher, she is often depicted as a huntress, with power over the natural world, or as a charioteer, driving on the changing seasons.*

Royal death mask *of a 4th-century BC Thracian ruler found near Kazanlûk, in the Valley of the Thracian Kings. It is likely that the king had some religious function as mediator between men and gods.*

KAZANLÛK FRESCO

Kazanlûk, in central Bulgaria *(see pp166–7),* is the site of this richly decorated chieftain's tomb. Dating from around the 4th century BC, it consists of a domed burial chamber covered by a large mound of earth. The frescoes that adorn the tomb depict a funeral feast, with the deceased accompanied by one of his wives. The Thracians appear to have had a positive view of the afterlife, and the transition from this world to the next was the cause for celebrations as well as mourning.

THRACIAN TOMBS

To date, over 50 tomb complexes have been excavated in Bulgaria and many more are certain to be discovered. Believing in an afterlife, the Thracians built an eternal house for a dead king and filled it with weapons, jewellery and even horses or dogs. Animal sacrifice was an important part of the ritual, although whether this was for food or to accompany them is not known. These royal tombs became temples or sacred places.

Burial mounds *such as Mogila Ostrusha, near Kazanlûk, dot the Bulgarian countryside. Mogila Ostrusha dates from the 5th century BC and has five chambers. The ceiling is carved with reliefs of people, plants and animals.*

The Great Mother Goddess is portrayed offering a tray of pomegranates, the fruit of death, to the deceased.

The deceased is shown seated, crowned with a ceremonial wreath and holding his wife's hand.

A wife would compete for the honour of being killed and buried with her lord, according to Greek historian Herodotus.

THRACIAN ART

Because of the lack of a writing system, most information about the Thracians has come from archaeological finds. It is clear that Thrace was greatly influenced by her neighbours. From Persia came the stylized depictions of mythical creatures that adorn Thracian gold and silver vessels. From Greece came more naturalistic portrayals, as in the frescoes in Thracian tombs.

Gold Amazon-head rhyton *or wine-cup from Panagyurishte. The Amazon wears a veil over her neat hair and a necklace. At the top of the handle stands a Persian-style figure of a flying sphinx. The frequency of wine-cups in burials reveals the importance of wine in such rituals.*

Heracles *is shown on this 4th-century BC silver plate from Rogozen in a natural Greek style. A hero who came back from Hades, Heracles was a cult figure among the Thracians.*

A WARRIOR NATION

Greek and Roman historians portrayed the Thracians as superior fighters – tough, mobile and with excellent cavalry. To the ancient Greeks, Thrace was a hostile and wild place, home of Ares, god of war. The Romans had a type of gladiator named after the Thracians – lightly armed with a curved sword and circular shield. Spartacus, the gladiator who started a revolt that nearly overthrew Rome *(see p115)*, was Thracian.

Thracian helmet *made of bronze and dating from around the end of the 3rd century BC. Examples of helmets have been found with leather inserts to ensure a firm fit to the skull. Other finds include breastplates, swords, spears and greaves, or shin guards.*

Ruins of the Roman baths complex in Varna

THE ROMANS

From the 2nd century BC, the Romans gradually replaced the Macedonians as the main power in southeastern Europe. By AD 50, they had taken control of the region, obliterating the old Thracian kingdoms and creating the provinces of Moesia and Thrace in their place. The Romans also built roads, founded new cities, and turned existing towns such as Philippopolis and Serdika (modern Sofia) into great metropolises.

In AD 330, Constantine the Great's establishment of a new imperial capital at Constantinople (Byzantium) boosted southeastern Europe's importance, bringing renewed vibrancy to the cities

Detail of a Roman mosaic, History Museum, Pleven

of Thrace. However, the Roman world's prosperity was increasingly threatened by barbarian invasions. The Visigoths ravaged the Danube region in 378, and the Huns sacked Serdika in about 450. In many cases the Byzantine authorities had no choice but to allow these migrating tribes to settle. The main beneficiaries of this policy were the Slavs, who came from northeastern Europe to the Balkans in the 6th century, and soon made up the majority of the rural population.

BIRTH OF THE BULGAR STATE

The Slavs lived peacefully under Byzantine rule until the arrival of the Bulgars, a warlike Turkic tribe whose origins lay in central Asia. In 681, a group of Bulgars under the leadership of Khan Asparuh crossed the Danube into what was to become Bulgaria. The Bulgars established a capital at Pliska, and gradually extended their rule over the Slavs already settled in the region. Unable to resist the Bulgars, Byzantium was forced to recognize their nascent state. Under Asparuh's successors, notably Khan Krum (803–14), Bulgaria's borders were extended southwards at Byzantium's expense.

The ruling Bulgar aristocracy adopted the language and culture of the Slavs, and the two communities merged to form the Bulgarian nation. This process was accelerated by Khan

Ancient pottery, Archaeological Museum, Sofia

Boris's conversion to Christianity in 865. Boris invited the Slav-speaking monks Kliment and Naum to spread the faith, ensuring the primacy of the

TIMELINE

AD 50 Southern Thracian lands become the Roman province of Thrace	**2nd century AD** The Romans build the city of Nikopolis ad Istrum, north of present-day Veliko Tŭrnovo.	*Roman funerary sculpture, Archaeological Museum, Varna*	**AD 447** Philippopolis is sacked by the Huns	**AD 550** Slav tribes begin to settle in the Balkans

0 AD	150	300	450	600

| **AD 6** The Romans absorb the northern Thracian lands and create the province of Moesia | **4th century** Christianity becomes the dominant religion in the Roman Empire. The first churches are built in Serdika (Sofia) | *St John Chrysostom, Archaeological Museum, Sofia* | **681** Khan Asparuh leads the Bulgar tribes into what is now Bulgaria |

Slav language. In order to translate the gospels into the Slav tongue, Kliment and Naum developed a new alphabet, which they named Cyrillic in honour of their mentor, St Cyril. With the new script, Bulgaria became a major centre of manuscript production, and the new spiritual and intellectual centre of the Balkans.

Ceramic icon of St Todor Stratilat, Archaeological Museum, Preslav

THE FIRST BULGARIAN KINGDOM

Bulgarian power reached its peak under Tsar Simeon (893–927), who pushed the Byzantines back to Constantinople, and extended the country's borders to the Black Sea in the east and to the Aegean in the west. However, Byzantine resurgence then halted further Bulgarian expansion. Bulgarian society was also weakened by a rift between the Church and a breakaway group of heretical preachers known as the Bogomils.

Squeezed by the Byzantines in the south and by Prince Svyatoslav of Kiev in the north, the Bulgarian kingdom fragmented in the late 10th century. A feeble Bulgarian state, under Tsar Samuil, survived in what is now Macedonia until 1014, when the Byzantine emperor Basil the Bulgar-Slayer destroyed Samuil's army at the Battle of Strumitsa. Four years later, Samuil's capital, Ohrid, fell to the Byzantines.

THE SECOND BULGARIAN KINGDOM

Byzantine rule brought peace and stability to Bulgaria. However, heavy taxation, and the replacement of Bulgarian priests with Greek-speaking clergy, led to discontent. In 1185 Petur and Ivan Asen led local *boyars* (nobles) in a revolt against Byzantine rule. After a struggle for independence, Ivan Asen was crowned tsar in 1187 and Veliko Tûrnovo became the capital of the reborn kingdom.

The fall of Byzantium to the Crusaders in 1204 gave the Bulgarian kingdom the opportunity to consolidate and grow. Under Ivan Asen II (1218–41), Bulgaria's territorial expansion resumed but in 1240 the Mongols swept through the Balkans, pillaging as they went. A group of Mongols (later known as the Tatars) settled on the northern Black Sea coast. With the revival of the Byzantine Empire after 1261, Bulgaria was once again at the mercy of its neighbours.

To stay in power, Bulgarian tsars often needed the support of either the Byzantines or the Tatars. The rebel and mystic Ivailo the Swineherd (1277–80) won the Bulgarian throne by promising to rid the country of Tatar influence, but in the end he fled to the Tatar court.

Medieval fortress in Shumen

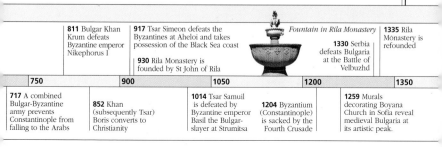

811 Bulgar Khan Krum defeats Byzantine emperor Nikephoros I

917 Tsar Simeon defeats the Byzantines at Aheloi and takes possession of the Black Sea coast

930 Rila Monastery is founded by St John of Rila

Fountain in Rila Monastery

1330 Serbia defeats Bulgaria at the Battle of Velbuzhd

1335 Rila Monastery is refounded

| 750 | 900 | 1050 | 1200 | 1350 |

717 A combined Bulgar-Byzantine army prevents Constantinople from falling to the Arabs

852 Khan (subsequently Tsar) Boris converts to Christianity

1014 Tsar Samuil is defeated by Byzantine emperor Basil the Bulgar-slayer at Strumitsa

1204 Byzantium (Constantinople) is sacked by the Fourth Crusade

1259 Murals decorating Boyana Church in Sofia reveal medieval Bulgaria at its artistic peak.

Bulgaria's decline as a major Balkan power was sealed by the rise of Serbia. The Bulgarian emperor, Mihail Shishman, tried to take advantage of the Byzantine civil war and attacked Serbia, but was defeated in 1330. Under his nephew Ivan Aleksandûr (1331–71) Macedonia was surrendered to the Serbs.

Tombul Mosque and minaret in Shumen

THE RISE OF THE OTTOMAN TURKS

Anatolia in the early 14th century was made up of a patchwork of Turkish tribal states, the most successful being the Ottoman Turk. Gradually absorbing Byzantine territory, they established a foothold in Europe in 1354. The effective light cavalry of the Ottomans soon made inroads into the Bulgarian kingdom.

Rather than outright conquest, the Ottomans made the Bulgarian tsars their vassals. Tsar Ivan Shishman's attempts to throw off this vassal status provoked a brutal response. In 1393 Sultan Bayezid sacked Veliko Tûrnovo, killed Ivan Shishman, and effectively wiped Bulgaria from the map.

In the anti-Ottoman crusade of 1396, King Sigismund of Hungary sought to liberate Bulgaria but was defeated by Bayezid at Nikopol. Another crusade, led by King Wladyslaw Jagiello of Poland, met a similar fate at Varna in 1444. Nine years later, the fall of Constantinople, last outpost of the Byzantine Empire, left the Ottomans in control of the Balkans.

BULGARIA UNDER OTTOMAN RULE

The Ottomans initially used cruel measures to assert their control of Bulgaria. Nobles were imprisoned or executed, and their subjects deported or enslaved. The Orthodox Church was allowed to carry on its activities, but the Ottoman legal system gave precedence to Muslims over Christians.

Under the Ottomans, cities such as Sofia, Plovdiv, Shumen and Varna emerged as major trade and administrative centres, endowed with fine mosques, covered bazaars, drinking fountains and prestigious public buildings. With a population that included Bulgarian artisans, Greek traders, merchants from Armenia and Dubrovnik, and civil servants from all over the Ottoman Empire, these cities became highly cosmopolitan.

Interior of the Church of Nativity, Arbanasi, with 17th-century frescoes

TIMELINE

1393 The Ottomans capture Veliko Tûrnovo, capital of Bulgaria

1396 The Ottomans take the fortress town of Vidin, confirming their mastery of Bulgaria

The Ottoman citadel of Baba Vida, in Vidin

1576 The Banya Bashi mosque in Sofia is completed by the master architect Hadji Mimar Sinan.

1350	1400	1450	1500	1550

1444 The crusade led by Wladyslaw Jagiello of Poland is crushed at the Battle of Varna.

1492 Sephardic Jews are expelled from Spain. Many of them subsequently settle in the Ottoman-ruled Balkans.

St George fighting the Ottoman

Some Bulgarian communities converted to Islam, perhaps to preserve their social status. Ottoman dervishes, who offered an accessible version of the Muslim faith, were key in making Islam attractive to potential converts. Those who adopted Islam were called *Pomaks* (Helpers) by their countrymen. Their descendants still inhabit the south of the country.

Ottoman bureaucracy was staffed almost entirely by slaves. These were usually collected under the *devshirme* system, by which the sultan's agents toured Christian villages, taking away an agreed proportion of boys aged between seven and 14. These were then forcibly converted to Islam, and educated in special schools before joining the army or the civil service. The brightest gained prestigious jobs. The Sultan's Grand Vezir (chief minister) was often a former *devshirme* boy. Cruel though it may have been, the *devshirme* system was broadly popular among Christian villagers because it offered their offspring an otherwise unimaginable degree of social mobility.

The Bulgarian nobility largely faded away, although a few rich landowners who cooperated with the regime retained their wealth. The inhabitants of highland villages, such as Kotel, Elena and Koprivshtitsa, also prospered. The Ottomans granted them privileges in return for keeping local mountain passes free of bandits and for supplying the Ottoman army with Balkan-reared sheep and wool.

Interior of the Ebu Bekir Mosque at Yambol

By the late 18th century, central authority in the Ottoman Empire had started to weaken. Bandits known as *kurdzhali* roamed the Balkan region with impunity, attacking wealthy villages and sacking monasteries. By their failure to act, the authorities appeared to favour the bandits, and relations between Christian Bulgarians and their Muslim rulers deteriorated.

Long drawn-out wars with Austria and Russia had also weakened the Ottoman Empire. Educated Bulgarians began to look to the Russians, fellow Orthodox Christians who spoke a similar Slavic language, as their potential liberators from Ottoman rule. This coincided with a new interest in Bulgarian history and culture. In 1762 the monk Paisii of Hilendar wrote his *Slavo-Bulgarian History*, which opened Bulgarians' eyes to their country's pre-Ottoman greatness. The authorities forbade the printing of Paisii's history, but it circulated in manuscript form and played a key role in awakening Bulgarian patriotism.

Decorated niche in the Bairakli Mosque, Samokov

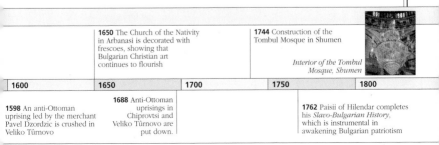

1600	1650	1700	1750	1800

1650 The Church of the Nativity in Arbanasi is decorated with frescoes, showing that Bulgarian Christian art continues to flourish

1744 Construction of the Tombul Mosque in Shumen

Interior of the Tombul Mosque, Shumen

1598 An anti-Ottoman uprising led by the merchant Pavel Dzordzic is crushed in Veliko Tŭrnovo

1688 Anti-Ottoman uprisings in Chiprovtsi and Veliko Tŭrnovo are put down.

1762 Paisii of Hilendar completes his *Slavo-Bulgarian History*, which is instrumental in awakening Bulgarian patriotism

THE NATIONAL REVIVAL

Bulgarian merchants who had grown rich from the wool trade began to fund patriotic cultural projects, such as the publication of books in the Bulgarian language, and to support schools where pupils were taught in Bulgarian. Funds were also raised for the refurbishment of historic monasteries such as Rila, Troyan and Bachkovo, and the best Bulgarian architects, icon painters and woodcarvers were commissioned to work on them.

Iconostasis detail, Museum of Icon Painting and Woodcarving, Tryavna

This patriotic upsurge in education and the arts was later dubbed the National Revival. Many Bulgarian merchants built themselves lavish family houses that reflected the new taste for fine architecture and woodcarving. This gave rise to a National Revival style of domestic architecture.

The patriotic spirit gradually spread from the cultural to the political sphere. From the earliest days of their rule, the Ottomans had placed the Orthodox Church in the hands of Greek-speaking priests and patriarchs.

Bulgarian community leaders now pressed for the creation of a separate branch of the Church, a Bulgarian exarchate free of Greek control. The sultan conceded to these demands in 1872.

Frustrated by the slow pace of reform, Bulgarian intellectuals proposed more radical tactics. In 1871, patriots of the younger generation formed a pro-independence organization from the safety of the Romanian capital, Bucharest. The revolutionary leader Vasil Levski (1837–73) set about organizing an underground anti-Ottoman movement in Bulgaria itself, but was captured and executed in 1873. Meanwhile, young revolutionary ideologues like Lyuben Karavelov and Hristo Botev continued to pin their hopes on a mass uprising.

FROM UPRISING TO LIBERATION

This was the April Rising, which began in 1876 in Koprivshtitsa, a mountain village at a safe distance from the Ottoman-controlled lowland towns. The Ottomans easily quashed the rebellion, but used undisciplined auxiliaries known as *bashibazouks* to restore order. Outraged by the indiscriminate massacres carried out by the *bashibazouks*, public opinion in Russia and western Europe fell solidly behind the Bulgarian cause.

In April 1877 Russia declared war on the Ottoman Empire. Despite Ottoman resistance, Russian forces

Rila Monastery, focus of restoration during the National Revival

Monument to martyrs of the April Rising, Koprivshtitsa

soon overran Bulgaria and forced the sultan to accept defeat. In March 1878, under the terms of the Treaty of San Stefano, an independent Bulgarian state was created. Besides core Bulgarian territory, it included large parts of Thrace and Macedonia.

Britain, France, Germany and other Western powers suspected that Russia would use the new Bulgarian state to increase its influence in the Balkans. In June 1878, at the hastily called Congress of Berlin, "Greater Bulgaria" was dismembered. A Principality of Bulgaria, still nominally subject to the Ottomans, was created north of the Balkans, with its capital at Sofia. Bulgaria south of the Balkans became a self-governing province of the Ottoman Empire, called Eastern Rumelia, with Plovdiv as its capital. Macedonia still remained a part of the Ottoman Empire, without self-governing status. For staunch Bulgarian patriots, the Congress of Berlin represented a major defeat, and their dream of reuniting the territories assigned to Bulgaria at the Treaty of San Stefano became the dominant theme of Bulgarian politics for the next 70 years.

INDEPENDENT BULGARIA

Having played a key part in the Liberation, Russia expected to have a guiding role in the new Bulgaria. The Bulgarian army and civil service also desperately needed an influx of Russian bureaucrats to help the fledgling state get on its feet. Alexandûr Batenberg, a German aristocrat who had served as a volunteer in the Russian army, was chosen to become the principality's new ruler. A natural autocrat, Prince Alexandûr had difficulty in dealing with Bulgaria's radical politicians, many of whom had been republican revolutionaries before the Liberation. He also had problems with Bulgaria's Russian masters.

In 1886 Bulgarian nationalists took control of Eastern Rumelia and unilaterally declared its union with the Principality of Bulgaria. The Russians, enraged that they had not been consulted, kidnapped Prince Alexandûr and tried to provoke a pro-Russian coup. Alexandûr was released, but was forced to abdicate. Another central European aristocrat, Ferdinand of Saxe-Coburg-Gotha, became the principality's new head, and Bulgaria's foreign policy was reoriented towards Germany and Austria-Hungary.

Evacuation of wounded from the Shipka Pass, 1877

Bulgarian National Revival

By the early 19th century, 400 years of Ottoman rule had forced Bulgarian culture into the background. Very few could read or write, and monasteries were the only places where scholarship lived on. However, a new generation of wealthy merchants wanted a Bulgarian-language education for their children, and raised money for teachers and schools. Before long, a cultural renaissance was under way, reawakening an interest in Bulgarian history and culture, and unleashing new energies in art and architecture. This was the National Revival, and by the mid-19th century its effect was felt in the political sphere, too, with radical young patriots demanding political change. Bulgarians dared to dream of a liberated future. A growing national consciousness swept through Europe. Greece gained independence from the Ottoman Empire in 1829, and Russia, long a friend to Bulgaria, was ready to take on the Turks and their allies.

National Revival woodcarving from Tryavna

THE BEGINNING OF THE REVIVAL

Spiritual godfather of the Bulgarian National Revival was Father Paisii of Hilendar (1722–73), a Bulgarian monk from Mount Athos. Dismayed by the Greek clergy's stranglehold on the Bulgarian Church, which used Greek as its official language, Paisii penned a patriotic manuscript entitled the *Slavo-Bulgarian History*, which eulogized Bulgaria's medieval rulers in stirring fashion. It was, in essence, a manifesto of Bulgarian nationalism – a history of the Bulgarian state and Church. Although the Greek-controlled Church authorities forbade the printing of Paisii's book, it was widely circulated, and became required reading for subsequent generations of Bulgarian patriots.

The *Slavo-Bulgarian History* *had three major chapters: On the Bulgarian Kingdom, On Bulgarian Saints and On Slav teachers.*

Father Paisii of Hilendar *distributed his pamphlet, urging people to study their own history and look after important national monuments. "The Lord has left only Rila Monastery to exist in our times...it is the duty of all Bulgarians to guard it, and to give alms to the sacred Rila Monastery."*

EDUCATIONAL REFORM

One of the main popularizers of Father Paisii's work was Neofit Rilski (1793–1881), a Bansko-born monk who devoted himself to the promotion of Bulgarian-language education. His *Bulgarian Grammar* (1835) was one of the first-ever text books in the language. He also translated a huge quantity of religious texts from Greek into Bulgarian, and spent decades working on a huge *Greek-Slavic Dictionary*. Most importantly, Neofit Rilski headed the first secondary school in Bulgaria, founded by Vassil Aprilov in Gabrovo in 1835. He went on to found a similar school two years later in Koprivshtitsa, introducing modern secular teaching methods later taken up across the whole of Bulgaria.

Aprilov High School, Gabrovo, built in 1835 to resemble the Rishelyov Lyceum in Odessa

The gravestone of Neofit Rilski *at Rila Monastery, where he first worked as a teacher before becoming involved with schools. After teaching in Samokov, Gabrovo and Koprivshtitsa, Rilski returned to Rila for the last 29 years of his life, eventually becoming* Igumen, *or head monk.*

ECCLESIASTICAL ARCHITECTURE

Relatively unharmed by the Ottomans – and the only form of public construction permitted, churches acquired civic functions, becoming keepers of the national identity. As the only outlet for Bulgarian nationalism, a wave of church building activity swept the country during the 1830s and 1840s. The renovation of Rila Monastery was one of the great patriotic projects of the era, funded by contributions from Bulgarians keen to turn Rila into a national spiritual landmark. One of Neofit Rilski's most famous followers was Zahari Zograf, a Samokov-born painter whose work can be seen in churches and monasteries throughout the country. Among his best-known works are the icons inside Rila monastery church, and frescoes in the church's porch.

Zahari Zograf (1810–53), *the artist, portrayed in the semi-Asiatic attire of a 19th-century Bulgarian gentleman.*

Rila Monastery's frescoes *are a lively mix of Orthodox icon painting styles, European realism and traditional Bulgarian folk art.*

DOMESTIC ART AND ARCHITECTURE

The upsurge in Bulgarian culture was accompanied by changes in lifestyle. Wealthy merchants were travelling widely and building large family houses, often using traditional Bulgarian crafts in their design and construction. House painters used Bulgarian folk art as the inspiration for the colourful floral designs with which they covered outer façades and reception rooms. Wood carvers incorporated floral motifs, bird shapes and sunburst patterns into intricate fretted ceilings. This all maintained a link with the past and reinforced a national identity. This increasing demand for artists in turn led to the development of schools of art – at Tryavna, Samokov and Boyana for example. This artistic legacy remains and can still be seen in Plovdiv, Koprivshtitsa, Tryavna, Veliko Tûrnovo and elsewhere.

Lyutov House, *Koprivshtitsa, has ceilings with ornate flower motifs and paintings of exotic cities visited by the owner, a yoghurt merchant.*

Oslekov House, *Koprivshtitsa, is exquisitely decorated (see p175). The owner, Nincho Oslekov, took part in the April Uprising, and was later killed by the Ottomans.*

THE WILL FOR POLITICAL CHANGE

Bulgaria's newly literate population was unwilling to put up with the administration imposed by the Ottoman Empire. Radicals like Georgi Sava Rakovski (1821–67) established the country's first anti-Ottoman armed group, inspiring intellectuals and freedom fighters such as Lyuben Karavelov (1834–79), Vasil Levski (1837–73) and Hristo Botev (1848–76) to organize pockets of resistance. In April 1876 a large-scale uprising against the Ottomans was launched but was brutally put down (see p174). However, news of the massacres resulted in universal condemnation, the start of another Russo-Turkish War and ultimately independence for Bulgaria in 1878.

The Battle at Shipka Pass *resulted in a Russian victory in the Russo-Turkish War of 1877–8. The ostensible cause for war was to help the Bulgarians but Russia had long been looking for a way of gaining access to the Mediterranean and ousting the Ottomans from the Balkans.*

Vasil Levski, leader of the struggle for independence

In 1903 the Macedonian Revolutionary Organization (IMRO) staged an uprising in Macedonia against Ottoman rule. The revolt was brutally put down, sending another wave of Macedonian exiles into Bulgaria. In 1908 the Ottoman Empire was again convulsed, this time by the Young Turks, a group of Western-oriented radicals who tried to introduce a modern liberal regime. Bulgaria took advantage of Ottoman weakness to declare itself an independent kingdom, with Ferdinand becoming Tsar Ferdinand I.

THE BALKAN WARS TO WORLD WAR I

Eager to force the Ottomans from their remaining European possessions in Macedonia and Thrace, Bulgaria was drawn into an anti-Ottoman alliance with Serbia and Greece. In the First Balkan War of 1912, these three Balkan states inflicted a crushing defeat on the Ottomans but disagreed on how to divide their conquests. The Greeks and Serbs occupied much of Macedonia, which Bulgaria regarded as rightly hers. Bulgaria responded by declaring war on her former allies, but was roundly defeated in the Second Balkan War of 1913.

Expulsion of occupying Bulgarian forces, perceived as invaders, by Macedonian civilians

BULGARIANS AND MACEDONIANS

After the Congress of Berlin, many Macedonians, who saw Bulgaria as their main ally in the struggle against Ottoman rule, came to Sofia as exiles. Because of ethnic and linguistic similarities between Bulgarian and Macedonian Slavs, many people from both groups claimed that they were historically one nation. The Bulgarian court and the country's armed forces also sought closer links with Macedonian factions.

Prime minister Stefan Stambolov angered the court by trying to clamp down on the Macedonian lobby, and was dismissed by Prince Ferdinand in 1895. The following year Stambolov was murdered in Sofia by Macedonian revolutionaries. This was the first of many political assassinations linked to Macedonian émigré groups.

Bulgarian soldiers in a trench during the Balkan Wars

TIMELINE

1913 The Second Balkan War, in which Bulgaria is driven out of Macedonia by Greeks and Serbs

1912–13 The First Balkan War, in which Bulgaria defeats the Ottomans

1915–18 Bulgaria joins in World War I on the German side

1923 Stambolyiski is overthrown and murdered

1900	1905	1910	1915	1920

1903 The Ilinden Uprising in Macedonia ends in defeat, forcing many Macedonians into exile in Bulgaria

1919–23 Aleksandŭr Stambolyiski's radical government tries to create a peasant-ruled state

Bulgarian irregular troops in World War I

Bulgaria's involvement in World War I was an even greater disaster. Once again lured by the chance to occupy Macedonia, Bulgaria joined the war on the German-Austrian side in 1915. Three years later a Greek-French-British army invaded Macedonia, sweeping the Bulgarian army aside. With the country in a state of collapse, Tsar Ferdinand abdicated in favour of his son Boris III, and Aleksandûr Stambolyiski, radical leader of the Agrarian Party, became prime minister.

King Boris III of Bulgaria with his family

THE INTER-WAR YEARS

Stambolyiski's policy of giving power to the peasants enraged the urban middle classes. He also lost the support of Bulgarian nationalists by failing to oppose Macedonia's becoming part of Yugoslavia. In 1923 Stambolyiski was murdered by embittered Macedonian exiles and their Bulgarian allies. An uprising by Bulgarian Communists was put down, leaving power in the hands of the authoritarian right.

Throughout the 1920s, Macedonian revolutionary factions continued to influence Bulgarian politics. They ran southwestern Bulgaria as a virtual gangster-state. Eager to bring the Macedonians under control, a group of intellectuals and Bulgarian army officers staged a coup in 1934. Tsar Boris III imposed a royal dictatorship the following year.

WAR AND REVOLUTION

In 1941, two years after the outbreak of World War II, Bulgaria joined the Axis, judging that an alliance with Germany would allow her to re-occupy Macedonia. By 1943, however, it was apparent that German victory was not assured, and Bulgarian politicians sought other options. In

1944 Bulgaria switched sides, hoping to head off an invasion by the Soviet Red Army. However, the Red Army invaded, providing the Bulgarian Communist Party with the opportunity to seize power.

The Communists' first priority was to banish all other political forces. Politicians sympathetic to the Communists were cajoled into joining the Fatherland Front, an umbrella organization controlled by the Communists. Anti-Communist politicians were denounced as traitors who were sabotaging the country's postwar reconstruction. Elections held in 1945 gave the Communists a landslide victory. A staged referendum in 1946 voted to abolish the monarchy, and Bulgaria became a republic. Persecution of the Communist Party's opponents culminated in 1947 with the trial of Agrarian leader Nikola Petkov, who was executed for allegedly plotting with foreign intelligence services.

1925 Communist extremists bomb Sofia's cathedral, killing 150

Adolf Hitler and Tsar Boris III of Bulgaria

1935 Christo, the artist famous for wrapping up huge buildings, is born Hristo Yavachev in Bulgaria

March 1941 Bulgaria forms an alliance with Nazi Germany

September 1944 Bulgarian Communists, supported by the Soviet Red Army, seize power

1925	1930	1935	1940	1945

1934 Intellectuals and army officers involved in the secret organization Zveno ("Link") launch a bloodless coup

May 1943 Anti-government demonstrations save Bulgaria's Jewish community from deportation to the death camps

Liberation of Sofia, 1944

model Stalinist society in which political, economic and cultural life was tightly controlled. Agriculture was collectivized and the development of heavy industry fed economic growth. The death of Stalin in 1953 was followed by the fall of his close associates in Eastern Europe, and in 1956 Chervenkov stepped down in favour of Todor Zhivkov. Although he allowed greater cultural freedom, Zhivkov remained a hardline Communist loyal to the Soviet Union.

By the early 1980s, the Bulgarian economy was stagnating and Zhivkov could no longer rely on full employment and improving standards of living to ensure continuing support. He also launched a policy of bringing Bulgaria's Turks into the national fold. Turks were made to adopt Bulgarian surnames, and the use of the Turkish language in public places was discouraged. The policy was justified by the dubious theory that Bulgaria's Turks were ethnic Bulgarians, forcibly Turkicized during Ottoman rule.

German forces on the streets of Sofia, after the Bulgarian government's alliance with the Axis powers

Bulgaria was forced to accept the loss of Macedonia, which became a federal republic within Communist Yugoslavia. The BKP leader Georgi Dimitrov considered solving the Macedonian question by forming a Bulgarian-Yugoslav Confederation, of which Macedonia would be a constituent part. However, Stalin disapproved, and Dimitrov died in mysterious circumstances in 1949.

Under his successor, Vulko Chervenkov, Bulgaria became a

Celebrations marking the Russian Revolution in Sofia in 1947

THE COLLAPSE OF COMMUNISM

By the 1980s, across Eastern Europe confidence in the Communist system was ebbing away. While the Soviet leader Mikhail Gorbachev addressed the problem through policies of *glasnost* (openness) and *perestroika* (restructuring), Zhivkov was unwilling to follow his lead. Instead, he opted to whip up nationalist passions by stepping up his anti-Turkish campaign. As a result, some 360,000 Bulgarian Turks fled to Turkey in 1989. The exodus led to catastrophic labour shortages, and crops remained unharvested.

TIMELINE

1946 Bulgaria becomes a republic and young Tsar Simeon II is forced to leave the country

1953 The death of Stalin in Moscow leads to a political thaw throughout Eastern Europe

1954–6 Chervenkov is removed from government, to be replaced by new party secretary Todor Zhivkov

1975 Todor Zhivkov's daughter Lyudmila becomes Minister of Culture

1945   1955   1965   19

1949 Communist Georgi Dimitrov is succeeded by the Stalinist Vulko Chervenkov

Georgi Dimitrov, Communist leader

1965 Zhivkov survives coup by nationalist army officers

1974 The Kozlodui nuclear power station in northern Bulgaria comes into operation

At the same time, Bulgarian dissidents became increasingly active, forming pressure groups such as the environmentally ethical Ecoglasnost, and the embryonic trade-union movement Podkrepa. The fall of the Berlin Wall in November 1989 suddenly changed Eastern Europe's political landscape. The Bulgarian Communist leadership forced Todor Zhivkov to resign, and embarked on a reformist path. Soon after, the anti-Communist opposition united to form the Union of Democratic Forces (UDF), led by the dissident intellectual Zhelyu Zhelev. Bulgaria's ethnic Turks, allowed political expression for the first time, founded the Movement for Rights and Freedoms (MRF).

Communist leader Todor Zhivkov

CONTEMPORARY BULGARIA

Under a new name, the Bulgarian Socialist Party (BSP), the Communists won the first free elections in Bulgaria in 1990. They were, however, greeted by a wave of protest, and were forced to accept the veteran anti-Communist Zhelyu Zhelev as president. Fresh elections in 1991 brought the UDF to power, but its radical programme of economic reform was halted when coalition partners, concerned by the social cost of free-market policies, deserted the government.

The BSP re-established itself as the dominant force in Bulgarian politics in 1994. However, economic mismanagement led to runaway inflation and food shortages, provoking mass protests. The UDF was returned to power in April 1997, but it failed to stamp out government corruption, and in 2001 Bulgaria turned to a new, non-ideological party formed by Bulgaria's former Tsar, Simeon of Saxe-Coburg-Gotha.

Simeon II's National Movement continued the programme of economic stabilization initiated by the UDF. But despite economic growth, prosperity failed to reach most of the populace, who returned the BSP to power in 2005.

Despite these frequent changes in government, most political parties agreed that Bulgaria's most important priority was its smooth integration into Western organizations. Bulgaria joined NATO in 2004, and signed the European Union Accession Treaty in 2005. Bulgaria's entry into the EU in 2007 marked a significant new phase in the country's voyage from post-Communist chaos to political and economic stability.

Welcome for Bulgaria, new member of NATO, in 2004

1978 Bulgarian dissident Georgi Markov is assassinated with a poisoned umbrella in London	1984–5 Bulgarian Turks are made to adopt Bulgarian names		2001 Simeon of Saxe-Coburg-Gotha (Simeon II) is elected prime minister	2005 Simeon of Saxe-Coburg-Gotha loses power to the Socialist Sergei Stanishev
		November 1989 Todor Zhivkov is forced to resign	*Tsar Simeon II*	
	1985		**1995**	**2005**
	1981 An attempt on the life of Pope John Paul II is linked to the Bulgarian secret service	1989 Mass exodus of Bulgarian Turks to Turkey, as anti-Turk campaign is stepped up	December 1994 The Socialist Party returns to government, but is forced out after two years due to economic incompetence	2004 Bulgaria joins NATO 2007 Bulgaria joins the EU

The beautiful Pirin Mountains, southwestern Bulgaria ▷

BULGARIA
AREA BY AREA

Bulgaria at a Glance

Combining long sandy beaches with bustling
cities, rich history and dramatic landscapes,
Bulgaria is one of Europe's most varied
destinations. Its two main cities, Sofia and
Plovdiv, are urban centres rich in historical
relics, contemporary cultural events and year-
round nightlife. The mountains offer superb
hiking opportunities, beautiful scenery and
highland valleys, and are home to the traditional
villages and monasteries that kept Bulgaria's
culture alive during five centuries of Ottoman
rule. The Black Sea coast has something for
everyone, from beachside resorts
pulsating with dusk-to-dawn nightlife to stretches of wild coast with
beautiful, unspoiled villages.

Svetlin Rusev Gallery in Pleven
*is largely devoted to the work of
Sveltin Rusev, a native of the town
(see p185). The building, in the
Neo-Byzantine style, was originally
a public baths complex.*

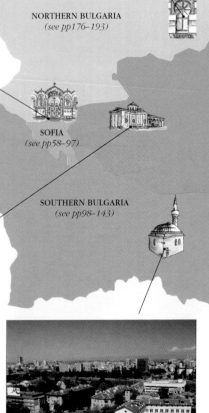

NORTHERN BULGARIA
(see pp176–193)

SOFIA
(see pp58–97)

SOUTHERN BULGARIA
(see pp98–143)

Russian Church in Sofia
*was built for the community
of Russians that settled in
the city (see p71). It is based
on the design of 16th-century
Muscovy churches and was
consecrated in 1914.*

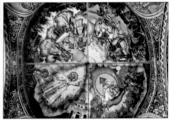

Frescoes at Troyan Monastery
*exemplify Bulgaria's 19th-century
artistic renaissance. The monastery
(see p149) is one the country's largest.*

Plovdiv, *an important cultural and
commercial metropolis, is Bulgaria's
second-largest city (see pp134–9). The
historic centre is notable for its fine
National Revival houses.*

Basarbovo Monastery, *whose name means "Cut in the Rock", lies in the canyon-like valley of the River Lom (see p188). The waters of the monastery's well, which is said to have been dug by St Dimitûr himself, are supposed to have healing powers.*

Kamen Briag *is one of the wildest and most beautiful spots on the Black Sea coast (see p202). The rocky coastline here is riddled with caves and the area is rich in archaeological remains, including the vestiges of a Roman and Byzantine fortress.*

CENTRAL BULGARIA *(see pp144–175)*

BLACK SEA COAST *(see pp194–213)*

0 kilometres 50

0 miles 50

The Stone Forest *stands in a barren landscape near the Black Sea coast. It consists of several groups of pillar-shaped formations (see p205). They were probably formed by accumulations of chalk and sand 50 million years ago.*

Eastern Rhodope Mountains *feature spectacular rock formations formed by the erosive action of wind and rain. Some of the more striking clusters are known by such names as the Stone Mushrooms and Stone Wedding (see p141).*

INTRODUCING SOFIA

Exploring Sofia

The capital of Bulgaria since 1879, Sofia was laid out on a grid plan by 19th-century urban planners. A royal palace, parliament house and various government ministries were built in the eastern part of the centre, providing Sofia with a quarter of fine buildings which still exists today. The Roman, medieval and Ottoman-era buildings that also dot Sofia give some idea of the city's ancient origins. Monumental public buildings from the Communist period add a melancholy grandeur to downtown squares and intersections. The main social artery of modern Sofia is Bulevard Vitosha, a permanently bustling shopping thoroughfare with cobbled residential streets on either side. Outside the city centre, Sofia is dominated by residential suburbs broken up by attractive swathes of green parkland and the looming presence of Mount Vitosha.

Changing of the Guard at the Presidency

KEY

- ▢ Street-by-Street area: see pp62–3
- ▢ Major sight
- ⓘ Tourist information
- ✝ Church
- Ⓜ Metro station
- Ⓟ Parking
- ░ Pedestrian street

```
0 metres        500
0 yards         500
```

KEY

- ▢ Area of the main map

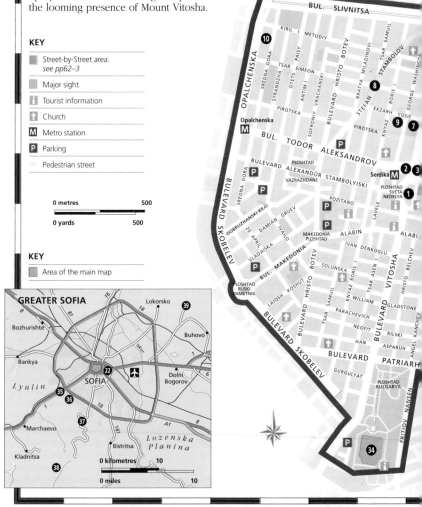

SIGHTS AT A GLANCE

Places of Worship

Aleksandûr Nevski Memorial Church pp72–3 ⑰
Banya Bashi Mosque ⑥
Boyana Church ㊱
Church of Sveta Petka Samardzhiiska ③
Church of Sveta Sofia ⑱
Church of Sveti Sedmochislenitsi ㉗
Dragalevtsi Monastery ㊲
Monastery of St George ㊴
Rotunda of Sveti Georgi ④
Russian Church ⑯
Sofia Synagogue ⑨
Church of Sveta Nedelya ①

Museums and Galleries

Archaeological Museum pp68–9 ⑪
City Art Gallery ㉚
Ivan Vazov House-Museum ㉘
Military Museum ㉒
National Art Gallery ⑭
National Gallery of Foreign Art ⑳
National History Museum pp84–5 ㉟
Natural History Museum ⑮
Peyu Yavorov Museum ㉜
National Polytechnic Museum ⑩
Slaveykov Museum ㉝

Theatre

National Theatre ㉙

Historic Streets and Squares

National Assembly Square ㉑
Slaveykov Square ㉛
Zhenski Pazar Market ⑧

Palaces, Historic Buildings and Monuments

Central Market Hall ⑦
Mausoleum of Prince Aleksandûr Batenberg ㉓
Mineral Baths ⑤
Monument to the Soviet Army ㉔
Monument to Sveta Sofia ②
National Palace of Culture ㉞
Party House ⑬
Red House ㉕
Presidency ⑫

Parks and Gardens

Borisova Gradina ㉖
Botanical Garden ⑲
Mount Vitosha pp88–9 ㊳

SEE ALSO

• *Street Finder* pp92–7
• *Where to Stay* pp218–20
• *Where to Eat* pp234–6

GETTING AROUND

Central Sofia is easy to explore on foot, although you may need public transport to reach outlying museums. An efficient tram network covers the city centre and the inner suburbs, while buses and trolleybuses are a convenient means of reaching Sofia's outer fringes. Taxis are numerous and inexpensive. The metro system, currently a single line running west from Serdika station to the suburb of Lyulin, will probably be extended eastwards in 2009.

Aleksandûr Nevski Memorial Church

Street-by-Street: The Historic Centre

Many cultures have shaped Bulgaria, and nowhere is this more visible than in Sofia's historic heart. Orthodox churches, a 16th-century mosque and an Art Nouveau synagogue just around the corner bear witness to a rich religious heritage. The parade of 19th-century buildings along ulitsa Tsar Osvoboditel attest to the mood of optimism and energy that invigorated Bulgaria after the Liberation of 1878. In stark contrast are the stern office blocks around ploshtad Nezavisimost, the legacy of Communist power. Today, Sofia is a centre of growing consumer culture, which is at its most tangible along bulevard Vitosha, the city's vibrant main shopping street.

Party House
Built to house the Central Committee of the Bulgarian Communist Party, this is Sofia's most imposing example of Stalinist-era architecture. ⓭

Presidency
This 20th-century building is the Bulgarian president's office. A Changing of the Guard ceremony takes place hourly at the entrance. ⓬

National Art Gallery
This fine 19th-century former palace displays paintings by Bulgaria's best artists. ⓮

MOSKOVSKA

KNYAZ AL.
BATENBERG
SQUARE

KNYAZ AL. BATENBERG

SABORNA

DYAKON IGNATI

IVAN VAZOV

GEN. GURKO

GEORGI

★ **Archaeological Museum**
A converted mosque, the museum has a dazzling array of ancient and medieval treasures. ⓫

City Art Gallery ㉚

National Theatre
Built in an opulent Neo-Classical style, the National Theatre is home to Bulgaria's leading state drama company. ㉙

Ivan Vazov Museum
honours the great poet, novelist and playwright. ㉘

Natural History Museum
has a collection ranging from rocks to snakes. ⓯

KEY

– – – Suggested route

★ Russian Church
Built in 1914 to serve Sofia's Russian community, the Russian Church is modelled on Muscovite church architecture. **16**

★ Aleksandûr Nevski Memorial Church
This stupendous Orthodox cathedral commemorates Russia's role in the Liberation of 1878. **17**

Church of Sveta Sofia
This small church has Roman origins. **18**

Botanical Garden
A tidy collection of exotic and fragrant flora. **19**

OBORISHTE

BUL. TSAR OSVOBODITEL

IS. TI NOEMVRI

KOVSKI

National Gallery of Foreign Art
With exhibits ranging from Burmese sculpture to Indian miniatures, the gallery has an eclectic and fascinating collection. **20**

National Assembly
Completed in 1928, this relatively plain building is in a restrained Classical Revival style, with Grecian motifs. **21**

Kristal Park
This green square is named after the café on its south side.

0 metres   100
0 yards   100

Monument to the Liberators
Commemorating the heroes of the National Liberation of 1878, the monument is crowned with an equestrian statue of Alexander II of Russia, the "Tsar Liberator".

STAR SIGHTS

★ Aleksandûr Nevski Memorial Church

★ Archaeological Museum

★ Russian Church

Church of Sveta Nedelya, built on the site of earlier churches and an important focus of Christian worship in Sofia

Church of Sveta Nedelya ❶
Църква "Света Неделя"

pl. Sveta Nedelya. **City Map** *1 B4.*
Ⓜ *Serdika.* 🚌 *1, 2, 7.* 🚻

Set on an island in central Sofia, the Church of Sveta Nedelya ("the Blessed Sunday") has long been one of the city's principal places of worship. It was built on the site of a 10th-century church. In Ottoman times it was known as the Church of Sveti Kral ("the Blessed King") because it held the relics of Stefan Urosh II Milutin, a 14th-century Serbian ruler who defeated the Bulgarian emperor, Mihail Shishman *(see p44).* The bones, believed to have miraculous healing powers, are kept in a casket beside the iconostasis.

The church was rebuilt in 1856–63 but was almost completely destroyed in 1925 when Communist extremists bombed it during a funeral service attended by Tsar Boris III and his family. The arcades on the north side and the gilt iconostasis survived. Frescoes executed in the 1970s and a marble floor added in the 1990s give the interior a contemporary look. The seat of the bishops of Sofia, the church has cathedral status.

Monument to Sveta Sofia ❷
Паметник "Света София"

pl. Nezavisimost. **City Map** *1 B4.*
Ⓜ *Serdika.* 🚌 *1, 2, 7.*

From a lofty pedestal, Georgi Chapkunov's statue of a golden-skinned, black-robed figure towers over Sofia's busiest crossroads. The Monument to Sveta Sofia ("Holy Wisdom"), erected in 2000 to stand as a millennial symbol of the city, was inspired both by the Orthodox Church's concept of Holy Wisdom (typically symbolized by a saintly-looking woman), and Athena, Greek goddess of wisdom. The crowned figure holds a laurel wreath (symbol of blessing) and an owl (symbol of knowledge) perches on her shoulder. The statue stands on the spot once occupied by a sculpture of Lenin, removed in 1990.

Church of Sveta Petka Samardzhiiska ❸
Църква "Света Петка Самарджийска"

pl. Nezavisimost. **City Map** *1 B4.*
Ⓜ *Serdika.* 🚌 *1, 2, 7.* 🚻

This tiny historic church, in an underground shopping mall just below the Monument to Sveta Sofia, is dedicated

The apse and high altar at the Church of Sveta Petka Samardzhiiska

to St Petka Paraskeva, a 3rd-century Christian girl from Asia Minor who was martyred during the reign of the emperor Diocletian. In the Ottoman period, the Guild of Saddlers financed the church's upkeep, and this accounts for its full name: Church of Sveta Petka of the Saddlemakers.

Entry to the church is via the crypt, which is thought to date from Roman times. A modern spiral staircase leads to the nave, built in the 11th century but strengthened with concrete in the 20th. Fragments of colourful 16th-century frescoes depicting scenes from the New Testament survive. The best-preserved are those on the north wall; they show a touching Deposition, and the resurrected Christ appearing to the disciples on Mount Tabor, bathed in divine light.

Rotunda of Sveti Georgi ❹
Ротонда "Свети Георги"

pl. Sveta Nedelya. **City Map** *1 B4.* Ⓜ *Serdika.* 🚋*1, 2, 7.* ⏱ *8am–5pm.*

Set in a courtyard between the Sheraton Hotel and the Presidency (see p70), this graceful red-brick rotunda probably stands on the site of a pre-Christian temple. The building has been used as a church since the 6th century. The church was converted into a mosque in the 16th century, and briefly served as a mausoleum for Aleksandûr Batenberg, independent Bulgaria's first prince.

The interior of the church is sumptuously decorated with medieval frescoes. A 14th-century depiction of Christ Pantokrator, accompanied by angels and symbols of the four evangelists, fills the cupola. Stretching round the drum that supports the cupola is a frieze containing 22 portraits of the prophets, clad in flowing robes. Below is a further tier, with figures of 16 other prophets. Fragments of 10th-century frescoes, including some beautiful angels' heads, also survive. Behind the Rotunda is a small

Rotunda of Sveti Georgi, with a plain exterior and colourful frescoes within

park where archaeological excavations have revealed the remains of 2nd-century Roman Serdica (see p42).

Mineral Baths ❺
Минерални Бани

City Map *1 C3.* Ⓜ *Serdika.* 🚋 *1, 2, 7, 20, 22.* 🔧 *for renovation.*

Warm mineral springs rise in the centre of Sofia, and, to exploit them, both the Romans and the Ottomans built extensive public baths here. The present-day Mineral Baths (Mineralna banya) were built in 1913. The architects, Petko Momchilov and Friedrich Grünanger, drew inspiration from Byzantine church architecture. The result is a highly distinctive building crowned by three egg-shaped domes. The Art Nouveau tiles running on the façade provide a feast of colour.

The Mineral Baths, based on the design of an Oriental building

Due to the dilapidated state of the roof, the baths closed in 1986, and are currently undergoing renovation. While the south wing will re-open as the City Museum, the north wing will be developed as a spa centre. Just north of the baths, on the opposite side of ulitsa Ekzarh Iosif, there are public taps, which people use to fill bottles and cans with spa water.

Banya Bashi Mosque ❻
Джамия "Баня Баши"

bul. Knyaginya Mariya Luiza. **City Map** *1 B3.* Ⓜ *Serdika.* 🚋 *1, 2, 7, 20, 22.*

The Mosque of the Central Baths is the only Muslim place of worship in Sofia that still serves its original function. It was built in 1576, possibly by the Ottoman master-builder Sinan, architect of the Suleiman Mosque, Istanbul. Like many mosques, it used to have the public bathhouse next door.

Constructed with large blocks of honey-coloured stone layered with terracotta bricks, this is a beautiful building. It has a finely proportioned cubic design, topped with an octagonal drum that supports a graceful dome 15 m (50 ft) in diameter. The mosque's most attractive features are its slender reddish minaret, and the arcaded porch at the entrance, crowned by a trio of small cupolas.

Central Market Hall ❼
Централни Софийски Хали

bul. Knyaginya Mariya Luiza 28. **City Map** 1 B3. **M** Serdika. 🚊 1, 2, 7, 20, 22. ⭘ 7am–10pm.

Boasting two huge floors of delicatessen stalls, food outlets, clothing shops and jewellery outlets, Central Market Hall (Tsentralni hali) is one of Sofia's busiest buildings. Built in 1909 and restored in the 1990s, it is also one of the most distinctive. The impressive Art Nouveau main portal bears Sofia's coat of arms and is topped by a dainty three-dial clocktower. The original mechanism, with shiny brass cogwheels and pendulum, is preserved in a glass case on the ground floor of the Hall. The Victorian-style iron pillars, balustrades and roofing beams of the cavernous interior convey a wonderful sense of period.

Central Market Hall, often simply called the Market Hall (Halite)

Colourful fresh produce at the popular Zhenski Pazar Market

Zhenski Pazar Market ❽
Женски Пазар

City Map 1 A2. 🚊 20, 22.

Five minutes' walk west of the synagogue, Zhenski pazar (Women's Market) is Sofia's biggest and most crowded open-air market, stretching for over half a kilometre (600 yards) along ulitsa Stefan Stambolov. Full of shoppers every day of the week, it represents a lively and traditional alternative to the shopping malls springing up elsewhere in the city. Fruit, vegetables and other foodstuffs are the main attraction, although you can also pick up all manner of inexpensive clothes, crafts, and kitchenware. Flower sellers congregate around the northern end of the market. Zhenski pazar is enduringly popular with Sofia's pensioners, as prices here can be rather significantly lower than elsewhere in the city. Pickpockets also operate here, so visitors should exercise extreme caution.

Sofia Synagogue ❾
Софийска Синагога

ul. Ekzarh Iosif 16. **City Map** 1 B3. **M** Serdika. 🚊 1, 2, 7, 20, 22. ⭘ 9am–5pm Mon–Fri, 9am–1pm Sat.

A spectacular Moorish design, one of the largest synagogues in Europe, this place of worship can hold as many as 1,300 people, although these days the numbers are far, far fewer. Designed by Austrian architect

Detail of the ornate Moorish exterior of the Sofia Synagogue

Friedrich Grünanger and completed in 1909, it is home to a magnificent and ornate brass chandelier weighing over 2,000 kg (4,400 lb). The interior also has some exquisite details in its Moorish mosaics, painted pillars and scalloped arches. It is not always possible to see inside the synagogue – knock at the door to see if a visit is possible – there is a Jewish Museum of History that tells the history of the Jews in Bulgaria.

National Polytechnic Museum ❿
Политехнически музей

ul. Opulchenska 66. **Tel** (02) 831 3004. **M** Opulchenska. 🚊 1, 5, 10. ⭘ 9am–5pm Mon–Fri. 🎟 **www**.polytechnic.hit.bg

Located about a fifteen-minutes' walk west of the centre, the National Polytechnic Museum (Natsionalen politehnicheski muzei) is Bulgaria's principal science museum, with a large and eclectic collection of various machines, laboratory instruments and gadgets through the ages. Everything from telescopes to the history of television is covered in the display, which also includes a handful of elegant vintage cars, and a pair of motorbikes made by the famous Plovdiv-based "Balkan" factory in the 1960s. There's also a fine display of early 20th-century porcelain and tableware, most of it donated by Bulgaria's former royal family, the Saxe-Coburg-Gothas.

Sofia's Jewish Community

The majority of Bulgaria's Jews were descended from the Sephardic community, who were allowed to settle in the Ottoman Empire after their expulsion from Christian Spain at the end of the 15th century. Sofia's Jews were respected for their contribution to the life of the city. This was recognized by Tsar Ferdinand in 1909, when he presided over the opening of the Sofia

A handwritten sacred text, the Sefer Torah

Synagogue. By World War II, the Jews made up about one fifth of Sofia's population. However, Bulgaria's alliance in 1941 with Nazi Germany led to an increasing spiral of anti-Jewish legislation despite protests from the Orthodox Church. Matters came to a head in 1943 when German officials asked their Bulgarian counterparts to deport 50,000 Jews to German-occupied Poland.

The unsung hero – Dimitûr Peshev
Dimitûr Peshev, from Kyustendil, was the Minister of Justice for Bulgaria, interested in safeguarding the constitution. However, at first he was supportive of the alliance with Germany, thinking that Bulgaria would regain the lands taken unjustly away after the Balkan Wars 1912–13. However, on learning of the plans to deport Bulgaria's Jews he and his colleagues pressurized the deputy Prime Minister to cancel the deportation order at the last moment. He and many others then wrote a formal letter of protest to the Prime Minister and the King.

Deportations from Thrace and Macedonia
However, the cancellation order did not reach Bulgaria's recently acquired territories of Thrace and Macedonia and over 11,000 Jews were rounded up and deported. The letter and threats of public demonstrations ensured that no more Jews from Bulgaria would be expelled. Two weeks later Prime Minister, Bogdan Filov sacked Peshev from his ministerial position. After the war Peshev was tried by the Communists and put in jail for being anti-Soviet as well as anti-Semite.

King Boris III
There is still controversy over King Boris's role during the war. He refused to hand over control to Germany on many matters, and in the end he did tell his ministers that somehow they must stop the deportation of Bulgarian Jews. However, some say he could have done more to prevent the Thracian and Macedonian deportations.

After the threat of Communism
After 1945, Bulgaria's atheist Communist rulers were profoundly hostile to traditional religions. Jewish community organizations were taken over by the state and synagogues were closed and left to fall into ruin. An increasing number of Jews chose instead to emigrate in the mid-1950s to the newly-established state of Israel rather than stay in Bulgaria. Today, probably fewer than 2,500 Jews still remain in Sofia, with an equal number spread throughout other major cities in the country.

Archaeological Museum ⓫
Археологически Музе

Many of Bulgaria's finest Thracian, Roman and
medieval treasures are preserved in Sofia's
Archaeological Museum (Arheologicheski
muzei). The building itself was once the
Buyuk Dzhamiya, or Grand Mosque, which
was built in 1494 and converted into the
present museum in 1894. The former prayer
hall, a lofty cube-shaped space beneath nine
graceful domes, provides the perfect ambience
in which to admire an open-plan display of
Greek, Roman and medieval sculpture. The
side rooms are devoted to a stunning sequence
of treasures dating from Bulgaria's prehistoric,
Thracian and medieval periods.

Macedonian Helmet
*This bronze helmet
of the 6th century
BC was found in
the grave of a
Macedonian
chieftain.*

★ Golden Burial Mask from Shipka
*Unearthed in 2004, this mesmerizing
portrait of a Thracian chieftain dates
from the late 5th century BC. Found
with a hoard of other items, it is finely
crafted from 673g (1lb 8 oz) of solid gold.*

Mezzanine III

Mezzanine II

Ground floor

★ Main Hall
*Roman sculptures, tombstones and floor mosaics are
arranged beneath a sequence of elegant arches.*

GALLERY GUIDE
*This is an unusually inviting museum – it is located
in an attractive building, the collection is not over-
whelmingly large and the labelling is informative.
After passing through the light and airy main hall,
visitors can head up to the top mezzanine to see
the Thracian gold, walk around the gallery
and then, if time allows,
simply explore at will.*

Mezzanine I

Main entrance

Thracian Rider
*Depictions of the
hunter-god often
adorn Thracian tombs.
In this example, of the 3rd
century BC, the rider is seated
on a lion-skin saddle, as his
horse tramples a wild beast.*

KEY TO FLOORPLAN

▢	Medieval Bulgarian Art
▢	Prehistoric Finds
▢	Iron Age Art
▨	Ancient Thracian Treasures
▢	Roman-era Art
▨	Non-exhibition space

For hotels and restaurants in this region see pp218–20 and pp234–6

Medieval Icons
This 17th-century Nativity scene from the Church of Sveta Petka in Krapets, southeast of Sofia, is just one of many valuable icons in the first-floor gallery.

VISITORS' CHECKLIST

ul. Suborna 2. **City Map** *1 C4.*
Tel *(02) 988 2406.* Ⓜ *Serdika.*
🚌 🚊 *1, 2, 7.* ⏰ *10am–6pm Tue–Sun.* 📷 📹 in museum annexe.

Laurel Wreath
Discovered in a princely grave dating from the 4th century BC, in Rozovets near Plovdiv, this delicate wreath features 63 leaves of gold.

Upstairs gallery

Ceramic Icon of Sveti Todor
Found in the ruined Patleyna Monastery near Preslav, this tiled icon is one of the high points of 10th-century Bulgarian art.

Medieval Bulgarian Pottery
From the 12th to the 14th centuries, Bulgaria's ceramics workshops produced bowls and jugs lavishly decorated with animal, bird and floral designs, and glazed in vivid yellows and greens.

Basement

STAR SIGHTS

★ Golden Burial Mask from Shipka

★ Main Hall

Roman-era sarcophagus
This 2nd-century AD Roman sarcophagus from Ratiaria (Archar) on the Danube river is decorated with cherubs and bulls' heads.

Presidency **⑫**
Президенство

ul. Lege. **City Map** *1 B4.* Ⓜ *Serdika.*
🚃 *1, 2, 7.* 🔵 *to the public.*

The Prezidentsvo, or office of
Bulgaria's president, is housed
in a 20th-century grey building that it shares with the
Sheraton Hotel on the north
side of ploshtad Nezavisimost.
The main entrance, on ulitsa
Lege, is guarded day and
night by soldiers dressed in
19th-century red-and-white
parade uniforms, complete
with braided jackets and
feathered hats. The Changing
of the Guard, in which one
shift of soldiers arrives and
another departs in ceremonial,
high-stepped marching style,
takes place every hour
throughout the day.

Party House, once the headquarters of the Communist Central Committee

Changing of the Guard ceremony
outside the Presidency

Party House **⑬**
Партиен Дом

pl. Nezavisimost. **City Map** *1 C4.*
Ⓜ *Serdika.* 🚃 *1, 2, 7, 20, 22.*

Diagonally opposite the Presidency is Party House (Partien
Dom), built in 1954 to serve
as the headquarters of the
Bulgarian Communist Party.
Intended to symbolize political power and prestige, it
dominates the wide open
space of ploshtad Nezavisimost, and is an immediately
visible landmark to anyone
approaching the city centre
from the west. The building's

monumental façade features a
lower storey of grey granite, a
cream Neo-Classical colonnade,
and a soaring spire that originally bore a huge red star.
    Following the political
changes of November 1989
(see p53), Bulgaria's Communists were advised to take the
red star down so as to avoid
provoking anti-Communist
sentiment. They failed to do
so, and in August 1990 an
angry mob attacked Party
House, setting fire to the lower
floors. The building has since
been renovated and it now
belongs to Bulgaria's Parliament, whose MPs have offices
and committee rooms here.

National Art Gallery **⑭**
Национална
Художествена Галерия

pl. Knyaz Aleksandûr Batenberg 1.
City Map *2 D4.* **Tel** *(02) 980 3325.*
Ⓜ *Serdika.* 🚃 *1, 2, 7.* 🔘 *10am–*
6pm Tue–Sun. 🏛 **Ethnographic**
Museum Tel *(02) 987 4191.*
🔘 *10am–6pm Tue–Sun.* 🏛 🔲

The National Art Gallery
(Natsionalna hudozhestvena
galeriya) occupies the west
wing of the former royal palace. It was built in 1873 for
Sofia's Ottoman rulers and
after 1877 was adapted for
independent Bulgaria's mon-
archs. The building's palatial
character persists. Many of
the exhibition halls have pre-
World War I parquet floors

and intricate stucco ceilings.
Bulgarian fine art grew out of
the icon-painting workshops
of the 19th century, and the
gallery's exhibition appropriately begins with works by
the greatest of all Bulgarian
religious artists, Zahari Zograf,
(see p106). Although he
devoted most of his life as an
artist to painting traditional
frescoes for the Orthodox
Church, Zograf also produced
a series of realistic portraits
that show great psychological
insight. Through these, he
effectively launched Bulgarian
painting on a modern European course. On display here
are Zograf's portraits of his
sister-in-law Kristina Zograf-
ska, the educationalist Neofit
Rilski *(see p48)*, and a simple
but charismatic self-portrait.
    The gallery's collection then
traces the development of
Bulgarian painting. Highlights
include a room devoted to the
work of local Impressionists,
which shows the impact of
Western artistic currents on
Bulgarian painting. Centrepiece of the collection is the
work of Bulgarian painters of
the interwar generation,
grouped together in the Red
Hall (the former palace ball-
room). These paintings show
how Bulgarian painters fused
modernist styles of painting
with traditional native themes,
creating a truly national style.
Foremost among them was the
mystically inclined Vladimir
Dimitrov-Maistor (1882–1960),
whose paintings of Bulgarian
peasant girls surrounded by

brightly coloured fruit exude a quasi-religious aura. Zlatyu Boyadzhiev (1903–76) is represented by some empathic portrayals of the poverty-stricken Bulgarian peasantry, while the magic realism of paintings of 19th-century Plovdiv by Tsanko Lavrenov (1896–1978) conjure up a seductively nostalgic vision of the Bulgaria of the past. Exhibitions of contemporary art are often held in the gallery's ground-floor rooms.

The Ethnographic Museum (Etnografski muzei) in the east wing has a small but absorbing collection of traditional Bulgarian costumes. It also mounts temporary exhibitions devoted to aspects of Bulgarian folklore and the museum shop offers a wide range of traditional craft items.

Natural History Museum ⓯
Национален Исторически Музей

bul. Tsar Osvoboditel 1. **City Map** 2 D4. Ⓜ Serdika. **Tel** (02) 987 4195. ☐ 10am–6pm daily. ▨ ▯ www.nmnh.bas.bg

East of the National Art Gallery, the Natural History Museum (Nationalen prirodonauchen muzei) is an enjoyable if rather old-fashioned museum, strong on geology and European fauna. Beginning with rows of rocks and crystals on

Entrance to the Natural History Museum on ulitsa Tsar Osvoboditel

the ground floor, the display moves on to a large collection of stuffed birds and mammals on the first and second floors, and an array of glass cabinets filled with butterflies and insects on the third. Walking up the staircase visitors pass glass tanks in which a variety of live snakes, lizards and rodents are kept. The museum shop has a small but fascinating selection of decorative stones and crystals.

Russian Church ⓰
Руска Църква

bul. Tsar Osvoboditel. **City Map** 2 D5, 4 D1. ☐ 7:30am–6pm daily. ▨

Standing beside the busy bulevard Tsar Osvoboditel, the Church of St Nicholas the Miracle-Worker (Tsurkva na Sveti Nikolai Chudotvorets),

popularly known as the Russian Church, is the most striking building in Sofia. It was built to serve Sofia's Russian community and was consecrated in 1914.

Modelled on 16th-century Muscovite churches, it boasts a cluster of shimmering gilt domes, one of which thrusts skywards at the tip of a pea-green spire. The porch, with a steeply pitched roof covered in bright green tiles, exudes a fairytale charm.

The church's interior is covered with frescoes derived from 17th-century paintings in Moscow and Yaroslavl. Rich in swirling arabesques, they reveal the influence of exotic Eastern styles on Russian art.

A door on the west side of the church leads down to the crypt, last resting place of Archbishop Serafim, leader of the Russian Church in Bulgaria from 1921 to 1950. Serafim's congregation was largely composed of Russian exiles who had fled their homeland after the Bolshevik Revolution, and his reputation for anti-Communism, his kindness and his dignity made him enormously popular with Sofians at large.

Such is Serafim's enduring spiritual stature that his tomb is considered to be capable of working miracles. Because of this a regular stream of worshippers visit the tomb to place handwritten prayers of intercession in a box beside his sarcophagus.

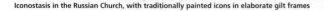

Iconostasis in the Russian Church, with traditionally painted icons in elaborate gilt frames

Aleksandûr Nevski Memorial Church ⑰

Храм-паметник "Александър Невски"

Mosaic portrait in the church

Crowned with a cluster of gilt domes, the Aleksandûr Nevski Memorial Church (Hram-pametnik Aleksandûr Nevski) was built in stages between 1882 and 1924, to commemorate Russia's military contribution to the War of Liberation of 1877–8. It is named after one of Russia's most revered medieval rulers, Prince Aleksandûr Nevski of Novgorod, who defeated the Teutonic Knights on the frozen waters of Lake Peipsi in 1242. Modelled on Russian Neo-Byzantine churches, it is built in pale Bulgarian limestone. The solemn interior is bathed in amber light, which pours in from the windows, and the soft glow of hundreds of flickering candles.

View of the Church
The church's domes are its outstanding feature. While the central dome and belfry are gold-plated, the others are plated with copper, which has weathered to a green hue.

West window

Entrance to the crypt

Clusters of Candles
Visitors to the church buy candles at the entrance, and light them as a symbol of prayer.

Main entrance

Mosaic of Christ
This mosaic of Christ, with arms outstretched, fills the tympanum over the portal's central arch.

STAR SIGHTS

★ Icon Gallery in Crypt

★ Iconostasis

For hotels and restaurants in this area see pp218–20 and pp234–6

Dome Fresco
God the Creator, with the Christ Child on his knee, looks down on the congregation. This church's frescoes were painted by Russian and Bulgarian artists.

VISITORS' CHECKLIST

ploshtad Aleksandûr Nevski.
1, 2, 4, 9, 10, 11.
Main Church *Tel* (02) 988 1704. winter: 7am–6pm daily; summer: 7am–7pm daily.
Icon Gallery *Tel* (02) 981 5775.
10am–5:30pm Tue–Sun.
Liturgy at 8am and 5pm daily. Evening vigil at 6:30pm Sat. Service at 9:30am Sun.

Gold-plated dome

★ **Iconostasis**
The marble, onyx and alabaster iconostasis features carvings of grapes, palms and peacocks. The icons include portraits of Christ and the Virgin.

Tsar's Throne
Built for Tsar Ferdinand (ruled 1886–1918), the throne is guarded by stone lions and crowned by a marble canopy. Behind is a portrait of the tsar and his wife.

★ **Icon Gallery in Crypt**
With icons dating from the 12th to the 19th centuries, and several delicately carved iconostases, the gallery contains the richest collection of religious art in Bulgaria.

Icons & Iconography

Icons play a major role in the Orthodox Church. Far from being mere depictions of Christ and the saints, icons are themselves sanctified objects that help the faithful to feel the presence of God. For this reason, icons are stylized, and are not intended to be realistic portraits.

Icons displayed on an iconostasis are usually arranged according to a strict hierarchy. Those of Christ, the Virgin Mary and St John the Baptist occupy central positions, with those of saints of particular importance to the individual church hung on either side.

St George
Among the most popular icons in Bulgaria are those of the dragon-slaying St George, the demon-slaying St Demetrius, and other mounted warrior-saints of the late Roman era, such as St Eustace, St Menas and St Todor Tiron. They symbolize the courage and perseverance that Christians must have to retain their faith in difficult times. Such icons were of great comfort to Orthodox Christians during the five centuries of Ottoman rule in Bulgaria.

St Nicholas (*Sveti Nikola*) is *the patron saint of seafarers and icons of him are prominently displayed in churches on the Black Sea coast. He is invariably portrayed as a kindly old man with long white beard, often with a ship in the background.*

St Constantine and St Elena
Constantine the Great was the Roman emperor who, in the 4th century, made Christianity the official religion of the Western Roman Empire. His mother Elena was said to have discovered a fragment of the cross of Christ during a visit she made to Jerusalem. She preserved the fragment as a holy relic. In icons, St Constantine and St Elena are often portrayed together.

St John of Rila
This 9th-century mystic and healer is the patron saint of Bulgaria. After his death, possession of his remains became associated with the legitimacy of kingship.

St Cyril and St Methodius (*SS Kiril i Metodii*) *were monks from Thessaloniki who set out to convert the Slavs of Moravia (now part of the Czech Republic) in the early 9th century. Their mission was only partially successful, but their work lived on through their disciples Kliment and Naum, who were responsible for converting Bulgaria's Khan Boris (later known as Tsar Boris) to Christianity in 865. The Cyrillic alphabet was named in honour of St Cyril, who did much preparatory work in developing the script.*

Church of Sveta Sofia, with a lion at the Tomb of the Unknown Soldier

Church of Sveta Sofia [18]
Църква "Света София"

pl. Aleksandûr Nevski. **City Map** 2 E4. 1, 2, 4, 9, 10, 11. 20, 22. 9am–7pm.

The origins of Sofia's oldest surviving Christian church go back to the 6th century. It was built on the site of two 4th-century churches, just outside the city walls. The spot was also the town graveyard of Serdika (as Sofia was known in ancient times), and the church remained Sofia's principal cemetery church well into the Middle Ages.

During the Second Bulgarian Kingdom (1185–1396), the church was probably the seat of the city's bishop, and the city itself (which was known in Bulgarian as Sredets) gradually took the church's name, which means "Holy Wisdom".

After the Ottoman conquest, the church became a mosque, but was abandoned when an earthquake struck in 1858.

The church takes the form of a three-aisled Byzantine-style basilica. The interior is lofty, calm and peaceful, and the beautiful exposed brickwork of the walls and arches is completely devoid of ornamentation. Some fragments of mosaic from one of the 4th-century churches can be seen in the floor of the south aisle.

Outside the church, just beside the south wall, is the Tomb of the Unknown Soldier, which commemorates the thousands of Bulgarian soldiers who fell during World War I. The monument is guarded by a stately bronze lion.

Botanical Garden [19]
Ботаническа Градина

ul. Moskovska 49. **City Map** 2 F4. **Tel** (02) 988 1797. 1, 2, 4, 9, 10, 11. 20, 22. May–Oct: 8am–5pm Tue–Sun.

Tucked away in a side street behind the Aleksandûr Nevski Memorial Church, Sofia University's Botanical Garden (Botanicheska gradina) has a small but inviting collection of Mediterranean flora, and a fragrant rose garden. There is also a glasshouse where a humid atmosphere has been created for the cultivation of such exotic species as palms, banana trees and coffee bushes. The garden's shop has a range of seedlings for sale.

National Gallery of Foreign Art [20]
Национална галерия за чуждестранно изкуство

pl. Aleksandûr Nevski 1. **City Map** 2 F4. **Tel** (02) 980 7262. 1, 2, 4, 10, 11. 11am–6pm Mon, Wed–Sun. www.foreignartgallery.org

The pristine white building behind the Aleksandûr Nevski Memorial Church houses the National Gallery of Foreign Art (Natsionalna galeriya za chuzhdestranno izkustvo). It opened in 1985, and its collection comprises gifts made

Main entrance to the National Gallery of Foreign Art

to the Bulgarian state, either by private individuals or by countries allied to the ruling Communist regime at that time.

On the ground floor are outstanding collections of African tribal sculpture and of Japanese woodblock prints. The display of 19th- and 20th-century painting upstairs seems rather mediocre in comparison. However, there are highlights, such as a pastel drawing by Renoir, a lithograph by Picasso, and some animated sketches by Eugène Delacroix. Thematic exhibitions are often held in the basement, where a barrel-roofed late-Roman tomb is also on display.

The building itself is a modern reconstruction of the State Printing House (1883), one of post-Liberation Bulgaria's finest Neo-Classical buildings, which was destroyed by Allied bombing raids in 1944.

The Botanical Garden on a sunny autumn day

The National Assembly building, on National Assembly Square

National Assembly Square ㉑

Площад "Народно Събрание"

City Map 2 E5, 4 E1. 🚇 1, 2, 5, 8–11.

At the eastern extremity of bulevard Tsar Osvoboditel, National Assembly Square (ploshtad Narodno sŭbranie) is a crescent-shaped space that takes its name from the National Assembly building on its northern side. Built in several stages from 1884 to 1928, the building is a plain, box-like structure, its decoration limited to a sparse row of Grecian-style urns atop the main façade. Above the portal at the entrance are the words *Obedinenieto pravi silata* ("Unity is Strength"), a dictum attributed to the 9th-century Bulgarian ruler Khan Krum.

At the centre of the square stands the Monument to the Tsar Liberator (Pametnik na Tsar Osvoboditel), an equestrian statue of Tsar Alexander II of Russia, whose war with the Ottoman Empire (1877–8) led to the liberation of Bulgaria after centuries of Ottoman rule *(see p47)*. Designed by the Italian sculptor Arnaldo Zocchi (1862–1940), the bronze statue portrays the tsar on horseback, holding Russia's declaration of war on the Ottomans in his outstretched hands. Clustered round the pedestal is a group of smaller statues of Russian troops and Bulgarian volunteer fighters being resolutely led into battle by a winged figure of Nike, the Greek goddess of victory.

Military Museum ㉒

Военноисторически музей

ul. Cherkovna 95. **Tel** (02) 946 1805. 🚇 120. 🕙 10am–6pm Wed–Sun. 📷

Set in the grounds of Bulgaria's military academy, 2 km (over 1 mile) east of the city centre, the Military Museum (Voennoistoricheski muzei) houses a colourful display of the uniforms worn by the Bulgarian army through the ages. The display begins with the home-made tunics worn by anti-Ottoman insurgents during the April Rising of 1876 *(see p172)*, and ends with the combat fatigues worn by Bulgarian armed forces today.

The most impressive aspect of the museum is the extensive walk-around display of military hardware set out in the yard outside. Visitors can examine at close quarters various pieces of artillery, as well as armoured cars, tanks, and MiG fighter jets. But the presence of a pair of SS23 missiles, once fitted with nuclear warheads and stored in silos near Sofia, may send a shiver down the spine.

Mausoleum of Prince Aleksandŭr Batenberg ㉓

Мавзолей на Княз Александър Батенберг

bul. Vasil Levski 81. **City Map** 4 E2. **Tel** (02) 523 969. 🚇 1, 2, 5, 8, 10. 🕙 9am–5pm Mon–Fri.

This charming domed pavilion with a Greek-style portico is the last resting place of Prince Aleksandŭr Batenberg, the German-speaking aristocrat (1854–93) who served as a volunteer in the Russian army before being chosen as the Bulgarian principality's first monarch in 1879 *(see p47)*. Incapable of maintaining a balance between the pro- and anti-Russian factions in Bulgarian politics, he was forced to abdicate in 1886, and spent the rest of his life in the Austrian town of Graz, where he died in 1893.

Two uniforms from the historic display at the Military Museum

Mausoleum of Prince Aleksandûr Batenberg

Aleksandûr's wish to be buried in Bulgaria was honoured by the Bulgarian government, who initially displayed his sarcophagus in the Rotunda of Sveti Georgi *(see p65)*, before moving it to its present purpose-built location.

The mausoleum is set in a tree-shaded park on the western side of bulevard Vasil Levski. The prince's tomb is carved from Carrara marble, and above the sarcophagus a portrait of the prince is held aloft by plump cherubs. On either side of the tomb are inscriptions referring to Aleksandûr's victories in the Serbo-Bulgarian war of 1885, when he was commander-in-chief of the Bulgarian army.

Monument to the Soviet Army ㉔
Паметник на Съветската Армия

Orlov most. **City Map** 4 F3. 🚌 72, 75, 76, 84. 🚊 4, 5, 8, 11.

Just five minutes' walk east of National Assembly Square, on the opposite side of bulevard Vasil Levski, is the Monument to the Soviet Army (Pametnik na Suvetskata armiya). It was unveiled in 1954, and is Sofia's finest Communist-era sculptural group. It consists of a granite pillar, 34 m (112 ft) high, on which stands an over-lifesize statue of a soldier of the Red Army, accompanied by a Bulgarian worker and a

peasant woman with a child in her arms. Reliefs at the base of the pillar show scenes from the Russian October Revolution of 1917 and from World War II.

About 100 m (330 ft) northeast of the pillar stand a pair of oblong stone blocks that bear another set of reliefs. These portray Bulgarian workers, peasants and partisans greeting their Soviet colleagues as liberators. Despite the heavy-handed ideological message that they convey, the sculptures themselves are filled with an expressive vitality rare in the political art of the period. In recent years, skateboarding and rollerblading parks have been set up around the base of the monument, turning it into an unlikely meeting point for Sofia's youth.

Immediately east of the monument is Orlov most (Eagle Bridge), an important Sofia landmark. This is where Bulgarian prisoners held in Ottoman jails re-entered the city on their return from captivity in 1878. Nicknamed the Eagles in recognition of their fortitude, the prisoners are commemorated by a quartet of eagle sculptures mounted on pillars beside the bridge.

Figures on the Monument to the Soviet Army

Red House ㉕
Червената къща

ul. Lyuben Karavelov 15. **City Map** 4 E4. **Tel** (02) 988 8188. 🚌 1, 2, 5, 8, 10. 🚊 2, 12. ⬜ 3–9pm, Tue–Sat. **www**.redhouse-sofia.org

The Red House (Chervenata kushta) is an independent cultural centre devoted to contemporary art, theatre and dance. It occupies one of Sofia's most famous modernist buildings, a flat-roofed, wine-red villa built in the 1930s for the sculptor Andrey Nikolov (1878–1959). Nikolov spent much of his professional life in Rome, and an Italian inscription *Voi ch'entrate qui, lasciate ogni cacattivo pensiero* ("Ye who enter here, leave all bad thoughts behind") stands above the main portal. Inside the house, the high-ceilinged rooms that Nikolov used as studio space now serve as an exhibition area for a programme of temporary exhibitions of modern art and photography. There is also a small permanent exhibition devoted to the life and work of Nikolov himself, featuring the portrait busts he made of prominent Bulgarians and a beautiful marble head of a woman entitled *Longing*. A life-size nude by Nikolov occupies a niche in the Red House's entrance hall.

Sculpture by Andrey Nikolov on display in a room of the Red House

Brightly coloured tiles on the exterior of the Russian Church, Sofia *(see p71)* ▷

A quiet corner of Borisova Gradina, the public park in southeastern Sofia

Borisova Gradina ㉖
Борисова градина

City Map *4 F4.* 4, 5, 8, 11.
2, 12.

Beyond the elliptical grey form of the Vasil Levski sports stadium that marks the southeastern fringes of the city centre, lies Borisova Gradina, Sofia's best-loved municipal park. It stretches out for some 2 km (just over 1 mile) beyond the stadium and was laid out by the Swiss garden designer Daniel Neff in 1884. It was later named Borisova Gradina (Boris's Garden) to mark the birth of Prince Boris (who was to become Tsar Boris III) in 1894.

Planted with elms, chestnuts, sycamores, limes and several species of conifers, and with large areas of oak forest at the far end, Boris's Garden has the atmosphere of semi-tamed woodland rather than that of a formal garden.

As well as the Vasil Levski stadium (the Bulgarian national football team's home ground) the park also has tennis courts, the CSKA football stadium, a velodrome and an open-air swimming pool.

Perhaps the most enjoyable part of the park is its northeastern section, parallel to Tsarigradsko shose. Here there is a children's play-park with climbing frames, and long avenues of limes leading towards the Bratska Mogila (Mound of Brotherhood). This obelisk, 42 m (138 ft) high, was raised in 1956 to commemorate those who died in the cause of communism. It is a typical piece of pro-Soviet propaganda, with statues of anti-Fascist partisans at its base, and bronze reliefs on the pedestal showing the Red Army being enthusiastically greeted by Bulgarian civilians.

Church of Sveti Sedmochislenitsi ㉗
Църква "Свети Седмочисленици"

ul. Graf Ignatiev. **City Map** *4 D3.*
2, 12.

In a small park beside ulitsa Graf Ignatiev, the Church of Sveti Sedmochislenitsi ("the Holy Seven") honours the seven saints (Cyril, Methodius and their five disciples) who brought both Christianity and literacy to the Balkan Slavs in the 9th century.

It was built as a mosque in the 16th century, during Ottoman times, and it was known as the Black Mosque because of the dark-coloured marble that was originally used to build its minaret (which no longer exists). After the War of Liberation of 1877–8 *(see p47)*, the Bulgarians used the mosque as a prison, and it was converted into a church in 1903. Using the famous 14th-century churches in the Black Sea town of Nesebûr *(see pp208–9)* as inspiration, the architects rebuilt the mosque's central dome and added many smaller cupolas and a bell tower.

The interior of the church is decorated with ravishing frescoes in which medieval and modern styles blend. The north wall shows an animated scene of Tsar Boris being given copies of

Mosaic of the Holy Seven, with the figure of Christ, above the entrance to the Church of Sveti Sedmochislenitsi

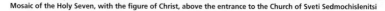

the scriptures by St Kliment and St Naum, followers of the priests Cyril and Methodius who brought Christianity to the Bulgarian court.

Portrait of the writer Ivan Vazov at the Ivan Vazov House-Museum

Ivan Vazov House-Museum ㉘
Къща - музей на Иван Вазов

ul. Ivan Vazov 10. **City Map** *4 D2*. **Tel** *(02) 988 1270*. ▣ *9*. ▣ *2, 12*. ◻ *1–5pm Tue–Thur, 11am–5pm Fri–Sat*. ▨

The life and work of Ivan Vazov (1850–1921), Bulgaria's best-loved novelist, poet and playwright, are honoured in this interesting and atmospheric museum. Most famous as the author of *Under the Yoke (Pod igoto)*, the epic novel of Bulgarian resistance to Ottoman rule, Vazov personified the patriotic spirit of Bulgarian literature in the years immediately after the Liberation.

Vazov was born in the central Bulgarian town of Sopot *(see p168)*. He lived as an exile in Romania during the final years of Ottoman rule, returning to post-Liberation Bulgaria to serve as a magistrate in the provincial town of Berkovitsa. However, Vazov had an uneasy relationship with Bulgaria's political leaders, and he spent time in both Plovdiv (then the capital of Eastern Rumelia) and in the Russian port of Odessa before finally settling in Sofia.

The publication of *Under the Yoke* raised Vazov to the status of a national figure, and he served as Minister of

Education in the late 1890s. His books still form an important part of today's school curriculum.

The museum occupies the house where Vazov lived from 1895 to 1921, and many of the rooms have been preserved intact. The upstairs bedrooms and sitting rooms, with Art Nouveau wallpaper and brightly coloured traditional carpets, are particularly seductive. Vazov's beloved dog Bobby, stuffed during the author's lifetime after an unfortunate incident with a tramcar, still enjoys pride of place in the study. In another room visitors can enjoy black-and-white photographs of places important to Vazov's life and career.

National Theatre ㉙
Народен театър

ul. Dyakon Ignatii 5. **City Map** *1 C5, 3 C1*. **Tel** *(02) 811 9219*. ▣ *9*. ▣ *2, 12*. **www**.nationaltheatre.bg

Presiding over a leafy oblong of park known as the City Garden, the National Theatre (Naroden Teatur) has a Neo-Classical splendour that few other buildings in Sofia can

Sculpture at the National Theatre

match. Built in 1907 by the Viennese architects Hermann Helmer and Ferdinand Fellner, the theatre has a colonnaded façade topped by a pediment that contains a relief of Apollo surrounded by luxuriantly reclining muses. Even more sensuous are the sculptural groups that crown the towers on either side of the pediment. They consist of trumpeters borne along in grand chariots, each of which is drawn by a trio of fierce lions.

Home to Bulgaria's leading state drama company, the theatre concentrates on a worthy repertoire of Bulgarian and international classics. Visitors should consider buying a ticket even if only to enjoy the opulent balustraded foyer and plush auditorium.

The City Garden (Gradskata gradina) in front of the theatre is Sofia's oldest park. It was laid out during the Ottoman period, when it served as the governor of Sofia's private garden. Now with neat lawns, a mixture of deciduous and evergreen trees and a modern fountain, it is a popular for relaxed strolling throughout the year.

The elegant Neo-Classical façade of the National Theatre

City Art Gallery ⓷⓪
Градска художествена
галерия

ul. Gûrko 1. **City Map** *1 C5, 3 C1.*
Tel *(02) 987 2181.* 🚊 *9.* 🚋 *2, 12.*
⏲ *10am–6pm Tue–Sat, 11am–6pm
Sun.* **www**.sghg.cult.bg

Standing at the southern end
of the City Garden, the
City Art Gallery (Grads-
ka Hudozhestvena
Galeriya) does not have
a permanent collection,
but hosts a regular pro-
gramme of prestigious
temporary exhibitions.
The main purpose of
these is to showcase
the excellent work of
contemporary Bulgari-
an painters and sculp-
tors, although some
challenging work by
international artists
is also shown here
from time to time.

**Sculpture of a female
figure, City Art Gallery**

Slaveykov Square ⓷⓵
Площад "Славейков"

City Map *3 C2.* 🚋 *2, 12.*

The broad pedestrianized
oblong of Slaveykov Square
(ploshtad Slaveykov), just a
short stroll southwards from
the City Garden, is famous for
hosting a large daily open-air
book market. Although most
of the books on sale here are
in Bulgarian, visitors will also
find a range
of richly illus-
trated books
in English on
Bulgarian
history

and culture. A daily book
market has been in the square
since the early 1990s. At that
time, many of Bulgaria's state-
owned bookshops had gone
bankrupt, and were replaced
by the informal network of
independent street stalls that
began to spring up in Sofia.
Most of these street stalls
eventually gravitated towards
Slaveykov Square.

The square is
named in honour of
the educationalist and
patriotic activist Petko
Slaveykov and his son,
the modernist poet
Pencho Slaveykov.
The lives and work
of both men are docu-
mented at the Slaveykov
Museum *(see below).*
The life-size bronze
statue of father and
son seated side by
side on a bench at
the western end of
the square is a
popular local landmark.

Peyu Yavorov Museum ⓷⓶
Музей на Пейо Яворов

ul. Rakovski 136. **City Map** *3 B3.*
Tel *(02) 988 0887.* 🚊 *9.* ⏲ *10am–
5pm Mon–Wed, 1–5pm Thu, 10am–
5pm Fri.* 📷

A short walk south of the
book market on Slaveykov
Square, this small but absorbing museum occupies the
apartment where the poet
Peyu Yavorov and his wife
Lora Karavelova lived in
1913–14.

Period furniture and original
Art Nouveau wallpaper
provide an intriguing insight
into the tastes of the period.
Most Bulgarians associate
this museum with the tragic
suicides of both Lora and
Peyu, and there are compelling references to both events
in the display. One glass cabi-
net holds a glamorous black
dress rent by a bullet, recalling the night of 29 November
1913 when a jealous Lora shot
herself with Yavorov's pistol.
In another room, a blood-
stained cushion still rests on
the couch where Yavorov
committed suicide a year later.
A statue of Yavorov, showing the seated poet in an atti-
tude of deep thought,
occupies the front garden.

**Room in the Slaveykovs' apartment,
now the Slaveykov Museum**

Slaveykov Museum ⓷⓷
Музей на Славейков

ul. Rakovski 138. **City Map** *3 B3.*
🚊 *9.* ⏲ *9am–5pm Mon–Fri.* 📷

Located in an undistinguished
apartment block next to the
Peyu Yavorov Museum, the
Slaveykov Museum honours
the Tryavna-born educationalist and publicist Petko
Slaveykov (1823–95), a key
campaigner for Bulgarian
political, religious and cultural
rights during the period of
Ottoman rule. The museum
also houses artifacts relating
to the life and work of Petko's
son Pencho (1866–1912), who
became one of Bulgaria's
foremost modern poets.

Life-size statue of Petko Slaveykov and his son Pencho in Slaveykov Square

For hotels and restaurants in this region see pp218–20 and pp234–6

The National Palace of Culture (NDK), a monolithic centre of the arts

Educated in Leipzig, Pencho introduced a new Western-European sensibility into Bulgarian literature. His name was about to be put forward for the Nobel Prize for Literature when he unexpectedly died in Switzerland.

The museum recreates the atmosphere of an early 20th-century Bulgarian home, with delicately embroidered tablecloths, traditional carpets and hand-painted storage trunks. The rooms are also lined with well-stocked bookshelves and photographs of members of the Slaveykov family.

National Palace of Culture ㉞

Национален дворец на културата (НДК)

pl. Bûlgariya. **City Map** 3 A5.
Tel (02) 916 6830. 🚋 1, 2, 5, 8, 9, 10. 🚋 1, 7.

Marking the southern end of bulevard Vitosha, Sofia's main shopping street, the National Palace of Culture (Naroden Dvorets na Kulturata, or NDK) is one of the city's modern landmarks. Begun in 1978, it was completed in 1981, when it opened in celebration of the 1,300th anniversary of Bulgarian statehood *(see p42)*. This monumental eight-storey hexagon of concrete and glass dominates the flagstoned open spaces and neat flowerbeds of ploshtad Bûlgariya.

The building was originally named in honour of Lyudmila Zhivkova, daughter of the dictator Todor Zhivkov *(see*

pp52–3). She was Bulgaria's Minister of Culture from 1975 to 1981. Zhivkova died of a brain tumour in 1981, and was much missed by Bulgarian intellectuals, who felt that she had broadened the horizons of Bulgarian culture beyond the ideological constraints of the Communist party. She was also active in promoting Bulgarian culture abroad.

Inside the NDK, the principal space is a concert hall with seating for 5,000 and other smaller concert halls and rooms. Beneath the building is an arcade filled with stalls selling clothes.

A footbridge behind the NDK leads across bulevard Bûlgariya to the Hilton Hotel and Yuzhen Park (South Park), an expanse of lawns, flowerbeds and untended grassy areas that stretches out for 3 km (2 miles) towards dense woodland. A conspicuous presence at the northern end of the park is the Thirteen Hundred Years Monument, an ugly, crumbling modernist sculpture. It stands as a reminder of 1,300 years of oppression, and bears the inscription "We are in time and time is in us", words attributed to Vasil Levski *(see p169)*.

PEYU YAVOROV (1878–1914)

Of all 20th-century Bulgarian poets, the one whose life and work most fascinates successive generations of readers is Peyu Yavorov. He began writing poetry while working at a provincial post office in the Black Sea town of Pomorie, and moved to Sofia when his work began to be published by the literary magazine *Misûl*. He is best known for the poems of obsessive love inspired by Mina Todorova, a teenage girl whose family considered Yavorov to be an unworthy suitor. Mina died of consumption in 1910, and Yavorov was immediately courted and captured by Lora Karavelova, an emancipated divorcée.

Yavorov was also a committed revolutionary, and his involvement in the guerrilla movement in Ottoman-occupied Macedonia made Lora feel abandoned and ignored. When in Sofia, Yavorov was constantly surrounded by female admirers, and Lora shot herself in a fit of jealous rage in 1913. Intending to commit suicide, Yavorov shot himself but survived. Lora's family accused Yavorov of her murder and pursued him through the courts. Abandoned by society, Yavorov finally committed suicide.

Statue of the poet at the Peyu Yavorov Museum

National History Museum ❸❺

Национален исторически музей

Bulgaria's largest collection of historic artifacts is located 7 km (4 miles) from the centre of Sofia, but, despite the distance, most visitors will think the trip worthwhile. The museum has a delightful setting in the foothills outside the capital and contains some truly remarkable objects – the 4th-century BC Thracian gold treasures from Panagyurishte are the highlight. But there is plenty more to see in this slightly eclectic collection: icons and frescoes recall the Bulgarian Church under the Ottomans, while modern history is covered by military uniforms and hardware, and theatrical memorabilia. The building was once a Communist Party palace, so touring the vast opulent rooms adds extra interest.

★ Panagyurishte Gold
The 3rd-century BC Panagyurishte treasure consists of eight richly decorated gold rhytons or drinking vessels. Five rhytons are in the form of animal heads, while three depict Amazon warriors.

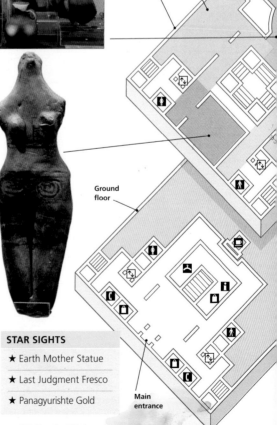

Second floor

First floor

Ground floor

Main entrance

Ceramics
The medieval cities of Pliska, Preslav and Veliko Tûrnovo were centres of ceramics manufacture, where vessels decorated with floral and animal motifs were made.

★ Earth Mother Statue
This clay figure was found near Targovishte, in north-eastern Bulgaria. It stands 14 cm (5½ in) high and is about 6,500 years old. The red and ochre spiral decorations indicate some sort of costume.

KEY

- Prehistory
- Ancient Thracians, Greeks and Romans
- Medieval Bulgaria
- Bulgaria under the Ottoman Empire
- Post-Liberation Bulgaria (post-1878)
- Folk Costumes and Craft
- Temporary exhibition
- Non-exhibition space

STAR SIGHTS

★ Earth Mother Statue

★ Last Judgment Fresco

★ Panagyurishte Gold

Kilim of Teteven
This example of a 19th-century hand-woven woollen kilim bears the colourful starburst design favoured by weavers in the town of Teteven.

VISITORS' CHECKLIST

ul. Vitoshko Lale, Boyana.
🚌 63, 11. 🚋 2. 🚇 M 21. 🚌
from Sofia. 🎫 (02) 955 4280.
www.historymuseum.org.
🕐 Nov–Mar: 9am–5:30pm (last
ticket 4:45pm); Apr–Oct: 9:30am–
6pm (last ticket 5:30pm).
🚫 1 Jan, 3 Mar, 24 May,
24 and 25 Dec. 🚫 📷 charge
applies. 📷 🚻 📁 🍴

Folk Costume
This collection features traditional dress from all over Bulgaria. Note the metal pafti or belt-buckles, frequently embossed with animals, figures of saints, or abstract designs.

Cinema Poster
Exhibits taken from the world of entertainment and popular culture add a touch of glamour to the display devoted to 20th-century life, on the second floor.

GALLERY GUIDE
The halls work well chronologically, so start with Prehistory before moving on to the Thracians – the stars of the show, they are often on loan to other museums. The Medieval hall is a little disappointing, but there are items of interest in the other halls. It is also rewarding to explore the building just to see how the Communist leaders lived.

★ Last Judgment Fresco
The Last Judgment was a favourite subject for Bulgarian religious artists. This 17th-century example shows the grisly punishments awaiting sinners in hell.

Wooden Icon Screen
The central doors of the icon screen, above, symbolize the divide between the material world and God's kingdom. The doors bear icons showing the Annunciation, framed by highly intricate woodcarving.

Fresco in Boyana Church, depicting scenes from the life of Christ

Boyana Church ㊱
Боянска църква

ul. Boyansko ezero 3. **Tel** (02) 959 0939. 🚌 64. ⬜ 9:30am–5:30pm, by prior arrangement. 📷

The village suburb of Boyana, on a hillside south of the National History Museum (see p71), is a relatively prosperous district of modern family houses and villas. However, just above the main square is Boyana Church (Boyanskata tsurkva), one of Bulgaria's most renowned medieval buildings. Covered from floor to ceiling with beautiful 13th-century frescoes, the church has been declared a UNESCO World Heritage Site.

The church's origins go back to the 11th century, when it was a compact building, roughly 6 m (20 ft) square. Two centuries later, it was enlarged by the addition of a two-storey annexe built onto its western façade. According to inscriptions, this enlargement was carried out in 1259 by Sebastokrator Kaloyan, a nobleman who also funded the church's interior decoration.

Painted by anonymous local masters, the church's frescoes display a quality of realistic portraiture unusual for the period. Western artistic

influences may have reached Bulgaria from Constantinople, which had been captured by Crusaders in 1204.

A glorious portrait of Christ Pantokrator fills the cupola, in the oldest section of the church. Lower down is a frieze with portraits of the Evangelists, followed by rows of armour-clad warrior-saints, including George and Demetrius.

Some of the finest paintings are in the 13th-century annexe. The ground floor contains 18 scenes from the life of St Nicholas, and one of the earliest known depictions of Bulgaria's patron saint, John of Rila (see p109). The portrayals of Christ, in scenes of the Last Supper, the Crucifixion and the Transfiguration, display a remarkable psychological depth.

On the south wall of the annexe are full-length portraits of Tsar Konstantin Asen (1257–77) and Irina, his queen. On the opposite wall are depictions of Sebastokrator Kaloyan and his wife Desislava, clad in fine clothes. Kaloyan is shown holding a model of the church, thereby indicating his status as the patron of its reconstruction.

Dragalevtsi Monastery ㊲
Драгалевски манастир

Dragalevtsi. 🚌 64, 93, 98.

On the wooded slopes of Mount Vitosha, just above the suburb of Dragalevtsi, stands a 14th-century monastery. Founded during the reign

Boyana Church, built in the 11th–13th centuries in Byzantine style

Draglevtsi Monastery, one-time refuge of the patriot Vasil Levski

of Tsar Ivan Alexandûr (1331–71), it was abandoned at the time of the Ottoman conquest, but was re-founded a century later thanks to the efforts of the local *boyar* (aristocrat) Radoslav Mavur. Frescoes in the monastery church depict Radoslav and his wife Vida, on the north wall of the vestibule. Also in the vestibule are scenes from the New Testament, including an impressive Last Judgment. Well-preserved frescoes of the apostles and of various saints line the walls of the nave.

The monks of Dragalevtsi frequently provided refuge to the Bulgarian patriot Vasil Levski *(see p169)* in 1871–2, when he was engaged in establishing a network of revolutionary cells throughout the country. Today, the monastery is home to a flourishing convent, and is used as a summer retreat by the Orthodox Church hierarchy.

From just above the suburb of Dragalevtsi, visitors can take a chairlift to the resort of Aleko, which provides panoramic views of Sofia sprawling over the plain. Aleko is an expanding winter sports destination. Its proximity to Sofia means that it can be quite busy at weekends, with city-dwellers coming to enjoy winter sports, and with walkers arriving in summer. It is therefore best to come here on a weekday.

Mount Vitosha ㊳
Витоша

See pp88–9

Monastery of St George ㊴
Манастир "Свети Георги"

Kremikovtsi. 🚌 *117.* ⬜ *irregular hours.* 📅 *St George's Day (6 May).*

In the 13th century Sofia was a major spiritual centre, and many monastic communities were established in the hills around the city. These outlying monasteries continued to flourish well into the Ottoman period, not least because they were some distance from the Turkish-dominated city centre.

The Monastery of St George, just above the village of Kremikovtsi, some 25 km (15 miles) east of Sofia, was one such focus of Bulgarian ecclesiastical life. In 1493 the local *boyar* Radivoy, grieving the loss of his children Todor and Dragana, funded the construction of a new monastery church. He also commissioned painters to decorate it with sumptuous frescoes. Radivoy and his family are portrayed in the narthex, the *boyar* presenting the model of the church to its patron, St George. The north wall of the nave bears an animated depiction of St George spearing a dragon. Elsewhere on the north wall are portraits of St George's fellow warrior-saints, such as Demetrius, Theodor Tyron, Theodor Stratilat and Mercurius, who is shown pulling an arrow from his eye. The monastery has irregular opening hours, but a key-holder is usually available to open the church. In the plain below Kremikovtsi, Bulgaria's largest steelworks presents an incongruous modern counterpoint to the monastery's medieval splendours.

Painting of St George and the Dragon at the Monastery of St George

Mount Vitosha ❸
Витоша

Rising above Sofia's southern suburbs, the granite massif of Mount Vitosha provides Bulgaria's capital with an easily accessible recreation area. The top of the mountain is relatively smooth, making it the ideal terrain for easy hikes. Acres of beech forest cover Vitosha's lower slopes, while spruce and pine predominate further up. The mountain's highest point, the 2,290-m (7,500-ft) Cherni Vruh (Black Peak), is surrounded by a plateau covered in grassland, juniper bushes and bogs. Protected as a nature park since 1934, Vitosha is a natural habitat for martens, deer, wild boar and, occasionally, brown bears.

Panorama of Sofia
For the best views of the city, which sprawls at the foot of Mount Vitosha, head for Kopitoto, or take a trip downhill on the Dragalevtsi chairlift.

Kopitoto (The Hoof)
is a ridge topped by the slender television and radio mast that can be seen from all over the city, and a restaurant with terrific views.

Boyar Churc
1348 m   1087 m
Boyana
Waterfall
1906 m
Boyana River

★ Stone River
This compelling natural attraction consists of huge boulders deposited by a glacier in the last Ice Age and smoothed by seasonal meltwaters.

ZLATNI MOSTOVE

Zlatni Mostove (Golden Bridges),
directly below the Stone River, is an area of meadows and forest clearings popular with picnickers.

1969 m

Torfeno Branisht Reserve

2041 m

2108 m

Mount Vitosha Plateau
West of the peak, this peat bog plateau supports rare wild flowers and insects. Much of it falls within the protected Torfeno branishte reserve, so hiking is discouraged.

Meteorological Observatory
This weather station was built in 1935 and has been monitoring the weather conditions ever since. In winter, when Sofia is in cold fog, an interesting inversion takes place and Vitosha enjoys the winter sun.

STAR SIGHTS

★ Cherni Vruh

★ Dragalevtsi Monastery

★ Stone River

For hotels and restaurants in this region see pp218–20 and pp234–6

★ Dragalevtsi Monastery

The Monastery of the Holy Virgin is set in deep forest just above the suburb of Dragalevtsi. Stunning 15th-century frescoes decorate the entrance hall of its church.

VISITORS' CHECKLIST

10 km S of Sofia. 🚌 🚌 66 to Aleko; 93 to Dragalevtsi; 122 to Simeonovo; 61 to Zlatni Mostove: all from Hladilnika bus terminus, (on tram route nos. 9 & 10). 🛈 ul. Antim I, 17, Sofia (02 989 53 77). www.park-vitosha.org

Simeonovo
Boasting fresh mountain air and plenty of green space, Simeonovo is one of Sofia's most affluent suburbs.

Cable Car
The cable car runs from the pleasant suburb of Simeonovo to Aleko, and provides excellent views over the city.

PERNIK

SOFIA

18

18

Dragalevtsi

PAZARDZHIK

Dragalevtsi Chairlift

862 m

Simeonovo Gondola

Bistritsa Lake

Goli Vrah 1837 m

ALEKO

Malak Rezen 2191 m

Cherni Vrah

Golyam Rezen 2277 m

0 kilometres   1

0 miles   1

Aleko Mountain Hut
Built in 1924, the Aleko mountain hut is a popular starting point for hikers in summer. In winter, Aleko becomes the centre of Mount Vitosha's busy ski scene.

★ Cherni Vruh
Vitosha's highest point is a popular destination for hikers. It is about an hour's walk up from Aleko, or a 30-minute walk above the last stop of the highest chairlifts, if they are running.

KEY

🟰	Major road
🟰	Other road
--	Trail
△	Peak
☀	Viewpoint
🚡	Cable car station
•—	Cable car line
🚡	Chairlift station
•—	Chairlift line
🚌	Coach park or terminus
▢	Urban area

ENTERTAINMENT AND SHOPPING

In terms of opera, classical music and drama, Sofia offers a great deal for a relatively low price. The city's bar and club scene is vibrant and stylish, but also slightly unpredictable, with many venues swiftly coming into vogue and going out of fashion again. Many of Sofia's most culturally authentic clubs, where live musicians and belly dancers often perform, are those devoted to the Oriental-influenced Balkan pop music known as *chalga*. Live rock music, however, is less common in Sofia than in other European capitals, although there are plenty of piano bars where you can dance to jazz and blues. Sofia also has a lively retail culture, with shops and markets staying open late into the evening seven days a week.

Traditional gourd-shaped bottle

ENTERTAINMENT

The music, opera and dance seasons usually run from October to June. Information and tickets for most cultural events in Sofia are available from the **Concert Bureau** or the National Palace of Culture.

OPERA, DANCE AND CLASSICAL MUSIC

Sofia's elegant opera house is home to the **National Opera and Ballet** (Natsionalna opera i balet), a very prestigious organization that puts on quality performances three to four times a week during the concert season. The regular programme is firmly rooted in the classics, although international companies often perform modern works.

The Sofia Philharmonic Orchestra gives performances at the **Bulgaria Concert Hall** (Zala Bulgariya) at least once a week. The concert hall is also a venue for recitals by soloists and chamber music concerts given by Bulgarian and international musicians.

Major orchestral concerts featuring international performers also take place at the **National Palace of Culture (NDK)** (Natsionalen dvorets na kulturata), a modern concert and congress centre whose main hall has excellent acoustics and seating for 3,800.

THEATRE

Sofia's leading theatre is the **Ivan Vazov National Theatre** (Naroden teatur Ivan Vazov), an opulent building that is the base of Bulgaria's best actors and directors. The programme is wide-ranging and includes Bulgarian classics as well as foreign contemporary drama. Modern plays are also put on by the **Sofia Drama Theatre** (Dramatichen teatur Sofia), the **Aleko Konstantinov Satirical Theatre** (Satirichen teatur Aleko Konstantinov), and **Tears and Laughter**, Sofia's oldest theatre.

The leading venue for fringe and experimental drama is the interesting **Sfumato Theatre Workshop** (Teatralna rabotilnitsa Sfumato).

Although performances are in Bulgarian, many are based on improvisation and movement rather than written text, so that they are accessible to non-Bulgarian speakers.

CLUBS AND BARS

Central Sofia is packed with clubs and bars, many of which have designer interiors and attract an equally dressed-up clientele. **Motto**, which serves cocktails and food in a stylish lounge-bar atmosphere, is typical of Sofia's contemporary music scene. There is also a growing number of pubs, which are popular with both Bulgarians and foreign visitors. Of these, **JJ Murphy's** is one of the longest-established.

Dance clubs are informal and inexpensive, with long-standing venues such as **Yalta** and **Chervilo** ("Lipstick") attracting international DJs and a youthful audience.

SHOPPING

Sofia's most glamorous shopping street is bulevard Vitosha, where brightly lit window displays feature clothing and accessories by modern international designers. Ulitsa Graf Ignatiev, just to the east, is also lined with shops, ranging from bakeries to bookstores.

ANTIQUES, CRAFTS AND SOUVENIRS

There is a daily antiques and bric-à-brac market on ploshtad Aleksandûr Nevski. A great range of items, from

A performance at the Ivan Vazov National Theatre, Sofia's main theatre

coins and old cameras to reproduction icons and folk costume, is on sale here.

For traditional woollen rugs, embroidered blouses and handmade jewellery, head for the **Ethnographic Museum Shop**. A colourful range of crafts and textiles is also on offer at **Traditzia**, which sells items made by the inhabitants of remote villages.

MARKETS

Central Sofia's liveliest market is **Zhenski pazar**, a vast open-air affair offering fresh fruit, vegetables and dairy produce, as well as clothes, textiles and kitchenware. Middle Eastern, Chinese and other exotic foodstuffs can be bought from shops in the narrow streets either side of the market.

The best place for indoor food shopping is **Tsentralni Hali** (see p66), an Art Nouveau covered market with stalls selling olives, cheeses, pickled vegetables, smoked meats and other delicacies. This is also a good place to buy Bulgarian wines and spirits.

Antiques and collectables at the market on ploshtad Aleksandŭr Nevski

BOOKS AND MUSIC

Sofia's principal open-air book-browsing location is ploshtad Slaveykov (see p82). An increasing number of high-street bookshops, such as **Booktrading** and **Helikon**, stock novels and guidebooks in English and other mainstream languages.

Orange stocks stationery, books and CDs of Bulgarian folk music. **Dyukyan Meloman** is another good place to seek out jazz and international music, including traditional Balkan sounds.

SHOPPING MALLS

Sofia's most famous shopping mall is **Tzum**, with four floors of upmarket shops selling clothing, accessories and luxury goods. Tzum (Tsentralen universalen magazin, or Central Universal Store) was built in 1955, as Sofia's main department store, and the building is still a city landmark. Two other malls, slightly outside the city centre, are **City Center Sofia** and **Mall of Sofia**. Both are filled with shops selling a range of international fashions.

DIRECTORY

OPERA, DANCE & CLASSICAL MUSIC

Bulgaria Concert Hall
ul. Aksakov 1. **Map** 2 D5.
Tel (02) 987 7656.

Concert Bureau
ul. Tsar Osvoboditel 2.
Map 1 C4. Open 8am–noon, 3–7pm Mon–Fri.

National Opera and Ballet
ul. Vrabcha 1. **Map** 2 D4.
Tel (02) 987 1366.
www.operasofia.com

National Palace of Culture
pl. Bulgariya 1. **Map** 3 A5.
Tel (02) 916 6830.
www.ndk.bg

THEATRE

Aleko Konstantinov Satirical Theatre
ul. Stefan Karadja 26.
Map 3 C2.
Tel (02) 987 6606.

Ivan Vazov National Theatre
ul. Dyakon Ignatii 5. **Map** 1 C5. *Tel (02) 811 9219.*
www.nationaltheatre.bg

Sfumato Theatre Workshop
ul. Dimitar Grekov 2.
Tel (02) 944 0127.
www.sfumato.info

Sofia Drama Theatre
bl. Y. Sakuzov 23a.
Tel (02) 944 2485.

Tears and Laughter
ul. Rakovski 127. **Map** 2 D5. *Tel (02) 987 5895.*
www.salzaismiah.com

CLUBS & BARS

Chervilo
bul. Tsar Osvoboditel 9.
Map 2 E5.
www.chervilo.com

JJ Murphy's
ul. Kurnigradska 6. **Map** 1 A5. *Tel (02) 980 2870.*
www.jjmurphys-sofia.com

Motto
ul. Aksakov 18. **Map** 2 E5.
Tel (02) 987 2723.
www.motto-bg.com

Yalta
bul. Tsar Osvoboditel 20.
Map 4 F2.
Tel (02) 987 3481.

CRAFTS & SOUVENIRS

Ethnographic Museum Shop
pl. Aleksandŭr Batenberg 1. **Map** 1 C4.

Traditzia
bul. Vasil Levski 36. **Map** 3 C4. *Tel (02) 981 7765.*
www.traditzia.bg

MARKETS

Bric-à-Brac Market
pl. Aleksandŭr Nevski.
Map 2 E4.

Zhenski pazar
ul. Stefan Stambolov.
Map 1 A2.

BOOKS & MUSIC

Booktrading
Graf Ignatiev 15.
Map 4 D3.

Dyukyan Meloman
ul. 6-ti septemvri 7a. **Map** 4 D1. *Tel (02) 988 5862.*

Helikon
bul. Nikolai Rakitin 2.
Tel (02) 97 1919.
www.helikon.bg

Orange
ul. Graf Ignatiev 18. **Map** 4 D3. *Tel (02) 980 8207.*

SHOPPING MALLS

City Center Sofia
bul. Arsenalski 2.

Mall Of Sofia
bul. Aleksandŭr Stamboliiski 100.

Tzum
bul. Knyaginya Mariya Luiza 2. **Map** 1 B3.

SOFIA STREET FINDER

All the map references given for sights, hotels and restaurants in Sofia refer to this section of the book. The key map below shows the area of the city covered by the Street Finder. The first figure of the reference indicates which map to turn to, and the letter and number which follow are for the grid reference. Street signs in Sofia often use two scripts, Roman and Cyrillic, but spellings may not always be exactly the same. The most common words used in addresses that the visitor should recognise are *ploshtad* for "square", *ulitsa* for "street" and obviously *bulevard* for "boulevard" (abbreviated to *pl.*, *ul.* and *bul.* respectively).

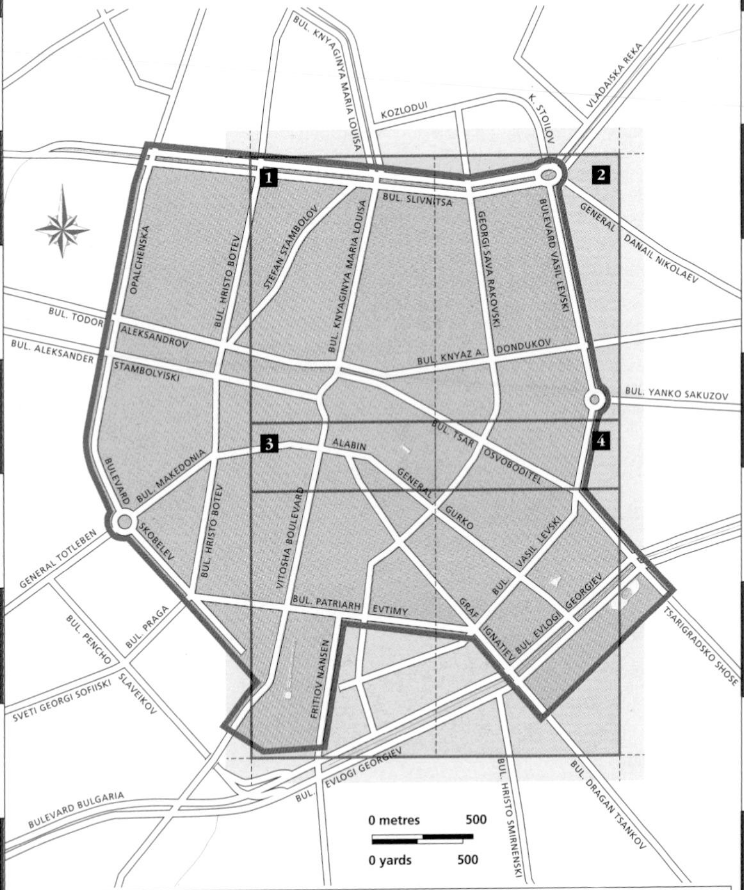

0 metres 500
0 yards 500

KEY

- ▣ Major sight
- ▣ Place of interest
- ▣ Other building
- Ⓜ Metro station
- ▣ Train station
- ▣ Car park
- ⓘ Tourist information point
- ✚ Hospital with casualty unit
- ▣ Police station
- ▣ Church
- ✡ Synagogue
- Ⓒ Mosque
- ⊠ Post office
- ═ Railway line
- ≈ Pedestrian street

SCALE OF MAP PAGES

0 metres 200
0 yards 200
1:14,000

Street Finder Index

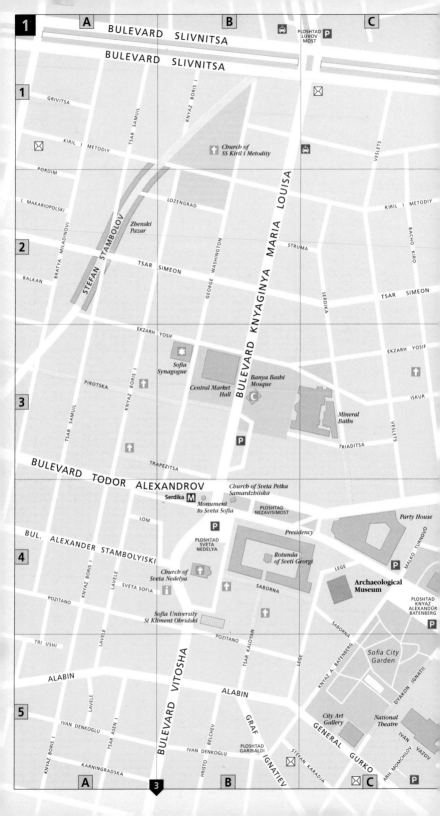

SOUTHERN BULGARIA

From December to April, most of this mountainous region is buried beneath thick snow, but the rest of the year it is an oasis of lush greenery and dense forests. The country's most spectacular scenery and most varied wildlife can be discovered here, and the architecture and folklore of this rugged landscape offer a fascinating insight into an intriguing and somewhat remote part of Bulgaria.

The highest peaks in the eastern Balkans rise in the Rila and Pirin mountain ranges. Both are national parks and both contain a great variety of flora and fauna, including wolves, bears, and many endemic plants. The Rhodopes, which cover a much greater area, are a largely undeveloped wilderness that, towards the east, tails off into the tobacco-growing Plains of Thrace. For centuries this area was inhabited by much of Bulgaria's Turkish community. In fact Palaeolithic flint tools discovered here show that human habitation of the region goes back 40,000 years. Thracians later settled in the area in large numbers. Smolyan's History Museum gives a superb overview of the region's past.

The Ottomans were largely tolerant of their Christian subjects, but there were isolated campaigns to force Bulgarians to adopt the Islamic faith. A small number of Bulgarians found refuge in the Rhodope Mountains, where they established villages that remained free of Turkish influence. Their untainted medieval Bulgarian language, music, costumes and customs served as a model for the National Revival movement of the 19th century.

Two great monasteries, Rila and Bachkovo, were also established in the Rhodopes. The monks kept Bulgarian heritage alive by preserving and copying the ancient manuscripts of the old Bulgarian kingdoms. These monasteries became a focus of the National Revival movement.

Glacial lake in the Pirin Mountains, one of three great massifs in southern Bulgaria

◁ Courtyard at Rila Monastery, founded in the 14th century and rebuilt in the 19th, in the Rila Mountains

Exploring Southern Bulgaria

Southern Bulgaria's stunning mountain ranges offer plenty of opportunities for hiking, biking and skiing. The region has a wealth of historic buildings, the finest of which are Bulgaria's two UNESCO-listed monasteries, Rila and Bachkovo. Birdwatchers can see vultures at Madzharovo Nature Reserve and many other rare breeds throughout the mountains. Much of the region has piping hot mineral springs, and a well established spa industry offering high-tech treatments.

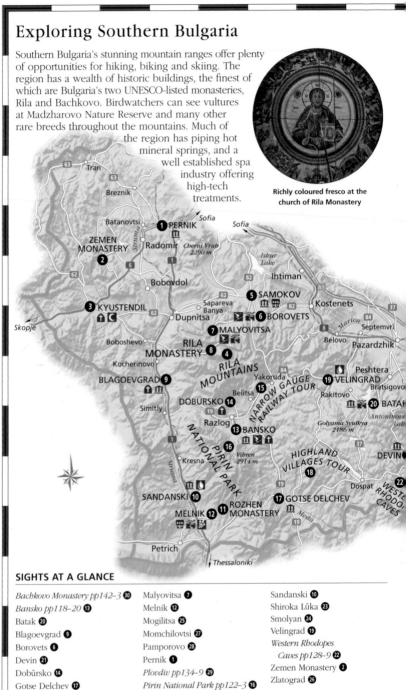

Richly coloured fresco at the church of Rila Monastery

SIGHTS AT A GLANCE

SEE ALSO

- **Where to Stay** pp220–24

- **Where to Eat** pp236–40

KEY

═══ Motorway

═══ Expressway

──── Main road

──── Other road

─┼─┼─ Railway

▪▪▪▪ International border

△ Peak

Church of Sveta Bogoroditsa at Bachkovo Monastery

0 kilometres 25

0 miles 25

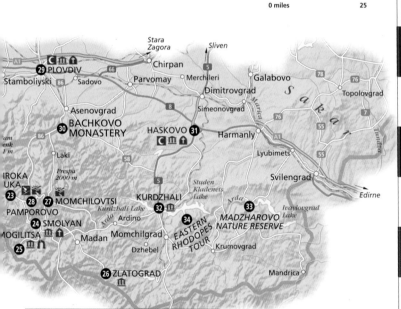

Madzharovo Nature Reserve, in the eastern Rhodopes

GETTING AROUND

Winding roads mean that visitors should allow plenty of time for journeys, especially if travelling by public transport. Buses cover the entire region, but services to remote villages are often limited to one bus a day. To explore the central and western Rhodope Mountains, hiring a car is the best option. Regular train services connect Sofia with Blagoevgrad and Sandanski, and a narrow-gauge track branches off the main Sofia–Plovdiv line, winding through the mountains to Bansko. From Plovdiv trains run to Haskovo and Kŭrdzhali.

Pernik ●
Перник

30 km (20 miles) SW of Sofia. **Map**
B3. 🏛 *86,000.* 🚉 🚌 🏨 🍴 📷
🎭 *Kukeri and Survakari Festival (end
Jan, even years).* **www**.surva.org

The history of Pernik, whose
name is derived from Perun,
the Slav god of thunder, dates
back to Thracian times. In
the 9th century AD, the now-
ruined fortress on Krakra
Pernishki hill, just outside the
town, played a key role in
repelling Byzantine attacks on
the First Bulgarian Kingdom.
The hill is named after Krakra,
a local feudal leader.
    After this turbulent period,
Pernik sank into obscurity
and was of little importance
until the 19th century, when
huge deposits of coal were
discovered nearby. It became
Bulgaria's largest coal mining
centre, but by the late 20th
century economic stagnation
and dwindling coal supplies
led to its decline.
    Today, Pernik's suburbs are
filled with crumbling tower
blocks and decaying Socialist-

The Church of St Ivan the Theologian, focal point of Zemen Monastery

era factories. The town centre
and the surrounding parks are
pleasant enough, but Pernik's
real attractions are the lively
biennial Kukeri and Survakari
festival *(see box)* and the
Mining Museum, in a shaft of
the town's first coal mine.

🏛 Mining Museum
pl. Sveti Ivan Rilski 1.
Tel *(076) 602 911, ext. 262.*
🕙 *10am–5pm, Tue & Thu.* 📷 📷

Zemen Monastery ●
Земенски манастир

3 km (2 miles) SW of Zemen. **Map**
A3. **Tel** *(077) 413 131.* 🚌 🕙 *9am–
5:30pm Mon–Wed, Fri–Sun.* 🎫 🚻

In a sheltered hillside spot
above the town of Zemen
stands Zemen Monastery.
Founded in the 11th century,
it was occupied until the
advent of Ottoman rule, and
was restored in the late 19th
century. It consists of modest
single-storey buildings set
around the small 12th-century
Church of St Ivan the Theologian, which contains fine
14th-century frescoes. Executed in the simple, bold style of
the Macedonian School of
early icon painters, they show
biblical scenes and portraits
of saints and of the monastery's patron, Konstantin
Deyan, and his wife Doya.

KUKERI AND SURVAKARI

Pernik is the venue for the Balkans' largest gathering
of Kukeri and Survakari dancers. Held alternate years, it
attracts over 5,000 participants from more than 90 national
and international folk groups. Survakari rites are winter
dances that take place in western Bulgaria on New Year's
Eve and New Year's Day. Kukeri rites are pre-spring dances
performed during Lent in the rest of the country. The
dancers wear outlandish costumes and frightening masks, or
cover their faces in charcoal. The costumes also incorporate
cow bells, which are worn on belts. By adopting a loping
gait, the dancers rhythmically jangle the bells to protect
themselves from the evil spirits that they must drive away
before celebrating the arrival of the new year or of spring.

The rituals, which date back to
Thracian times, are acted out
by male dancers. Both Kukeri
and Survakari rituals involve
midnight visits by dancers
carrying flaming torches to
every home in a town or village
so as to drive out evil spirits. In
the associated fertility rituals,
Survakari dancers celebrate
a symbolic wedding. Kukeri
pre-spring rituals involve
symbolically impregnating the
earth with wooden ploughs
and sowing it with seed amid
a cacophony of jangling bells,
drums and joyful uproar.

Group of Kukeri dancers

Fresco in the Church of St Ivan the
Theologian at Zemen Monastery

Kyustendil ❸
Кюстендил

88 km (50 miles) SW of Sofia.
Map A3. 🏛 *50,000.* 🚉 🚌 🚍

Thanks to its thermal springs, Kyustendil was known as the "town of baths" in Roman times. Later, the Turks built hammams here, and today Kyustendil is a popular spa resort. Although it no longer has a Muslim population, vestiges of its former Oriental culture remain.

The hefty Ahmed Bey Mosque houses the town's small **History Museum**, in which archaeological artifacts discovered in the region are displayed. The mosque is surrounded by the remains of the Pautalia Roman baths, Bulgaria's second-largest baths complex after that in Varna *(see p199)*. Built in the 2nd century AD it covered more than 1,000 sq m (11,000 sq ft) and had an unusual system of vaulted brick corridors to heat the building's floors.

Chifte Bathhouse is a 20th-century conversion of the Ottoman baths that were built over part of the Pautalia baths. It has separate pools for men and women, with a year-round water temperature of 36–40° C (98–104° F).

Beyond the mosque, on the corner of ploshtad Velbuzhd, is the pretty three-domed Church of Sveta Bogoroditsa. In obeisance to the Ottoman ruling that Christian churches should not cause offence to Muslims, it was set slightly below ground level.

Just off bulevard Bulgaria is a large **Art Gallery** devoted to the work of the local painter Vladimir Dimitrov-Maistor (1882–1960), who is known to Bulgarians as "Maistora" (the Master). His work is characterized by vivid colours and broad brushstrokes, and his bold portraits often feature peasant girls framed by the region's ripe fruits, echoing the Madonnas depicted by medieval icon painters. Several bearded self-portraits are on display, revealing a wild look in the eyes of a man who disdained city life in favour of a monastically simple village existence.

Immediately behind the gallery is the **Dimitûr Peshev House-Museum**. Dimitûr Peshev *(see p67)* was a prominent Kyustendil politician and vice-chairman of the Bulgarian parliament in the 1940s. When Nazi Germany put pressure on Bulgaria to deport its Jews, Peshev orchestrated a campaign to protect them. Although over 11,000 Jews from Bulgaria's newly occupied territories were sent to German concentration camps, a letter signed by 43 Bulgarian MPs, combined with the adamant support of the Orthodox Church, persuaded the Tsar and the government to defy Hitler by refusing to deport the country's 50,000 Jews.

Incredibly, following the Communist takeover in 1944, the signatories to the letter were arrested. Twenty were

Dimitûr Peshev, national hero

Detail of Ahmed Bey Mosque in Kyustendil, built in the 16th century

executed and the rest imprisoned. Peshev was sentenced to 15 years' hard labour; he only served one year but had his property confiscated and lived an ignominious existence until his death in 1973. However, his reputation was posthumously restored after the fall of Communism in 1989. The museum, in a building reconstructed in 2002 as a replica of his house, documents his story.

The wooded Hisarlûk hill that overlooks the town can be reached on foot along marked pathways, or by car following a road that snakes up the hillside. Close to the summit are the ruined walls of the once formidable Hisarlûk fortress. It was built in the 4th century and, with 14 towers and walls 2 m (6 ft) thick, it was a secure place of refuge during both the first and second Bulgarian kingdoms *(see p43)*. It was destroyed by the Ottomans in the 15th century.

🏛 **History Museum**
Ahmed Bey Mosque, ul. Stefan Karadzha, 2. **Tel** *(078) 550 124.*
⏰ *8:30am–5:30pm Tue–Sat.* 📷

🏛 **Art Gallery**
ul. Patriarch Evtmii, 20. **Tel** *(078) 550 029.* ⏰ *9am–noon & 2–6pm Tue–Sun.* 📷 📷

🏛 **Dimitûr Peshev House-Museum**
ul. Tsar Simeon I, 11. **Tel** *(078) 551 811.* ⏰ *9am–5pm daily.* 📷 📷

Three hexagonal domes on the Church of Sveta Bogoroditsa, Kyustendil

Rila National Park ❹

Национален парк "Рила"

The source of several Balkan rivers, this massif, Bulgaria's largest national park, derives its name from the Thracian word *rula*, meaning "abundance of water". Its dense forests of spruce, fir, and Macedonian pine are home to wolves, bears, boar, Balkan chamois and *suslik* (ground squirrels) as

Wolf in the Rila Mountains

well as the rare wallcreeper and the Alpine chough. No fewer than 57 endemic plant species, including the divine primrose, Rila pansy and Bulgarian avens, also thrive here. A network of hiking paths crisscrosses the park, reaching the imposing peaks of Musala and Malyovitsa and the Seven Lakes.

LOCATOR MAP

☐ Rila Mountains

— Area Illustrated

★ Seven Lakes

One of the Rila Mountains' most popular hiking trails follows this series of small glacial lakes, which are set amid spectacular scenery. The lakes, formed by melted glaciers, are set at ascending levels.

★ Mount Malyovitsa

At the head of a valley, the mountain rises to 2,729 m (8,957 ft). A cliff near Malyovitsa hikers' hut offers a tough challenge to rock climbers. A nearby rock is studded with memorials to those who failed.

Rila Monastery Forest Reserve

Created in 2000, the reserve covers more than 27,000 ha (67,000 acres) around Rila Monastery (see pp108–11). It includes a large beech forest.

STAR SIGHTS

★ Mount Malyovitsa

★ Seven Lakes

★ Mount Musala

KEY

═ Main road

═ Other road

-- Trail

— Railway

△ Peak

Map labels:
SAMOKO
Sofia
Pernik
Razardzhik
Blagoevgrad
SOFIA
Sapareva Banya
62
6204
Dupnitsa
Bistritsa
Seven Lakes
Malyovitsa 2729 m
Kalin Lake
Rila Monastery Forest Reserve
1005
Rila
Rilska R.
Rila Monastery
Bab 2608 m
107
Struma
Dzherman
Kocherinovo
Bistritsa
1
106
1006
Blagoevgrad
SANDANSKI
Kapatnik 2169 m

Shtrashnoto Lake
Set at an altitude of 2,465 m (8,090 ft) the lake is ringed by the dark granite cliffs of the Kupenite peaks. A hikers' hut on the lakeside provides basic accommodation.

VISITORS' CHECKLIST

Map B4. **Getting there:** *bus from Samokov (Borovets).* campsites, and chalets bookable via Bulgarian Tourism Union. **www**.rilanationalpark.org/en/index.phtml **www**.bulgariannationalparks.org

Musala Lakes are a set of pretty glacial pools set below the peak. The "Icy Lake" is the highest in the Balkans at 2,709 m (8,900 ft).

★ **Mount Musala**
At 2,925 m (9,600 ft) Mount Musala is the highest peak in the eastern Balkans. On a clear day, the arduous hike to the summit is rewarded by stunning views of the Pirin and Rhodope mountains to the south and of Mount Vitosha to the north.

SAMOKOV · Raduil · KOSTENETS · Govedartsi · Borovets · Kostenets · Musalevski Lakes · Ibar Reserve · Central Rila Reserve · Musala 2925 m · Belmeken 2626 m · Belmeken Lake · Chaira Lake · Beli Iskur Lake · Ribni Lakes · Golyam Mechi Vrah 2618 m · Parangalitsa Reserve · Bela Mesta · Yakoruda · VELINGRAD · Belitsa · RAZLOG

0 kilometres 5
0 miles 5

DUNOVISTI

A mystic religion based on the teachings of the priest-philosopher Petur Dunov (1864–1944), Dunovism caught on in 1900, when his book *The Seven Conversations* was published. Dunov toured Bulgaria expounding his cosmic view of life. He advocated worship in the open air and daily meditation with a ritual of greeting the rising sun. Dunov won international renown, but under Communism his message was suppressed. Since then Bulgarians have rediscovered his teachings and hundreds of his white-robed followers still gather at the Seven Lakes around 19 August to celebrate the Dunovist new year's day.

Group of white-robed Dunovists in a ritual

Parangalitsa Reserve
This reserve, on the southwestern slopes of the Rila Mountains, was established in 1933 to protect some of Europe's oldest spruce forests. It is now a UNESCO Biosphere Reserve.

Samokov **5**

Самоков

65 km (40 miles) south of Sofia.
Map B4. 🏛 *27,500*. 🚌 🚖

Although the town centre is
an unattractive sprawl of drab
concrete buildings, Samokov
has a pleasant setting close to
the Rila Mountains and the ski
resort of Borovets. Established
in the Middle Ages as a major
centre of mining and manufacture, Samokov retained its
industrial importance until the
Liberation in the late 19th
century. Today the town is
the centre of Bulgaria's largest
potato-producing region.

During the National Revival
(see p46), Samokov's thriving
schools of icon painters and
woodcarvers made a significant contribution to the
decoration of religious and
civic buildings throughout the
country. They also left their
mark in the town itself. Just
off the main square stands
Bairakli Mosque, a building
constructed in a style typical
of the National Revival period.
The eaves of the mosque's
red-tiled dome and roof are
decorated with floral motifs,
as are its interior walls. The
entrance, fronted by wooden
columns, is set into a delightful façade of trompe-l'oeil
murals depicting theatrical
stages. This decorative scheme
is a fine example of Samokov
artists applying their skills in
a context other than that of
traditional icon painting.

ICON PAINTERS OF SAMOKOV

When he added floral motifs to a series of icons that he had
painted for the consecration of Samokov's Metropolitan
Church in 1793, Hristo Dimitrov unwittingly founded what
became known as the Samokov School of icon painters.
He subsequently trained his sons Dimitûr (1796–1860) and
Zahari Zograf (1810–53) and, with Samokov's other icon-
painting family, the Obrazopisovs, they produced a large
number of icons and murals during the National Revival.

During his short lifetime, Zahari Zograf attained legendary
status as the creator of a new kind of secular art. Defying
the rules of medieval icon painting, he introduced landscapes and naturalistically rendered floral and animal motifs,
and his grotesque scenes of Hell became a standard feature
of church and monastery murals during the National
Revival. The fact that he signed his works, and even added
self-portraits to some of them, indicates that he considered
his painting to be an art rather than a
mere craft carried out by lowly and
anonymous hands, as painting
had been seen for centuries.
His best works are on display
at the monasteries of Rila,
Troyan, Preobrazhenski and
Bachkovo, and outside
Bulgaria, in the western
Balkans and Mount Athos,
in Greece. His most famous
self-portrait is in the National
Art Gallery, Sofia (see pp70–71).

Fresco by Zahari Zograf, Rila Monastery

The **History Museum** occupies
a National Revival-style building set in a quiet garden. The
highlights of its relatively
small collection are two working replicas of Samokov's
medieval forges. They were
modelled on Saxon furnaces,
and have water-powered
bellows and huge hammers
called *samokovi*, which gave
the town its name. Enormous

antique anvils stand beside the
forges. Upstairs, a display of
faded photographs documents
Samokov's more recent past.

Five minutes' walk from the
museum are the high stone
walls that enclose **Sarafina
House** (Sarafska Kushta). In
the 19th century it was the
home of a wealthy Jewish
family, and after restoration it
was opened as a museum

Bairakli Mosque in Samokov, with floral decoration typical of the National Revival style of mural and icon painting

A room at Sarafina House in Samokov, once the home of a wealthy family

house. Its elaborate ceilings and floral wall paintings were executed by Samokov's woodcarvers and painters.

At the opposite end of the town, towards the Rila Mountains, is the Metropolitan Church (1793), a long stone building with a copper-clad bell tower. The church has a superbly detailed iconostasis by Samokov woodcarvers, and icons by Hristo Dimitrov, *(see box, opposite).*

🏛 Bairakli Mosque
pl. Zahari Zograf. *Tel* (072) 266 712. ⭘ 8:30am–5:30pm Mon–Fri.
🏛 History Museum
ul. Profesor Vasil Zahari 4. *Tel* (072) 266 599. ⭘ 8:30am–5:30pm daily.
🏛 Sarafina House
ul. Knyaz Dondukov 11. *Tel* (072) 260 301. ⭘ 9am–5pm Mon–Fri.

Borovets ❻
Боровец

70 km (43 miles) south of Sofia.
Map B4.

One of Bulgaria's three major ski resorts *(see pp30–31),* Borovets is located below the majestic peaks of the Rila Mountains. Its untidy centre is cluttered with large hotel blocks and lines of wooden huts that house nightclubs, bars, restaurants, ski shops and souvenir stalls.

During the winter season, visitors crowd the resort's network of ski runs and lifts and gather in its central bars and clubs for rowdy late-night partying. In summer the main

gondola lift whisks visitors up to Yastrebets, a peak that rises to 2,369 m (7,775 ft). From here hikers can follow a path to Musala refuge and the lofty summit of Musala (2,925 m/ 9,600 ft), the highest peak in the Balkans. The Sitnyakovo Express, a chairlift that operates at week-ends only, takes visitors up to the highest point of the Sitnyakovo ski runs. A pleasant path leads back down to Borovets.

The resort also offers a range of summer activities, including pony trekking, motorized safaris, guided hiking, climbing and abseiling, most of which can be arranged through the large hotels here.

Apart from its attractions as a ski resort, Borovets's only feature of real interest is **Bistritsa Palace**. It was built as

Detail of Bistritsa Palace, Borovets

a hunting lodge for Prince Ferdinand in the late 19th century, making Borovets the country's oldest mountain resort. The palace's interior decor is a mix of luxurious Victorian fittings, elaborate Samokov woodcarving and hunting trophies.

🏛 Bistritsa Palace
15 minutes' walk from central Borovets. *Tel* (0750) 32710. ⭘ 10:30am–3:30pm Tue–Sun.

Malyovitsa ❼
Мальовица

10 km (6 miles) W of Borovets.
Map B4.

The small mountain resort of Malyovitsa consists of little more than a hotel, car park and mountain refuge. It has two drag lifts and a few pistes for beginners and intermediate skiers. As such it offers a nice contrast to the bustle of Borovets in the winter sports season.

In summer Malyovitsa is a convenient base for exploring the Rila Mountains *(see pp104–5).*

From the resort a path leads up to Malyovitsa refuge and the looming peak of Malyovitsa mountain (2,729 m/8,957 ft). From the refuge hikers can continue along marked paths that lead westward to the Seven Lakes, or southward to Rila Monastery *(see pp108–11).*

View into the valleys below Malyovitsa, in the Rila Mountains

Rila Monastery ❽
Рилски манастир

Established in the 10th century by St Ivan of Rila
(Sveti Ivan Rilski), Rila Monastery is Bulgaria's
most impressive example of National Revival
architecture. Generously supported by successive
kings, the monastery flourished until Ottoman raids
destroyed it in the late 15th century. While the
Russian Church sponsored its renovation, Rila's
monks played a crucial role in preserving Bulgaria's
language and history during the most repressive
periods of Ottoman rule. Devastated by fire in 1833,
the monastery was rebuilt with funding from wealthy
Bulgarians intent on cultivating national pride at a
time of great hope for liberation from the Ottomans.

Rila Monastery *nestles in a*
valley at the foot of thickly
forested mountains. It is
protected by fortress-like
walls 20 m (65 ft) high.

★ **Murals**
The murals in the arcade
vividly depict sinners thrown
into an apocalyptic vision of
Hell. This contrasts with the
arcades' graceful structure
of arches, slender columns
and blind cupolas.

CHURCH OF THE NATIVITY
The exquisite Church of the Nativity,
which stands proudly in the middle
of Rila Monastery's courtyard, is the
largest monastery church in Bulgaria.
Its exterior is a busy but harmonious
confection of layers of stripy colours
and curved domes and arches set at
different levels. Take some time to
appreciate the outside thoroughly
before entering the main part of
the church.

Entrance
to church

★ **Murals**
Magnificent murals
adorn the church walls,
illustrating characters
and episodes from the
Bible. Zahari Zograf
(see p48), Bulgaria's
greatest 19th-century
painter, is the only one
of the artists responsible
to have signed his work.

Arcades decorated with
some of the finest murals

★ Holy Relic of St Ivan

A silver casket holds the nation's holiest relic, St Ivan of Rila's preserved left hand. In the 16th century, the right hand was taken on a tour of Russia to raise funds for the monastery.

The three main cupolas contain murals of the Holy Trinity

★ Iconostasis

This masterpiece was created by a team of Samokov woodcarvers working under Atanas Telador between 1839 and 1842. The 10-m (33-ft) wide iconostasis, covered in gold leaf, is elaborately decorated with complex carvings of stylized floral elements, symbolic human and animal images, biblical scenes and wild animals.

Grave of Tsar Boris

The heart of Tsar Boris III, who was allegedly poisoned by the Nazis in 1944 for saving Bulgarian Jews, is buried in this chapel.

STAR SIGHTS

★ Holy Relic of St Ivan

★ Iconostasis

★ Murals

ST IVAN OF RILA

The medieval hermit St Ivan of Rila (880–946), retreated into the Rila Mountains to escape what he saw as the moral decline of society. He was venerated for his wisdom and as a healer, and was persuaded by his followers to establish a monastery. After his death, pilgrims came to view his remains, which were believed to possess curative powers.

Exploring the Rila Monastery

Deep in the heart of a forest reserve, Rila Monastery has an imposing external presence. Enter by the west (Dupnitsa) gate, crossing over ancient stone slabs worn smooth by pilgrims' feet, then savour a first taste of the colourful treat to come. Several floors of wooden balconies enclose the courtyard and the central Church of the Nativity, with Hrelyo's Tower to one side. To the right of the west gate is the Treasury Museum, located in the south wing. The north wing, to the left of the west gate, contains the old kitchen and leads to the east (Samokov) gate, which conceals the entrance to the Monastery Farm Museum and leads out to a cluster of restaurants and souvenir shops.

Raphael's Cross

One of over 100 intricately carved scenes on Raphael's Cross

CHURCH OF THE NATIVITY

Construction of the Church of the Nativity began in 1835, two years after the monastery had been devastated by fire. The work directed by the master builder Pavel, from Krimin, who had previously worked on Mount Athos, in Greece.

The church's design was intended to be innovative and original, as befitted the National Revival period. For the interior, emphasis was placed on spatiality so as to draw worshippers into the centre of the building. The three large domes were positioned to allow maximum light to fall on the spectacular gilt iconostasis, while still keeping the rest of the interior in typically sombre darkness. The murals on the interior are also typical of the period and were executed by the country's best painters. The biblical scenes that cover the walls are brightly painted and show an attention to detail that was the hallmark of the National Revival movement. Among the many artists who painted these scenes were Zahari Zograf and his brother Dimitûr, of the Samokov School *(see p106)*.

The walls are also busy with delightful displays of icons, some produced by 19th-century artists from Samokov and Bansko. Others date from much earlier times. On the left-hand side of the church as you enter, usually hidden away in a wooden drawer, is the serene 12th-century Icon of the Virgin.

A chapel on the right of the church contains a smaller iconostasis and the simple grave of Tsar Boris III, marked with a plain wooden cross.

TREASURY MUSEUM

Raphael's Cross is certainly the star of this fine collection. Just 81 cm (32 in) high, the cross bears a series of biblical scenes carved with needles, each one enclosed in silver-plated frames no larger than a fingernail. The work, completed in 1802, took 12 years and cost the monk Raphael his eyesight. The collection includes about 20 other miniature crosses, as well as jewelled silver boxes that contain ancient bibles, a ruby-encrusted communion cup and other church silver.

The lower floor has varied exhibits, including a 2-m (6-ft) musket and several swords and pistols. Nearby is a collection of books from the monastery library. The oldest dates back to the 10th century and is written on parchment in the Glagolitic script of the old Slavonic languages. Opposite is the Suchava Tetra, a large bible produced in 1529. Its embossed gold and enamel cover depicts Christ on the cross, with the four evangelists watching from each corner. Several other ancient Bibles are on show below some extravagantly jewelled icons.

A neighbouring glass case is filled with a selection of 19th-century gold church plate. At the far end of the room is a 14th-century ivory-inlaid bishop's throne that belonged to the original monastery church. Alongside are the skilfully carved original doors of Hrelyo's Tower and a pair of 14th-century icons of St Ivan of Rila *(see p109)*.

Church of the Nativity, dominant feature of the monastery's courtyard

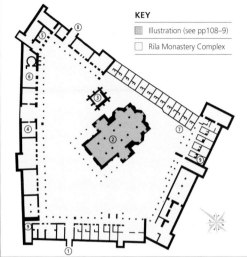

KEY

■ Illustration (see pp108–9)

□ Rila Monastery Complex

RILA MONASTERY PLAN

① Western Entrance (Dupnista Gate)

② Church of the Nativity

③ Hrelyo's Tower

④ Monastery Kitchen

⑤ Farm Museum

⑥ Oven

⑦ Treasury Museum

⑧ Eastern Entrance (Samokov Gate)

⑨ Public Toilets

MONASTERY COMPLEX

In contrast to the monastery's stern exterior, the courtyard is light and open; an elegant tracery of red, white, and black striped arches deftly frame more than 300 monks' cells and mirror the façade of the Church of the Nativity. **Hrelyo's Tower** is the monastery's oldest surviving structure. It was built by Hrelyo Dragoval, a feudal lord, in 1334. A small chapel on the top floor, with 14th-century frescoes, is occasionally open to the public. Today, access to this mini-fortress is via wooden steps to the first floor, but was originally by a removable stepladder.

An intriguing section of the north wing contains the **Monastery Farm Museum**. It is entered via the old guard house, off Samokov Gate. Here, muskets used by the guards are displayed, alongside their red and white uniforms with metal breastplates featuring a portrait of St Ivan of Rila and the monastery. Next door is a bare-walled room that houses the monastery's water-powered mill, and where hollow logs once used as sewage pipes are displayed. A 19th-century see-saw water pump used for

fire-fighting embodies the precautions taken after the fire that devastated the monastery in 1833. The enormous domed brick oven that takes up most of the next room is an impressive sight. Like the huge pots and cauldrons of the old kitchen, and the giant wooden ladles in the adjoining room, the oven's great size was essential if food was to be provided for the hundreds of monks and pilgrims at the monastery. The kitchen's ceiling curves into a huge blackened chimney that tapers elegantly through the four floors of the north wing.

Hrelyo's Tower

AROUND RILA MONASTERY

The **Chapel of St Ivan of Rila** and the dark cave where he spent the remainder of his life are an hour's walk north of the monastery and worth a visit just to get out into the surrounding countryside. Tourists can clamber through the narrow opening of the cave ceiling, a task once expected of visiting pilgrims: supposedly only the pure of heart will get through.

About 7 km (4 miles) northeast of the monastery, **Kiril Meadow** is an attractive leafy green picnic spot with cafés and a few places offering accommodation.

The Chapel of St Ivan of Rila, in countryside near the monastery

Detail of the Rila Monastery's colourful and detailed frescoes ▷

The Church of the Annunciation, built in 1841, in Blagoevgrad's old town

Blagoevgrad ❾
Благоевград

97 km (60 miles) S of Sofia.
Map B4. 🏛 71,000. 🚗 🚌 Ⓜ 🚕

Studious youngsters clutching notepads and textbooks populate much of this bustling town, which is home to both the American University in Bulgaria (AUB) and Southwest Neofit Rilski University. It was the location's pleasant climate and hot mineral springs that attracted Thracian, then Roman, settlers here. Under Ottoman rule, when it was known as Gorna Dzhumaya, the town was predominantly Muslim but was integrated into the new Bulgarian state in 1912 (*see p50*). Later, Gorna Dzhumaya's Turkish inhabitants were replaced by Bulgarian refugees from Macedonia and the Aegean, and in 1950 the town was renamed Blagoevgrad after Dimitûr Blagoev, founder of the Bulgarian Communist Party.

Ploshtad Georgi Izmirliev Makedoncheo, the pedestrianized hub of the town centre, is a spacious square with pleasantly babbling fountains and an abundance of trees. On one side stands the huge AUB building, which served as the Communist Party's headquarters until 1989. To the east is ploshtad Bulgaria, a lively square lined with cafés and restaurants.

Across the river is the cavernous **History Museum**, with thousands of artifacts exhibited on several floors. Minerals, stuffed animals and birds, ethnographic displays, and historic photographs fill the upper levels, but the most intriguing items are tucked away in the basement, where the museum's archaeological collection is laid out. Among the exhibits here is an array of votive figurines, dating from the 6th century BC and simply modelled in clay. They are thought to have been used in rituals connected with fertility, fruitfulness and the concept of Mother Earth. Also notable are a pair of Thracian bronze helmets of the 4th century BC, each with moulded beard and moustache, and a pair of bronze knee and shin protectors.

Fresco in the Church of the Annunciation, Blagoevgrad

Behind the museum lies the Varosha quarter, Blagoevgrad's old town. Here, renovated National Revival buildings cluster around the boldly decorated **Church of the Annunciation**, with an eye-catchingly patterned façade. The porch is decorated with frescoes of biblical scenes, and inside is a stunning iconostasis with carvings of angels, birds, fruit and flowers by master-craftsmen from Bansko and Samokov (*see p106*).

🏛 **History Museum**
ul. Rila, 1. **Tel** (073) 885 370.
⏱ 9am–6pm Mon–Sat. 🈺 🚻

🕆 **Church of the Annunciation**
Varosha quarter. ⏱ 6:30am–8pm daily. 🕆 8am daily.

Sandanski ❿
Сандански

162 km (100 miles) south of Sofia.
Map B5. 🏛 26,500. 🚗 🚌 🚕 🚕
ℹ Palace of Culture (0746-22549).

Sandanski is a pleasant town set in a sheltered, sunny valley with hot mineral springs. About 4,000 years ago, this favourable location attracted Thracian settlers of the Medi tribe, but it was much more intensively developed by the Romans, who arrived in the early centuries AD. The baths and residential complexes that they built have been discovered under the modern town.

Sandanski's residents make much of the possibility that Spartacus, the Thracian slave famed for leading a slave

Hot mineral pool at Sveti Vrach Park, in southeastern Sandanski

For hotels and restaurants in this region see pp220–24 and pp236–40

revolt against the Roman Empire in the 1st century BC, was born in the town, which in Roman times was known as Desudava. A statue of him stands just outside the town.

The centrepiece of the **Archaeological Museum**, built over an excavated Roman villa, is a mosaic floor with a swastika and other geometric motifs. Upstairs is a collection of marble reliefs that depict Thracian horsemen, as well as portraits, a child's tomb and brief information on archaeological sites discovered in the region. Next door to the museum are the ruins of a 4th-century Christian basilica and paving slabs from the town's original main street.

Running parallel to this street is Sandanski's present-day main thoroughfare, ulitsa Makedonia. Lined with clothes shops and cafés and set with fountains, it bisects the town centre. To the southeast it leads to Sveti Vrach Park, a vast wooded park with an outdoor spa pool filled with water heated to 31° C (88° F), and over 200 species of exotic trees. Nearby, steaming hot mineral water spouts from fountains, where local people queue to fill bottles and containers. The town's larger hotels also use this water in the various hydrotherapy treatments that they offer to guests.

Rozhen Monastery, sited on a plateau above the village of Rozhen

Tomb, Archaeological Museum, Sandanski

🏛 **Archaeological Museum**
ul. Makedonia 55. **Tel** (0746) 32380. 🕐 9am–noon, 2–5pm Mon-Sat. 📷

Rozhen Monastery ⓫
Роженски манастир

Above Rozhen village, 7 km (4 miles) NE of Melnik. **Map** B5. **Tel** (07437) 222. 📷 🕐 7am–7pm daily. 🚌 8am daily. 🎪 local fair (8 Sep).

Rozhen Monastery occupies a tranquil spot high in the hills with dramatic views of the region's sandstone cliffs. It was established in 1220 by Aleksei Slav, a 13th-century overlord, but soon fell into disrepair, remaining neglected until it was restored in 1597. During the period of Ottoman rule, the Orthodox Church used the monastery as a convent until it passed back into Bulgarian hands in 1912, after the First Balkan War. Dispute over the monastery's ownership led the Macedonian revolutionary Yane Sandanski to begin the construction of the nearby Church of SS Kiril i Metodii (1914) for Bulgarian worshippers who were debarred from Rozhen by the Orthodox clergy. The church stands a short distance down the hill from the monastery, and behind it lies Sandanski's large marble grave.

The monastery's simple brick buildings form an irregular hexagon, fronted by rickety wooden balconies, around the 16th-century Church of the Birth of the Holy Virgin. A porch protects the church's exterior frescoes, which show believers ascending a ladder to Heaven with the help of angels, while devils endeavour to hurl them into the mouth of a fiery monster.

In a side chapel inside the church is a miracle-working icon of the Virgin, which is paraded around the monastery on 8 September, feast of the Birth of the Virgin. The church also contains well preserved frescoes of saints and a fantastic gilt iconostasis with bold icons and intricate woodwork that gleams in the semi-darkness. The refectory, with a long wooden dining table and vestiges of frescoes, is also open to the public.

SPARTACUS THE THRACIAN

Leader of the Gladiatorial War of 73–71 BC against Rome, Spartacus and his army of runaway slaves and gladiators terrorized Italy for two years. Born in Thrace, Spartacus served in the Roman army but was disgraced and sold into slavery, where he trained as a gladiator. With other slaves, Spartacus escaped, and began a campaign of plunder and pillage. Joined by still others, the group grew into an army of some 120,000 men, who overcame successive Roman legions sent to destroy them. The rebels were eventually defeated and put to death.

Defeat of Spartacus by the Roman general Crassus, 71 BC

Melnik ⑫
Мелник

182 km (113 miles) south of Sofia.
🚍 243. 🚌 *from Sandanski.*

The enchanting small town of Melnik is tucked away in a valley formed by rocky, arid hills crowned with pyramidal sandstone formations. Once a thriving centre of winemaking and the capital of a principality, Melnik is now a quiet town with a much reduced population. However, it attracts coachloads of visitors, who come to admire the intriguing rock formations here, and to taste the famous Melnik wine, which is still produced by a few local families.

Wine has been Melnik's major export since the 13th century, when production was increased to take advantage of tax-free trade with Dubrovnik. During this period, the despot Aleksei Slav made Melnik the capital

Melnik and its square *konak*, the town hall during Ottoman rule

of his principality, funding the construction of churches and monasteries in the vicinity.

After the Ottoman conquest, Melnik fell into decline, but its fortunes revived in the 19th century, when the town's

largely Greek population of 20,000 began to prosper from exporting tobacco and wine. Much of Melnik was destroyed during the Second Balkan War of 1913 and its remaining Greek residents left as a result

Melnik Wine Tour

Renowned throughout Bulgaria, Melnik wine is made from the dark blue grapes of the Melnik broad-leaved vine, an indigenous Bulgarian variety grown in the volcanic soil of the sunny Struma Valley, near Melnik. There once were 19 wine cellars *(izbe)* in Melnik, where pressed grapes were left to ferment and where wine was stored in wooden barrels. Today only four of these cellars are open to the public and only a handful of families still produce wine. The Damianitza winery, just outside Melnik, is now the only large producer of Melnik wine.

Rodina Hotel ①
Though it advertises itself as a wine cellar, the Rodina Hotel does not have its own *izba*. It does, however, have a small *vinarna*, where visitors can sample the owner's Merlot wine.

Traditional Bulgarian wine vessel

Melnishka
Rozhenski Dol
Town Hall
Pashovata Kushta
Vinarna Melnik
Konak
①
Rodina Hotel
②
SANDANSKI
Bus Stop
20 m (18 yards)
SS Petur and Pavel Church

Vinarna Melnik ②
Although the Vinarna Melnik does not have an *izba*, it offers tastings of its Melnik, Merlot and Cabernet wines.

Lumparova Kushta ③
This pleasant family-run hotel has a rock-cut *izba* with a mineral spring and tables and chairs for visitors who come to taste Melnik wine.

For hotels and restaurants in this region see pp220–24 and pp236–40

of ensuing anti-Greek sentiment. Today, with a population of less than 250, Melnik is officially Bulgaria's smallest town.

Melnik's restored stone houses are clustered on either side of a dry river bed that rises eastwards into the mountains. Most of Melnik's attractions are at the top of the town. The **History Museum** occupies the upper floor of Pashovata Kushta, the house from where Yane Sandanski *(see p115)* announced Melnik's liberation from Ottoman rule in 1912. The museum's exhibits include examples of locally made terracotta wine vessels and a small collection of regional costumes and photographs.

A little further on is **Kordopulov House** (1754), a wonderful example of early

National Revival architecture in which Western and Oriental motifs are combined on a grand scale. The decorative wooden façade sits atop high stone walls. While the lower windows are in the traditional Bulgarian style, the stained-glass windows on the top floor show Oriental influences. The house's interior features a central salon with an intricately carved wooden ceiling and an Ottoman-style raised seating area. Doors lead off to a spacious sitting room lit by many windows, and to a dining room with a secret inner chamber concealed behind a bookcase. Downstairs is a small *mehana* connected to the house's labyrinthine wine cellar.

Beyond Kordopulov House, a footpath leads to the remains of Bolyarskata Kushta, Aleksei Slav's once

Glazed terracotta wine vessels at Melnik's History Museum

formidable fortress. On the opposite side of the valley, another footpath leads uphill from the 18th-century Church of Sveti Nikolai Chudotvorets to Nikolova Gora and the ruins of the Church of Sveti Nika (1756).

Bottle of wine from **Kordopulov House**

🏛 **History Museum**
Pashovata Kushta. **Tel** (07437) 216. 🕐 9am–6pm daily.

🏛 **Kordopulov House**
Kordopulov House. **Tel** (07437) 265. 🕐 8am–8pm daily. 🖼 🍴 🚻

Pri Mitko Shestaka ④
Carved deep into the rock, the wine cellars here were created over 250 years ago. The main cavity is used for storing and tasting wine. The Melnik wines stored here have been produced by the same family for 150 years.

A taste of Melnik wine at one of the town's *izbe*.

TIPS FOR VISITORS

Tour length: approximately 1.5 km (1 mile).

Tips: There are no banks in Melnik so be sure to have some cash already with you. It is illegal to drive after drinking any alcohol.

Kordopulov Kushta ⑤
This house overlies Melnik's oldest and largest *izba*. Labyrinthine passages snake into the hillside, and vast rock-cut wine cellars are filled with huge barrels.

| 0 metres | 100 |
| 0 yards | 100 |

KEY

– – – Suggested route

Litova Kushta ⑥
An 800-year-old *izba*, cut deep into the rock, lies beneath this hotel. Red Melnik wine, and white Keratzuda, Misket and Bouquet wines are stored in massive barrels here.

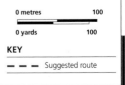

(Map labels)
Lumparova Kushta
Rozhenski Dol
Bolyarskata Kushta
Sv. Antonii Church
Zlatolistki Dol
Pri Mitko Shestaka ④
Old Turkish Baths
Kordopulov Kushta ⑤
Sv. Nikolai Chudotvorets Church
Sv. Barbara Church
Litova Kushta ⑥

Bansko
Банско

The small mountain town of Bansko lies just below the jagged peaks of the Pirin Mountains. It was founded in the 9th century, but remained obscure until the 19th century, when its prospering merchants began to fund the building of churches here. As the birthplace of Neofit Rilski, the town is also closely associated with Bulgarian nationalism. Another of its famous sons is Father Paisii (1722–73), whose *Slavo-Bulgarian History* was to provide the impetus for the beginnings of the National Revival.

Statue of Father Paisii in Bansko

Bansko's historic centre consists of a labyrinth of cobbled streets running between high stone walls that conceal hefty 19th-century timber and stone houses. Its suburbs, which are mostly filled with new hotels and apartment complexes, reflect its more recent development into a prosperous ski resort and weekend retreat.

Painting and inscription in the Church of Sveta Troitsa

🔒 Church of Sveta Troitsa
pl. Vûzhrazhdane. 🕐 8am–6pm daily. 🔔 9am Sun.
Hidden by a stone wall 4 m (12 ft) high, the massive Church of Sveta Troitsa owes its existence to a bribe that local merchants offered Ottoman officials so as to secure their consent for its construction. A miracle-working icon, so the story went, had been found on the site, and this qualified it as a suitable place to build a Christian church. The wall that surrounds the church was built to conceal its eventual dimensions, which exceeded the limit set by the Ottomans.

Work on the church began in 1832. It was built in the distinctive smooth, rounded stones characteristic of the region, each framed by red bricks to relieve the monotony of an otherwise featureless exterior. The bell tower was added in 1850.

The church's gloomy interior is lit by small windows, and a large gilt iconostasis shines in the flickering candlelight. Topped with dragons, fruit and birds of prey, the iconostasis was made by the master-craftsman Velyan Ognev, from Debûr, in Macedonia. Dimitûr and Simeon Molerov created the icons. Hefty columns support the wood-panelled ceiling and a latticework screen at the rear of the nave hides a balcony where female worshippers were segregated from the male congregation.

Part of the stone- and timber-built Neofit Rilski House-Museum

🏛 Neofit Rilski House-Museum
ul. Pirin 17. **Tel** (0749) 88272. 🕐 9am–noon, 2–5pm daily.
An attractive garden dotted with modern sculptures is the setting for the former home of Neofit Rilski, the 19th-century

NEOFIT RILSKI (1793–1881)
The scholar Neofit Rilski is revered as the founder of modern education in Bulgaria and for his leading role in the National Revival movement. He was born Nikola Popetrov Benin in Bansko and studied teaching, icon painting and Greek at Rila Monastery. In 1835, he published the *Bulgarska Gramatika*, the first grammar of modern Bulgarian and an essential tool in the campaign to create a national, standardized Bulgarian education. That year he also became head of the first school to teach pupils in Bulgarian. It was opened in Gabrovo by Vasil Aprilov and followed the Bell-Lancaster system whereby pupils of all ages studied together, with older children helping to teach their younger classmates. By the time of the Liberation in 1878, there were some 2,000 such schools in Bulgaria. In 1852 Rilski returned to Rila Monastery, where he became abbot. He further contributed to the National Revival movement by translating the New Testament into Bulgarian and compiling the first Greek–Bulgarian dictionary.

Sculpture of Neofit Rilski, one of Bansko's famous sons

scholar who, through his promotion of the Bulgarian language and reform of the education system, became one of Bulgaria's national heroes. Now restored and opened as a museum, this beautiful National Revival house documents Rilski's achievements, and illustrates aspects of daily life in the 19th century.

The building centres around a tree-shaded courtyard. The low ceilings of the kitchen rooms on the ground floor are blackened with soot from the bread oven. Next to the oven is a secret room where the family hid from the Ottoman authorities in times of trouble. Upstairs is a covered terrace that overlooks the courtyard, and rooms that illustrate 19th-century family life. In one of them, a small classroom, similar to those that Rilski would have taught in, has been re-created. The sand boxes here were for the use of younger pupils, who would learn to write by tracing words with their fingers or with wooden sticks. On the opposite side of the courtyard is a display of photographs, letters and texts relating to Rilski's life.

Velyanov House

ul. Velyan Ognev 2. *Tel* (0749) 88274. ☐ 9am–noon, 2–5pm Mon–Fri. ⌨

This fine stone house was reputedly built for Velyan Ognev, the craftsman from Debûr, in Macedonia, who came to Bansko to create the iconostasis for the Church of Sveta Troitsa, and who then settled in the town.

Built in local stone and surrounded by high walls, Velyanov House (Velyanova Kûshta) is typical of comfortable 19th-century Bansko dwellings, and it is filled with

furniture and carpets of the period. Of particular interest are the elaborate wood-carvings with which Ognev decorated the house, and the rich murals in the Blue Room, which he is thought to have painted for his wife, the daughter of a local priest.

Velyanov House, a 19th-century family home, with a summer veranda

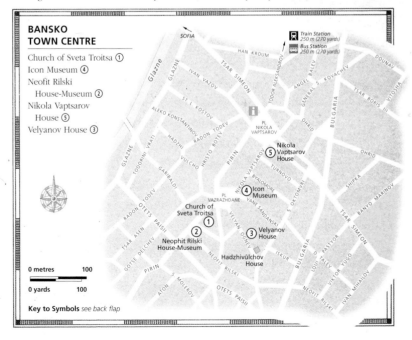

BANSKO TOWN CENTRE

Church of Sveta Troitsa ①
Icon Museum ④
Neofit Rilski House-Museum ②
Nikola Vaptsarov House ⑤
Velyanov House ③

0 metres 100
0 yards 100

Key to Symbols see back flap

Icon Museum
ul. Yane Sandanski. ***Tel** (0749) 88273.*
9am–noon, 2–5pm Mon–Fri.
The glowing works of art in the Icon Museum's collection line the walls of the converted dormitories and barn of a former hostel for travelling nuns. The buildings, which date from 1749, are set round a peaceful courtyard, and the complex is enclosed by the sturdy walls that typify Bansko's old town architecture.

As visitors cross a creaky wooden balcony to enter the museum's first room a comprehensive audio tour introduces artists of the Bansko School of painting. The leading light of this school, which flourished in the 19th century, was Toma Vishanov-Molera (born c.1750). He studied in Vienna with Hristo Dimitrov, founder of the Samokov School *(see p106)*. Like his son Dimitûr Molerov and his grandson Simeon Molerov after him, Toma Vishanov-Molera executed paintings for several churches in and around Bansko.

A portrait of Christ in the Icon Museum

Nikola Vaptsarov House-Museum
pl. Nikola Vaptsarov. ***Tel** (0749) 88304.*
The home of the poet Nikola Vaptsarov (1909–42) honours the memory of a young man who died for his opposition to Fascism, and who was posthumously idolized by Bulgaria's Communist government. Vaptsarov grew up in Bansko, and after studying in Varna, he worked in Sofia. Here he wrote poems that enthused about the modern age. But his eager involvement with the Communists during World War II led to his arrest for anti-Fascist activities. While awaiting execution, he wrote this poem: *The fight is hard and pitiless/The fight is epic, as they say;/I fell. Another takes my place –/ Why single out a name!/After the firing squad – the worms./Thus does the simple logic go./But in the storm we'll be with you/My people, for we loved you so.*

The museum's rooms contain family photographs and personal possessions. There is also a re-creation of the room where the poet's mother read Bulgarian classics to him as a child.

Nikola Vaptsarov House-Museum, childhood home of the anti-Fascist poet

Dobursko ⓮
Добърско

23km (14 miles) north of Bansko.
Map B4. *450.*

The road heading north from Bansko into the Rila Mountains leads to the sleepy village of Dobursko. According to legend, this is where Tsar Samuil's army came in 1014. Its men had been blinded by the Byzantine emperor Basil the Bulgar Slayer, but they found a cure in the mineral springs here.

Today, Dobursko is an increasingly popular centre of rural tourism. Besides this, its main attraction is the 17th-century **Church of SS Teodor Tiron and Teodor Stratilat**. Its well-preserved frescoes include a depiction of the Ascension with Christ framed by a curious triangular construction that has been likened to a space rocket.

Church of SS Teodor Tiron and Teodor Stratilat
8am–5pm Mon–Fri.

The mountain village of Dobursko, a centre of rural tourism with legendary mineral springs

Narrow-Gauge Railway Tour ⑮

Three trains a day make the scenic five-hour journey, following a stunning route through mountains. The line begins at Dobrinishte, but visitors are more likely to board at Bansko. From here the train leaves the Pirin Mountains and begins a gradual ascent of the Mesta River valley, set between the Rila Mountains and the western Rhodopes. After traversing a landscape of villages and meadows, it stops at Yakoruda. From there the route ascends into pine forests, then descends to Velingrad and follows a valley down to Septemvri.

TIPS FOR VISITORS

Map B4.
Tour length: 50 km (30 miles).
Departure points: Dobrinishte, Bansko or Septemvri. Mainline trains run between Septemvri and Plovdiv or Sofia.
Stopping-off places: There are hotels and restaurants at larger halts along the route.

Septemvri ⑥
This is the end station of the narrow-gauge line. From here, passengers can travel on the main line to Sofia or Plovdiv.

Yakoruda ④
A pleasant Pomak (Bulgarian Muslim) logging town. Its mosque and church come into view from a distance as the train rumbles past logs piled high for the saw mills.

Belitsa ③
From the station at Belitsa village, visitors can take a taxi to the Belitsa Dancing Bear Park, 10 km (6 miles) away. This is a refuge for bears rescued from a captive life as trained dancing bears, now illegal.

Velingrad ⑤
With many hot mineral pools, the spa resort of Velingrad makes a welcome stop. Most of the pools are located within hotel complexes but are usually open to members of the public for a small fee.

0 kilometres 10

0 miles 10

KEY

---	Narrow-gauge Railway
—	Railway
🚉	Railway station
===	Main road
==	Other road
△	Peak

Razlog ②
Razlog's brand-new golf course is its principal asset for visitors. The town comes alive when *kukeri* rites are performed on 1 January.

Dobrinishte ①
The starting point of the narrow-gauge railway line is at this quiet town at the foot of the Pirin Mountains. Plans to merge it with the ski resort of Bansko will open it to tourism.

Pirin National Park ⑯

Национален парк "Пирин"

This rugged landscape of granite and limestone peaks, glacial lakes and steep-sided valleys makes up one of Bulgaria's wildest national parks. Its forested valleys offer plenty of scope for hiking but, with 45 mountains over 2,500 m (8,200 ft) high, this is also Bulgaria's most rugged terrain. The habitat of wolves, bears, foxes, wild cats and mountain goats, the park also shelters hundreds of rare plants, including Pirin thyme, the yellow Pirin poppy, and the Urumov milk vetch. Although it is a UNESCO World Heritage Site, the park is under threat from the expansion of the ski resort of Bansko.

Campanula, a Pirin flower

LOCATOR MAP

☐ Pirin National Park

— Area Illustrated

Bayuvi Dupki Dzhindzhiritsa Nature Reserve
The largest nature reserve in the Pirin Mountains was established in 1934 to preserve relict Balkan pine and Bosnian pine forests. It is also home to many rare plants, including the lake quillwort and the great yellow gentian.

★ **Koncheto**
This ridge connects a series of peaks, which rise up between steep valleys. The ridge is just 1 m (3 ft) wide in places and, despite the steel cable to assist hikers, walking it should only be attempted in good weather, and by experienced climbers.

★ **Vihren**
At 2,914 m (9,564 ft), Vihren is the Pirins' highest peak. From Vihren hut, the climb to the summit, on a marked path, takes two and a half hours.

Mount Sinanitsa
The white limestone mass of Mount Sinanitsa, 2,516 m (8,257 ft) high, dominates the picturesque valley below.

★ **Baikousheva Mura**
Some 1,300 years old, this massive Bosnian pine (Pinus heldreichii) *is Bulgaria's oldest tree.*

EXPLORING THE PARK

With plenty of hotels and restaurants, Bansko is the obvious choice for a base. With a good map, you can follow day-long trails into the park. For longer excursions, book a stay in a *hizhi*, or mountain hut. Bansko gets busy at weekends, but is quiet during the week.

VISITORS' CHECKLIST

Bansko. **Map** B4. 🚌 from Blagoevgrad or Gotse Delchev.
🚃 narrow-gauge from Septemviri (see p121) linking to mainline. www.visitpirin.net
www.pirin-np.com

KEY

═	Main road
═	Other road
– –	Trail
─	Railway
△	Peak

Damyaritsa Valley
Coniferous forests on the valley's lower slopes give way to picturesque alpine meadows and lakes at the foot of Mount Todorka, 1,895 m (6,200 ft) high.

Lake Popovo
Surrounded by towering peaks, Popovo is the largest of Pirin's 186 glacial lakes. Windsurfers use the lake for high-altitude practice.

0 kilometres	5
0 miles	5

THE BROWN BEAR

The semi-open, mountainous terrain of the Pirin Mountains is an ideal habitat for brown bears. The animals once thrived here but, as elsewhere in Europe, their populations are now dangerously small. Until quite recently, dancing bears were a common sight on the streets of Bulgaria. This cruel practice was outlawed in 1998, and in 2000 the Belitsa Dancing Bear Park *(see p121)* began collecting the bears, paying their mainly Gypsy owners compensation. The 12-ha (30-acre) park, funded by Four Paws of Austria and the Brigitte Bardot Foundation, includes forest, pools and caves where the bears hibernate. Visitors can observe the bears from covered walk-ways, and there are regular guided tours.

Inhabitant of Belitsa Dancing Bear Park, refuge for maltreated bears

BLAGOEVGRAD

Bansko

19

GOTSE DELCHEV

Glazne

ikusheva ura

dorka 746 m

silishki Lakes

Yulen Reserve

Damyanitsa

Popovo lake

Polezhan 2850 m

Kremenski Lakes

anska Bistritsa

Kamenitsa 2816 m

Kamenitsa

Toufcha

Pirinska Bistritsa

STAR SIGHTS

★ Vihren

★ Koncheto

★ Baikousheva Mura

Gotse Delchev ⑰
Гоце Делчев

52 km (32 miles) SE of Bansko.
Map B5. 🏔 24,500. 🚌 🚗 ℹ️ *ul. Tsaritsa Yoana.* ⬜ *variable.*

Thanks to crisp mountain air combined with warm winds blowing along the Mesta valley from the Aegean Sea, Gotse Delchev has a pleasant climate. It lies in the shadow of the Pirin but, despite this, the town is free of snow for most of the winter.

The National Revival-style Rifat Bey House-Museum, in Gotse Delchev

The area, known as Nestos in ancient times, was settled in about 5000 BC. Thracians arrived in 2000 BC and in the 2nd century AD Romans built Nikopolis ad Nestrum, which became the region's first major settlement. The poignant ruins, overgrown with vegetation, are 5 km (3 miles) from Gotse Delchev, on the main road to Kovachevitsa. After the decline of Nikopolis in the 6th century, a new settlement, named Nevrokop, was established nearby, on the banks of the Delchevska River. In 1950 the town was renamed Gotse Delchev in honour of the Macedonian revolutionary *(see box)*. The recently re-opened Greek border crossing into Greece, 20 km (12 miles) southeast of the town, has revived the

Bust of Vasil Levski in Gotse Delchev

trading route that was once a major link between Serdika (ancient Sofia) and the Aegean.

Gotse Delchev is a useful base for exploring the highland villages of the northern Rhodopes *(see opposite)*. It is a quiet, pleasant town, with a pedestrianized centre that gives it a relaxed air. Its main attraction for visitors is the **History Museum**, in an impressive National Revival house. The exhibits include several early Thracian clay figurines dating from 1000 BC and the metal wheels and

axles of a Roman chariot discovered near the town. The museum's ethnographic collection features a display of 19th-century cow bells and a *kazan*, or still, for making the potent spirit *rakiya*, as well as local costumes, instruments and antique tools.

Also of interest is the **Rifat Bey House-Museum**, on the riverside. Its exhibits illustrate the daily life and artistic tastes of the National Revival period.

🏛 **History Museum**
ul. Hristo Botev 26. **Tel** (0751) 60287. ⬜ 8:30am–noon, 1:30–5:30pm Mon–Sat. 📷

🏛 **Rifat Bey House-Museum**
⬜ 8:30am–noon, 1:30–5:30pm Mon–Sat. 📷

Room at the History Museum, Gotse Delchev, with ethnographic items

MACEDONIAN REVOLUTIONARIES

The euphoria that swept Bulgaria after the Liberation of 1878 and the subsequent creation of a large Bulgarian state, which included most of Macedonia, was soon dashed when the Berlin Congress ordered the return of Macedonia to the Ottoman Empire. From this, two distinct groups emerged, both determined to free Macedonia from Turkish rule. One was the Internal Macedonian Revolutionary Organisation (IMRO), whose leader was Gotse Delchev (1872–1903). He believed in the creation of a separate Macedonian state. A group of influential Macedonian émigrés based in Sofia formed the Supreme Macedonian Committee (SMC), which argued for Macedonia's incorporation into Bulgaria. Both endeavours failed, but Delchev remains a hero. The towns of Gotse Delchev in Bulgaria and Delchevo in Macedonia were named after him.

Statue of Gotse Delchev, fighter for Macedonia's sovereignty

Highland Villages Tour ⑱

Over 300 years ago, Christian Bulgarians fleeing an aggressive Ottoman campaign to convert them to Islam sought refuge in the remote highlands. Here they established villages, using local materials to build fine stone houses. Almost deserted in the 1950s, these beautiful and still remote villages have recently become popular with city-dwellers in search of tranquillity. Both Kovachevitsa and Dolen are now protected as architectural reserves.

TIPS FOR DRIVERS

Map B4.
Length: about 40 km (25 miles).
Getting there: The easiest way is by car or taxi. There are limited bus services from Gotse Delchev.
Stopping-off points: There are B&Bs and inns at all villages.
Walks from Kovachevitsa: Various paths lead out of the village. One (2 km/1 mile) leads to the top of a hill within reach of the small Church of Sveti Georgi. Another (19 km/12 miles) crosses the mountains to Dolen.

Kovachevitsa ①
Here, massive stone houses are set on the steep hillside. Their windowless ground floors sheltered animals and produce and served as defences against Ottoman raids.

0 kilometres   5

0 miles   5

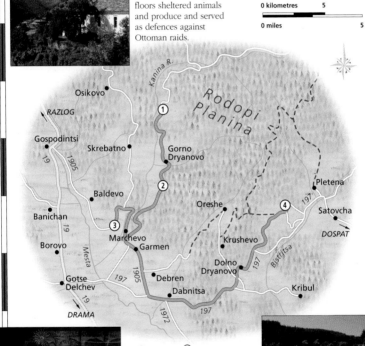

Ognyanovo ③
The outdoor pools of Ognyanovo are popular in winter, when bathers can rub themselves with snow after a hot bath. A pleasant large indoor pool is filled with steaming warm spa water.

Leshten ②
This tiny mountain hamlet, where visitors can stay, has been restored. The houses have original wooden floors, thick stone walls, and modern bathrooms and heating. The roofs are tiled with slabs of local stone.

KEY

━━ Tour route

═══ Main road

──── Other road

- - - Trail

Dolen ④
Unlike Kovachevitsa and Leshten, Dolen is still a working agricultural village. The inhabitants keep animals and work the land. Tobacco leaves are hung out on wooden frames and people can be seen sorting beans and corn on their doorsteps.

Swimming pool, filled with spring water, at one of Velingrad's spa hotels

Velingrad ⑲
Велинград

50 km (32 miles) W of Plovdiv.
Map B4. 🚶 *24,800.* 🚃 🚌 🏨 🚗
ℹ *pl. Svoboda (0359-58401).*
www.velingrad.bg

This sprawling spa town owes its popularity to the springs that supply its many hotels, swimming pools and bath-houses with steaming hot mineral water. Wooded parks and a pleasant pedestrianized centre also contribute to making this one of Bulgaria's principal spa resorts. The most popular of Velingrad's many public baths are in the Chepino quarter, east of the town centre, where visitors can also hire rowing boats for excursions on a lake fed by the Kleptuza spring. Most of the town's larger hotels have their own mineral pools and offer hydrotherapy.

Besides this, the town's main point of interest is its **History Museum**, in the Kamenitsa quarter. It contains displays of black-and-white photographs, local costumes and jewellery, and painted Easter eggs.

Velingrad is also a station stop on the narrow-gauge railway from Septembri to Dobrinishte *(see p121).*

🏛 **History Museum**
ul. Vlado Chernozemski 2.
Tel *(0359) 52591.* 🕐 *9am–5:30pm Mon–Sat.* 📷

Batak ⑳
Батак

45 km (30 miles) SW of Plovdiv.
Map C4. 🚶 *4,000.* 🚌 🚗

This unassuming Rhodopean logging town would have remained as anonymous as its neighbours were it not for the infamous events of April 1876, which inspired Ivan Vazov to write: "It goes without saying that without Batak there would not be a free Bulgaria." One of several towns that supported the revolutionary cause, Batak was punished with exceptional ferocity following the dismal failure of the April Rising *(see p174).* Ottoman mercenaries known as *bashibazouks,* together with local Bulgarian Muslims, slaughtered 5,000 people in an indiscriminate attack. The local rebel Trendafil Kerelov was tied to a tree and set alight.

Bust of Trendafil Kerelov in Batak

Newspaper reports by English journalist J.A. MacGahan, who witnessed the aftermath, prompted international outrage, and ultimately led to pressure being put on Turkey to recognize Bulgaria's independence.

Much of Batak's **History Museum** is devoted to documenting the massacre. The names and ages of the victims cover a wall, while alongside are numerous photographs of skulls and bones piled next to elderly survivors. Muskets and woodsmen's axes used in the attack are on display, as are the crude cherry-tree cannons built by the revolutionaries.

Across the main square is the small **Church of Sveta Nedelya**, surrounded by a walled compound where Batak's inhabitants once sought refuge. In a report for *The Daily News* in August 1876 MacGahan described the scene as he entered the compound: "The whole church-yard for three feet [1 m] deep was festering with dead bodies… The church was still worse. The floor was covered with rotting bodies… I never imagined anything so fearful."

The church stands as a shrine to Batak's victims, with charred beams, signs pointing to bullet holes, and a pit dug by mothers desperate to find water for their children.

The nearby **Ethnographic Museum**, in a 19th-century farmhouse, makes no reference to the atrocities. Its covered courtyard contains displays of antique farming implements and logging equipment. The simple living quarters upstairs are laid out much as they would have been in the 19th century.

Batak Reservoir, the picturesque artificial lake near Batak

History Museum
pl. Tsentral. **Tel** (03553) 2329.
8:30 am–5:30pm Mon–Fri.
Joint ticket for History Museum,
Church of Sveta Nedelya and
Ethnographic Museum.

Church of Sveta Nedelya
pl. Tsentral. 8:30am–5:30pm
Mon–Fri. See History Museum.

Ethnographic Museum
Off pl. Tsentral. 8:30am–5:30pm
Mon–Fri. See History Museum.

Environs
Picturesque **Batak Reservoir**
lies 6 km (4 miles) north of
Batak. The lake is surrounded
by meadows, and only a small
part of the lakeside has been
developed for tourism, leaving
plenty of unspoilt open space.

Devin ㉑
Девин

80 km (50 miles) S of Plovdiv.
Map C4. 7,500.

Besides the bottled mineral
water for which Devin is well
known, this small town's
greatest merit is its thermal
pools and baths. The Orpheus
Hotel, in the town, has an
outdoor thermal pool that is
open to the public.
    Devin also has a **History
Museum**, with a collection of
exhibits illustrating folklore of
the western Rhodopes.

History Museum
pl. Osvobozhdenie. 10am–noon,
3–5:30pm Mon–Sat.

Western Rhodopes
Caves ㉒
Западни Родопи пещерите

See pp128–9.

Shiroka Lûka ㉓
Широка Лъка

90 km (56 miles) S of Plovdiv.
Map C4. 800. Kukeri
carnival (1st weekend in Mar);
International Bagpipe Festival (Aug)

This quaint and atmospheric
village is deservedly popular
with visitors. It clings to the
side of a steep valley washed
by a small river, and looks

GAIDA, BULGARIAN BAGPIPES
The Rhodope Mountains are thought to be the home of
Bulgaria's oldest folk music tradition. Central to this is
the *gaida*, or Bulgarian bagpipes. A *gaida* consists of a
goatskin with a blowpipe attached to the neck hole and
two other pipes – the drone and the melody chanter –
attached to each of the front leg holes. Holding it under his
arm, the player blows into the bag, forcing air out through
the pipes. A feature of the *gaida* is the "flea hole", a smaller
hole usually covered by the
player's index finger. When
uncovered, it raises any
note by a semitone to create
the unique ornamentation
of Bulgarian folk music.
    Folk singers are often
accompanied by a *kaba
gaida*, a large, low-pitched
bagpipe. Bands of 60 to
100 pipers, known as *sto
kaba gaidi*, produce a
tremendous sound.

**Gaida players at the International
Bagpipe Festival in Shiroka Lûka**

across to densely wooded
slopes on the opposite side.
Picturesque houses with bare
stone foundations, timber and
whitewashed walls, and roofs
of roughly hewn stone slabs
perch on terraces cut into the
hillside. A network of cobbled
streets threads through the
town's haphazard layout.
    The **Church of the Assump-
tion** (1834), reached by crossing an ancient stone bridge
on the western side of the
village, is decorated with
colourful naïve frescoes of a
funeral procession and biblical scenes. Across the road
from the church is the Sgurov
Konak (Sgurov House), built
by a wealthy local family in
the late 19th century. Now the
Town Hall, the building houses

the **Ethnographic Museum**,
filled with original furnishings
and other exhibits that illustrate the daily lives of members of the Sgurov family.
    Shiroka Lûka has a strong
association with folk culture.
It is one of the best places to
see a *kukeri* carnival (*see p102*).
The village is also the home
of the National School of
Folklore Arts, which organizes
performances of folk music
for tour groups, and it hosts
the International Bagpipe
Festival (*see p35*).

Church of the Assumption
rarely. Enquire in the village.

Ethnographic Museum
Tel (0899) 465170. summer:
9am–6pm Mon–Tue, Thu–Sun;
winter: by prior arrangement.

Houses at Shiroka Lûka, on a hillside above the Shirokolûshka river valley

Western Rhodopes Caves ②
Западни Родопи пещерите

The road southwest from Devin leads into the spectacular, pine-forested Rhodope Mountains, where it forks to either the spectacular Trigrad Gorge or the winding Buzhnov Gorge and Yagodina Cave. This remote border region is dotted with tiny villages dependent on small-scale farming. The locals are a mix of Christian Bulgarians and Muslim Bulgarians *(pomaks)* who have coexisted peacefully for many centuries; many villages here have both a church and a mosque. The area is excellent for hiking, mountain biking and bird watching, and pony-trekking tours can also be arranged from Trigrad. Although they are accessible by limited public transport, it is far easier to reach the villages and caves by car.

Western Rhodopes
This picturesque and diverse geography of mountains, caves, forests, rivers, lakes and valleys is home to a wide variety of flora and fauna.

Cave-dwelling Bats
Large colonies of bats – 28 out of the 35 bat species known in Europe – live in the Rhodope Mountains. All of them are under the protection of the law. In colder months they live deep in the caves but can roost in old buildings and trees in summer.

Haberlea Rhodopensis
This rare alpine flower is endemic to Bulgaria and enjoys the wet rocky climate of caves – so much so that it is also known as Orpheus's flower.

ORPHEUS IN THE UNDERWORLD

Orpheus, the mythological hero of Thrace, sang and played the lyre so beguilingly that his music charmed trees and animals. When his beloved wife Eurydice died, Orpheus descended into the Underworld to seek her. Moved by his music, Hades agreed to return Eurydice on condition that Orpheus did not set his eyes on her until they had reached the Overworld. But Orpheus looked back, and lost his wife forever. Heartbroken, Orpheus roamed the Rhodope Mountains, singing mournfully of his loss. He was killed by Thracian women and his head and lyre were thrown into a river. Lodged in a rock, his head became an oracle.

The death of Orpheus at the hands of a Thracian woman

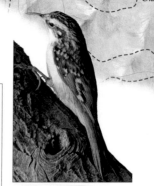

Treecreeper
These are attractive little birds that hop around tree trunks, looking for insects, in steady little spirals working their way to the top, before flying off to the next tree flashing a golden wing bar.

★ Yagodina Cave
Stretching for 10 km (6 miles) over five levels, Yagodina Cave is the longest and deepest in the Rhodopes. Tunnels lead visitors through stunning galleries with interestingly shaped rock formations and evidence of prehistoric occupation.

VISITORS' CHECKLIST

Trigrad 30 km (20 miles) SW of Devin. **Map** C5. 🚌 🚐 from Devin. 🎭 *Orphic Mysteries Folk Music Festival, Trigrad (Aug).* **Devil's Throat Cave** ◯ daily. 🕐 *30 mins.* 🎫 **Yagodina Cave** ◯ daily. 🕐 *45 mins.* 🎫

Buzhnov Gorge
Following the winding Boinovska River, this gorge is less precipitous than Trigrad Gorge, but is still worth a visit.

Grohotno
DEVIN

astraklii
Reserve

197

197   Teshel

Kazanite
Reserve

Gyovren

Trigradska

Bosnovska

Yagodina

Trigradsko
Zhdrelo
Reserve

Trigrad

★ Trigrad Gorge
This gorge ascends gradually towards the Devil's Throat, where its steep walls narrow dramatically and the Trigradska River plunges into the cave.

★ Devil's Throat Cave
A long corridor leads into a vast cavern 110 m (360 ft) long and 35 m (115 ft) high traversed by walkways. A noisy 45-m (150-ft) waterfall reveals where the Trigradska River dives underground. Three hundred steep steps lead up to the cave mouth.

0 kilometres   2

0 miles   2

KEY

═══ Main road

═══ Other roads

– – Trail

⋔ Cave

Trigrad Village
This picturesque village is notable for the sight of a church and a mosque side by side. Birdwatchers should look out for the wallcreepers often spotted on rocks nearby.

STAR SIGHTS

★ Devil's Throat Cave

★ Trigrad Gorge

★ Yagodina Cave

The mountain town of Smolyan, one of the highest in Bulgaria

Smolyan ㉔
Смолян

103 km (64 miles) S of Plovdiv. **Map** C5. 🚶 *33,000.* 🚌 Ⓜ 🚗 🚖 **ℹ** *bul. Bulgaria Administratsiya Komplex (0301-62530).* **www**.smolyan.com

Smolyan is a narrow strip of a town strung out between densely forested mountains at an altitude of about 1,000 m (3,300 ft). The air here is crisp and fresh, and the climate pleasantly sunny.

Smolyan has a relatively short history. The original local settlement of Ezerovo, situated beside the lakes above the town, was destroyed by the Ottomans in the 17th century as a reprisal against those of its inhabitants who refused to adopt Islam. While they fled to the mountains, those that agreed to convert settled along the Cherna River, where they founded the villages of Smolyan, Ustovo and Raikovo. In 1960 the three settlements were amalgamated to form Smolyan, now the cultural and administrative capital of the central and western Rhodopes.

The town's modern centre was laid out in the 1980s. Its great central thoroughfare and enormous civic buildings, many of which appear to be underused, seem out of proportion to the relatively modest size of its population.

Icon of St John the Theologian, Smolyan

The **History Museum**, however, makes good use of its space. Its captivating exhibits begin with the earliest human presence in the central Rhodope Mountains. Flint tools from the Palaeolithic period are followed by objects from later prehistory, such as spindle weights and other stone implements. One room is devoted to the Thracians, who were most active in the region during the Iron Age. Objects in this section include ceramic vessels, bronze and iron clasps, swords and arrows, a bronze helmet with bearded cheek guards, and a delightful bronze oil lamp in the shape of a doe.

Most of these objects were found in the many Thracian necropolises that have been discovered in the Rhodopes. Later exhibits relate to the Ottoman campaign to convert local villagers to Islam. Evidence of outward acceptance of Islam that concealed continued Christian belief is shown in such pieces as an Islamic gravestone with a cross carved on the underside. Upstairs, the museum's displays continue with beautiful fleecy rugs, woven in goat's wool coloured with vivid natural dyes.

The town's **Art Gallery**, opposite the museum, has an absorbing collection of paintings that includes romantic Rhodopean landscapes and modern works by local artists.

Further along bulevard Bulgariya is the modern Church of Sveti Vaserion Smolyanski, topped with eyecatchingly large copper-clad domes. Across the road are the somewhat smaller domes of the **Planetarium**, which has daily shows in English and other languages.

🏛 **History Museum**
bul. Bulgariya, Administratsiya Komplex. *Tel (0301) 62727.* ◯ 9am–5pm Tue–Sat. 🈳

🏛 **Art Gallery**
bul. Bulgariya, Administratsiya Komplex. *Tel (0301) 62328.* ◯ 9am–5pm Tue–Sat. 🈳

🏛 **Planetarium**
bul. Bulgariya 20. *Tel (0301) 83074. Shows in English at 2pm daily.* 🈳 **www**.planetarium-sm.org

Part of Agushev Konak, a fine fortified manor house in Mogilitsa

Mogilitsa ㉕
Могилица

20 km (12 miles) SW of Smolyan. **Map** C5. 🚶 *500.* 🚌 🚗

An easy day trip from Smolyan is the quiet village of Mogilitsa. It was once home to the wealthy Agushev family, who grew rich from sheep farming. The **Agushev Konak**, their winter residence, is one of the best surviving examples of a Rhodopean fortified manor house. It was begun in 1812 and completed in 1842 and, with a total of 221 windows, 86 doors and 26 chimneys, it is an imposing presence in the village. The complex is divided into three walled compounds, which were inhabited by Agushev's eldest sons and their families.

The comfortably furnished interior has large panelled rooms with intricately carved ceilings and a huge hall. According to a local legend, Agushev cut off the architect's right hand to prevent him from designing such a beautiful building for anyone else.

Environs

About 3 km (2 miles) east of Mogilitsa is **Uhlovitza Cave**. The descent to the mouth of the cave, down steep steps, is rewarded by the dramatic sight of underground waterfalls and fascinating mineral formations. The cave can quite easily be reached by car, or on foot via a hiking trail.

🏛 **Agushev Konak**
◯ 9am–5:30pm Wed–Sun. 🖼

⋔ **Uhlovitza Cave**
◯ 9am–5pm Wed–Sun. 🖼

Zlatograd ㉖
Златоград

50 km (31 miles) SE of Smolyan.
Map D5. 🏠 8,000. 🚌 Ⓜ 🚗

Under Communism, Zlatograd (Gold Town) was a thriving mining centre. But by the late 1990s, rising costs and other factors had made its mines uneconomical and all were closed. More recently, however, Zlatograd has begun to recover, attracting visitors to its newly opened **Ethnographic Museum Complex**.

This ensemble of restored National Revival buildings houses traditional workshops, an Ethnographic Museum, and an Education Museum.

A piste on the forested slopes above the ski resort of Pamporovo

At the Water Mill Museum, visitors can watch huge water-powered hammers processing woollen material. The complex also includes a guest house.

🏛 **Ethnographic Museum Complex**
1 km (¾ mile) west of bus station.
Tel (03071) 4474. ◯ 9am–6:30pm daily. 🖼 🍴 🖥 🏠 ✎

Momchilovtsi ㉗
Момчиловци

90 km (56 miles) S of Plovdiv. **Map** C5. 🏠 450. 🚌 🚉 🛈 (03023) 2803.

This pretty Rhodopean mountain village lies at an altitude of 1,200 m (4,000 ft). With stunning views and great tranquillity, it has become popular as a weekend retreat for wealthy townspeople. Its nearby snowboard park also attracts winter visitors, and the area is used as a base by hunters visiting Kormisosh, Bulgaria's largest hunting reserve, 15 km (9 miles) away.

Pamporovo ㉘
Пампорово

85 km (53 miles) south of Plovdiv.
🚌 Ⓜ 🚗 www.pamporovo.net

With Borovets and Bansko, Pamporovo forms part of the trio of major Bulgarian ski resorts. Second-largest of the three, it is also the southernmost and the sunniest. It was purpose-built under Communism, with large hotels set at the base of pine-forested pistes. While the resort covers a larger area than Borovets (*see p107*), it lacks the village atmosphere of Bansko (*see pp118–20*), and has fewer après-ski facilities.

As it is geared to catering for large groups, the resort has long attracted Western European tourists on cheap package holidays. With gentle slopes, Pamporovo is suitable for beginners and intermediate skiers, but offers little to challenge the more advanced.

With snow from December to mid-April, the resort is crowded during the winter season. In summer, by contrast, it is virtually deserted, despite the beauty of the landscape at that time of year and the efforts of tour operators to promote mountain biking and hiking here.

For spectacular views at any time of year, visitors can take the chairlift to Mount Snezhanka. The **Television Tower** on the summit, at a height of 1,926 m (6,320 ft), has an observation gallery.

🗼 **Television Tower**
Mount Snezhanka.
◯ 9am–5pm daily. 🖥

Part of the Ethnographic Museum Complex in Zlatograd

Rock formation known as the Stone Wedding near Kŭrdzhali ▷

Plovdiv ㉙

Пловдив

The three hills on which Plovdiv's Old Town stands were settled by Thracians in the 5th millennium BC. Philip II of Macedon captured the town in 342 BC and from the 1st to 4th centuries AD it was held by the Romans. It thrived, but was largely destroyed by Huns in 447. In the 6th century, Plovdiv was occupied by Slavs. It then passed back and forth between Byzantines and Bulgarians before the Ottomans took control of it in the 14th century. After the Liberation of 1878, Plovdiv was returned to the Ottomans as part of Eastern Rumelia but in 1885 it was reunified with Bulgaria. Now Bulgaria's second-largest city, Plovdiv is a pleasant town, with a pedestrianized centre, mosques, churches, Roman ruins and National Revival mansions.

Statue in the Roman Stadium

⋔ Roman Stadium

pl. Dzhumaya.
Crumbling marble terraces and tumbled columns oddly incorporated into the concrete foundations of modern Plovdiv are almost all that remain of the town's once huge Roman stadium. It was built in the 2nd century AD, and could seat 30,000 spectators.

☪ Dzhumaya Mosque

pl. Dzhumaya.
Although the imposing nine-domed Friday Mosque is currently undergoing much needed structural repairs, it is still open to visitors. The central focus of its pale blue interior is a fountain surrounded by four massive pillars. It is thought to have been built as early as 1364, during the reign

of Sultan Murad I. A café that abuts the mosque's outer wall serves Turkish coffee and *baklava* (syrupy cake).

The Archaeological Museum, in a redundant revenue building

⛫ History Museum

pl. Suedinenie. **Tel** *(032) 229 409.*
◯*10am–5:30pm Mon–Sat.* 📷 ♿
The History Museum is housed in what was intended to be Eastern Rumelia's new parliament building. It was completed in 1885 but, with the unification of Bulgaria with Eastern Rumelia later that year, Sofia became the capital of Bulgaria. The building lost its purpose, and it has been a museum ever since. Consisting of declarations, weaponry, uniforms and photographs of soldiers and ragged rebels, its collection documents the unification of 1885 *(see p47).*

The diamond-patterned minaret of Dzhumaya Mosque

⛫ Archaeological Museum

pl. Suedinenie
The museum has an excellent collection of antiquities from all periods. Unfortunately it is currently closed and undergoing refurbishment. The only exhibits visible are a few marble pillars in the gardens, inscribed with Greek proclamations.

[map]

Key to Symbols *see back flap*

KEY

▨ Street-by-Street *pp136–7*

☪ Imaret Mosque

ul. Han Kubrat.
Dating from 1445, this is one of more than 50 mosques built in Plovdiv during the Ottoman period. *Imaret* means "shelter for the homeless", and this was the mosque's original function. Its square walls support a central dome and a minaret with unusual zigzag brickwork.

🏛 Natural History Museum

ul. Hristo Danov 34. **Tel** (032) 626 683. ◯ 8:30am–noon, 1–5pm Tue–Sun. 📷

A stuffed deer at the museum entrance sets the scene for the remarkable collection of stuffed mammals, birds and reptiles that lie within. Among

SIGHTS AT A GLANCE

many notable exhibits are a camel and an anaconda. Downstairs is an aquarium where visitors can see live turtles and fish, including piranhas.

Other rooms contain displays of minerals and giant crystals, fossilized trees, mammoth tusks and teeth, and tiny fossils of organisms that lived millions of years ago.

🏛 City Art Gallery

ul. Knyaz Alexander I 15. **Tel** (032) 624 221. ◯ 9am–5:30pm Mon–Fri, 10am–5pm Sat. 📷

This gallery displays the work of Bulgarian and international artists in continually changing displays. It also has a permanent collection of 19th-century art. Another of Plovdiv's permanent art collections is kept at the State Gallery of Fine Arts (see p138).

Cloisters at the 18th-century Church of Sveta Marina

🛐 Church of Sveta Marina

ul. Dr Vulkovich 7.

The present Church of Sveta Marina was built in 1783, on the site of a 16th-century church, which was destroyed by fire. It is renowned for its intricate iconostasis, which is decorated with tiny figures painted by artists including Zahari Zograf (see p106).

🏛 Hristo Danov House

ul. Mitropolit Paisii. ◯ 9am–noon, 2–5pm Mon–Fri. 📷

Built on Taxim Tepe (Taxim Hill), Hristo Danov House overlooks Plovdiv. Steep steps lead up to it. Its arched gable is supported by four columns, and trompe-l'oeil pillars adorn the façade. The house's symmetrical interior is typical of

VISITORS' CHECKLIST

145 km (90 miles) SE of Sofia.
Map C4. 🏙 338,000. 🛬 ⊠ 🚉
🚏 🚎 🚌 🚕 🚢 daily. 🎭 Folk
Festival (Aug), Intnl. Fair (May,
Sep). **www**.plovdivguide.com

National Revival architecture, with rooms each side of the main drawing room.

Hristo Danov, founder of organized book publishing in Bulgaria, lived here from 1868 until his death in 1911. Danov was largely responsible for the first large-scale publication of school textbooks in Bulgarian. As well as Danov's study, and books printed before and during the National Revival, the house contains a re-created 19th-century classroom.

🛐 Church of Sveta Bogoroditsa

ul. Metropolit Paisii. ◯ 7:30am–6:30pm daily. 🛐 8am daily.

This imposing stone church has a distinctive pink and blue bell tower that was added with Russian assistance in 1880, after the Liberation. Its murals echo the mood of the late 19th century. They depict Bulgarian Orthodox saints alongside leaders of the Liberation movement. To the right are priests, intellectuals and peasants chained together under the whip of a cruel Turk. To the left are children being taught by a benign Bulgarian schoolmaster. The church's interior is lit by arched windows, and hefty columns lead towards a bright gilt iconostasis.

Murals with a political message, in the Church of Sveta Bogoroditsa

Street-by-Street: Plovdiv Old Town

One of the most picturesque of Bulgaria's historic urban centres, Plovdiv's Old Town consists of steep cobbled streets lined with fine National Revival houses, many of them built for wealthy merchants. Colourfully rendered exteriors protrude majestically over high walls, and within are breathtakingly opulent interiors. Mostly built in the mid-19th century, these houses gradually fell into decay as the cost of maintaining them outstripped their owners' means. However, state restoration projects in the 1970s did much to preserve these houses, several of which are now museums. Most of the Old Town is also under state protection as an architectural reserve.

★ Icon Museum
The beautiful icons on display here were painted in the 15th and 16th centuries, and come from churches in the vicinity of Plovdiv.

Zlatyu Boyadzhiev House
The rooms of this grand house are filled with paintings by Zlatyu Boyadzhiev (1903–76). These large-scale, colourful and impressionistic works were inspired by village life, and often depict peasants. The artist produced his most interesting works after 1951, when partial paralysis forced him to paint with his left hand.

Apteka Hipokrat
This pharmacy museum gives a fascinating insight into the treatment of common ailments in the 19th century.

Georgi Bozhilov-Slona Gallery
The work of Bulgarian modernist painters fills the rooms of this gallery.

STAR SIGHTS

★ Church of SS Konstantin & Elena

★ Icon Museum

★ Kuyumdzhiogh House

★ **Church of SS Konstantin & Elena**
Richly coloured frescoes decorate both the entrance to this church and its interior. There is also an iconostasis partly decorated by Zahari Zograf.

VISITORS' CHECKLIST

Map C4. 🏛 8,602.
🛈 pl. Tsentralen 1 (032-656 793). 🚃 🚌 🚕 *Winter Festival of Symphonic Music (first 2 weeks of Jan); International Trade Fair (early May and last 2 weeks of Sep); International Folklore Festival (Aug); City Holiday (6 Sep).*
www.plovdivguide.com

★ **Kuyumdzhiogh House**
This beautiful house is one of the Old Town's showpieces. Built in 1847, it is now an Ethnographic Museum, with regional costumes and a traditional rose-oil distiller.

ULITSA TSANKO LAVRENOV

ARH. PEEV HRISTA

P. R. SLAVEYKOV

NEKTARIEV

Nedkovich House
Secluded behind a high wall, Nedkovich House was built for a textile merchant in 1863. The rooms contain many of the house's original furnishings, imported from East and West to create a blend of European and Oriental styles.

Georgiadi House
Built for a wealthy Turkish merchant in 1846, this grand house has rooms with projecting box windows. Among objects on display here is the bell that tolled during the April Rising of 1876.

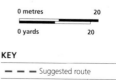

| 0 metres | 20 |
| 0 yards | 20 |

KEY

– – – Suggested route

Exploring Plovdiv

Plaque, Hipokrat Pharmacy

With narrow cobbled streets leading off in all directions, Plovdiv's Old Town can be disorientating at first, but with the help of a good map visitors should be able to find their way around. The easiest approach is to enter from ulitsa Saborna, off ploshtad Dzhumaya. This street leads through the old town, passing many museum-houses and galleries, all the way up to Nebet Tepe, from where there are stunning views of Plovdiv. Ulitsa Tsanko Lavrenov passes both the History Museum and Nedkovich House, and joins ulitsa Kiril Nektariev, which leads to Lamartine House and on towards the Roman Theatre. From here there is a sweeping view of the city and the Rhodope Mountains beyond.

�
 Philippopolis Art Gallery
ul. Saborna 29. ☐ 10am–7pm daily.

This appealing gallery occupies an elegant house with fine furnishings. Downstairs is a collection of late 19th- and early 20th-century Bulgarian portraits and landscapes, most of which are for sale.

The permanent collection fills the spacious rooms upstairs. Many of the works have romantic themes. Ivan Trichkov's *The Sower* (1920) portrays a ragged, bare-footed peasant sowing in an ochre landscape, while a large canvas by Dimitar Gyudzhenov (1975) depicts a gathering of revolutionaries bathed in the light of a setting sun.

⊞ State Gallery of Fine Arts
ul. Saborna 14a. ☐ 9am–5:30pm Mon–Sat.

In a grand old building that was once a school, the State Gallery of Fine Arts has a

The State Gallery of Fine Arts, in an imposing Neo-Classical building.

comprehensive collection of 19th- and 20th-century Bulgarian paintings. Solemn 19th-century portraits hang alongside idyllic scenes such as Ivan Angelov's *Women Gathering Hay* (1903), and some typically vibrant works by Vladimir Dimitrov-Maistor. Large, bold canvases on the second floor represent more recent Bulgarian painting. Among the works here is *The Fire* (1977) by Svetlin Rusev, a monumental canvas in which a figure walks away from a furnace carrying a glowing ember into the darkness.

⊞ Hipokrat Pharmacy
ul. Saborna ☐ 10am–5pm Mon–Fri.

The fascinating Hipokrat Pharmacy (Arteka Hipokrat) has been preserved virtually as it was when it was a working pharmacy. It is lined with wooden drawers, and contains bottles and jars neatly labelled in Latin.

⊞ Georgi Bozhilov-Slona Gallery
Knyaz Tseretelev 1. ☐ 10am–6pm daily.

This attractive blue and white house contains a collection of paintings by Georgi Bozhilov-Slona (1935–2001). The artist, a key member of the Bulgarian Modernist movement, often painted abstract pictures of familiar objects, such as a still life with a chair, a stove and a cup. By using thick layers of oil paint and by blending textures and media he created striking images

charged with emotion. Few of the paintings exhibited here are named or dated.

⊞ Icon Museum
ul. Saborna, 22. ☐ 9am–12:30pm, 1–5:30pm Mon–Sat.

This interesting museum is home to a valuable array of icons from the Plovdiv eparchy collection that was collected from churches under threat during the Communist years.

Icon of St Cyril and St Methodius in the Icon Museum

⌂ Nedkovich House
ul. Tsanko Lavrenov, 3. ☐ 9am–noon, 1–5pm Mon–Fri.

This grand house is a fine example of the symmetrical architecture so loved during the National Revival. An interesting feature is the courtyard structure with a window to the street known as the *clukarnik* (literally "gossip room") where the inhabitants could drink tea and chat to passers-by. The first floor salon boasts a raised stage where musicians would entertain guests.

Room in Nedkovich House, built for a textile trader in 1863

Detail of one of the murals of European cities at Hindliyan House

Hindliyan House

ul. Artin Gidikov 4. 9am–5pm
Mon–Fri.

This elegant house, its pale
blue outer walls decorated
with floral motifs, looks onto
a peaceful courtyard garden.
It was built in 1835–40, for
Stepan Hindliyan, a wealthy
Armenian merchant. The interior features murals depicting
the European cities that he
visited. The house also has a
hammam with a marble floor,
hot and cold water, and a
domed ceiling with tiny windows. The spacious first-floor
salon has a stunning panelled
ceiling and a marble fountain.

Nebet Tepe

Dilapidated houses line ulitsa
Dr Chomakov, the street that
leads up to the equally ram-
shackle Nebet Tepe (Prayer
Hill). As the city's highest
point, the summit was the site
of a citadel. Today it is an
overgrown wasteland strewn
with boulders and the barely
visible foundations of the
ancient fortress. Even so, it is
easy to understand why the
hill was so prized by successive invaders. Situated close
to the Maritsa River, it stands
prominently in the centre of
the plain between the Rhodope
and Stara Planina mountains.
It is a good vantage point
from which to view most of
the city, spread out below.

Lamartine House

ul. Puldin. to the public.

This attractive house is named
after the French poet Alphonse
de Lamartine, who stayed here
briefly in 1833, in the course
of travels that he described
in *Voyage en l'Orient*.

The house, now owned by
the Union of Bulgarian Writers,
is not open to the public, but
from the outside visitors can
admire its projecting floors
supported by wooden ribs.

**Lamartine House, named after the
French poet who stayed here**

Roman Theatre

ul. Hemus 9am–6pm daily.

This impressive marble amphitheatre, set in the hillside
overlooking the city and the
Rhodope Mountains beyond,
was discovered during construction work in 1972. It was
built in the 2nd century AD,
when Trimontium (Roman
Plovdiv) was at its height, and
formed part of the acropolis.
Today the theatre is used for
concerts and plays.

Trakart Cultural Centre

Podlez Arheologicheski. **Tel** (032)
631 303. 9am–7pm daily.
www.trakart.org

Most pedestrians using the
Archaeological Underpass
(Podlez Arheologicheski) to
cross bul. Tsar Boris Osvoboditel will not know that it
is a Roman street, paved with
huge stone slabs, dating back
to the 3rd–4th centuries AD.
Alongside the underpass is
the Trakart Cultural Centre,
which exhibits the foundations and mosaic floors of a
4th-century Roman house
uncovered in the mid-1980s.
Supporting columns carved
with crosses date the building
to the late 4th century, when
Emperor Theodosius I made
Christianity the official religion.

The mosaics, preserved in
situ, are in remarkably good
condition. They include a
portrait of a woman thought
to be Penelope, the pagan
goddess of peace, who was
adopted by Christians as
St Irene. The lead pipe that
supplied water to the fountain
in the house's main reception
room also survives. Beside
the fountain is a mosaic with
the words "happiness" and
"welcome" and geometric
designs bordered by bands of
swastikas and other motifs.
The remains of a corridor with
underfloor sewage channels
lead from the main entrance
to a room with a patterned
mosaic floor. An east-facing
apse was added later, as a
meeting room or chapel.

The centre, which is funded
by the US Embassy, also hosts
art exhibitions, and sells replicas of ancient ceramics.

The well-preserved Roman Theatre, with seating for 6,000 spectators

Bachkovo Monastery ㉚
Бачковски манастир

See pp142–3

Haskovo ㉛
Хасково

75 km (47 miles) E of Plovdiv.
Map D5. 🏠 *80,300.* 🚉 🚌 🚖
🏧 🚗 🛈 *daily.*

With pedestrianized streets, neat flowerbeds and plashing fountains, Haskovo has an appealing town centre. It was established in the 14th century, and was predominantly Muslim until the overthrow of Ottoman rule in 1912 led to an influx of ethnic Bulgarians.

Of the town's original seven mosques only two remain. One of them, the **Eski Mosque**, is the oldest in the Balkans, although its plastered façade and wood-panelled interior largely conceal the building's original features.

Haskovo was a centre of southern Bulgaria's once-thriving tobacco industry. This period of the town's history is documented in the **History Museum**, which has a display of machinery used to process tobacco. Other rooms contain collections of antique cigarette boxes and photographs.

On the other side of the town, on bulevard Bulgariya, is the 19th-century **Church of Sveta Bogoroditsa**, a simple stone building with an intricately carved iconostasis and bishop's throne. Nearby

Street in Haskovo, with the minaret of Eski Mosque in the background

is the **Paskalevata Kûshta** , a National Revival house with period furnishings and a small art gallery. It is the birthplace of Aleksandûr Paskalev, who laid the foundations of publishing in Bulgaria.

🇨 Eski Mosque
ul. Sveti Stefan 12.

🏛 History Museum
pl. Svoboda 19. *Tel (038) 624 501.*
🕐 *9am–12:30pm, 2–4:30pm Tue–Fri.*

⛪ Church of Sveta Bogoroditsa
Corner of bul. Bulgariya and ul. Berkovski. 🕐 *7:30am–6:30pm daily.* 🕐 *8am Fri, Sun.*

🏠 Paskalevata Kûshta
ul. Yanko Sakerzov 4. 🕐 *9am–noon, 2–6pm Mon–Sat.* 📷

Islamic-style building in Kûrdzhali, now the town's History Museum

Kûrdzhali ㉜
Кърджали

53 km (33 miles) south of Haskovo.
Map D5. 🏠 *45,600.* 🚉 🚌 🏧 🚗
www.kardjali.bg

Named after the legendary Turkish commander Kûrdzha Ali, who died during an attack on the eastern Rhodopes in the 14th century, Kûrdzhali has always been a mainly Muslim town. Today, ethnic Turks make up 62 per cent of its population. Many have migrated to Turkey, as reduced demand for the region's tobacco in recent years has lead to economic decline. The main attraction for visitors to Kûrdzhali is the **History Museum**, in a splendid Islamic-style building. Originally a Muslim college, it has rows of arched windows flanking a grand

central balcony topped with a lead dome. The museum's excellent archaeological, natural history, and ethnographic collections are laid out on three floors. Highlights include a nephrite swastika pendant of the 6th millennium BC, and an impressive bronze statue of Apollo of the 3rd century BC. Others include a replica of a hefty metal-plated battle catapult, and a collection of medieval iron and bronze crosses found at Perperikon.

🏛 History Museum
ul. Republikanska 4. *Tel (0361) 63584.* 🕐 *9am–noon, 1–5pm Tue–Sun.* 📷 🛈
www.kardjali-museum.org

Madzharovo Nature Reserve ㉝
Защитена местност около Маджарово

35 km (22 miles) southeast of Haskovo. **Map** D5. 🚌 🛈
🕐 *9am–5pm daily.* 🅿 🍴 📷 🛒
Accommodation and guided tours should be booked in advance.

One of the few European breeding grounds for black, Egyptian and griffon vultures, this reserve is of great interest to birdwatchers. The vultures nest on steep crags beside the meandering Arda River, and so as to maintain, or even increase, their numbers, a diet of carrion is provided by the reserve warden.

Eight species of falcon and nine of woodpecker, as well as many other birds, also inhabit the reserve.

Rocky cliffs in Madzharovo Nature Reserve, habitat of vultures

Eastern Rhodopes Tour ㉞

As they descend eastwards towards Kûrdzhali, the Rhodope Mountains become less dramatic. This dry, hilly landscape is dotted with extraordinary rock formations, most of which were formed by volcanic activity some 40 million years ago and slowly shaped by the erosive action of wind, sand and rain. This region, with small villages among tobacco fields and flocks of sheep and goats, was the first part of Bulgaria to be conquered by the Ottomans, and it still has a large population of ethnic Turks.

TIPS FOR DRIVERS

Road Map D5.
Starting point: Stone Mushrooms, near Beli Plast, 20 km (12 miles) north of Kûrdzhali.
Length: 140 km (87 miles).
Getting there: Perperikon (from which the Stone Mushrooms are one hour's walk away) and Tatul (where the ruins are just outside the village) are accessible by bus. The other rock formations are best reached by car.

Stone Mushrooms ①
The puffy pink Stone Mushrooms (Kamenite gûbi) are up to 2.5 m (8 ft) high. The green hue of their caps and their brown flecks are produced by traces of iron, manganese and other oxides.

Stone Wedding ③
Gently moulded columns of pink tufa make up the Stone Wedding (Vkamenenata svatba). The "bride" and "groom" are surrounded by other formations, their "guests".

Rock Window ④
The massive Rock Window (Skalen Prozorets) is 10 m (33 ft) high and 7 m (23 ft) wide. More of a table than a window, it consists of a limestone slab on two fat columns.

Rocks at Ustra ⑤
Perhaps the most impressive of the eastern Rhodopes' rock formations, the Rocks at Ustra (Skalite na Ustra) have been sculpted by the elements into huge pillars and cones.

HASKOVO
Chernoochene
Yavorovo
Varbentsi
Stremtsi
Zayhar 507 m
Most
Dazhdovnitsa
Chiflik
Perperek
Padartsi
Enchets
Kurdzhali Lake
Kûrdzhali
Studen Kladenets Lake
Shiroko Pole
Volovartsi
Gruevo
Raven
Nanovitsa
Mishevsko
Momchilgrad
Lale
Dzhebel
KOMOTINÍ
Pripek
Mrezhichko
General Geshevo
Boynik planina

Perperikon and Ahridos ②
Cut deep into a rocky hilltop, Perperikon was a settlement founded in 6000 to 5000 BC. The spectacular ruins include a fortified acropolis. At the foot of the hill are the remains of Ahridos, thought to have been the capital of the eastern Rhodopes c.AD 1000.

Stone Forest ⑦
This collection of rock stumps, up to 4 m (13 ft) wide and 1.5 m (5 ft) high, is known as the Stone Forest (Vkamenenata gora). The stones may be fossilized tree trunks or, more likely, the result of intense underwater volcanic activity during the early Eocene period.

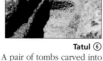

Tatul ⑥
A pair of tombs carved into the rock crown this site, once a Thracian hilltop temple. Other remains include a circular altar, a Roman wall, and a deep grain store.

KEY

▬▬ Tour route
══ Main road
── Other road
╼╾ Railway
△ Peak

0 kilometres 10
0 miles 10

Bachkovo Monastery ⑳
Бачковски манастир

At the foot of the forested slopes of the Rhodope Mountains lies Bachkovo Monastery, its serene courtyards filled with flowerbeds, exotic trees and drinking fountains. The monastery was founded in 1083 by Grigori and Abbasi Bakouriani, Georgian brothers who were commanders in the Byzantine army. In the 13th century, the monastery was sponsored by Tsar Ivan Assen II and his successor Ivan Aleksandûr. Destroyed by the Ottomans in the 16th century, it was restored by the 17th century. Because of its fine architecture and frescoes, this great monastery, the second-largest in Bulgaria after Rila Monastery, is a UNESCO World Heritage Site.

The Ossuary
This is the only surviving part of the 11th-century monastery. The frescoes inside are so delicate that it is not open to visitors.

★ **Last Judgment**
In the porch of the Church of Sveti Nikola is a dramatic fresco of the Last Judgment by Zahari Zograf, with sinners falling into the fires of Hell.

Church of Sveti Nikola
A door to the left of the main courtyard leads to the Church of Sveti Nikola, which was built in 1834. It contains frescoes by Zahari Zograf and other renowned painters.

STAR SIGHTS

★ Iconostasis

★ Last Judgment

★ Refectory

Fresco in the Dome
The dome of the Church of Sveti Nikola is decorated with a fresco of Christ Pantocrator, encircled by exquisitely painted portraits of saints.

Church of Sveta Bogoroditsa
This 17th-century church is richly decorated with frescoes. Themes include the Devil addressing Christ from the mouth of a monster, and Death shadowing an angel.

VISITORS' CHECKLIST

Bachkovo, 30 km (19 miles) S of Plovdiv. **Map** C4.
Tel *(03327) 277.* *from Plovdiv or Asenovgrad.*
7am–9pm daily. *for the Refectory.*

★ Iconostasis
The Church of Sveta Bogoroditsa also contains a highly ornate 17th-century gilt iconostasis, which gleams in the soft light of hundreds of flickering candles.

Miracle Icon of the Virgin
Worshippers gather here to kiss the silver-plated Icon of the Virgin, painted in 1310.

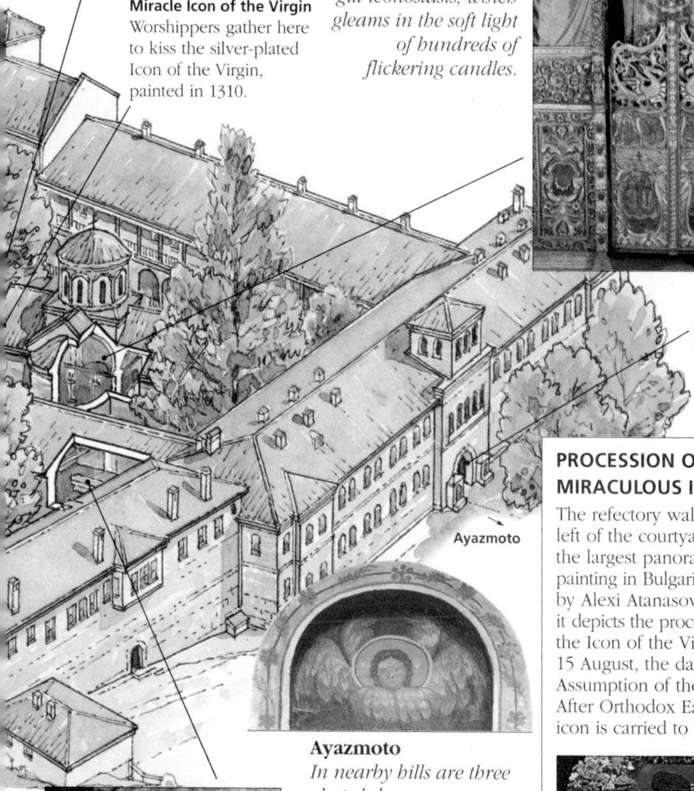
Main entrance
Ayazmoto

Ayazmoto
In nearby hills are three chapels known as Ayazmoto. The Icon of the Virgin was once hidden from the Ottomans here.

★ Refectory
A solid stone table and wooden benches stretch the length of the 17th-century refectory. The vaulted ceiling is covered with frescoes by pupils of Zahari Zograf.

PROCESSION OF THE MIRACULOUS ICON

The refectory wall on the left of the courtyard bears the largest panoramic wall painting in Bulgaria. Painted by Alexi Atanasov in 1846, it depicts the procession with the Icon of the Virgin on 15 August, the day of the Assumption of the Virgin. After Orthodox Easter, the icon is carried to Ayazmoto.

Procession of the Miraculous Icon of the Virgin Mary

CENTRAL BULGARIA

*T*he Stara Planina Mountains form a mighty wall across the heart of Bulgaria. To north and south lie wooded hills, fertile plains and the vast rose fields of the Sredna Gora valley. The region is renowned both for its natural beauty and its ancient remains, which include Neolithic settlements, Thracian tombs, the Roman towns of Nikopolis ad Istrum and Hisarya, and the majestic citadel of Tsarevets.

The Ottoman policy of granting regional towns local autonomy and tax privileges in return for guarding mountain passes allowed places such as Koprivshtitsa, Tryavna, Troyan and Kotel to prosper both financially and culturally. Merchants grew rich from sheep and cattle farming, and from the export of such goods as leather items, woollen cloth, pottery, rose oil and silk.

In the early 19th century, turning the weakened state of the Ottoman Empire to their advantage, these merchants used their wealth to establish and fund Bulgarian language schools and to restore long-neglected churches and monasteries. This fostered the sense of national identity that was to become the keystone of the National Liberation movement.

From the 1860s, central Bulgaria was a hotbed of revolutionary activity. The rebel leader Vasil Levski established secret revolutionary committees throughout the region, and it was from Koprivshtitsa that the April Rising of 1876 began. In 1877, the region witnessed the bloodiest battle of the War of Liberation when a Russian army, supported by Bulgarian militias, dug in at the Shipka Pass, from where they eventually defeated the Ottomans.

Though the *kurdzhali* raids of the early 19th century destroyed much of the area's architectural heritage, restored buildings in several picturesque museum towns and villages give an insight into 18th- and 19th-century rural life. The region's natural beauty has also been safeguarded by the creation of the reserves that form the Central Balkan National Park.

Traditional shuttered windows of a National Revival-style house in Koprivshtitsa

◁ The elegant octagonal vestibule, with wrought-iron gallery, of Sarafkina House in Veliko Tŭrnovo

Exploring Central Bulgaria

The Central Balkan National Park, a paradise
for wildlife as well as for hikers, dominates the
western part of the region. Central Bulgaria is
also rich in archaeological sites, including the
Valley of the Thracian Kings, near Kazanlûk,
and the Roman town of Nikopolis ad Istrum
and fortress of Hisarya. The region has many
historic towns such as Bozhentsi, Tryavna and
Koprivshtitsa, each with outstanding architecture
not to mention four famous monasteries.
Bulgaria's famous rose fields, at their best in
May and June, line the valley between
Kazanlûk and Karlovo, below the
towering Stara Planina mountains.

**Ritual drinking vessel from the
Valley of the Thracian Kings**

SEE ALSO

• *Where to Stay* pp224–6

• *Where to Eat* pp240–42

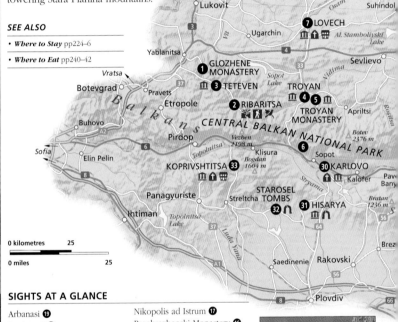

0 kilometres   25

0 miles   25

SIGHTS AT A GLANCE

**Sveta Troitsa Convent, on the
Yantra River, north of Arbanasi**

GETTING AROUND

The main Sofia–Burgas road runs west to east, via Karlovo, Kazanluk and Sliven, along the southern slopes of the Stara Planina Mountains. The Sofia–Veliko Tûrnovo road runs north of the mountains. These two routes are connected by the Zlatishki, Troyan and Shipka passes. A railway runs parallel to the Sofia–Burgas road, with a branch veering north beyond Kazanlûk to Veliko Tûrnovo. Troyan and Lovech have rail connections, but most of the northern half of the region can only be reached by bus.

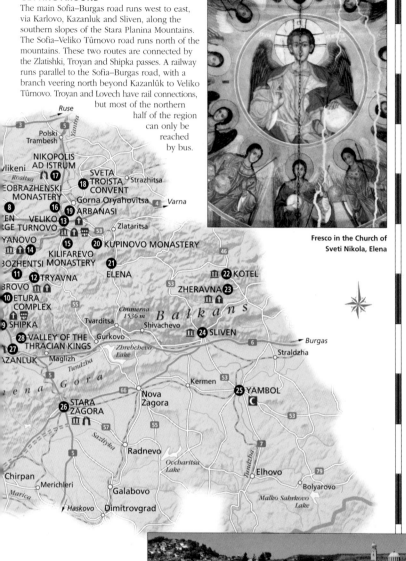

Fresco in the Church of
Sveti Nikola, Elena

Ruse

Polski
Trambesh

Yantra

NIKOPOLIS
AD ISTRUM ⑰
Mlikeni
Rositsa

SVETA
TROISTA ⑱
CONVENT   Strazhitsa

EOBRAZHENSKI
MONASTERY ⑯   Gorna Oryahovitsa
8   Varna
EN   VELIKO ⑲ ARBANASI
GE TURNOVO ⑬
Zlataritsa
YANOVO   ⑮   ⑳ KUPINOVO MONASTERY
⑭
KILIFAREVO   46
BOZHENTSI MONASTERY   ⑳
⑪   ⑫ TRYAVNA   ㉑
ELENA
BROVO   53
⑩ ETURA   ZHERAVNA ㉓   ⑳ KOTEL
COMPLEX
9 SHIPKA   Chumerna   Balkans
1536 m
Tvarditsa
㉘ VALLEY OF THE   Shivachevo
㉗ THRACIAN KINGS   Gurkovo   ㉔ SLIVEN
AZANLUK   Maglizh   Zhrebchevo   6
Lake   Burgas
ena Gora   Tundzha   Straldzha
66
Nova   Kermen   53
5   Zagora
㉖ STARA   ㉕ YAMBOL
ZAGORA   57   55   53
Sazliyka   7
5   Radnevo
Ovcharitsa
Lake
Chirpan   Merichleri   Elhovo   79
Marica   Bolyarovo
Galabovo   Malko Sahrkovo
Haskovo   Dimitrovgrad   Lake

KEY

═══ Motorway

═ ═ Motorway under construction

═══ Expressway

─── Main road

═══ Other road

┼─┼ Railway

▬▬ International border

△ Peak

Part of Veliko Tûrnovo, once the historic capital of Bulgaria

Glozhene Monastery ❶

Гложенски манастир

11 km (7 miles) NW of Teteven.
Map C3. *Tel* (01960) 388.
◑ 8am–9pm daily. ✦ 6pm daily. ▣

Of all Bulgaria's many monasteries, this one probably has the most impressive setting. It perches on sheer cliffs that tower high above the Vit River valley. The monastery's fortress-like stone lower walls support rickety wooden upper storeys roofed with the roughly cut stone slabs characteristic of the region.

Founded in 1224, the monastery was dedicated to St George the Victorious by Prince Glozh, a Ukrainian who brought with him a miracle-working icon of St George from Kiev Monastery. The icon now in the monastery church is a copy; the original is in Lovech bishopric.

In the 13th and 14th centuries Glozhene Monastery was a thriving centre of learning, with schools for the study of literature and religion. The residential buildings around the central courtyard were built in 1858. It was here, in a secret underground chamber, that Vasil Levski hid from the

Ottoman authorities *(see p168)*. The trapdoor to this hideout is now part of the **History Museum**, which also contains the room in which Bishop Kliment was imprisoned in 1893 after falling out with the Stambolov government. His meagre diet of salt fish and water was secretly supplemented by monks, who passed him a supply of food through a hole in the ceiling.

The earthquake of 1913 destroyed the old monastery church, although its 16th-century gilt iconostasis survives. The present church dates from 1931.

Tour sign, Tsarichina Reserve, near Ribaritsa

🏛 **History Museum**
◑ 9am–6pm daily. 📷

Ribaritsa ❷

Рибарица

12 km (7 miles) SE of Teteven.
Map C3.

The village of Ribaritsa lies on the picturesque Vit River. It is popular as a weekend retreat for Bulgarians, who stay in the village's many hotels or their villas on the wooded slopes of the Stara Planina Mountains.

Although Ribaritsa's main industry is tourism, it also benefits from cultivating raspberries and cattle farming. Fishing is a popular pastime here, as are pony trekking, hunting and walking in the neighbouring Tsarichina Reserve, part of the Central Balkan National Park *(see pp 150–51)*. The beech, fir and spruce forests in the reserve are the habitat of Bulgaria's seven species of owl as well as wolves, brown bears, red deer and otters *(see pp26–7)*.

South of the village is the Benkovski Monument, which marks the spot where Georgi Benkovski was killed by the Ottomans after his participation in the fateful April Rising of 1876 *(see p174)*. The event is re-enacted each year on 25 May.

Teteven ❸

Тетевен

72 km (45 miles) SW. **Map** C3. of Lovech. 🚶 11,500. 🚌 📆
ℹ *pl. Sava Mladenov (0678-4217)*. 📅 Sat. **www**.teteven.bg

The forested peaks and rocky cliffs of the Stara Planina Mountains loom over Teteven, a quiet town that straddles the Vit River. Under Ottoman rule, Teteven, like several other settlements in the region, was granted self-government in return for providing troops to guard the mountain passes.

This relative autonomy boosted the town's craft-based economy, and its merchants profited from the export of locally made goods to Western Europe and Asia. In recognition of its skilled goldsmiths, the town became known as Golden Teteven, but this attracted the unwelcome attention of marauding *kurdzhali* bandits, who pillaged the town in 1801, supposedly killing over 5,000 and leaving only three houses standing.

Apart from its picturesque setting, the town's main attraction for visitors is its **History Museum**. The large collection begins with an

Interior of Glozhene Monastery church, with a 16th-century iconostasis

Teteven, set in a valley amid the peaks of the Stara Planina Mountains

array of Neolithic stone tools and clay figurines, Roman silverware, bronze coins and medieval swords, spears and axes, and flintlock rifles and pistols used by 19th-century revolutionaries. Teteven rugs, with typical diamond patterns in red, yellow and green, and 19th-century Bulgarian costumes make up much of the ethnographic display upstairs.

🏛 **History Museum**
pl. Sava Mladenov 3. **Tel** (0678) 2005. ◯ summer: 9am–noon, 2–5pm daily; winter: 9am–noon, 2–5pm Mon–Fri. 🖼 🖻

Troyan ❹
Троян

36 km (22 miles) S of Lovech.
Map C3. 🚶 26,000. 🚇 🚌 🚕
🛈 ul. Vasil Levski 133 (0670-35064).
🎪 Rakiya Festival (last Sat in Sep).
www.troyan-bg.com

Thracians founded a settlement at this spot on the slopes of the Stara Planina Mountains about 3,000 years ago. In the 14th century Troyan grew into a centre of craftsmanship, exporting goods to Serbia, Romania and Constantinople. Today it is known for *Troyanski rakiya* (fruit brandy), which is celebrated at an annual festival.

It was the clay from the banks of the Ossum River that enabled potters to create Troyan's famed ceramics. They developed skilled techniques, including mixing metal oxides with the clay to produce a wider range of colours. *Angoba*, the resulting

brown ceramics with horizontal bands of colour and ripple effects have long been seen as a very traditional type of Bulgarian pottery.

The **Museum of Traditional Crafts** provides an excellent overview of the town's great potting industry. Other displays are devoted to woodcarving, and to Troyan's production of *kalpakchiite,* the bullet-shaped fur hats worn by men in the 18th and 19th centuries. The **History Museum**, next door, documents the exploits of local citizens during the April Rising *(see p174)*.

Glazed jug at Troyan's History Museum

🏛 **Museum of Traditional Crafts**
pl. Vazrazhdenie. **Tel** (0670) 22062.
◯ 9am–5pm daily. 🖼 🖻

🏛 **History Museum**
pl. Vazrazhdenie. **Tel** (0670) 62062. ◯ 9am–5pm daily. 🖼 Admittance by request at Museum of Traditional Crafts.

Troyan Monastery ❺
Троянския манастир

10 km (6 miles) E of Troyan. **Map** C3.
Tel (06952) 2866. 🚌 🚗 ◯ 8am–10pm daily. 🔼 5pm daily. 🖻 🖻 🛍

Its central cobbled courtyard lined by wooden balconies bedecked with flowers, Troyan Monastery has an atmosphere of peaceful intimacy. One of Bulgaria's largest monastic establishments, it was founded in 1600 but most of its existing buildings date from the mid-19th century.

The main Church of Sveta Bogoroditsa was completed in 1835. Zahari Zograf *(see p106)* painted many of the church's superb exterior and interior murals and his brother Dimitûr was responsible for the realistic portraits that adorn its elaborate Tryavna iconostasis. The façade features Zahari's signature scenes of Hell: devils torture sinners before rivers of fire sweep them into the jaws of monsters, while haloed saints surrounding Christ look down from Heaven.

In the outer courtyard is the **Hiding-Place Museum**, where visitors can see the room and secret cupboard where Vasil Levski *(see p169)* hid from the Ottomans while attempting to set up a revolutionary committee in the monastery. In an adjoining room is a display of assorted ecclesiastical objects.

🏛 **Hiding-Place Museum**
◯ 9am–6pm daily. 🖼

Detail of a fresco by Zahari Zograf at Troyan Monastery

Central Balkan National Park ➏

Централна Стара планина "Централен Балкан"

Established in 1991, the Central Balkan National Park was created to preserve specific wildlife habitats. Covering a narrow strip stretching 85 km (53 miles) from east to west along the central Stara Planina, it includes nine reserves with magnificent granite and limestone peaks, as well as deep gorges, sheer cliffs, cave systems and sub-alpine meadows. Ancient forests of beech and fir constitute over half the park's extent. Bears, wolves, wild cats, otters, martens and 224 species of birds make up the animal population, and rare plants include nine locally endemic species and 67 endemic to the eastern Balkans. A network of paths and mountain huts allow hikers to enjoy this rugged and pristine wilderness.

Golden eagle, one of the park's rare birds

Balkan chamois on the steep slopes of the Kaloferska Planina

Mount Vezhen, at 2,198 m (7,214 ft), is one of the highest peaks in the park. Its challenging ascent attracts experienced mountaineers.

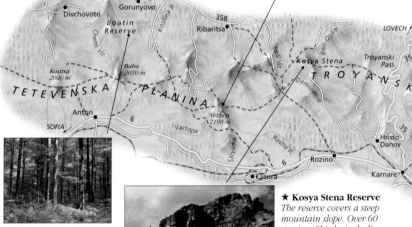

Boatin Reserve
With trees over 250 years old, the reserve has one of the largest protected beech forests in Europe. It is home to brown bears, wolves and wild boar.

★ Kosya Stena Reserve
The reserve covers a steep mountain slope. Over 60 species of birds, including the black woodpecker and Ural owl, nest here. There are also more than 40 species of rare plants, such as moonwort, edelweiss, and mountain avens.

Sub-alpine ecosystems
At lower altitudes, a gentler climate allows grassy vegetation to grow and provide a superb habitat for wildlife. In spring and early summer, the meadows are carpeted with wildflowers.

STAR SIGHTS

- ★ Dzhendema Reserve
- ★ Kosya Stena Reserve
- ★ Raiskoto Praskalo

Steneto Reserve
Established to protect the Steneto Gorge, this reserve consists largely of lush beech forest. It is home to the greatest diversity of bird species in the Balkans. These include golden and booted eagles, eagle owls, and woodpeckers.

★ Raiskoto Praskalo
Bulgaria's highest waterfall, Raiskoto Praskalo (Paradise Gusher) cascades 124 m (407 ft) over sheer cliffs below Mount Botev. The park's other great waterfalls are Vidimskoto Praskalo (80 m/263 ft) and Kademliskoto Praskalo (72 m/236 ft).

VISITORS' CHECKLIST

Map C3. 🛈 *Central Balkan National Park Directorate, Bodra Smyana 3, Gabrovo (066-801 277) and information centres at entry points around the Central Balkan National Park; Stara Planina Tourist Association, ul. Raicho Karolev 4, Gabrovo (066-809 161).* ✉ **www**.staraplanina.org

EXPLORING THE PARK

The park and the reserves within it have a network of marked footpaths and a small number of mountain-biking trails, and chalets and lodges that offer basic to comfortable accommodation. As this is wild, harsh terrain, with an unpredictable climate, walkers should be suitably equipped before setting off on hikes.

Spectacular cliffs and dramatically eroded rock formations, which are frequently shrouded in swirling mist, gave Dzhendema its name, Hell Reserve.

The Singing Rocks in Peeshti Skali Reserve, on the easternmost side of the park, are a cluster of rock formations that emit a melodious sound when the wind blows.

★ Dzhendema Reserve
Stark granite and limestone cliffs, dramatic gorges, and thundering waterfalls make up Dzhendema Reserve, the largest in the park. At lower altitudes there are ancient beech and fir forests as well as sub-alpine meadows.

```
0 kilometres    5
0 miles         5
```

KEY

═ Major road
─ Other road
-- Trail
▬ Railway
△ Peak
⤬ Pass

Pokritya most, or Covered Bridge, across the Osûm River at Lovech

🏛 **Ethnographic Museum**
ul. Marin Pop Lukanov.
◯ 8am–noon, 1–5pm daily.

🏛 **Vasil Levski Museum**
ul. Marin Pop Lukanov. **Tel** (068)
601 407. ◯ 8am–noon, 1–5pm
daily.

⛪ **Church of the Assumption**
ul. Marin Pop Lukanov.
◯ 7am–10pm daily.

Lovech ➐
Ловеч

35 km (22 miles) S of Pleven. **Map**
C2. 👥 44,100. 🚌 🚐 🏛 🚐
www.lovech.bg/EN

Because its position gave it control of the Troyan Pass, to the south, the site that Lovech occupies has been inhabited since Thracian times. In the 16th century the town's population was swelled by the arrival of thousands of Ottoman Turks, who stamped their mark on Lovech's cultural life by building mosques and Muslim schools here. Lovech's Bulgarian minority remained in the Varosh quarter, the old town on the slopes of Hisarya hill. Pokritya most ("Covered Bridge"), across the Osûm River, links Lovech's old and new quarters. It was built in 1874 by National Revival architect Kolyo Ficheto and is now filled with souvenir shops.

Many of the National Revival houses in the Varosh quarter form part of an architectural preservation area. The town's **Ethnographic Museum** occupies two of them, one filled with 19th-century European furniture and Ottoman floor cushions and low tables, the other furnished in early 20th-century style. The cellars contain wooden wine barrels, a wine press and a still for making *rakiya*, a potent spirit.

Further along the street is the **Vasil Levski Museum**. In 1870 Levski *(see p169)* made Lovech the headquarters of Bulgaria's Central Revolutionary Committee and the town contributed significantly to the Liberation movement.

The museum contains a huge mural of the legendary rebel leader, as well as his dagger, sword and pistol, and other items relating to his life. The **Church of the Assumption** (1834) overlooks the museum. The murals in its simple interior are undergoing restoration.

A huge statue of Levski stands on Hisarya hill next to Hisar fortress. Originating in the 9th century, the fortress was prominent during the Second Bulgarian Kingdom (1185–1393) but fell into disrepair after the Ottoman invasion and is now in ruins.

Emen Gorge ➑
Еменски каньон

Emen village, 25 km (16 miles) W of
Veliko Tûrnovo. **Map** D2. 🚐

The magnificent Emen Gorge was carved out by the action of water over thousands of years. From Emen village, visitors can follow a trail that leads deep into the gorge via rocky paths and wooden walkways. The trail, which takes two hours to walk, culminates at Momin skok waterfall. Here cascades spill over a 10-m (30-ft) drop into a small lake that is suitable for swimming. This pristine area was declared a nature reserve in 1980.

Dramatic cliffs of Emen Gorge, carved out by the Negovanka River

Gabrovo 9
Габрово

46 km (29 miles) SW of Veliko Tŭrnovo. **Map** D3. 🏯 67,000. 🚍 🚍 🚌 ♻ (066) 818 4068. 🎭 *Festival of Humour and Satire (May).* **www**.gabrovo.bg

Officially Bulgaria's longest town, Gabrovo is strung out along the Yantra River for over 10 km (6 miles). Thanks to its textiles industry, which flourished during the 19th century, it became known as the Manchester of Bulgaria.

Gabrovo has long been the butt of jokes about its citizens' thriftiness. According to one anecdote, the townspeople avoid paying for musicians by dancing in soundless sheepskin slippers to tunes being played in neighbouring Sevlievo. Gabrovo has shrewdly encouraged this image. In 1972, it opened the **House of Humour and Satire**. The intriguing displays here include humorous paintings, cartoons, clownish costumes and photographs from around the world, and some comical cost-saving devices.

A visit to the **Museum of Education** is a more sobering experience. It is in the Aprilov School – Bulgaria's first secular school, founded in 1835. Starting with early monastic schools, the museum charts the development of Bulgaria's education systems. Across the river is **Detchko House**, the smartly restored National Revival home of Hadzhi Detchko, a local merchant.

The **History Museum** traces the town's development from

Copperware and other traditional objects in the History Museum, Bozhentsi

its origins in the 13th century to the 1940s. The museum also has a gallery of paintings by 20th-century local artists.

🏛 **House of Humour & Satire**
ul. Bryanska 68. *Tel* (066) 807 229.
◻ 9am–6pm daily. 🏷 ♿
www.humorhouse.bg

🏛 **Museum of Education**
ul. Aprilovska 15. *Tel* (066) 806 461. ◻ 8:30am–5pm daily. 🏷 ♿

🏛 **Detchko House**
pl. 10 Yuli 2. *Tel* (066) 806 905.
◻ 9am–5pm daily. 🏷

🏛 **History Museum**
ul. Nikoloayevska 10. *Tel* (066) 809 767. ◻ 9am–noon, 1–5pm Mon–Fri. 🏷

Etura Complex 10
Етъра

9 km (6 miles) S of Gabrovo. **Map** D3. *Tel* (066) 801 831. 🚌 🚗 ◻ 9am–6pm daily. 🏷 📷 ♿ ♻

This open-air museum was created to preserve Gabrovo's crafts heritage. It is laid out as a village where visitors can see craftsmen at work using the water-powered machinery that once drove Gabrovo's booming economy. In openfronted workshops spread out along the banks of the Sivek River, they work with wood, metal, clay, silver and cloth to produce the souvenirs that are sold in the bazaar quarter. Shops also line a cobbled street of re-created National Revival buildings. A church, a clock tower and stone fountains add detail to this fascinating reconstruction of 19th-century town life.

An exhibit at the House of Humour and Satire in Gabrovo

Bozhentsi 11
Боженци

16 km (10 miles) E of Gabrovo. **Map** D3. 🏯 50. 🚌 ♻ (066) 804 422.

This enchanting village of cobbled streets and stone-roofed houses nestles among woods in the Stara Planina Mountains. It was founded by Bulgarians seeking a safe haven after the fall of Veliko Tŭrnovo to the Ottomans in 1393. For centuries the village prospered from its weaving and potting industries, but declined in the early 1900s as its inhabitants left in search of work.

In 1962 the village was declared a listed site. Since then over 100 houses have been restored and are now museums, guest houses, inns and shops. The **Museum of History** contains farming and domestic implements that illustrate daily life. A beautiful old house on the other side of the village contains the **Doncho Popa Museum**. Constructed over a cavernous barn, the first floor has a cosy open hearth, Ottoman-style wall benches and a baby-sized hammock. The flat sink stones in the balcony allowed dirty water to be disposed of. Marked footpaths connect the village with Gabrovo, Tryavna and Dryanovo Monastery.

🏛 **Museum of History**
◻ 9am–6pm daily. 🏷 📷
Admittance by request at tourist information office.

🏛 **Doncho Popa Museum**
◻ 9am–6pm daily. 🏷 📷
Admittance by request at tourist information office.

Tryavna ⑫
Трявна

Daskalov House, sculpture in the park

Tryavna's eminence as a crafts town is evident both in the remarkable houses of its old quarter and in its traditional workshops, which now produce souvenirs. The town was founded in the 15th century and, because good arable land was scarce, its inhabitants turned to crafts. By the late 18th century silk, rugs, rose oil and gold jewellery underpinned the town's flourishing economy. Tryavna's builders and woodcarvers earned fame for the quality of their workmanship, and its painters provided icons for many of the churches and monasteries that were built during the National Revival period.

🏛 Shkoloto
pl. Kapitan Dyado Nikola 7. **Tel** *(0677) 2278.* ⬜ *9am–5pm daily.* 📷 📱
Entered through a low stone archway off the main square, Shkoloto is a beautiful old building that was originally a school. It opened in 1839, and has a galleried courtyard lined with rooms that once provided accommodation for teachers and pupils from distant villages.

The long school room now contains an exhibition of paintings by Dimitûr Kazakov (1933–92) and wooden sculptures by his brother Nikola (b. 1935). Dimitûr's moody works, which often feature strong lines and limited colours, depict simple figures in abstract landscapes. Nikola's sculpture include intriguing wooden figures with a naïve character.

An adjoining room contains a small collection of antique clocks. The oldest, made in 1700, has a mechanism that is weighted with stones.

🏚 Raikov House
ul. Profesor Raikov 1. ⬜ *summer: 9am–6pm daily; winter: 8am–5pm daily (entry via Shkoloto).* 📷
This imposing residence, roofed with rough stone slabs, was the home of Professor Pencho Raikov, who is considered to be the father of Bulgarian chemistry. The house was built in 1846, and its whitewashed façade has large windows that light the spacious rooms within. The furnishings and paintings that fill the house indicate a comfortable middle-class lifestyle.

⛪ Church of the Archangel Michael
pl. Kapitan Dyado Nikola. **Tel** *(0677) 3442.* ⬜ *7am–7pm daily.* 📱 *8am Sun.* 📱
Founded in the 12th century and rebuilt in 1821, this charming church is set below ground level, in accordance with Ottoman requirements. The projecting roof, of rough stone slabs, almost reaches to the ground. The interior has a curved balcony for female worshippers. The iconostasis, by members of the Vitanov family of Tryavna, is superbly decorated with carvings of fruit and flowers. On the walls are frescoes by members of the Zahariev family.

Church of the Archangel Michael, with paintings and woodcarvings

🏚 Daskalov House
ul. Slaveykov 27a. **Tel** *(0677) 2166* ⬜ *summer: 9am–6pm daily; winter: 8am–4:30pm daily.* 📷 📱
Walled gardens surround this beautiful house, built in 1804 for Hristo Daskalov, a wealthy rose oil and silk merchant. The symmetrical building consists of two separate dwellings connected by a veranda. The interiors feature a pair of panelled ceilings, each with a finely carved sun motif.

The ceilings are result of a competition held between a master woodcarver, Dimitûr Oshanetsa, and his apprentice, Ivan Bochukovetsa. While the latter's work is notable for its swirling central rays, the master framed his sun with floral motifs. Oshanetsa was declared the winner, but the woodcarvers' guild recognized Bochukovetsa as a master.

An adjacent building contains an absorbing exhibition of Tryavna woodcarving. Items include icon frames, walking sticks, portrait busts, and statues of knights and bishops.

🏚 Slaveykov House
ul. Slaveykov 50. **Tel** *(0677) 2166.* ⬜ *summer: 9am–6pm; winter: 9am–5:30pm Wed–Sun.* 📷 📱
Two literary giants lived in this cozy house set in bushy gardens. Petko Slaveykov (1827–95) was an important National Revival figure who published Bulgarian-language newspapers and magazines.

Open cobbled courtyard at Shkoloto, once Tryavna's school house

He contributed significantly to the campaign for an autonomous Bulgarian church. Pencho (1866–1912), the youngest of his nine children, published a modernist literary magazine. He was the director of Sofia's national theatre and library, and was nominated for the Nobel Prize (see pp82–3).

The house, which is simply furnished, contains a display of family portraits, book covers, and other literary items.

🏛 Museum of Icon-Painting
ul. Breza 1. *Tel (0677) 3753.*
⬜ *summer: 10am–6pm daily; winter: 8am–noon, 12:30–4:30pm daily.* 🖼 🚻

This museum, in a churchlike building in a park above the town, contains a large and captivating collection of boldly coloured 19th-century icons.

The Tryavna School of icon-painting, Bulgaria's oldest, originated in the late 17th century. It continued the style of medieval Bulgarian art, with some elements of Renaissance realism. Over two centuries, more than 200 icon painters were trained at Tryavna, and many were from the Vitanov

Portrait of the Madonna and Child at the Museum of Icon-Painting

and Zahariev families. While the Vitanovs were painters and woodcarvers who worked in the classic Tryavna style, the Zaharievs had a tendency towards greater realism and innovation. Much of these artists' early work was lost during *kurdzhali* attacks on churches and monasteries in the 18th century.

🏚 Angel Kûnchev House
ul. Angel Kûnchev 39. *Tel (0677) 2398.* ⬜ *summer: 9:30am–1:30pm, 2–6pm Mon, Wed–Sun; winter: entry via Shkoloto.* 🖼

Angel Kûnchev (1850–72) was a leading rebel who, with Vasil Levski (see 169), worked to

VISITORS' CHECKLIST

245 km (150 miles) E of Sofia.
Map D3. 🚶 *11,900.* 🚌 🚉 🚐
ℹ *ul. Angel Kûnchev 33 (0677-2247).* **www.**tryavna.bg

set up revolutionary cells around the country. He shot himself after his arrest in 1872 to avoid divulging secrets.

The house where he was born was built in typical Tryavna style, with low doorways and ceilings, and ample wood panelling. There is also a display of rifles and pistols, bullet belts and swords.

Room at Angel Kûnchev House, with hearth and woven rug

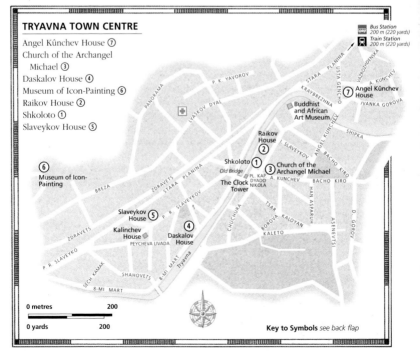

TRYAVNA TOWN CENTRE

Angel Kûnchev House ⑦
Church of the Archangel
   Michael ③
Daskalov House ④
Museum of Icon-Painting ⑥
Raikov House ②
Shkoloto ①
Slaveykov House ⑤

Bus Station 200 m (220 yards)
Train Station 200 m (220 yards)

P. K. YAVOROV
STARA PLANINA
USTA GENCHO
VAZROZHDENSKA
A. KUNCHEV
KRAYBREZHNA
PANORAMA
LYASKOV DYAL
⑦ Angel Kûnchev House
IVANKA GOROVA
Buddhist and African Art Museum
SHIPKA
Raikov House ②
I. SLAVEYKOV
ANGEL KÛNCHEV
BACHO KIRO
⑥ Museum of Icon-Painting
BREZA
ZDRAVETS
STARA PLANINA
P. R. SLAVEYKOV
Shkoloto ① Old Bridge
③ Church of the Archangel Michael
PL. KAP. DYADO NIKOLA
A. KUNCHEV
The Clock Tower
BACHO KIRO
HAN ASPARUH
Slaveykov House ⑤
Kalinchev House
④ Daskalov House
PEYCHEVA LIVADA
CHUCHURA
TSAR KALOYAN
KALETO
BOROVA
ZDRAVETS
SECH KAMAK
P. R. SLAVEYKO
SHAHOVETS
8-MI MART
8-MI MART
Tryavna
ASENEVTSI
D. GOROV

0 metres   200
0 yards   200

Key to Symbols see back flap

Veliko Tûrnovo

Велико Търново

With a picturesque hillside setting, fine architecture and a wealth of historic sights, Veliko Tûrnovo is one of Bulgaria's most beautiful cities. Tall, narrow houses teeter on sheer cliffs that rise high above the meandering Yantra River, and to the east are the ruins of the majestic fortress of Tsarevets. The city has a proud history as the mighty capital of the Second Kingdom (1185–1393), and later as the seat of liberated Bulgaria's first National Assembly. By day Veliko Tûrnovo bustles with local people, students and visitors. After dark, the focus switches to the city's lively bars and nightclubs.

Detail of the Asenid Monument

steeply above the old town. The attractive stone houses that line the bazaar's narrow cobbled streets are now occupied by souvenir shops selling local craft items.

Samovodska Charshiya, the bazaar in the Varosh quarter of the city

House of the Little Monkey
ul. Vustanicheska 14.
to the public.
This house, one of many in Veliko Tûrnovo designed by the great local architect Kolyo Ficheto (1800–81), dates from 1849. It is set on a hillside, with the ground floor accessible at street level, and entrances to the two projecting upper floors at the rear. It features a pair of bay windows, attractive red and white brickwork, and a tiny statue of a monkey that gives the house its name.

Church of SS Kiril i Metodii
ul. Slaveykov, Varosh quarter.
8am–7pm daily. 8am Sun.
High up in the hills, in the city's old Varosh quarter, this small church was built by Kolyo Ficheto in 1860, but lost its dome and belfry during the earthquake of 1913. A curved wooden balcony at the back of the church was designed for the segregation of female worshippers.

Church of Sveti Nikola
ul. Shipka, Varosh quarter.
8am–7pm daily. 8am Sun.
This sturdy church, with a simple stone exterior and a red-tiled roof, was designed by Kolyo Ficheto. The iconostasis, with dragons, eagles and a central sun motif lighting the church's gloomy interior, is a stunning example of the work of the Tryavna School (see pp154–5). The bishop's throne features an allegorical carving of a dragon (Turkey) attacking a lion (Bulgaria) that is being suffocated by a snake (the Orthodox Church).

Samovodska Charshiya
Varosh quarter.
It was in the 19th century that Samovodska Charshiya developed into a thriving bazaar, with stalls, workshops and a caravanserai for visiting merchants. The bazaar is in the pleasant historic Varosh quarter of the city, which rises

Asenid Monument
Asenovtsi Park.
Unveiled in 1985, to mark the 800th anniversary of the founding of the Second Bulgarian Kingdom, this monument features a mighty sword, with Asen, Petûr, Ivan Asen II and Kaloyan astride horses. The four tsars ruled the kingdom from 1185 to 1241. The monument is an excellent point from which to admire the city's old houses, precariously perched on the cliffs opposite.

Art Gallery
Asenovtsi Park. Tel (062) 638 941.
10am–6pm Tue–Sun.
Bulgarian painting of the 19th and 20th centuries makes up this fine collection. Charcoal landscapes by Boris Denev (1883–1969) fill much of the ground floor. In the upper rooms are works by Dimitûr Kazakov (1933–92), with sharply outlined figures in abstract compositions. Among several monumental works are Veliko Tûrnovo in the Past by Naiden Petkov (1918–89) and People Say Goodbye to Patriarch Evtimii by Svetlin Rusev (b. 1933).

Sarafkina House
ul. Gûrko 88. 9am–12 noon, 1–6pm Mon–Fri.
With stone walls below and whitewashed walls above, shuttered windows and a tiled roof, this house is typical of

Church of Sveti Nikola, built by the 19th-century architect Kolyo Ficheto

Luxurious interior of Sarafkina House

the city's 19th-century domestic architecture. It was built in 1861 for Dimitûr Sarafkina, a wealthy banker, and is set on sheer cliffs above the river. The wood-panelled interior has Western-style furniture, and a display of family photographs and period outfits.

⛫ Archaeological Museum

ul. Pikolo 6. *Tel (062) 601 528.*
⭘ 9am–5:15pm Tue–Sun. 🎟️
The courtyard of this grand old building is littered with Classical columns and busts. Although several of the museum's most precious artifacts were stolen in 2006, most of this absorbing collection remains in place.

The well-guarded centrepiece is a replica of a burial known as Kaloyan's Grave.

It was discovered in 1972, by the Church of the Forty Martyrs in the Asenova quarter *(see p160).* On the skeleton was a gold ring and seal with the name Kaloyan, which suggested these may be the remains of Tsar Kaloyan (1197–1207). In an adjoining room the gold seal of Tsar Ivan Asen II (1218–41) is displayed under a magnifying glass. Downstairs are finds from the Roman city of Nikopolis ad Istrum *(see p162).*

Archaeological Museum, a fine arcaded building with a courtyard

VISITORS' CHECKLIST

220 km (137 miles) NE of Sofia.
Map D3. 🚏 *66,900.* 🚉 🚌
🚇 🚏 🛈 *ul. Hristo Botev 5
(062-622 148).*
www.velikoturnovo.info

⛫ Museum of the National Revival and Constituent Assembly

pl. Suedenenie 1. *Tel (062) 629 821.*
⭘ 9am–6:30pm Mon, Wed–Sun. 🎟️
Built by Kolyo Ficheto for the city's Ottoman governor in 1872, this vast edifice became Bulgaria's first parliament building after the Liberation. A copy of the new state's first constitution, signed in 1879, is on display. A huge array of material relating to the revolt against Ottoman rule fills the ground floor.

⛫ Modern History Museum

pl. Suedenenie. ⭘ 8am–noon, 1–5pm Mon–Fri. 🎟️
Housed in a former prison, the museum's exhibits cover the Balkan Wars and Bulgaria's role in the First World War. A small display recalls the life of the prime minister Stefan Stambolov, who was born in Veliko Tûrnovo.

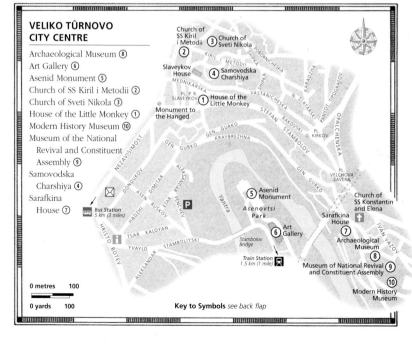

VELIKO TÛRNOVO CITY CENTRE

Archaeological Museum ⑧
Art Gallery ⑥
Asenid Monument ⑤
Church of SS Kiril i Metodii ②
Church of Sveti Nikola ③
House of the Little Monkey ①
Modern History Museum ⑩
Museum of the National
  Revival and Constituent
  Assembly ⑨
Samovodska
  Charshiya ④
Sarafkina
  House ⑦

Church of SS Kiril i Metodii ②
Church of Sveti Nikola ③
Slaveykov House
Samovodska Charshiya ④
House of the Little Monkey ①
Monument to the Hanged
Asenid Monument ⑤
Asenovtsi Park
Art Gallery ⑥
Stambolov Bridge
Sarafkina House ⑦
Church of SS Konstantin and Elena
Archaeological Museum ⑧
Museum of National Revival and Constituent Assembly ⑨
Modern History Museum ⑩

Bus Station 5 km (3 miles)
Train Station 1.5 km (1 mile)

0 metres   100
0 yards   100

Key to Symbols *see back flap*

Tsarevets
Царевец

The impressive hilltop fortress of Tsarevets occupies a commanding position on a rocky hill that is nearly completely encircled by the Yantra river. This vantage point was occupied almost continuously from the 4th millennium BC, and in 1186, Tsar Petûr made it the capital of the Second Bulgarian Kingdom. From that time, the kings of Bulgaria inhabited the Royal Palace and many aristocrats and foreign diplomats set up residence in the citadel. When the Second Kingdom fell to the Ottomans in 1393, Tsarevets was reduced to rubble. Of the original 400 buildings and 22 churches only a small number have been fully restored.

★ **Light Show**
A fantastic light show, with a rousing sound track, takes place almost every night in summer. Waves of colour light up the fortress, and the spectacle culminates with bell ringing and fireworks.

Church of Sveti Georgi
This small church contains frescoes of Orthodox saints. The paintings, badly damaged and heavily restored, once covered almost the entire interior.

Church of the Dormition

Church of the Forty Martyrs

To Veliko Tûrnovo

Main Gate

Asenova Gate
Reconstructed in 1976, this three-storey gate tower was used by the artisans and clerics who lived in the Asenova Quarter below the fortress.

0 metres	50
0 yards	50

STAR SIGHTS:

★ Baldwin's Tower

★ Light Show

★ Royal Palace

★ **Baldwin's Tower**
Named after Emperor Baldwin of Flanders, who was held here in the 13th century, this tower guarded the rock's southernmost point. Earlier, it was known as the Frenk Hisar Gate, and was used by foreign merchants living outside the complex.

Church of Sveti Dimitûr
The church is dedicated to St Demetrius, patron saint of the Second Bulgarian Kingdom. Medieval frescoes, repainted at a later date, decorate the interior.

Church of SS Petûr i Pavel
This medieval church is notable for its openwork capitals, frescoes of St Peter and St Paul, to whom it is dedicated, and depiction of the Pietà.

Rock of Execution
At the northernmost point of the fortress, the Rock of Execution juts out above sheer cliffs and the River Yantra far below. It was from here that traitors and criminals were pushed to their deaths.

★ Royal Palace
Built in the 12th century, the Royal Palace was an enclosed complex with a central courtyard. Now a partially reconstructed ruin, it has modern concrete staircases that visitors can climb for magnificent views of the surroundings.

Patriarchate
Perched at the rock's highest point is the 13th-century Church of the Patriarchate. Defended by thick walls, it was once part of the patriarch's residential complex. Startling modern murals adorn the interior.

Asenova Quarter

Асенова махала

This quiet district of Veliko Tûrnovo straddles the banks of the Yantra River, below the towering fortress walls of Tsarevets. For centuries, the quarter was inhabited by a thriving community of artisans and clerics, but they were forced to abandon it after an earthquake struck in 1913. This tremendous cataclysm flattened Asenova's old houses and seriously damaged its precious medieval churches.

Church of the Forty Martyrs, burial place of Bulgarian tsars

🔒 Church of the Forty Martyrs

ul. Mitrolpolska. ⏰ 9:30am–6pm daily. 📷 🚻

Recently opened after lengthy reconstruction, the church has a gleaming marble iconostasis and bright new icons. It was built in 1230 to commemorate Tsar Ivan Asen II's triumph over the Byzantines at Klokotnitsa, on the Feast of the Forty Martyrs. Of the six stone pillars that support the church's roof, three bear inscriptions by Bulgarian tsars.

The most famous, opposite the entrance, is by Khan Omurtag (ruled 816–31). It reads: *"A man, no matter how happy his life, eventually dies and another is born. May the man born later, while looking at this inscription, remember the man that made it."* The pillar on the left opposite the entrance has an inscription by Khan Krum (ruled 803–14) and was brought from his frontier fortress of Rodesto. That to the right of the entrance was inscribed by Asen I with a list of his conquests.

🔒 Church of the Dormition

ul. Mitrolpolska. ⏰ 9am–6pm daily. ⛪ 8am Sun.

This simple church, dedicated to the Dormition of the Virgin, was built in 1923 on the site of a 14th-century nunnery. Its plain interior walls are offset by a large wooden iconostasis with many portraits of saints.

🔒 Church of SS Petûr i Pavel

ul. Mitrolpolska. ⏰ 9am–6pm daily. 📷

This small 13th-century church lost its roof in the terrible earthquake of 1913, but was later carefully restored. Two rows of stone columns flank the central aisle and fragments of original frescoes, depicting haloed saints, can be seen in an archway to the left of the entrance.

Frescoes in a side chapel at the Church of SS Petûr i Pavel

The biblical scenes on the south wall were painted in 1441, and the exterior wall, covered by a gallery, was painted with frescoes in the 17th century. It was at this church that the Ottomans slaughtered 110 Bulgarian nobles when they conquered Veliko Tûrnovo in 1393.

🔒 Church of Sveti Georgi

ul. Tsar Ivan Asen II. ⏰ 9am–6pm daily.

According to an inscription in Greek at the entrance, this small church was built with funds provided by a local man and his wife, and it was constructed in no more than two months, in 1616. It stands on the foundations of a medieval church. The paintings in the interior include original frescoes that depict various Orthodox saints.

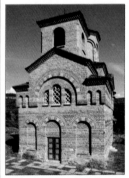

Church of Sveti Dimitûr, dedicated to the First Kingdom's patron saint

🔒 Church of Sveti Dimitûr

ul. Patriarh Evtimii. ⏰ 9am–6pm daily.

From this church in 1185, the year of its consecration, two local noblemen, Petûr and Asen, launched a revolt against Byzantine rule. As a result, the Second Bulgarian Kingdom was established, with Petûr ruling as tsar, and Sveti Dimitûr became the new kingdom's patron saint.

Reduced to ruins by the earthquake of 1913, the church was painstakingly restored. Its walls consist of alternating layers of stone and brick, and the arches of its blind niches are ornamented with coloured ceramics. Its twin towers stand out above Asenova's houses.

Dryanovo Monastery, with craggy cliffs behind

Dryanovo ⑭
Дряново

25 km (16 miles) southwest of
Veliko Tûrnovo. **Map** D3.
🏛 *8,700.* 🚌 🚗 🚕 🛈 *ul. Stefan
Stambolov 7 (0676-2332).*
www.dryanovo.com

Named after the cornel tree
(dryan), Dryanovo was
founded in the 12th century.
It was its school of National
Revival woodcarvers and stone
masons that made the town
famous in the 19th century.

Today Dryanovo is known
chiefly as the birthplace of the
itinerant master builder Kolyo
Ficheto (1800–81), who constructed many houses, public
buildings, churches and
bridges in the region. He
began an apprenticeship in
Teteven at the age of 10,
studied stonemasonry in
Albania in his teens, and
later learnt the art of building
churches, bell towers and
bridges. He achieved the
status of master builder at
the age of 36.

Dryanovo's **History Museum**
is devoted to Ficheto's life
and work. The exhibits
include models of his most
important projects, which
include the covered bridge at
Lovech *(see p152),* the bridge
at Byala, and the Church of
Sveti Nikola in Dryanovo.

Environs
A little to the south of town
lies **Dryanvo Monastery**. After
a troubled history, its present
iteration consists of a cluster
of whitewashed buildings set
around pretty gardens and a
church. Founded in the 12th
century, the monastery became
a centre of Hesychasm *(see
p163)* in the 14th century.
Ottoman troops torched it early

in the 15th century
and again in the
17th century after it
had been restored.
It was rebuilt in the
1840s and later
became a secret
meeting place for
Veliko Tûrnovo's
Central Revolution-
ary Committee,
headed by Vasil
Levski *(see p169)*.
After the April Rising of 1876,
a group of 100 rebels led by
Priest Hariton and Bacho Kiro
held out in the monastery for
nine days against an over-
whelming Ottoman force.
Most were killed and the
monastery burned once again.

A path beside the monas-
tery leads to **Bacho Kiro Cave**,
with a gallery some 1,200 m
(4,000 ft) long. Evidence of
Palaeolithic occupation has
been discovered here.

🏛 **History Museum**
ul. Shipka 82. *Tel (0676) 2332.*
⏰ *9am–noon, 1–5pm daily.* 📷

🛈 **Dryanovo Monastery**
4 km (3 miles) south of Dryanovo.
⏰ *7am–10pm daily.* 🛏 *6pm daily.*
🍴 ♦

🦇 **Bacho Kiro Cave**
500 m (550 yards) beyond
Dryanovo Monastery. *Tel (0676)
2332.* ⏰ *9am–6pm daily.* 📷 📷

Kilifarevo
Monastery ⑮
Килифаревски манастир

14 km (9 miles) south of Veliko
Tûrnovo. **Map** D3. 🚌 ⏰ *8am–9pm
daily.* 🛏 *7pm daily.* 🍴 ♦

Now a nunnery, this attractive
riverside monastery was
founded in the 14th
century by Teodosi
Tûrnovski, with funds
from Tsar Ivan Asen II.
In 1350 the Kilifarevo
Literary School, a
leading promulgator of
Hesychasm *(see p163),*
was established here.
Medieval literature
was copied and stud-
ied at the school, and
it was also where
Evtimii, last patriarch
of the Second Kingdom,
received his education.

The monastery was several
times destroyed and rebuilt
during the Ottoman period.
Its principal church, dedicated
to St Demetrius of Salonika,
was built by Kolyo Ficheto in
1842. It incorporates two
16th-century chapels.

**Fresco by Zahari Zograf inside
Preobrazhenski Monastery's church**

Preobrazhenski
Monastery ⑯
Преображенски манастир

7 km (4 miles) north of Veliko
Tûrnovo. **Map** D2. 🚌
⏰ *8:30am–8pm daily.*

Set below rocky cliffs high in
the hills above the Yantra
River, the monastery was
founded in the 14th century.
It was destroyed during the
Ottoman period, and its
reconstruction began in 1825.

The master builder Dimitûr
of Sofia began work on the
Church of the Transfiguration
in 1834 but, in 1835, his impli-
cation in a plot to overthrow
the Ottomans led to his execution. Kolyo Ficheto was
commissioned to complete
the work. In 1863 he added
the tower, with a bell
donated by Alexan-
der II of Russia. Many
of the icons and
murals were painted
by Zahari Zograf *(see
p106)*. He also paint-
ed the bold Wheel of
Life, turned by angels
while devils cast sin-
ners into a monster's
mouth, on the façade.

The monastery's
other buildings have
suffered damage from rock
falls and are rather dilapidated.

**Elderly monk at
Preobrazhenski**

Broken columns of a building at the Roman town of Nikopolis ad Istrum

Nikopolis ad Istrum ⓱
Никополис ад Иструм

20 km (12 miles) N of Veliko Tûrnovo.
Map D2. 🚗 🔘 *9am–6pm daily.*

This once magnificent Roman town was founded by the emperor Trajan in AD 102. It had temples, baths and theatres, and gladiatorial games were held here. By the 3rd century the town had developed into the most powerful settlement between the Danube to the north and the Stara Planina Mountains to the south. However, in the 6th century much of the town was destroyed by Goths and Slavs and many of its inhabitants resettled in present-day Veliko Tûrnovo *(see pp156–7)*.

Nikopolis ad Istrum has been partially excavated but the site is neglected and overgrown. Even so, the ancient paved road that leads into it, and the surviving columns, walls and tombs give a good idea of its ancient glory. Artifacts from the site are on display in Veliko Tûrnovo's Archaeological Museum.

Sveta Troitsa Convent ⓲
Манастир "Света Троица"

4 km (3 miles) N of Veliko Tûrnovo.
Map D2. 🚗 🔘 *8am–7pm daily.*

Sveta Troitsa Convent stands on the site of an 11th-century monastery that rose to prominence in the 14th century,

when pilgrims seeking spiritual guidance flocked to the nearby cave inhabited by the hermit Teodosi Tûrnovski. Patriarch Evtimii, a pupil of Tûrnovski, established the Tûrnovo School of Literature here, dedicated to the study of medieval Bulgarian, Greek and Russian texts. When the Second Bulgarian Kingdom fell in 1393, the monastery's 300 monks were put to death by the Ottomans for refusing to convert to Islam. According to legend, Evtimii himself was spared when the Ottomans seemingly received a divine warning, and decided to send him into exile instead.

In 1847 a new church was built on the site, but it was destroyed in the earthquake of 1913. The present convent buildings date from 1927.

Arbanasi ⓳
Арбанаси

4 km (3 miles) NE of Veliko Tûrnovo.
Map D3. 🏛 *300.* 🚌 🚗 ❙ *Val Turs (062-602 5758).* **www***.valturs.com*

The verdant pastures that surround Arbanasi were once densely populated by the cattle from which local merchants grew rich. Set on a limestone plateau overlooking Veliko Tûrnovo *(see pp156–7)*, the picturesque town consists of an intriguing warren of dusty streets and massive fortress-like houses.

It is thought that Arbanasi was established either by Ottomans for the resettlement of Christian Albanian prisoners of war in the 15th century, or by ethnic Bulgarians who chose to speak Greek and take Greek names until the Liberation of 1878. In return for guarding the pass giving access to Veliko Tûrnovo, Arbanasi's inhabitants were granted autonomy and fiscal

Sveta Troitsa Convent, set against rocky cliffs in the Yantra River

The colourfully decorated interior of the Church of the Nativity, Arbanasi

privileges. This benefited its merchants, who prospered from exporting locally produced leather as far as India and Persia. The sturdy houses that they built to protect them in times of trouble failed to shield them from the brutal attacks of *kurdzhali* in 1798. Continuing insecurity in subsequent years led many of Arbanasi's residents to move to Veliko Tûrnovo. Today the town attracts large numbers of visitors and its restored houses have become retreats for wealthy Bulgarians.

One of the finest of Arbanasi's residential buildings is the 17th-century **Konstantsliev House**, west of the centre.

Hefty stone foundations support a wooden upper floor, where various wood-panelled rooms are filled with period furniture. The upstairs toilet simply consisted of a hole in the floor through which human waste was delivered to hungry pigs below.

Southeast of the centre is the 17th-century **Church of the Archangels Michael and Gabriel**, which is decorated with 18th-century murals. But Arbanasi's greatest attraction is the **Church of the Nativity**, southwest of the centre. The simple exterior of this 17th-century church belies its fantastic interior. Strikingly colourful murals depicting

saints and biblical scenes, interspersed with inscriptions in Greek, cover the walls and barrel-vaulted ceiling.

Further west is the **Monastery of Sveta Bogoroditsa**, which was founded as a convent in the 13th century. It was abandoned in 1393, after the end of the Second Kingdom, but was reopened in 1680 only to be destroyed by marauding *kurdzhali* bandits in 1798. The present cluster of simple stone buildings topped with red tiles dates from the mid-19th century, when the monk Daniel of Troyan launched the convent's restoration. The monastery church's miracle-working icon depicting a three-handed Madonna attracts a constant stream of pilgrims.

🏛 **Konstantsliev House**
Tel (062) 621 572. ⏰ 9am–6pm daily. 🖼 If closed, admission by request at Church of the Nativity.

🔒 **Church of the Archangels Michael and Gabriel**
⏰ 9am–6pm daily. 🖼 If closed, admission by request at Church of the Nativity.

🔒 **Church of the Nativity**
⏰ 9am–6pm daily. 🖼 🎥 🛈

🔒 **Monastery of Sveta Bogoroditsa**
⏰ 8am–6pm daily.

Kûpinovo Monastery ❷⓪
Капиновски манастир

18 km (11 miles) SE of Veliko Tûrnovo. **Map** D3. ⏰ 8am–8pm daily.

This sturdy stone structure was rebuilt in 1825 with defence in mind, as the original 13th-century monastery was repeatedly destroyed under Ottoman rule. The church was built in 1835 and features icons by the Vitanov family of Tryavna. Above its entrance is a glowing Last Judgment mural (1845) by Yovan Popovich. It shows Christ flanked by legions of haloed saints watching devils poke sinners into a river of fire that sweeps them into hell. The monastery was a key educational and cultural centre during the National Revival movement of the 19th century.

HESYCHASM

Developed by the monks of Mount Athos, in Greece, in the early 14th century, Hesychasm, a mystic Orthodox religion, was propagated from Kilifarevo Monastery by Sveti Teodosii Tûrnovski. Demanding the rejection of social activity, it was based on silent contemplation. Hesychasts constantly repeated prayers in the hope of reaching an ecstatic state in which they might experience God's divine light. Hesychasm's widespread popularity has sometimes been blamed for further weakening the declining Second Kingdom at a time when citizens were needed to defend the state rather than retreat into prayer.

Portal at Kilifarevo Monastery, once a centre of Hesychasm

Elena ㉑
Елена

40 km (25 miles) SE of Veliko Tŭrnovo.
Map D3. 6,500.

Set amid forested hills, Elena was founded in the 15th century. Under Ottoman rule it was granted autonomy in exchange for guarding mountain passes in the vicinity, and this allowed it to prosper and develop as a centre of learning. It was here that Bulgaria's first teacher-training college was established, in 1843.

Much of Elena's quaint old town was consumed by fire during the War of Liberation (1877–8), but some fine houses and churches in the National Revival style survived. A notable example is **Ilarion Makariopolski House**, a handsome riverside mansion with dark wooden walls and a large veranda. Ilarion Makariopolski was born here in 1812. As Bishop of Constantinople, he played a key role in persuading the Ottoman authorities to establish an independent Bulgarian exarchate in 1870 (*see pp22–3*), a significant step towards liberation.

The National Revival Complex, a nucleus of fine 19th-century buildings above the town square, is centred on the large hilltop Church of the Assumption. Next to it is the smaller 16th-century **Church of Sveti Nikola**, whose barrel-vaulted interior glows with bright murals. In a former inn further down the hill is the **Ethnographic Museum**, with a display of Elena's colourful fleecy rugs, and garments made from *aba*, a locally produced coarse woollen cloth.

🏛 **Ilarion Makariopolski House**
ul. Doino Gramatik 2. **Tel** *(06151) 2214.* ⏱ *9am–5pm daily.*

⛪ **Church of Sveti Nikola**
National Revival Complex, ul. Tsarkovna 1. **Tel** *(06151) 2129.* ⏱ *9am–5pm daily.*

🏛 **Ethnographic Museum**
National Revival Complex, ul. Tsarkovna 1. **Tel** *(06151) 2129.* ⏱ *9am–5pm daily.*

Colourful carpets and weaving instruments at the Carpet Exhibition, Kotel

A vivid scene of the Last Judgment at the Ethnographic Museum, Elena

Kotel ㉒
Котел

54 km (34 miles) NW of Sliven.
Map E3. 6,900.

Founded in the 16th century as a sheep-farming centre, Kotel enjoyed relative autonomy under Ottoman rule in return for guarding a local mountain pass and providing the Ottoman authorities with sheep. While Kotel's shepherds tended their flocks, the womenfolk wove the carpets for which Kotel is renowned.

A variety of these beautiful examples of traditional handicraft is on display at the **Carpet Exhibition** in the old Galata quarter. The exhibition is housed in Kotel's former school house (1869), one of the few wooden buildings to have survived a fire that swept through the town in 1894. More of Kotel's colourful carpets are displayed at the **Ethnographic Museum** nearby, in a house built in 1872. Its wood-panelled rooms are furnished in the comfortable domestic style of the late 19th century.

The large modernist stone building in the town centre is the **Pantheon**, dedicated to Kotel's most illustrious sons, Dr Petŭr Beron (1799–1871) and Georgi Rakovski (1821–67). Preserved here is the pickled heart of Dr Beron, who contributed greatly to the country's education system. Another room contains the bones of Georgi Rakovski, one of Bulgaria's first active revolutionaries.

West of the town is Izvorite Park, with bubbling springs and woodland, and the **Natural History Museum**, with an array of stuffed wildlife.

🏛 **Carpet Exhibition**
ul. Izvorska 17. **Tel** (0453) 2316.
◯ 9am–6pm daily.

🏛 **Ethnographic Museum**
ul. Altunlu Stoyan 5. **Tel** (0453) 2315. ◯ 9am–6pm daily.

🏛 **Pantheon**
pl. Vuzrazhdanie. **Tel** (0453) 2549.
◯ 9am–6pm daily.

🏛 **Natural History Museum**
Izvorite Park. ◯ 9am–6pm daily.

Zheravna ㉓
Жеравна

14 km (9 miles) S of Kotel. **Map** E3.
🏃 525.

With cockerels and goats wandering at liberty, and donkeys that pick their way along cobbled streets, this museum-village owes its charm to its authenticity. Like Kotel, Zheravna was granted autonomy by the Ottomans in return for guarding a local mountain pass. This helped to preserve the town's Bulgarian customs and culture.

Most of Zheravna's inhabitants were sheep or cattle farmers, and several museum-houses offer an insight into their lives. One is Sava Filaretov House, built in the early 19th century, with carved wood panelling in its rooms. Next to the hearth is a raised floor where the family slept during the winter. The early 18th-century Russi Chorbadzhi House is of a similar design, with arched doorways and intricately carved panelling. The cellar contains an ethnographic exhibition and a display of Zheravna carpets.

Another highlight of the village is the small stone Church of Sveti Nikolai, with a beautiful gilt iconostasis topped with dragons and eagles. Yovkov House celebrates the life and work of Yordan Yovkov (1880–1937), author of *Legends of the Stara Planina Mountains*, in which he described Zheravna.

Sliven ㉔
Сливен

110 km (68 miles) W of Bourgas.
Map E3. 🏃 100,350.

Although undistinguished, this large town is pleasant enough. It is of interest chiefly through its association with *haidouki*, or Bulgarian rebels (mountain bandits who fought the Ottomans). The *haidouk* Hadzhi Dimitûr, who was born here in 1840, made frequent raids from Romania into Bulgaria before he was killed by Turkish soldiers in 1868. The **Hadzhi Dimitûr Museum**, in a 19th-century building that was the family house, is devoted to his life. The town also has an interesting **History Museum**, where exhibits include the skeleton of a horse from a Thracian tomb.

Window in Ebu Bekir Mosque, Yambol

Sliven's other main attraction is its proximity to the Blue Rocks (Sinite Kamûni), in the Karandila area on the eastern side of the town. The rocks, once the hideout of *haidouki*, can be reached by means of a chair lift (12:30–6:30pm Mon, 8:30am–6:30pm Tue–Sun).

🏛 **Hadzhi Dimitûr Museum**
ul. Asenova 2 (off bul. Stefan Karadzha). **Tel** (044) 622 496. ◯ 9am–noon, 2–5pm daily.

🏛 **History Museum**
bul. Tsar Osvoboditel 18. **Tel** (044) 622 494. ◯ 8am–noon, 1–5pm daily.

Yambol ㉕
Ямбол

28 km (17 miles) SE of Sliven. **Map** E3. 🏃 82,600.

Signs of ancient settlement discovered near Yambol show that the vicinity has been inhabited since Neolithic times. Yambol's immediate predecessor was the Thracian town of Kabile, located about 10 km (6 miles) to the northwest.

Under Roman rule, Yambol was enlarged, and in AD 293 it was renamed Diospolis by Emperor Diocletian. In the 4th century the town was destroyed by invading Goths, and through the Middle Ages its name changed several times as it came under the control of different peoples. Yambol still has a sizeable Turkish minority, whose presence here dates back to Ottoman times, and its oldest buildings are Islamic. The **Ebu Bekir Mosque**, off the town's central square, was built in 1413. Its massive stone walls support a single dome and minaret and, inside, a small section of the original murals has survived. Another notable Islamic building is the Bezisten Bazaar, opposite the mosque. Built in the 15th century, it is an elegant arched structure crowned with domes.

🇨 **Ebu Bekir Mosque**
pl. Osvobodzhenie. ◯ daily.

Hadzhi Dimitûr Museum, Sliven, with cobbled courtyard and open veranda

Stara Zagora ㉖
Стара Загора

90 km (56 miles) NE of Plovdiv.
Map D3. 🚶 143,500. 🚉 🚌 🚕
🏨 🏧 🛈 *bul. Ruski 27.*
www.city.starazagora.net

Having been destroyed during the War of Liberation, Stara Zagora was rebuilt at the end of the 19th century. Although it is a rather undistinguished town, it is of interest for its important Neolithic site.

In the grounds of the hospital west of the modern town, this site consists of several **Neolithic Dwellings** (*Neolitni zhilishta*). Two have been preserved, and such features as hearths can be made out. The dwellings were largely destroyed by fire in about 5500 BC but enough remains for visitors to gain an insight into daily life 8,000 years ago. There is also a museum, where many of the objects unearthed at the site are displayed.

Memorial to the defenders of Stara Zagora, Russo-Turkish War 1877–8

A building that dates from a much later phase in Stara Zagora's history is the **Roman Theatre**, near the town centre, with partially restored marble columns and tiered seating. Nearby, modern buildings surround the **Museum of 19th-Century Town Life**. The period furnishings and other objects on display here provide an overview of middle-class life during the National Revival period. A few streets south is the large, domed Eski Mosque, built in 1409. It is currently closed.

🏛 **Neolithic Dwellings**
District Hospital (Okruzhna bolnitsa).
Tel (042) 622 109. 🕘 9am–noon,
2–5pm Tue–Sun. 🖼 📷 🛈

𝄐 **Roman Theatre**
Bul. Mitropolit Metodii Kusev 33.

🏛 **Museum of 19th-Century Town Life**
ul. Dimitûr Naumov 68.
Tel (042) 623 931. 🕘 9am–noon,
2–5pm Tue–Sat. 🖼

Kazanlûk ㉗
Казанлък

36 km (22 miles) NW of Stara
Zagora. **Map** D3. 🚶 53,700. 🚉
🚌 🏨 🚕 🛈 *ul. Iskra 4 (off
ploshtad Sevtopolis).* 🎭 *Rose
Festival (1st week in Jun).*
www.tourism.kazanluk.net

Though famed as the capital of Bulgaria's rose-oil industry, Kazanlûk is also the centre of an area of Thracian settlement

---

Detail of the painting on the cupola of the Kazanlûk Tomb in Kazanlûk

now known as the Valley of the Thracian Kings. The valley is dotted with Thracian tombs that date from the 5th to the 3rd centuries BC (*see opposite*). Many were found to contain superb wall paintings and exquisite gold and silver objects. These are displayed in the **Iskra Museum**.

In Tyulbe Park, in the northeast of the town and within walking distance of the centre, is the **Kazanlûk Tomb**. The original tomb, whose exceptionally fine frescoes shed light on Thracian rituals, is closed to the public, but visitors can see an exact replica nearby.

Aspects of life in Kazanlûk's much more recent history are presented at the **Kulata Ethnographic Complex**. The restored 19th-century houses here include the home of a rose-farming family and a peasant dwelling. Kazanlûk's rose-oil industry is documented at the small **Museum of the Rose-Oil Industry**, next to a rose field on the outskirts of the town.

🏛 **Iskra Museum**
Corner of il. Kiril i Metodii and
ul. Slaveykov. **Tel** (043) 163 762.
🕘 9am–5pm daily. 🖼 🛈

🏛 **Kulata Ethnographic Complex**
ul. Nikola Petkov 18. **Tel** (043) 165
733. 🕘 9am–5pm daily. 🖼

𝄐 **Kazanlûk Tomb**
Tyulbe Park. **Tel**.(043) 121 733.
🕘 9am–5pm daily. 🖼 📷 🛈

🏛 **Museum of the Rose-Oil Industry**
bul. Osvobozhdenie 49. **Tel** (043)
125 170. 🕘 9am–5pm daily. 🖼 🛈

BULGARIA'S ROSE-OIL INDUSTRY

Rosa damascena, the red rose from which attar of roses, or rose oil, is made, was introduced to central Bulgaria by the Turks in the 19th century. The region's soil and climate were perfect for its cultivation and, by the 20th century, production of rose oil had developed into a major industry. The roses, which are grown in plantations that stretch for over 30 km (20 miles) along the valley between Karlovo and Kazanlûk, bloom from late May until mid-June, and the flowers are

Girl in traditional costume at the Kazanlûk Rose Festival

harvested before dawn so as to preserve their oil content. About 3.5 tonnes of petals produce 1 kilo (just over 2lb) of rose oil, which is worth about €6,000 (£4,200). The week-long Kazanlûk Rose Festival culminates on the first weekend of June, with music, dancing and the election of a Rose Queen.

Valley of the Thracian Kings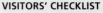

Тракийска гробница – Казанлък

The Tundzha Valley, northwest of Kazanlûk, was a holy place for the inhabitants of Seuthopolis, the capital of Seuthes III, who ruled the powerful Odrysae tribe in the 4th century BC. It was in this valley that many Thracian kings and nobles were buried, in elaborate stone tombs that were sealed and covered with earth. Excavation of these burial mounds *(mogili)*, some of which seem to have been used as places of ritual and sacrifice, has shed light on Thracian rituals. About 15 of the tumuli have so far been excavated, but only a few are open to visitors.

VISITORS' CHECKLIST

About 20 km (12 miles) NW of Kazanlûk, on the road to the Shipka Pass. **Map** D3. *Visits to the tombs can be arranged through the Iskra Museum in Kazanlûk; tel (0431) 163 762.* *for visitors without their own transport, the tombs are best reached by taxi from Kazanlûk.* **www**.bulgariatravel.org/eng/sights.php

★ **Mogila Shoushmanets**
A pair of stone doors with carvings of sun discs open into the burial chamber. A single column topped by a stone disc thought to symbolize the sun supports the domed ceiling.

Mogila Griffin
A corridor leads deep into the tumulus. The stone seats in its circular central chamber suggest that it was used as a temple. There are even iron hooks for the priests' robes.

★ **Mogila Helvetia**
Named after Switzerland, which provided the funds for its excavation, this tomb contains a temple and an antechamber where horses were regularly sacrificed and where priests made divinations from their blood.

Mogila Golyama Arsenalka
As it was found to be empty when it was excavated, this tomb is thought to have been plundered in ancient times. A corridor leads to a circular domed chamber with a concave central floor tile that represents the sun.

Mogila Golyama Kosmatka
This tomb consists of three linked chambers, one of which contains the sarcophagus of Seuthes III and some remarkable gold and silver treasures.

Kazanlûk Tomb

0 kilometres   5
0 miles   5

★ **Mogila Ostrousha**
Beneath a mound 20 m (65 ft) high, the Ostrousha Tomb contains six chambers. The northern room was carved from a single block of stone. The paintings on its walls include this tiny portrait of a red-haired girl.

STAR SIGHTS

★ Mogila Helvetia

★ Mogila Ostrousha

★ Mogila Shoushmanets

KEY

— Main road

— Other road

-- Trail

— Railway

⋒ Thracian tomb

Freedom Monument, Shipka Pass, a memorial to Russian and Bulgarian soldiers

Shipka ❷❾
Шипка

12 km (7 miles) north of Kazanlŭk.
Map D3. 🏛 *2,500.* 🚌

The gleaming golden domes of **Shipka Memorial Church** pinpoint the village of Shipka from afar. Sheltered by dense forest, this magnificent church was built in 1902 as a memorial to Russian and Bulgarian soldiers who died in the War of Liberation (see p47).

Environs
From Shipka village a winding mountain road leads up to Shipka Pass. It was here that General Gûrko and his Russian army, supported by Bulgarian militia using cherry tree cannons and rocks for weapons, repulsed fierce Ottoman attacks in 1877. From the pass, several hundred steep steps lead up to the **Freedom Monument**, which crowns the summit of Mount Shipka, at an altitude of 1,326 m (4,352 ft). Standing 32 m (105 ft) high and built of roughly cut stone, the grand

memorial contains a small museum, with a collection of weapons and illustrations of the battle. A lofty observation platform offers stunning views of the memorial's mountainous surroundings.

🛉 **Shipka Memorial Church**
🕐 8am–6pm daily. ✝ 8am Sun. 📷
🏛 **Freedom Monument**
🕐 9am–7pm daily. 📷

Karlovo ❸⓪
Карлово

35 km (22 miles) N of Plovdiv. **Map** C3. 🏛 *25,500.* 🚉 🚌 🚕 🚗 🚖 ℹ *ul. Vodopad 35.* **www**.karlovotur.hit.bg

The highest mountains in the Central Balkans loom over Karlovo, birthplace of Vasil Levski, Bulgaria's most celebrated revolutionary. The town's 19th-century quarter is a pleasant jumble of National Revival buildings and cobbled streets centred on the rough stone **Church of Sveta Bogoroditsa** (1851). Its bright blue bell tower was added in the late 19th century.

The pink-walled **History Museum**, housed in a former boys' school, stands off ulitsa Vasil Levski, just south of the church. The museum's collections include various prehistoric artifacts, traditional costume, weaponry used by Bulgarian revolutionaries, and woollen socks made in Karlovo. Kurshum Mosque, at the top of ulitsa Vasil Levski, was built in 1485, with large blocks of stone framed by red bricks, but its large wood-panelled porch was added in the late 19th century. The mosque is disused and is not open to visitors.

A few streets to the west is the **Vasil Levski Museum**, in the house where Levski (see box) grew up. It features the dyeing room used by Levski's widowed mother, the family's winter quarters, with low tables and stools, and open first-floor summer rooms adorned with family photographs and portraits. A small chapel in the grounds contains a lock of Levski's hair sealed inside a glass case.

Environs
The small town of **Sopot** straddles the busy Sofia–Burgas road. Its main point of interest is the **Ivan Vazov Museum**, in the house where Bulgaria's literary hero was born. Ivan Vazov (1850–1922) is best known for his novel *Under the Yoke*, in which he described village life at the time of the April Rising. The building is a typical 19th-century house, and the

Fresco of Vasil Levski in the Church of Sveta Bogoroditsa, Karlovo

exhibits include a quirky set of costumed manikins playing musical instruments while one of their number shaves himself in a barber's chair.

🏛 Church of Sveta Bogoroditsa
ul. Vasil Levski. ◯ *8am–7pm daily.* 🏛 *9am Sun.*

🏛 History Museum
ul. Vazrozhdenska 4. *Tel (0335) 94728.* ◯ *8am–noon, 1–5pm daily.* 📷

🏛 Vasil Levski Museum
ul. General Kartsov 57. *Tel (0335) 93489.* ◯ *8:30am–1pm, 2–5pm daily.* 📷

🏛 Ivan Vazov Museum
pl. Ivan Vazov, Sopot. *Tel (03134) 2070.* ◯ *8:30am–5.30pm daily.* 📷

Kamilite Gate, one of four gates into the ancient town of Hisarya

Hisarya ❸❶
Хисаря

43 km (27 miles) N of Plovdiv. **Map** C3. 🚶 *8,400.* 🚆 🚌 🚗

Hisarya lies in a depression at the eastern end of the Sredna Gora Mountains. Springs drew Thracian settlers here in the 1st millennium BC, and later the Romans developed the settlement into a luxurious spa town. In AD 251 Hisarya was devastated by invading Goths, but it was rebuilt, with the addition of colossal walls, as much as 10 m (33 ft) high in places, and four gates. Of these, only one, the Kamilite Gate (named after the camel caravans that passed through it), remains.

In AD 293 the Romans renamed the town Diocletiano-polis in honour of Emperor Diocletian, and prosperity returned until the collapse of the Byzantine Empire in the 6th century. One thousand years later, the town recovered its fortunes when the Ottomans rediscovered its healing mineral springs.

One of the temple-tombs near Starosel, burial place of Thracians

Today Hisarya's town walls enclose gardens, outdoor cafés and fountains. The small **History Museum** contains objects found during excavations of the town, including artifacts made by the Bessi, a Thracian tribe of the 1st millennium BC, votive tablets from the Roman period, and a marble bust of Diocletian.

🏛 History Museum
ul. Alexander Stamboliiski 8. *Tel (0337) 62796.* ◯ *8am–noon, 1–4:30pm daily.* 📷

Starosel Tombs ❸❷
Тракийска гробница – Старосел

N of Starosel village. **Map** D3. 🚌 🚶 ◯ *9am–5pm daily.* 📷 📹 🚻

Of the 120 tumuli in the vicinity of Starosel, only a few have been fully excavated, but six of those were discovered to be Thracian temple-tombs. Their close proximity suggests that the area was particularly sacred to Thracians. Only two of the tombs are open to the public.

The Horizont tomb lies 3 km (2 miles) outside the village of Starosel. In 2002 archaeologists uncovered a rectangular Thracian temple with steps leading to the entrance, and ten stone pillars that once supported the roof. The temple dates from the 5th century BC and was later used as the tomb of an unknown Thracian ruler, who was buried with a collection of arrowheads, silver beads and leather armour covered with plates of beaten gold.

The Chetinyova tomb, excavated in 2000, is 3 km (2 miles) further on. It dates from the 6th century BC and is thought to have been the burial place of the legendary Thracian ruler Sitalkes. The entire hilltop site is encircled by a wall of dressed granite. Granite steps lead up to the tomb's outer entrance, where a corridor opens onto a burial chamber 5.4 m (18 ft) in diameter, the largest so far discovered in Bulgaria.

The complex's early use as a temple is indicated by the wine trough for ritual libations behind the hill, the sacrificial pits dug near the entrance, and the fact that the site is aligned in such a way that, at the winter solstice, a shaft of sunlight beams into the central chamber.

VASIL LEVSKI (1837–73)

One of Bulgaria's most active revolutionaries, Vasil Levski fervently believed that the only way for Bulgaria to win freedom was for its own people to rise up against Ottoman rule rather than await foreign intervention. Levski was a prominent member of the Central Revolutionary Committee and spent many years establishing secret revolutionary organizations in towns and villages throughout Bulgaria. His arrest and execution for treason in 1873 dealt a mighty blow to the liberation movement.

Monument to Vasil Levski in Karlovo

Koprivshtitsa ➌

Копривщица

Detail of murals in Lyutov House

Thanks to its many fine National Revival houses, Koprivshtitsa is one of Bulgaria's most attractive towns. It was founded in the 14th century, as a rich centre of cattle farming. Under Ottoman rule its citizens were granted autonomy in return for collecting taxes on behalf of the Ottoman Empire. In the early 19th century, Koprivshtitsa's prosperity attracted bandits *(kurdzhali)*, who plundered and torched the town on several occasions. However, it quickly recovered, and it is during that period of reconstruction that its colourfully painted wood and stone houses were built. Koprivshtitsa was also the home of several of Bulgaria's leading revolutionaries, and it was here that the momentous April Rising of 1876 was declared.

🏛 Debelyanov House

ul. Dimcho Debelyanov. ☐ *9:30am–5:30pm Tue–Sun.*

This delightful house has a picturesque setting above the town, against a backdrop of forested hills. Its projecting red-tiled roof contrasts with bright blue lower walls and the dark wood of the upper storey.

It is the birthplace of the Symbolist poet Dimcho Debelyanov (1887–1916), who was killed in action during World War I.

The house contains personal possessions, such as books, that Debelyanov took with him to war, photographs of friends and family, and paintings, including a portrait of him by Georgi Mashev. In the garden is a brooding statue of his mother, awaiting the son who was never to return.

Statue in the garden of Debelyanov House

🔒 Church of Sveta Bogoroditsa

ul. Dimcho Debelyanov 26.
☐ *irregular hours.* 🔔 *8am Sun.*
The blue-walled Church of Sveta Bogoroditsa played a memorable role in Bulgarian history. On 20 April 1876, its bell rang out to announce the beginning of the April Rising.

The church was built in 1817, on the site of an earlier church that was destroyed by *kurdzhali* bandits. Surrounded by thick stone walls, it was built slightly sunken into the ground so as to comply with Ottoman regulations governing the height of Christian churches. The three-storey bell tower was added in 1896.

The church's interior is plain, but it has a superb iconostasis by woodcarvers of the Tryavna School, with biblical scenes interwoven with animals and flowers. Some of its icons were painted by Zahari Zograf *(see p106)*. Tragically, the church's original murals were destroyed in the course of misguided renovation, and replaced with newly painted icons.

🏛 Kableshkov House

ul. Todor Kableskov 8. ☐ *9:30am–5:30pm Tue–Sun.*
The upper floor of this imposing residence juts out over the stone wall round its cobbled courtyard. It was built in 1845, to a symmetrical design, the central salons on both floors flanked by identical rooms. With stepped windows and a decorated ceiling, the central bay on the upper floor makes a pleasant summer sitting area.

*Train Station
12 km (7.5 mi)*

① Debelyanov House

⑥ Oslekov House

Apriltsi Mausoleum

DEBELYANOV

GARANILO

Cemetery

② Church of Sveta Bogoroditsa

③ Kableshkov House

PURVA PUSHKA

④ Bridge of the First Shot

NIKOLAI BELODEZHDOV

⑤ Lyutov House

0 metres   100
0 yards   100

Key to Symbols *see back flap*

The Church of Sveta Bogoroditsa, whose bell proclaimed the April Rising

Kableshkov House, elegant home of the leader of the April Rising

VISITORS' CHECKLIST

110 km (68 miles) E of Sofia.
Road Map C3. 3,000.
pl. 20 April (07184-2191).
Fri. Re-enactment of the
April Rising (1–2 May),
International Folk Festival (every
five years, next in summer 2010).
www.koprivshtitsa.info

This was the home of Todor Kableshkov (1851–76), leader of the April Rising *(see p174)*. After studying in Plovdiv and Istanbul, where he became fluent in French, Greek and Turkish, he returned to Koprivshtitsa to chair the town's secret revolutionary committee. On 20 April 1876 he declared the start of the uprising with his infamous Bloody Letter, written in the blood of the revolutionaries' first Turkish victim. In the aftermath of the uprising's failure, Kableshkov was captured and imprisoned in Gabrovo, where he shot himself. He was buried at the Church of the Assumption in Koprivshtitsa.

🚧 Bridge of the First Shot
ul. Todor Kableshkov
Over a small stream in a quiet location southwest of the town centre is the Bridge of the First Shot. As the spot where the first Turk was killed during the April Rising, the humpbacked bridge is a hallowed site in Bulgarian history. A statue of Todor Kableshov, leader of the April Rising *(see above)*, stands nearby.

Detail of a room at Lyutov House, with elaborate painted decoration

🏛 Lyutov House
ul. Nikola Belovezhdov 2. 9:30am–5:30pm Mon, Wed–Sun.
With a huge curved gable, symmetrical layout and decorative features, Lyutov House typifies Plovdiv architecture. It was designed and built in 1854 by master-craftsmen from Plovdiv, and in 1906 it was acquired by Petko Lyutov, a Koprivshtitsa milk merchant, who decorated the building with the Viennese furniture on display here today.

A double staircase leads up to the central salon on the first floor. The room has an impressive elliptical vaulted ceiling edged with murals of the cities that Lyutov visited on his travels. The rooms on either side of the salon are furnished with Ottoman-style benches as well as European furniture. The walls feature niches and coving painted with elaborate floral motifs and further cityscapes.

On the ground floor is an exhibition of 18th- and 19th-century grey felt rugs, made in Koprivshtitsa.

Bridge of the First Shot, an historic spot

🏛 Karavelov House

ul. Hadzhi Nencho Palaveev 39.
🕐 9:30am–5:30pm Wed–Mon. 🖼

Home to one of the National Liberation Movement's key ideologists, Karavelov House consists, in fact, of two separate buildings. The winter quarters were constructed in 1810, while the summer house, built over the main entrance, was added in 1835.

Lyuben Karavelov, born here in 1834, was a prolific writer, publisher and fervent revolutionary. He spent time among Bulgarian émigrés in Bucharest, where he published the influential *Liberty* and *Independence* newspapers and chaired the Bulgarian Revolutionary Central Committee. The printing press that he bought in Serbia in 1871 is on display in the winter

Panorama of Koprivshtitsa as seen from the Benkovski monument

quarters along with the some of the various publications he put together with Vasil Levski and Hristo Botev. During the Russo-Turkish War of 1877–8, he returned to Bulgaria before succumbing to tuberculosis within a year. Petko, his younger brother, was three times prime minister of the new Bulgarian state that emerged after the war.

Benkovski monument, unveiled in 1908

🏛 Benkovski House

ul. Georgi Benkovski 5.
🕐 9:30am–5:30pm Wed–Mon. 🖼

Its rickety wooden façade and pretty garden give Benkovski House the appearance of a fairytale cottage and the homely interior suggests that

Pretty exterior and courtyard of Karavelov House, Koprivshtitsa

the Hlutev family led a modest and cozy existence. The asymmetrical design consists of low winter quarters topped by summer rooms grouped around a pleasant veranda that now displays a replica of one of the cherry-tree cannons used in the April Rising. Adjoining rooms contain Benkovski's revolutionary district flag, uniforms, and his Winchester rifle as well as faded photographs of him and his family.

He was born Gavril Hlutev and grew up here, studying to become a tailor before moving abroad at the age of 22. In Romania he was revolutionized by a group of Bulgarian émigrés and returned to Koprivshtitsa in 1875 under the assumed name of Georgi Benkovski. He formed what was to become the legendary "winged" cavalry detachment that rallied support from local villages during the April Uprising. The detachment managed to escape to the Balkan Mountains following the failure of the uprising, but Benkovski was betrayed and later killed on 25 May 1876.

The massive granite monument on the hillside above Benkovski House portrays a cloaked Benkovski astride a leaping horse looking over his shoulder to rouse his rebel army. The words *"Stavaite robove az neshta yarem"* (Rise up slaves, I don't want a yoke) are carved boldly across its base.

THE APRIL RISING, 1876

Initially planned for May, the April Uprising of 1876 relied upon the local populace to rise up against the Ottomans when called upon. Itinerant revolutionary agitators had spent several years priming and arming local groups in preparation for the revolt. Kableshkov, chairman of Koprivshtitsa's revolutionary committee, was forced to declare an early start on 20th April when Turkish officials tried to arrest him. The uprising disastrously failed to raise the support it needed from locals too fearful of Turkish retribution; villages that did participate were brutally punished – the most notorious case being at Batak (*see p126*). Though many died in this apparently fruitless sacrifice, universal international outrage at the barbaric Ottoman reprisals lead to Russia's declaration of war on Turkey a year later and Bulgaria's liberation in 1878. The Apriltsi Mausoleum was built in 1928 in Koprivshtitsa's main square to honour those who died.

The Apriltsi Mausoleum

Oslekov House

Ослековата къща

Commissioned by the wealthy merchant and tax collector Nincho Oslekov, the house was built in 1856 by Samokov craftsmen. Because of space restrictions, it is asymmetrical, but is otherwise typical of National Revival buildings. The ground-floor winter quarters have low ceilings and small windows to conserve heat. The first floor, used in summer, has a spacious salon with large windows and adjoining rooms. Oslekov's support for the National Liberation movement brought him a death sentence after the April Uprising. He was hanged in Plovdiv in 1876.

VISITORS' CHECKLIST

ul. Garanilo 4. Tel (07187) 2191. 9:30am–5:30pm Tue–Sun (may close for lunch). one ticket allows entry to the six main National Revival houses.

★ Red Room
Like other rooms in the house, the Red Room has a fretted wooden ceiling. On the walls are paintings of mansions and the original symmetrical plan for Oskelov House.

Men's Room
This was where Oslekov would receive his guests and engage in business. The murals throughout the building reveal foreign places he visited while on business.

The women's room displays a colourful collection of woollen socks along with a horizontal loom and a spinning wheel.

First floor

Ground floor

Main entrance

Ground floor salon

The ground-floor living room, decorated with murals of female musicians, was used in winter. The mix of eastern and western influences is typified by the European dining table with Turkish-style wall benches.

First-Floor Salon
Cloth-covered benches line the walls of this impressive room. This was a weaving workshop, but was also used for festivities and family events. It was here that rebel uniforms were clandestinely produced for the April Rising.

STAR SIGHTS

★ Main Façade

★ Red Room

★ Main Façade
Views of Venice, Padua, Rome and other European cities, painted by Kosta Zograf of Samokov, decorate the façade. The columns are of cedarwood imported from Lebanon.

NORTHERN BULGARIA

With dramatic contrasts, northern Bulgaria encompasses jagged mountains and pine forests in the northwest and fertile sunflower-covered flatlands and low vine-covered hills near the banks of the Danube. The region also has a rich cultural heritage, with Stone Age cave paintings, medieval castles and Muslim holy sites that illuminate the complex fabric of Bulgarian history.

Much of the region is mountainous, with the eastern spurs of the Balkan range presenting a formidable obstacle to the main transport routes leading north from Sofia. The trip through Iskûr Gorge, just north of the capital, is one of Bulgaria's classic journeys, past a tortured sequence of rocky outcrops. The limestone cliffs of Vratsata Gorge are no less dramatic, although little beats the sandstone pillars of Belogradchik. Further north, the prehistoric paintings of Magura Cave are evidence of one of Europe's earliest cultures.

North and east of the mountains lie flatlands watered by the tributaries of the Danube, a river that has played a major role in Bulgarian history. The stately fortress of Baba Vida at Vidin defended the state from northern invaders, while the city of Ruse grew rich on the profits of river trade. Ruse is the gateway to the Rusenski Lom, a twisting canyon where medieval monks turned caves near Ivanovo into a unique community of rock-cut monasteries. Above the southern end of the Rusenski Lom hovers the cliff-top citadel of Cherven, one of Bulgaria's most atmospheric medieval sites.

Further east, Lake Sreburna is a famous feeding ground for migrating birds, including Dalmatian pelicans. Rolling hills of pasture and fruit trees provide an idyllic setting for Sveshtari, a site whose Thracian tombs and Muslim shrines still radiate a spiritual aura. The major urban centre of the northeast is Shumen, a former fortress town whose modern café-lined boulevards have a delightfully relaxing feel.

Belogradchik fortress, first built in Roman times using the natural terrain to maximum advantage

◁ Cherepish Monastery, founded in the 14th century, at the time of the Second Bulgarian Kingdom

Exploring Northern Bulgaria

A region that embraces the eastern spur of the Balkan mountains, the Danubian Plain and the rolling hills of the northeast, northern Bulgaria has some of the country's most varied terrain. The mountains of the northwest offer plenty of opportunities for hiking, especially around the karst outcrops of the Vrachanski Balkan and the rock pillars of Belogradchik. Vidin and Pleven are historic towns, but it is the 19th-century port of Ruse that offers the best urban attractions. The cluster of tombs near Sveshtari are among the finest Thracian sites in the country, and the enigmatic Madara Horseman, near Shumen, is equally unmissable. Lake Sreburna, in the east, is one of the country's top birdwatching sites.

Kilims at Chiprovtsi, with typical geometric motifs woven in bright colours

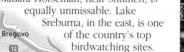

Negotin
Bregovo
12
♙ 🏛 VIDIN **1**   Craiova →
Kula   Dunavci
14   Gramada
Lom
Dimovo **11**   **11**   Kozloduy
2   Oryahovo   Danube (Dunav)
MAGURA   Valchedram   Miziya   **11** ♙   NIKOPOL
CAVE **1**   **3** BELOGRADCHIK   Gulyantsy   **34**
♙ 🏛 🗡   **81**   Oguşta   Knezha   Isker
Midžur
2168 m   Boychinovtsy   **15**   **13**   Pelovo   Dolna   Slavyanov
CHIPROVTSI   Byala   Dolni   Metropolija   **3**
6 🏛   **4** MONTANA   Slatina   Dabnik 🏛 **10**
🏛   Krivodol   Koynare   PLEVEN   Pordim
BERKOVITSA   Cherven
🏛 **5**   Varshets **7** VRATSA   Bryag
VRACHANSKI   **8** Mezdra   Lukovit   **35**
Todorini   BALKAN TOUR   Roman
kukli   **16**
Nish   Godech   1785 m   Yablanitsa **3**
ISKUR GORGE TOUR
Dragoman   **9**
8   **81**   Botevgrad   Pravets **37**
Kostinbrod   Etropole
Bankja   Novi Iskar

0 kilometres   25

0 miles   25

KEY

═══ Motorway

= = Motorway under construction

═══ Expressway

─── Major road

═══ Other road

-·- Railway

▬▬▬ International border

△ Peak

Rock formations, once used as a stronghold, above Belogradchik

SIGHTS AT A GLANCE

Belogradchik **3**
Berkovitsa **5**
Chiprovtsi **6**
Madara **19**
Magura Cave **2**
Montana **4**
Nikopol **11**
Pleven **10**
Ruse pp186–7 **13**
Shumen **18**
Silistra **17**

Sreburna Nature Reserve **16**
Sveshtari **15**
Svishtov **12**
Veliki Preslav **20**
Vidin **1**
Vratsa **7**

Tours

Iskûr Gorge Tour **9**
Rusenski Lom Tour **14**
Vrachanski Balkan Tour **8**

SEE ALSO

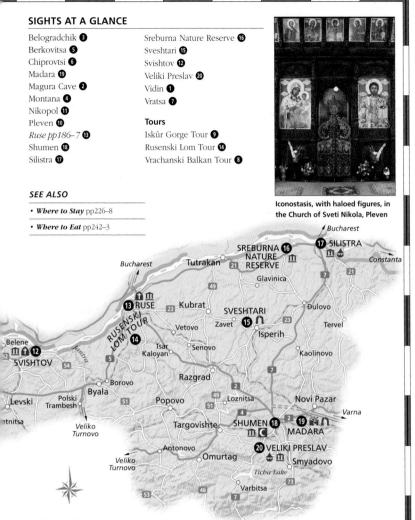

Iconostasis, with haloed figures, in the Church of Sveti Nikola, Pleven

GETTING AROUND

The principal routes through the region are the main road and rail lines running north from Sofia to Vratsa, Montana and Vidin, and those running northeast from Sofia to Pleven and Ruse. From Ruse, onward travel to either Silistra or Shumen is fairly easy. Shumen itself is connected to the Black Sea city of Varna by a fast stretch of dual carriageway. Some of the most scenic parts of northern Bulgaria, such as Iskûr Gorge, the rock formations near Belogradchik and the Rusenski Lom, can only be reached on minor roads, where progress may be slow. Unfortunately, the river Danube has little potential as a tourist itinerary: there is no passenger transport on the river itself, and the roads along its banks are in poor condition.

Ornately decorated cupola of Tombul Mosque in Shumen

Vidin ❶
Видин

200 km (125 miles) N of Sofia.
Map A1. 🚶 53,625. 🚉 from Sofia.
🚌 from Sofia.

Set on the Danube, Vidin is Bulgaria's westernmost port and of strategic importance to successive waves of settlers. First were the Celts, who arrived in the 3rd century BC, followed by Romans, Byzantines, Ottomans and Bulgarians. Today Vidin is an important river crossing, with ferries shuttling across the Danube to the Romanian port of Calafat.

Central Vidin centres around ploshtad Bdin, a broad square lined with modern buildings. A short walk northeastwards along ulitsa Turgovska is the **History Museum**, in the much-modernized residence of Vidin's governor in Ottoman times. The museum contains an absorbing collection of floor mosaics and marble sculpture from the 2nd-century Roman settlement of Ratiaria, a frontier fort 25 km (16 miles) southeast of Vidin, near the village of Archar.

Northeast of ploshtad Bdin, and parallel to the banks of the Danube, are the Riverside Gardens, with lawns and trees. On the western side of the gardens is Vidin's only surviving mosque, built by the soldier and governor Osman Pazvantoglu in the 1790s. The attractive domed building in the mosque's enclosed garden originally served as a *kitabhane*, or Koranic library.

Dominating the northern end of the park are the imposing towers and bastions of **Baba Vida**, the 13th-century fortress that once guarded the north-western approaches to the medieval kingdom of Bulgaria. Baba Vida is one of the best-preserved castles in Bulgaria, largely because it was so valuable to successive Ottoman occupiers that it remained in constant use. The core of the castle, with towers and turrets, is still largely intact. From here visitors can enjoy sweeping views of the river.

Walking back towards central Vidin along ulitsa Knyaz Boris I, visitors will pass the Cross-shaped Barracks (Krustata kazarma) built during the reign of Osman Pazvantoglu. The barracks now contain the town's **Ethnographic Museum**. Its collection includes local costumes, textiles woven by the nomadic, sheep-rearing Vlachs, a local ethnic minority who speak a language similar to modern Romanian.

Behind the nearby Church of Sveti Nikolai is one of Vidin's oldest churches, Sveti Panteleimon, built by the 17th-century Despot of Wallachia, Ioan Matei Basarab, whose portrait graces the entrance.

🏛 **History Museum**
Tel (094) 601 710. ◯ 9am–5pm Mon–Fri, 10am–5pm Sat–Sun. 📷

♣ **Baba Vida**
Tel (094) 601 705. ◯ 9am–5pm Mon–Fri, 10am–5pm Sat–Sun. 📷

🏛 **Ethnographic Museum**
Tel (094) 601 709. ◯ 9am–5pm Mon–Fri, 10am–5pm Sat–Sun. 📷

Prehistoric rock paintings of men and animals at Magura Cave

Magura Cave ❷
пещерата "Магура"

Rabisha village, 35 km (22 miles) SW of Vidin. **Map** A2. ◯ 9am–5pm daily. 📷 🍴 ♿ 🖥 www.magura.hit.bg

Both on account of its mineral formations and its prehistoric paintings, this is one of Bulgaria's most spectacular limestone caves. It is located just outside Rabisha, a village in the foot-hills of the Western Balkan range. The cave has unusually large galleries, some with ceilings 25 m (80 ft) high, and zestful rock paintings that date from the 2nd millennium BC.

The route descends 2 km (over 1 mile) down the cave, with some steep and slippery sections. The first two caverns, the Triumphal Hall and Gallery of the Stalactones, contain stunning stalactites and stalagmites. A tunnel-like side chamber off the main route leads to the Gallery of Drawings, where paintings executed in bat droppings show stylized sun and star shapes, hunters wielding bows, and a variety of exotic beasts. Most striking are the scenes of ritual celebration, in which female figures dance with their arms above their heads, observed by sexually excited males.

Along the main route visitors will come to the Chamber of the Fallen Pine. It is named after the tapering stalagmite, 11 m (36 ft) long and 6 m (20 ft) in diameter, which collapsed in the chamber.

The cave is also near Lake Rabisha, which is popular with local fishermen because of its rich stocks of catfish and carp.

The fortress of Baba Vida, built to defend the Danube crossing at Vidin

The natural fortress above Belogradchik, transformed into a citadel by Romans, Bulgarians and Ottomans

Belogradchik ❸
Белоградчик

50 km (31 miles) SW of Vidin.
Map A2. 🚶 6,685. 🚌 *from Vidin.*

The small hillside town of
Belogradchik is surrounded
by some of the most dramatic
rock formations in Bulgaria.
The Belogradchik rocks
(Belogradchiskite skali) were
formed millennia ago, when
thick deposits of sandstone
were forced upwards by the
movement of tectonic plates.
Erosion by wind and rain then
shaped them into an other-
worldly assortment of pillars,
cones and mushroom forms.

The hill above the town is
crowned by a particularly
dramatic circle of rocky pin-
nacles. Forming a natural
fortress, they were used as an
almost impregnable citadel by
Romans, Bulgarians and Ottomans. The inner stronghold
commands stunning views of
the surrounding landscape. Yet
more spectacular rock formations, with names such as the
Bear, the Horseman and the
Monks, can be seen by
following footpaths through a
vale west of Belogradchik.

In a glade outside the town
is a **Natural History Museum**,
with stuffed examples of birds
and forest-dwelling mammals
of northwestern Bulgaria.

🏛 **Natural History Museum**
Tel (0936) 3231. 🕐 8am–noon,
2–5pm Mon–Fri. 🖼

Montana ❹
Монтана

80 km (50 miles) SE of Vidin; 90 km
(56 miles) N of Sofia. **Map** B2.
🚶 46,902. 🚌 *from Sofia.*

Although it grew from the
Roman fort of Castra ad Mon-
tanesium, modern Montana
has the appearance of a 20th-
century town. The spacious
main square, with fountains
and flowerbeds, is an example of Communist urban planning. Just off the square is a
small **History Museum**, with
traditional costumes of the
Karakachani, nomadic shepherds of the western Balkans.
Few genuine Karakachani
now remain, as most have
adopted settled lifestyles.

🏛 **History Museum**
Tel (096) 305 393. 🕐 8am–noon,
2–5pm Mon, Wed–Sat. 🖼

Fountains in Montana's large
pedestrianized main square

Berkovitsa ❺
Берковица

24 km (15 miles) south of Montana.
Map B2. 🚶 16,818. 🚋 *from
Montana.* 🚌 *from Sofia.*

In the 19th century Berkovitsa
was a prosperous centre of
woodworking and pottery-
making. It became a minor
health resort in the early 20th
century, when Sofians discovered its pure mountain air. The
town is also the starting point
of a hiking trail to Mount Kom,
12 km (7 miles) to the west.

Evidence of Berkovitsa's
19th-century heritage is displayed in the **Ivan Vazov
Museum**, in the house where
the novelist lived while serving
as magistrate. Appointed in
1879, Vazov *(see p81)* soon left
to pursue a writing career in
Plovdiv. His former home
features handsomely carved
wooden ceilings, luxurious
carpets and some copperware.

The **Ethnographic Museum**
celebrates Berkovitsa's ceramics
industry with a display of pots
and jugs glazed in vivid yellow
and green. Local craftsmanship
can also be seen in the Church
of the Birth of the Virgin,
which contains a beautifully
carved wooden iconostasis.

🏛 **Ivan Vazov Museum**
ul. Berkovska Reka. *Tel* (0953) 2235.
🕐 8am–noon, 1–5pm daily. 🖼

🏛 **Ethnographic Museum**
ul. Poruchnik Grozhdanov.
🕐 8am–noon, 2–5pm Mon–Fri. 🖼

Ruins of the Cathedral of Sveta Maria, Chiprovtsi

Chiprovtsi ❻
Чипровци

25 km (16 miles) W of Montana.
Map A2. 🏠 2,915.

Wedged into an attractive
mountain valley, Chiprovtsi is
a small, unassuming town that
betrays few signs of its former
greatness. From the 13th
century, when it was populated
largely by Saxon immigrants
of Catholic faith, Chiprovtsi
was one of the most important
centres of gold- and silver-
mining in the Balkans. Its
prosperity survived the Ottoman
conquest, and the town
became a great centre of
Catholic learning. After an un-
successful uprising against the
Ottomans in 1688, the town
was laid waste and its inhabitants banished. Chiprovtsi was
not repopulated until 1737. It
was then that carpet-weaving
became the town's main
industry, as it still is today.

The **Town Museum**, in a
former schoolhouse, illustrates
aspects of Chiprovtsi's past.
Exhibits include examples of
the intricate jewellery that

was made by the
town's goldsmiths in
the 17th century.
There is also a
display of brightly
coloured Chiprovtsi
kilims, and an
example of the
vertical looms on
which carpets are
still woven in the
town today.

Next door to the
museum is the
Church of the
Ascension, which
contains a fine 19th-century
iconostasis. Nearby are the
meagre ruins of the medieval
Cathedral of Sveta Maria, razed
by the Ottomans in 1688.

🏛 **Chiprovtsi Town Museum**
⏰ 9am–5pm Mon-Fri, 10am-4pm
Sat–Sun. 📷

Vratsa ❼
Враца

110 km (68 miles) N of Sofia.
Map B2. 🏠 63,858. 🚌

Vratsa is an ideal starting point
for touring the Vrachanski
Balkan (see opposite) whether
by foot or car. However, it
should not be overlooked as
an attraction in its own right.

Vratsa's main square is
dominated by a statue of the
poet and revolutionary Hristo
Botev (1848–76). In May
1876, Botev entered Ottoman-
occupied Bulgaria at the head
of a band of patriot exiles. He
and all his followers perished,
having made their last stand
on Mount Okolchitsa, just
outside Vratsa.

Botev is also remembered
at Vratsa's **History Museum**.
However, the real attraction
here is some of finest Thracian
gold and silver yet discovered
in northern Bulgaria. A room
is devoted to the Rogozen
Treasure (Rogozensko
sukrovishte), a collection of
more than 150 silver ewers
and bowls discovered in
1983. Made for a Thracian
noble family between the
5th and 4th centuries BC, the
vessels are richly decorated,
some with abstract swirls and
stripes, others with mythological subjects and hunting
scenes. A particularly
impressive piece is a pitcher
with a powerful portrait of
the Thracian mother-goddess
astride a lion.

Another room contains the
Vratsa Treasure (Vrachanska
sukrovishta), a collection of
artifacts from the grave of a
Thracian noblewoman.
Notable pieces include an
exquisite gold wreath and a
bronze shin-guard bearing
the tattooed face of a deity.

Vratsa's **Ethnographic
Museum**, in a restored 19th-
century schoolhouse, contains
a collection of colourful
Bulgarian costumes. There
is also a display of musical
instruments that illustrates
the history of brass bands
in northern Bulgaria.

🏛 **History Museum**
pl. Hristo Botev. ⏰ 8am–noon,
1–5pm daily. 📷

🏛 **Ethnographic Museum**
ul. Turgovska. ⏰ 9am–6pm
Tue–Sun. 📷

**Traditional costumes at the
Ethnographic Museum, Vratsa**

CHIPROVTSI CARPETS

**Brightly coloured
Chiprovtsi carpets**

Chiprovtsi is one of the few Bulgarian
villages where carpet weaving is still
widely practised, and where skills are
passed down from mother to daughter.
Woven on vertical looms, the carpets
feature brightly coloured patterns
that feature a centuries-old repertoire
of stylized motifs. Many of these
originated as fertility symbols. They
include bird motifs known as *piletata*
(chickens), abstract zig-zags known
as *lozite* (vines), and the mysterious
cluster of black triangles known as
karakachka (black-eyed bride).

Vrachanski Balkan Tour ⑧

The highland region that stretches out to the west of Vratsa is known as the Vrachanski Balkan. Its landscape, most of which is protected as a nature park, consists of pasture-covered hills, forested valleys and jagged outcrops of limestone. The region's most dramatic feature is the deep Vratsata Gorge, which starts just west of Vratsa. The hills on either side of the gorge provide lush grazing for cows and sheep, and from their milk local dairies produce some of the best Bulgarian yoghurt.

TIPS FOR DRIVERS

Map: B2.
Starting point: Vratsa.
Length: 60 km (37 miles).
Stopping-off places: There are several hotels, restaurants and cafés in Vratsa, and you can get light refreshments at villages such as Pavloche and Chelopek. There is a hostel at Ledenika.
Ledenika Cave 🕘 9am–5pm daily. 🖼 🚻

Vratsata Gorge ②
Cutting a great swathe through the landscape, Vratsata Gorge is formed by sheer cliffs that rise almost vertically from the valley floor. The terrain above consists of pasture and majestic outcrops of rock.

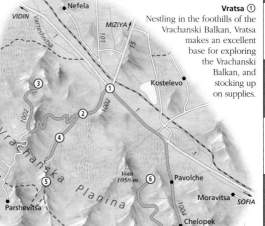

Vratsa ①
Nestling in the foothills of the Vrachanski Balkan, Vratsa makes an excellent base for exploring the Vrachanski Balkan, and stocking up on supplies.

Ledenika Cave ③
Formed by seeping rainwater over a period of 2 million years, the cave contains a sequence of subterranean halls, with spectacular stalactites and stalagmites. The cave is also inhabited by a large colony of bats.

Zgorigrad ④
Largely agricultural and with horses and carts still serving as a popular mode of transport, Zgorigrad is a pleasant example of a northwest Bulgarian village.

Vrachanski eco-trail ⑤
Upstream from the village of Zgorigrad, this well-signed nature walk (*Eko puteka*) ascends a narrowing ravine, passing through forests of lime, beech and walnut.

Okolchitsa ⑥
This historic peak, where the poet and revolutionary Hristo Botev was killed, has a cross at the top and panoramic views overlooking the valley.

KEY

▬	Tour route
═	Main road
=	Other road
- -	Trail
▬	Railway
△	Peak

0 kilometres   5

0 miles   5

Iskûr Gorge Tour ⑨

Rising on the slopes of Mount Vitosha, the Iskûr River flows north to join the Danube just west of Nikopol. Its course cuts through the limestone of the western Balkans to form the Iskûr Gorge, a defile that runs for 156 km (97 miles) between Sofia and Mezdra, where the river emerges onto the open plains. The gorge is famous for its dramatic rock formations, and the monasteries nearby are important places of pilgrimage.

TIPS FOR DRIVERS

Map B3. Length of tour: *approximately 105 km (65 miles).* **Getting there:** *Road and rail routes follow the gorge, providing easy access to the scenic stretches.* **Stopping-off places:** *There are picnic spots and café-restaurants at Gara Lakatnik, right beneath the Lakatnik rocks.*

Cart Rails ①
These outcrops of limestone, near the north end of the gorge, run dramatically down the hillside in parallel lines, hence their name.

Lakatnik Rocks ④
One of the gorge's most dramatic features is this outcrop of rock, whose sheer cliffs rise above the village of Gara Lakatnik.

Proboinitsa River and Mountain Chalet ⑤
Visitors can stay in this mountain chalet, on the bank of the Proboinitsa River. It can be reached along a marked track.

Katina Pyramids ⑥
Rising dramatically against the skyline, these extraordinary rock formations have been shaped by the action of wind and rain.

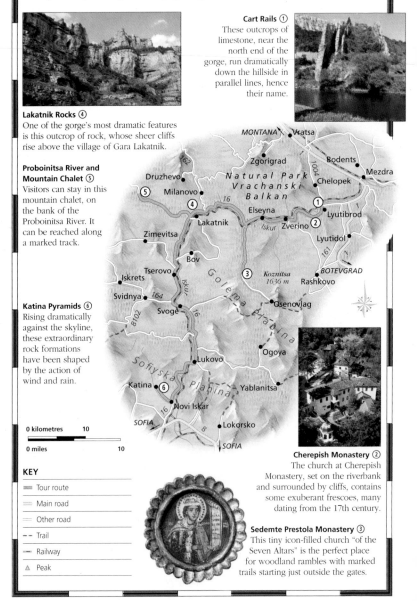

KEY

- ▬ Tour route
- ═ Main road
- ═ Other road
- -- Trail
- ▬ Railway
- △ Peak

Cherepish Monastery ②
The church at Cherepish Monastery, set on the riverbank and surrounded by cliffs, contains some exuberant frescoes, many dating from the 17th century.

Sedemte Prestola Monastery ③
This tiny icon-filled church "of the Seven Altars" is the perfect place for woodland rambles with marked trails starting just outside the gates.

The Panorama, one of several reminders of the Siege of Pleven

Pleven ❿
Плевен

160 km (99 miles) NE of Sofia.
Map C2. 🏛 *117,651.* 🚌 ▭

An important centre of trade in the 19th century, Pleven is remembered today primarily for the decisive role that it played in the Russo-Turkish War of 1877–8 *(see p17)*. In July 1877 the Russian army advanced on Pleven, but the Ottoman garrison, under the command of Osman Pasha, stood resolute. After a five-month siege, Pleven finally surrendered, and this was soon followed by the collapse of Ottoman resistance throughout Bulgaria.

Several public buildings in the town recall the event. A **Mausoleum** commemorating Russian casualties in the siege is the central feature of ploshtad Vuzrazhdane, Pleven's main square. Its hushed interior is filled with plaques engraved with the names of the fallen. Pleven's main shopping street, ulitsa Vasil Levski, leads northward to the **Museum of Liberation**, in which the Siege of Pleven is remembered through a colourful display of guns and uniforms.

Nearby is the 14th-century Church of Sveti Nikola. It was substantially rebuilt in 1834 after being pillaged by *kurdzhali*, roving bandits who preyed on town-dwellers. Inside the church are a wooden iconostasis delicately carved by Master Peter of Gabrovo, and icons by Dimitûr Zograf *(see p106).*

In a former barracks just south of the town centre, the **History Museum** displays more weaponry dating from the siege, as well as an extensive archaeological collection that includes mosaics and sarcophagi from the Roman settlement of Oescus, 35 km (22 miles) north of Pleven.

Roman sculpture in the History Museum, Pleven

On high ground west of the town centre, defensive earthworks dating from the Ottoman period underlie the lawns and trees of Skobelev Park. At its centre is the **Skobelev Museum**, which honours the Russian general who commanded Cossack detachments during the siege. At the northern end of the park is the **Panorama**, a cylindrical monument unveiled in 1977 to mark the centenary of the siege. Its interior is lined with a long panoramic painting that depicts the decisive moment when Osman Pasha tried to break the siege. Smaller paintings show other episodes of the siege.

🏛 **Mausoleum**
pl. Vuzrazhdane. ⬤ *9am–noon, 1–6pm daily.* 🖼

🏛 **Museum of Liberation**
ul. Vasil Levski. ⬤ *8am–noon, 1–5pm, daily.*

🏛 **History Museum**
ul. Doiran. ⬤ *9am–noon, 1–5pm daily.*

🏛 **Skobelev Museum**
Park Skobelev. ⬤ *9am–noon, 1–5pm daily.*

🏛 **Panorama**
Park Skobelev. ⬤ *9am–noon, 1–5pm, daily.* 🖼

Nikopol ⓫
Никопол

55 km (34 miles) N of Pleven.
Map C2. 🏛 *4,976.* 🚌

Situated in a cleft in a chalky escarpment over the Danube, Nikopol is a sleepy rural settlement that betrays few signs of its historical importance. In Roman times, when it was known as Nikopolis, it was a garrison town. It was later developed by Byzantine and Bulgarian

rulers, and by the Middle Ages, it was the most important fortress on the lower Danube. In 1396, Nikopol was the site of a significant battle, when Crusaders led by King Louis of Hungary were crushed by Ottoman forces. Today there are only scant remains of the fortress on the bluff, east of the town.

Svishtov ⓬
Свищов

95 km (59 miles) NE of Pleven.
Map D2. 🏛 *34,922.* 🚌 ▭

Now a quiet provincial town, in the 19th century Svishtov was the busiest ferry-crossing point on the Bulgarian stretch of the Danube (Dunav).

The most prominent building that recalls this golden age is the Church of Sveta Troitsa, built in 1867 by Kolyo Ficheto *(see p161)*. Down the hill from the church is the **Aleko Konstantinov House**, where the furniture and personal effects of Aleko Konstantinov, Bulgaria's greatest 19th-century satirical writer, are displayed. In 1897 Konstantinov was assassinated, and the remains of his bullet-perforated heart are preserved in a glass jar in the house.

🏛 **Aleko Konstantinov House**
ul. Klokotuitsa 6. **Tel** *(0631) 60467.* ⬤ *8am–noon, 1–5pm Mon–Fri.* 🖼

Church of Sveta Troitsa in Svishtov, built by Kolyo Ficheto

Ruse ⑬
Pyce

With handsome 19th-century municipal buildings and Art Nouveau villas, the Danube port of Ruse has a strong Central European flavour. Ruse owes much to Midhat Pasha, its governor from 1864 to 1868. This enlightened Turkish administrator transformed the Ottoman garrison town into a modern European city. After the Liberation, Western investment increased, and Ruse became Bulgaria's wealthiest city. Many of its most atmospheric neighbourhoods are in its northwesterly section, among the grid of streets between ulitsa Aleksandrovska and the Danube. Its focal point is ploshtad Svoboda, the central square traversed by the pedestrianized ulitsa Aleksandrovska, one of Bulgaria's most vibrant shopping streets.

⌂ Church of Sveta Troitsa
ul. Gorazhd.
Built in 1764, this church is an eyecatching blend of Baroque and Muscovite styles. Steps lead down to a nave that lies 4 m (13 ft) below street level, a reminder that, during the Ottoman period, churches could not rival mosques in height or magnificence. The church's main iconostasis bears some splendid Russian icons presented to it by the Sergiev Monastery in Moscow.

⊞ Ploshtad Svoboda
Central Ruse revolves around ploshtad Svoboda (Liberation Square), a broad pedestrianized area with well-kept lawns and shrubs. At its centre stands the Liberation Monument (1909), in the form of a soaring pillar topped by a figure symbolizing liberty.

On the southwestern side of the square is the Drama Theatre, built in 1900 as an entertainment and shopping centre. The ground floor was leased to shopkeepers, and it

Palace of Aleksandûr Batenberg, now the Regional History Museum

became known as Dohodnoto Zdanie (Revenue Building). The figure of Mercury on the roof is a city landmark.

⊞ Regional History Museum
pl. Aleksandûr Batenberg 3. ◻ 8:30am–noon, 1–5:30pm Mon–Fri. *Tel* (082) 825 002. 🖼
From Ploshtad Svoboda, a short walk southwest along ulitsa Aleksandrovska leads to ploshtad Aleksandûr Batenberg, one of Ruse's most elegant

squares. At its western end is the former palace of Prince Aleksandûr Batenberg, now the Regional History Museum.

The first floor is devoted to Bulgaria's prehistoric, Roman and medieval periods. The centrepiece is the Borovo Treasure, a ceremonial bowl and drinking horns made for Thracian rulers in the 4th century BC. Other rooms recall Ruse's belle époque, with re-creations of pre-World War I high-street shops. There is also an ethnographic section, with traditional wedding costumes.

⋒ Sexaginta Prista
ul. Tsar Kaloyan. ◻ 9am–5pm daily. 🖼
Just north of pl. Aleksandûr Batenberg, along ul. Tsar Kaloyan, a path leads to the site of Sexaginta Prista (Port of Sixty Ships). This Roman naval base was built in the 1st century, during the reign of the emperor Vespasian. Traces of its fortifications are visible, and there is a fascinating collection of Roman tombstones and inscriptions.

To the north lies Ruse's 19th-century port area, where luxury goods from western Europe arrived by barge, to be stored in the fine red-brick warehouses that still stand.

⛪ Zahari Stoyanov Museum
bul. Pridunavski 14. *Tel* (082) 820 996. ◻ 9am–noon, 1–5pm Mon–Fri. 🖼
From the port area, bulevard Pridunavski rises to a bluff above the Danube. Among the handsome villas on the landward side is the Zahari Stoyanov Museum, devoted to the revolutionary who took part in the April Rising and who wrote a stirring firsthand account of the event. With photographs, muskets, revolutionary banners and some of Stoyanov's personal belongings, the museum documents Bulgaria's struggle for liberation.

⛪ Kaliopa House
ul. Tsar Ferdinand 39. *Tel* (082) 820 997. ◻ 9am–noon, 1–5pm Mon–Fri. 🖼
A little way northeast of the Zahari Stoyanov Museum is the 19th-century villa once inhabited by Maria "Kaliopa"

Iconostasis with Muscovite icons, in the Church of Sveta Troitsa

For hotels and restaurants in this region see pp226–8 and pp242–3

An opulently furnished room at Kaliopa House

Kalitsch, wife of the Prussian consul. It is now home to the Museum of Urban Lifestyles.

Lavishly decorated by Kalitsch and a succession of subsequent owners, the house is a perfect example of how Ruse's upper classes lived prior to World War I. A fresco depicting Cupid and Psyche dominates the stairwell, while the upstairs rooms have stuccoed ceilings, hand-painted wall decorations and opulent furnishings.

🏛 Transport Museum

ul. Bratya Obretenovi 1. 🕐 *9am–noon, 1–5pm Mon–Fri.* 📷
Bulevard Pridunavski continues northeast along the riverfront towards the Ruse Transport Museum. Here Ruse's railway heritage is celebrated with a

display of historic locomotives. One of Midhat Pasha's most important initiatives was the construction of a railway line from Ruse to Varna (from where steamships sailed to Istanbul), thus opening up Ruse to international investment. Among the museum's exhibits is an opulently furnished carriage built for Empress Eugenie of France, who travelled through Ruse on her way to attend the opening of the Suez Canal in 1869.

🚇 Pantheon of National Revival Heroes

Park na Vûzrozhdentsite.
South of the Transport Museum lie two large parks, oases of peaceful green space. Park na Vûzrozhdentsite (Park of the Men of the Revival) is dotted with small mausolea commemorating those who fought for independence in the 19th century. Its main feature is the Pantheon of National Revival Heroes, a concrete ziggurat with a gilt dome. Inside, an eternal flame burns in memory

VISITORS' CHECKLIST

330 km (200 miles) NE from Sofia.
Map *D2.* 🚊 *154,556.* 🚉 *from Sofia, Pleven, Varna.* 🚌 *from Sofia.* 🎻 *March Music (classical).*

of those who fell in the struggle for freedom. There are also symbolic statues and tombs of guerrilla leaders and of Bulgarian volunteers who fought in the Russo-Turkish War. Because it was built over one of the city's oldest cemeteries, the Pantheon has aroused controversy. In 2001 the site was symbolically re-Christianized, when a cross was added to the Pantheon's dome.

Pantheon of National Revival Heroes, in Park na Vûzrozhdentsite

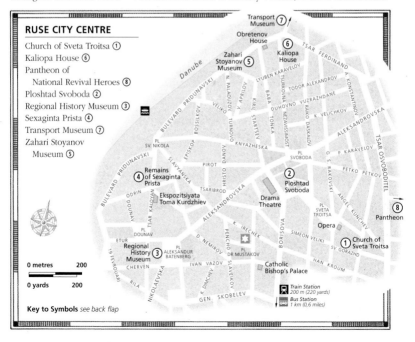

RUSE CITY CENTRE

Church of Sveta Troitsa ①
Kaliopa House ⑥
Pantheon of
    National Revival Heroes ⑧
Ploshtad Svoboda ②
Regional History Museum ③
Sexaginta Prista ④
Transport Museum ⑦
Zahari Stoyanov
    Museum ⑤

0 metres   200
0 yards   200

Key to Symbols *see back flap*

Rusenski Lom Tour ⑭

South of Ruse, the Rusenski Lom river winds its way through a dramatic series of çanyons. This unique and unspoiled natural environment is home to tortoises, lizards and snakes, eagles, buzzards and a few Egyptian vultures. The inaccessible nature of the valley made it popular with medieval hermits, who established monasteries in the caves, decorating them with sumptuous frescoes. Further up the valley at Cherven, medieval Bulgarian rulers built a magnificent cliff-top city, whose crumbling ruins are as dramatic as any in the country.

TIPS FOR DRIVERS

Map D2–E2.
Length: 40 km (25 miles).
Starting point: Ruse. Follow the main highway to Sofia as far as the city outskirts then take the turn-off to Basarbovo.
Stopping-off places: There is a restaurant and a couple of simple cafés in the village of Ivanovo. The parking lot at the entrance to the Ivanovo Rock Monasteries is the starting point for some relaxing riverside walks.

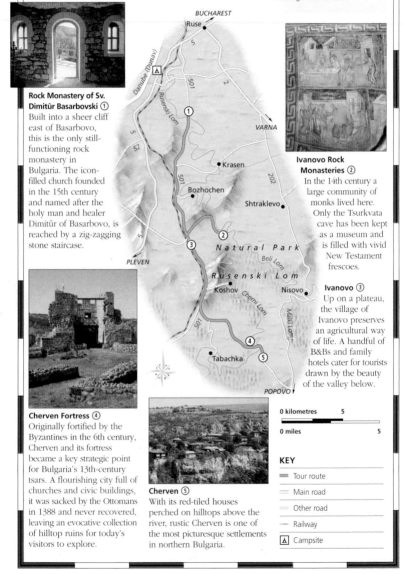

Rock Monastery of Sv. Dimitûr Basarbovski ①
Built into a sheer cliff east of Basarbovo, this is the only still-functioning rock monastery in Bulgaria. The icon-filled church founded in the 15th century and named after the holy man and healer Dimitûr of Basarbovo, is reached by a zig-zagging stone staircase.

Ivanovo Rock Monasteries ②
In the 14th century a large community of monks lived here. Only the Tsurkvata cave has been kept as a museum and is filled with vivid New Testament frescoes.

Ivanovo ③
Up on a plateau, the village of Ivanovo preserves an agricultural way of life. A handful of B&Bs and family hotels cater for tourists drawn by the beauty of the valley below.

Cherven Fortress ④
Originally fortified by the Byzantines in the 6th century, Cherven and its fortress became a key strategic point for Bulgaria's 13th-century tsars. A flourishing city full of churches and civic buildings, it was sacked by the Ottomans in 1388 and never recovered, leaving an evocative collection of hilltop ruins for today's visitors to explore.

Cherven ⑤
With its red-tiled houses perched on hilltops above the river, rustic Cherven is one of the most picturesque settlements in northern Bulgaria.

KEY

━━ Tour route
══ Main road
── Other road
── Railway
▲ Campsite

0 kilometres   5
0 miles   5

Mound of Ginina Mogila, most important of the Thracian tombs outside the village of Sveshtari

Sveshtari ⑮

Свещари

95 km (59 miles) SE of Ruse.
Map E2. 🚌 from Isperih. 🚗 with
driver, or hire a car.

The large number of Thracian
burial mounds around the
village of Sveshtari suggests
that the area was a major civic
and religious centre before the
Roman conquest. The largest
cluster of burial mounds
(mogili) are located just west
of the village, in an area that
is now the Sboryanovo History
and Archaeology Reserve. Visits
to the mounds are arranged
through the **Sveshtari Mogili
Information Centre** at the
entrance to the reserve.

There are 26 burial mounds
in all. Ginina Mogila, a tomb of
the 3rd-century BC excavated
in 1982 and now a UNESCO
World Heritage Site is the most
famous, and most important in
archaeological terms. Beyond
the ornately carved portal at
its entrance, a tunnel-like
passageway leads to the burial
chamber of a Thracian noble
and his wife. Ten caryatid-like
female figures, which may
represent an archetypal mother
goddess, line the walls. A
mural just below the barrel-
vaulted ceiling depicts the
deceased on horseback, being
presented with a wreath and
other gifts by a goddess and
her servants. On either side of
this main chamber are two
smaller chambers in which the
skeletons of ritually slaughtered
horses were found. Two of the
other tombs nearby are as
impressive in their construction,
but not as richly decorated.

Just beyond the tombs, a
path descends for 2 km (1¼
miles) towards Pette Pûrsta, a

natural spring at the bottom
of a cliff. The spring seems to
have been sacred to local
people since Neolithic times.

Beside the spring is **Demir
Baba Tekke**, the shrine of a
16th-century Muslim holy
man. Set beneath
cliffs, it consists of
a domed chamber
containing a stone
sarcophagus about
4 m (13 ft) long.
Demir Baba, a
semi-legendary
figure, is still
highly revered
by the mixed
Muslim-Christian
community around Sveshtari.
As a place of pilgrimage, the
tekke is particularly popular
among the Aliani, a local
community of Muslims whose
forebears came from Iran and
Azerbaijan. Aliani regularly
come to pray at Demir Baba's
shrine or to tie coloured
cloths to its window-frames to
bring them good luck.

A short distance beyond the
Pette Pûrsta locality are the
remains of a fortified city

**Entrance to Ginina Mogila,
in the side of the mound**

dating from the 3rd century
BC. It is thought to be the
capital of the Getae, who were
a strong Thracian tribe c. 5th
century BC. The Greek
historian Thucydides men-
tions the Getae in connection
with their prowess
in horsemanship.
This provides an
interesting link
with the horses in
Ginina Mogila,
which were
almost certainly
slaughtered to
provide the dead
with mounts in
the afterlife. Both
the accounts of Greek
historians and artifacts
recently discovered in the
tombs around Sveshtari have
thrown light on the Getae's
religious beliefs and rituals.

🏛 **Sveshtari Mogili
Information Centre**
1 km (¾ mile) W of Sveshtari.
Tel (08335) 279. ⏱ Mar–Nov:
9:30am–4:30pm Wed–Sun. 🎫 📷

🏛 **Demir Baba Tekke**
3 km (2 miles) W of Sveshtari.

Burial chamber inside Ginina Mogila, with stone couch and female figures

Shadirvan (fountain) in the Tombul Mosque courtyard, Shumen ▷

Lakeland and reed beds at Sreburna Nature Reserve

Sreburna Nature Reserve ⑯
резерват "Сребърна"

17 km (11 miles) W of Silistra.
Map F1. 🚌 *from Silistra.*

One of Bulgaria's richest wild-fowl habitats, this expanse of pristine wetland is a UNESCO Biosphere Reserve. At its centre is Lake Sreburna, a shallow stretch of fresh water cut off from the Danube by a narrow spit of sand and marshland.

Surrounded by reeds and rushes, and filled with frogs and insects, the lake makes an ideal feeding ground for a multitude of birds, many species of which are rarely seen elsewhere in Bulgaria. While it has a permanent population of several species of ducks and herons, Sreburna also attracts large numbers of cormorants, spoonbills and Dalmatian pelicans during the spring nesting season. So as not to disturb the birds, access to the lakeshore is restricted, but the **Natural History Museum** on the western side of the lake has a viewing terrace.

🏛 **Natural History Museum**
Tel (08515) 530. ◷ 9am–noon, 2–6pm daily. 📷

Silistra ⑰
Силистра

122 km (76 miles) NE of Ruse. **Map** F1. 🚶 *39,107.* 🚌 *from Sofia & Ruse.*

The easternmost of Bulgaria's ports on the Danube, Silistra has been important since the mid-1st century AD, when

Emperor Claudius made it the base of the 11th Legion. Under Byzantine rule, Silistra became an episcopal see and in the Middle Ages it served as the Bulgarian kings' foremost military base on the lower Danube.

While a scattering of Byzantine and medieval ruins can be seen in Silistra's riverside park, an overview of the city's past is provided by the **Archaeological Museum**, whose collection includes some fine Roman tombstones and a 1st-century stone sundial with a charming depiction of Orpheus.

Medzhditabiya Fortress, on a ridge 3 km (2 miles) west of the town centre, was built by the Ottomans in the 18th century. It has huge stone walls and angular bastions giving sweeping views of the river below.

🏛 **Archaeological Museum**
ul. G.S. Rakovski 24. ◷ *8am–noon, 2–6pm Tue–Sun.* 📷

Statue of Pegasus in Silistra

Shumen ⑱
Шумен

90 km (56 miles) SW of Dobrich; 106 km (66 miles) SE of Ruse.
Map E2. 🚶 *86,841.* 🚉 *from Sofia & Varna.* 🚌 *from Ruse and Varna.*

One of northeastern Bulgaria's major urban centres, Shumen is rich in monuments associated with the medieval Bulgarian state and later Ottoman rule. Bulevard Slavyanski, a

café-lined, tree-shaded strip, runs through the town centre. In a park nearby is the **History Museum**, where finds from the medieval cities of Veliki Preslav and Pliska, and a replica of a Thracian war chariot, are displayed.

Several attractive 19th-century buildings, which are open to the public 9am–5pm weekdays, line ulitsa Tsar Osvoboditel, which lies parallel to bulevard Slavyanski. Among the scattering of interesting small museums in this part of town is the House of Pancho Vladigerov (1899–1978), devoted to the life of Bulgaria's leading symphonic composer. Nearby, the Lajos Kossuth House-Museum honours the famous Hungarian nationalist leader who briefly made his home in Shumen in 1849. Also nearby is the Panaiot Volov Memorial House, family home of one of the leaders of the ill-fated April Rising of 1876.

To the west of the town centre are two reminders of the Ottoman era. One is the Bezisten, an oblong, stone-built market hall where traders from Dubrovnik set out their stalls. The other is the huge **Tombul Mosque**, crowned by a huge dome. This masterpiece of Ottoman architecture is the largest functioning mosque in the country. It was built in 1744, and the interior is decorated with wall paintings in which plant motifs are entwined with lines from the Koran written in elegant Kufic script. In the west wing of the mosque is a Koranic school, with a beautiful arcaded courtyard in the centre of which is a canopied fountain for ritual washing.

Dominating the Ilchov bair ridge immediately south of the town centre (accessible via a steep flight of steps) is the **Monument to the Creators of the Bulgarian State**. This was erected in 1981 to mark the 1,300th anniversary of Bulgar Khan Asparuh's arrival in the Balkans *(see p42)*. Its central tower is adorned with reliefs of Asparuh and his successors. An audiovisual display describes the glories of the medieval kingdom of Bulgaria.

Crowning a hill about 3 km (2 miles) west of the town centre is **Shumen Fortress** (Shumenska krepost). This defensive construction was a major component of the ring of castles built to defend Pliska and Preslav, capitals of the First Bulgarian Kingdom. The outer walls have been partially rebuilt, and give an idea of what the fortress looked like in the 14th century. Visitors can wander the tight grid of medieval streets within.

🏛 **History Museum**
bul. Slavyanski 15. **Tel** *(054) 063 429.* ⬜ *9am–5pm Mon–Fri.* 🖼

🅒 **Tombul Mosque**
ul. Doiran. ⬜ *9am–6pm daily.* 🖼

🏛 **Monument to the Creators of the Bulgarian State**
Ilchov bair. ⬜ *8:30am–5pm daily.* 🖼

♣ **Shumen Fortress**
⬜ *8:30am–5pm daily* 🖼

Madara ⑲
Мадара

12 km (7 miles) E of Shumen. **Map** F2. 🚶 *1, 415.* 🚌 *from Shumen.*

With sheer cliffs towering above it, the village of Madara is one of the most compelling historical locations in Bulgaria. Central to the site's mystique is the Madara Horseman, an 8th- or 9th-century relief carved into the rockface just above the village.

The courtyard, with central fountain, at Tombul Mosque, in Shumen

It depicts a king on horseback, accompanied by a hunting dog, striking a lion with his spear. Inscriptions in Greek beside and below the relief refer to the military campaigns of three Bulgar Khans – Tervel, Krumesis and Omurtag. Both a statement of dynastic power and a tribute to the gods of hunting and horsemanship, it is a powerful and charismatic piece of sculpture.

To its right, a path leads to the Cave of the Nymphs, an atmospheric limestone cavern with moss and trickling water, used as a shrine by Thracians in the 4th century BC. To the left of the horseman, a steep rock-cut stairway leads to the top of the cliff and out onto a plateau, where the scant ruins of an 8th-century Bulgar fortress can be explored.

Veliki Preslav ⑳
Велики Преслав

20 km (12 miles) SW of Shumen. **Map** E2. 🚶 *10, 645.* 🚌 *from Shumen.*

Lying immediately south of the modern town of Preslav, the old city of Veliki Preslav (Great Preslav) was the capital of Bulgaria from 893 to 969. It emerged as Bulgaria's spiritual centre soon after the country's conversion to Christianity in 865. Tsar Boris I retired to a monastery here in 889, and his son Simeon probably trained as a monk here. Veliki Preslav's days as state capital ended when Prince Svyatoslav of Kiev sacked it in 969.

The ruins of Veliki Preslav include two rings of fortifications built with huge blocks of stone. Inside are traces of civic buildings, a palace complex and a rotunda known as the Golden Church because of the gold-plated dome that once crowned it. An **Archaeological Museum** at the northern end of the site has a rich collection of medieval pottery and coins, and some delicate gold jewellery from the grave of a medieval noblewoman.

🏛 **Archaeological Museum**
Veliki Preslav. ⬜ *9am–5pm daily.* 🖼

The Madara Horseman, an ancient relief carved in rock above Madara

BLACK SEA COAST

Golden sandy beaches with clear blue sea and hot summers with cloudless skies are the Black Sea coast's greatest attractions. Away from its resorts, which are crowded with visitors at the height of the season, lie stretches of wild coastline, small fishing villages and nature reserves that attract many migratory birds.

Sunny Beach, Golden Sands and Albena are the Black Sea coast's three major resorts. It is to these that the vast majority of summer visitors come. The coast's smaller resorts, such as Sveti Konstantin and Rusalka, cater for those in search of quieter, smaller-scale, family-oriented facilities.

In recent years, traditional fishing and farming towns along the coast have begun to exploit the possibilities offered by their own glorious stretches of sand. Here, hotels and apartment blocks have sprung up with startling alacrity, and tourism now accounts for much of the region's revenue. Although many of these newly built hotels are brash, large-scale commercial concerns, there are also smaller, family-run establishments. These usually offer a friendlier alternative to the large resorts.

In ancient times, the Black Sea Coast was a thriving hub of trade. Originally populated by sophisticated Thracians, it was later colonized by Greek traders until the Romans took control of much of the coast in the 1st century BC. The coast was conquered by both the First and Second Bulgarian Kingdoms, and it is to the latter period that Nesebûr's small 13th- to 14th-century churches belong. After the cultural stagnation of centuries of Ottoman rule, the National Revival of the mid-19th century inspired the construction of the picturesque half-timbered houses in Sozopol and Nesebûr.

Today, the region is still in a period of transition. Construction continues apace and, with massive investment in tourist facilities and infrastructure, the Black Sea coast seems set to maintain its popularity in the future.

The beach at Golden Sands, one of the largest and most popular resorts on the Black Sea coast

◁ Entrance to the Arabella restaurant, in a sailing ship on the beach at the resort of Albena

Exploring the Black Sea Coast

With long sandy beaches and a pleasant climate, Bulgaria's Black Sea coast is the country's main holiday region. Major resorts include Albena, Golden Sands, Varna and Sunny Beach. Away from these centres, the coastline is much less developed. To the north, it is wild and rocky, while to the south lies the wilderness of Strandzha Nature Park. The coast is also a stopping place for migrating birds, thousands of which rest or overwinter in the wetlands around Durankûlak, Pomorie and Burgas. Settled by Greek traders in the 6th century BC, the coast has a rich history. A glimpse of its fascinating past is revealed at the Archaeological Museum in Varna, and in the ancient towns of Kaliakra, Nesebûr and Sozopol, now popular holiday resorts.

Ceiling painting at the Church of Sveti Atanas in Varna

Steep cliffs on the headland at Cape Emona, between Obzor and Sunny Beach

SIGHTS AT A GLANCE

Tervel ㉑
Karapelit
Benkowski
Valtchi Dol
Sofia
Suvoro
Devny
Provadia
Dalgopol
Veselinovo
Tsonevo Lake
Varbicka Planina Bilka
Kamchiya Lake
Lyulyakovo
Kamchiys
Eminska
Beronovo
Iliica 684 m
Prosenik
Sungurlare
Lozarevo
Aytos
Sofia
Kableshko
Venets
Karnobat
Vetren
Kameno
Asparuhovo
BURGAS ⑯
Rusokastro
Burgas Lake
Mandra La
Zagortsi
Sredets
Karatepe
Fakiyska R.
Bos
Malko Tarnovo
Kirklareli

SEE ALSO
- *Where to Stay* pp228–9
- *Where to Eat* pp243–5

Beach at Golden Sands, one of Bulgaria's most popular resorts

Loznica
Krushari
Constanta
Obrudzba
General Toshevo
Spasovo
Durankulashko Lake
Constanta
BRICH ②
Senokos
Vranino
Shabla ③
NORTHERN BLACK SEA COAST TOUR
BALCHIK ⑥ ⑤ **KAVARNA**
④ **KALIAKRA**
⑦ **ALBENA**
ONE REST
Aksakovo
⑧ **GOLDEN SANDS**
⑨ **SVETI KONSTANTIN**
① **VARNA**
Beloslav
Galata Cape
ndel
Kamchiya
⑪ **KAMCHIYA NATURE RESERVE**
Dolni Chiflik
Staro Oryahovo
lanina
Byala
⑫ **OBZOR**
Banya
⑬ **SUNNY BEACH** *Emine Cape*
⑭ **NESEBUR**
eloy
⑮ **POMORIE**
B L A C K
S E A
⑰ **SOZOPOL**
OPOTAMO RIVER
⑱ *Malsen Nos Cape*
⑲ **PRIMORSKO**
⑳ **LOZENETS**
㉑ **TSAREVO**
STRANDZHA NATURE PARK TOUR
㉒ **AHTOPOL**
㉓ **SINEMORETS**
Rezovska R.
Rezovo
㉔

0 kilometres 25

0 miles 25

KEY

Motorway

Major road

Secondary road

Other road

Railway

International border

△ Peak

GETTING AROUND

Whether you reach the Black Sea coast by plane, train, bus or car, your starting point will be Burgas or Varna. Burgas is the gateway to Sunny Beach, Nesebûr, Sozopol and the Strandzha region, while from Varna a road leads north to Golden Sands, Albena, Balchik and beyond. The region has an extensive bus network, with frequent services between and around Burgas and Varna. Further north and south, however, bus services are progressively sparser and less frequent. In summer, these outlying regions are served by minibuses, although they run according to demand rather than to a set timetable. Taxis are ubiquitous, and all large towns and resorts have car hire agencies.

Wooden house in Sozopol's historic district, on the peninsula

Varna ❶

Варна

With wide pedestrianized boulevards, shady Sea Gardens, and a sandy beach, Varna has the tranquil air of a coastal resort, despite its being a centre of commerce and Bulgaria's third-largest city. As Varna's remarkable ancient necropolis shows, the city's history goes back to the 5th millennium BC. In the 6th century BC, it was settled by Greeks. The thriving colony fell to the Romans in the 1st century BC, but retained its role as one of the Black Sea's key ports. Varna became part of Bulgaria in the 8th century. It was taken by the Ottomans in 1393, but after the Liberation of 1878 it rapidly grew to become the bustling modern city, port and resort that it is today.

🏛 **Archaeological Museum**

bul. Maria Luisa 41. **Tel** (052) 681 011. ⬜ 10am–5pm Tue–Sun.

Over 100,000 ancient artifacts discovered in and around Varna fill this fascinating museum. It was founded in 1888 by the Czech archaeologist Karel Skorpil, who settled in Varna after the Liberation and pioneered the exploration of Bulgaria's ancient past.

The collection fills 40 rooms on two floors. The most intriguing section is that devoted to Varna's necropolis, west of the modern city. It was in use from 4400 to 4200 BC, and was discovered in 1972. Many of the 294 graves that were excavated contained some stunning gold objects, among which were some of the earliest examples of gold jewellery ever found. No fewer than 850 pieces, including gold animal figures, were found in a single grave. Visitors can also see the replica of a grave in which the body, of a powerful leader or a priest, was covered with gold items, including a penis sheath, and surrounded with copper and flint tools.

Another important exhibit is the gold jewellery of a Thracian noblewoman. Dating from the Hellenistic period (4th–1st century BC), it consists of a bull's-head pendant and two beautifully detailed earrings that are miniature statuettes of Nike, goddess of victory. Among the many

Archaeological Museum exhibit

Roman artifacts in the collection is a large array of marble tombstones carved with scenes of funeral banquets.

The museum's upper floor is devoted to the medieval period. Here visitors can see a fine display of pottery, weaponry, jewellery and religious art, including some superb altarpieces with silver motifs, and a collection of radiant icons of the 16th to the 19th centuries.

🛐 **Cathedral of the Assumption**

pl. Mitropolitska Simeon. **Tel** (052) 613 005. ⬜ 7:30am–7pm daily. 🕊 8:30am daily, also 6pm Sat.

The second-largest place of Christian worship in Bulgaria after the Alexander Nevski Memorial Church in Sofia (see pp72–3), the cathedral was built to commemorate the Russian soldiers who died in the fight for liberation from Ottoman rule. Its construction was funded by Varna's citizens, and it was

completed in 1886. Designed by the Russian architect Maas, with golden onion domes, the cathedral is similar to St Petersburg's cathedral. Its surprisingly compact interior is covered with over-life-size murals painted under the supervision of another Russian, Professor Rostovtsev, in 1949. Master craftsmen from Debur, in Macedonia, carved the splendid bishop's throne, which features a pair of winged panthers, and created the vast iconostasis in 1912. Hearing the cathedral's

0 metres 400

0 yards 400

Key to Symbols see back flap

Iconostasis, made by Macedonian craftsmen, Cathedral of the Assumption

male-voice choir, which sings at weekend services, is a memorable experience.

🏛 Ethnographic Museum
ul. Panagyurishte 22. **Tel** (052) 630 588. ⬜ 10am–5pm Tue–Sun. 📷 🚻

In an imposing 19th-century National Revival-style house surrounded by high stone walls, this is one of Bulgaria's largest ethnographic museums. The ground floor is dedicated to farming, with displays of

tools used for sowing, harvesting and threshing, and beekeeping and viniculture.

In the rooms upstairs, traditional costumes are on display. Among them are the single-colour costumes that were predominant in the Varna region until settlers introduced multicoloured outfits. This section includes a wedding scene of costumed dummies, with the bride in a wooden wedding sled, men in black hats, and the village matchmaker, who holds a black cockerel.

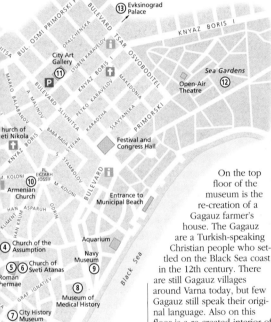

On the top floor of the museum is the re-creation of a Gagauz farmer's house. The Gagauz are a Turkish-speaking Christian people who settled on the Black Sea coast in the 12th century. There are still Gagauz villages around Varna today, but few Gagauz still speak their original language. Also on this floor is a re-created interior of the house of a wealthy early 20th-century family, furnished in a combination of Oriental and European styles.

🔒 Church of the Assumption
ul. Han Krum 19. **Tel** (052) 633 925. ⬜ 7:30am–6pm daily. ✝ 10am Sun. This tiny church is known to local people as the Little Virgin (*Malka Bogoroditsa*). It was built in 1602, and is set below ground level, in accordance with the requirement that churches should be no higher than a man on horseback, lest they outshine mosques. The church's attractive wooden bell tower was added after the Liberation.

SIGHTS AT A GLANCE

VISITORS' CHECKLIST

380 km (235 miles) E of Sofia.
Map G2. 🚶 326,200. ✈ ✕
🚉🚌🚊Ⓜ🚗🚻 ℹ pl. Musala
(052-654 519). 🏨 daily. 🎭
Varnensko Lyato (Varna Summer;
Jul–Sep). **www**.varna-bg.com
www.mitropolia-varna.org

The church contains Varna's oldest icon, a 13th-century depiction of the Virgin, whose silver plating has been worn smooth by the lips of believers who venerated and prayed to her. The elaborate iconostasis was carved by the Macedonian craftsmen who provided the woodwork for the Cathedral of the Assumption.

Part of the Roman Thermae, a baths complex of the 2nd–4th centuries AD

⛎ Roman Thermae
ul. Han Krum. ⬜ 10am–5pm Tue–Sun. 📷
A monument to the ingenuity of Roman architects, this huge public baths complex covers over 7,000 sq m (75,000 sq ft). It was built in the 2nd century AD for what was then the Roman city of Odessos.

Although in ruins, enough of the complex survives to give an idea of Roman bathing habits. Having disrobed in the *apodyteria* (dressing rooms), visitors would pass through to the *frigidarium* (cold pool), *tepidarium* (warm pool), and *caldarium* (hot pool), then repeat the process. Warm air circulated in cavities between the walls and under the floors, and doorways were staggered so as to prevent cold draughts. The cost of the baths' upkeep is thought to have caused their decline in the 3rd–4th centuries.

🔒 Church of Sveti Atanas

ul. Graf Ignatiev 19. *Tel (052) 639 711.* 🕐 *summer: 7:30am–6pm daily; winter 8am–5pm daily.* ✝ *9am Sun.*

Peaceful gardens next to the Roman Thermae *(see p199)* are the setting of this National Revival church. The focal point of the interior is a dramatic iconostasis that is completely covered with intricately carved figures and motifs. It was made in the 19th century by master woodcarvers from Tryavna, who also made the richly decorated bishop's throne and pulpit. Originally built in the late 17th century, the church was destroyed by fire in 1836 and was rebuilt in 1838.

🏛 City History Museum

ul. 8 Noemvri 3. *Tel (052) 632 677.* 🕐 *10am–5pm Tue–Sun.* 📷

This building, constructed in 1851 as the Belgian Consulate, is one of Varna's oldest surviving houses. The museum that it now accommodates traces the history of Varna from the late 18th century, when it was a neglected coastal town, to the mid-20th, when it had become a major port and popular seaside resort.

Some of the most interesting exhibits here are the tools and implements used by Varna's craftsmen and tradesmen of the past. Black and white photographs provide other historical documentation. Upstairs are the uniforms and military paraphernalia of Varna's citizens who fought in the Serbo-Bulgarian War, Balkan Wars, and both world wars.

Printing press at the City History Museum, Varna

🏛 Museum of Medical History

ul. Paraskeva Nikolao 7. *Tel (052) 639 729.* 🕐 *10am–4pm Mon–Fri.* 📷

The somewhat gruesome collection of the Museum of Medical History occupies a building that was once Varna's first hospital, opened in 1869. An array of 10th-century skulls and skeletons demonstrate mysterious practices such as deliberate deformation of the skull by binding it, and trepanation (the practice of drilling holes in the skull).

Upstairs is an exhibition of folk medicine, the only kind of medical treatment that was available under Ottoman rule. Surgical instruments of the last century are displayed alongside antique examination chairs and the re-creation of a 19th-century pharmacy.

🏛 Navy Museum

bul. Primorski 2. *Tel (052) 632 018.* 🕐 *10am–5:30pm Mon–Fri.* 📷

The prize exhibit here is the *Druzhki (Intrepid)*, a torpedo boat displayed outside the museum. In 1912, during the First Balkan War, the *Druzhki* secured the Bulgarian navy's only victory in the conflict when it sank a large Turkish cruise ship, the *Hamidie*. Inside the museum are exhibits relating to navigation on the Black Sea in ancient times, starting in the 6th century BC. There are also models of mines and battleships, and photographs of great naval figures.

The yard behind the museum is filled with an assortment of helicopters, artillery cannon and boats, and a working submarine periscope, through which visitors can admire views of Varna Bay.

Nave and main altar at the Armenian Church, Varna

🔒 Armenian Church

ul. Han Asparuh 15. *Tel (052) 619 382.* 🕐 *8am–6pm daily.* ✝ *10:30am Sun.*

Built in 1842, this light, airy church was renovated in 2003. Like most Armenian churches, the interior is quite plain, with no iconostasis, murals or icons. However, the walls are hung with naïve paintings of St Sargis, to whom the church is dedicated, and scenes from the life of Christ. Recordings of Armenian chanting, which play throughout the day, create a magical atmosphere.

A monument commemorates Ottoman atrocities against the Armenians in 1894 when an estimated 300,000 were killed. Known as the "Great Massacres", they were overshadowed by the 1915 genocide which claimed over 1.5 million lives.

🏛 City Art Gallery

ul. Petko Karavelov 1. *Tel (052) 612 363.* 🕐 *10am–6pm Tue–Sun.* 📷

This collection concentrates on the development of Bulgarian painting since the early 20th century. Several works by Vladimir Dimitrov (1882–1960) are on display, and there are also portraits by the 17th-century Flemish painter Anselmus von Hulme. The gallery also hosts temporary exhibitions of Bulgarian and international art. The main hall is often used as a venue for concerts and poetry readings.

The torpedo boat *Druzhki* at the entrance of the Navy Museum in Varna

Varna's popular Sea Gardens, above the town's long sandy beach

🌴 Sea Gardens

Aquarium *Tel (052) 632 064.*
🕐 *9am–8pm daily.* 📷 ✓
www.varna-bg.com
Planetarium *Tel (052) 684 441.*
✓ *Shows at 5pm and 7pm daily;
pre-booked groups only.* 📷
Zoo 🕐 *8am–8pm daily.* 📷 ♿
Dolphinarium *Tel (052) 302 199.*
🕐 *shows at 11am, 2pm, 3:30pm.*
📷 ✓ 📖 ✓ **www**.varna-bg.com
Terrarium *Tel (052) 302 571.*
🕐 *9am– 9pm daily.* 📷

The Sea Gardens' (Morskata
Gradina) first trees were
planted in 1862. The Czech
landscape architect Anton
Novak spent much of his life
laying out this urban park,
with trees and plants from
Bulgaria and from around the
Mediterranean. With neat
flowerbeds and shaded paths,
the gardens provide welcome
respite from the sweltering
summer heat.

Closest to the centre of the
gardens is the ivy-covered
Aquarium, whose graceful pair
of stingrays are the stars of a
somewhat neglected collection.
Further along is the recently
renovated **Planetarium**, which
offers daily shows in various
languages. To reach the **Zoo** it
is best to take the road train
that winds its way through the
park on a 2-km (1-mile) circuit.
The zoo's inhabitants range
from camels and deer to
emus and pelicans. Although
they seem content enough,
they are housed in fairly
cramped concrete quarters.
Nearby is the **Dolphinarium**,
where dolphins entertain
large audiences with games of
basketball and a variety of

tricks. A little way beyond is
the **Terrarium**, with a spine-
tingling collection of black
widow spiders and venomous
snakes, and a crocodile,
among other reptiles.

Varna's long sandy beach
stretches out below the Sea
Gardens. As it is lined with
outdoor restaurants, cafés and
bars, it is not particularly peaceful but it is ideal for sybaritic
days of swimming, sunbathing, eating and drinking. After
dark, the beach is one of the
Black Sea's liveliest spots,
with clubs pumping out loud
music until the small hours.

🏛 Evksinograd Palace

8 km (5 miles) north of central Varna.
Tel (052) 393 100. 🕐 *9am–3pm
daily, only for pre-booked groups of
at least 10.*

The spectacular Evksinograd
Palace and its beautiful gardens
are located in Varna's northern suburbs, on the main road
out of the city. The palace
grounds also incorporate the
Evksinograd winery, which
produces some of Bulgaria's
finest wines and *rakias*.

This chateau-like palace was
built for Prince Aleksandûr
Batenberg I *(see p47)* and was
completed in 1886. It was
designed by the Viennese
architect Rumpelmeyer and
its gardens were laid out by
French landscape designers
in the late 19th century.

The palace was the summer
residence of Bulgarian royalty
until the Communists came to
power in 1944. It then became
the holiday home of the party
élite. It is still state property.

Dobrich ❷
Добрич

93 km (60 miles) SE of Silistra,
55 km (34 miles) NW of Varna.
Map F2. 👥 *93,614.* 🚌 *from
Varna or Sofia.*

Dobrich lies at the centre of a
rich agricultural region that is
known as Bulgaria's bread-
basket. The largely modern
town centre encloses an open-
air ethnographic complex,
Stariya Dobrich (Old Dobrich).
It stands on the site of an
Ottoman bazaar and contains
about 30 workshops, where
artisans practise traditional
crafts, and a café that serves
Turkish coffee in copper pots,
accompanied by a spoonful
of *sladko* (cherry jam).

The small **Archaeological
Museum** in the complex contains gold jewellery from a
necropolis of the 5th millennium BC. The **Ethnographhic
Museum** has displays of folk
costumes and traditional
embroidery, and a traditional
cottage garden.

Dobrich's **Art Gallery** con-
tains paintings by many major
Bulgarian painters, including
Vladimir Dimitrov-Maistor and
Zlatyu Boyadzhiev.

🏛 Archaeological Museum
Stariya Dobrich. 🕐 *8am–noon,
1–5pm Mon–Fri.* 📷
🏛 Ethnographic Museum
bul. 25 Septemvri. 🕐 *9am–noon,
2–6pm daily.* 📷
🏛 Art Gallery
bul. Bulgariya. 🕐 *9am–noon,
1–5pm Mon–Fri.* 📷

Fertility, a painting by Keazim
Issinov at the Art Gallery in Dobrich

Northern Black Sea Coast Tour ❸

Thanks to its rocky shore and short summer, the northern Black Sea coast has escaped intensive development. In this flat landscape, fields of sunflowers and wheat stretch for miles in every direction. The coast is punctuated with sleepy villages, whose inhabitants still subsist from small-scale fishing and farming. Dramatic cliffs line the wide sandy beaches of Krapets. This part of the Black Sea coast is also rich in bird and plant life, and is littered with archaeological remains.

TIPS FOR DRIVERS

Map G2.
Length of route: approximately 40 km (25 miles).
Stopping-off points: There are hotels, guesthouses, campsites, restaurants and cafés along the route, but most especially in Kavarna, Shabla and Krapets.
Place of further interest: The Archaeological Park on an island in Durankulak Lake has remains of prehistoric habitation.

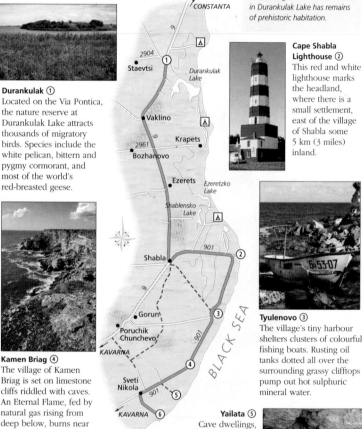

Cape Shabla Lighthouse ②
This red and white lighthouse marks the headland, where there is a small settlement, east of the village of Shabla some 5 km (3 miles) inland.

Durankulak ①
Located on the Via Pontica, the nature reserve at Durankulak Lake attracts thousands of migratory birds. Species include the white pelican, bittern and pygmy cormorant, and most of the world's red-breasted geese.

Tyulenovo ③
The village's tiny harbour shelters clusters of colourful fishing boats. Rusting oil tanks dotted all over the surrounding grassy clifftops pump out hot sulphuric mineral water.

Kamen Briag ④
The village of Kamen Briag is set on limestone cliffs riddled with caves. An Eternal Flame, fed by natural gas rising from deep below, burns near memorials to people who have fallen from the cliffs.

Yailata ⑤
Cave dwellings, a cliffside necropolis and a ruined medieval fortress are preserved in the archaeological park here. The park is also home to many plants, birds and snakes.

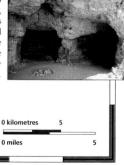

Rusalka ⑥
The Holiday Village here is a tranquil and isolated resort. It's much quieter than those further south and caters for all ages.

KEY

▬▬	Tour route
═══	Main road
═══	Other road
- -	Trail
🅰	Campsite

0 kilometres   5

0 miles   5

For hotels and restaurants in this region see pp228–9 and pp243–5

Kaliakra ❹
Калиакра

56 km (35 miles) from Dobrich.
Map G2. 🚌 🚐 ⬜ 10am–7pm
daily. 🎫 🍴 🔲 📷

Meaning "fine nose" in Greek, Kaliakra is a rocky promontory that extends 2 km (over 1 mile) into the sea. Locals attribute the reddish colour of its limestone cliffs to the blood of the many people who died in battles for control of this strategic point. The ruins of a grand fortress of the 4th century BC remain; it was successively held by Greeks, Romans, Bulgarians and Ottomans. According to legend, 40 maidens tied their hair together and jumped into the sea to escape a worse fate at the hands of invading Ottoman soldiers.

Ruins of the fortress at Kaliakra, subject of many legends

Kavarna ❺
Каварна

61 km (38 miles) north of Varna.
Map G2. 🏛 11,600. 🚌 🚉 🚐 ⛴
daily. **www**.kavarna.bg

Although its main street is dominated by dour Socialist-era architecture, Kavarna is a pleasant town, with lively cafés and bars. Its origins go back to the 6th century BC, when a settlement known as Bizone was founded by Greek colonists. Bizone thrived until it was flattened by an earthquake in the 1st century BC. Later rebuilt, it was ruled successively by Romans, Slavs and Ottomans.

Since the Middle Ages the town has been known as Kavarna. Liberated from Ottoman rule in 1878, the town became part of Romania in 1913, after the Balkan Wars. It was finally returned to Bulgaria in 1940.

Kavarna's **Ethnographic Museum**, in a National Revival house, features displays on the daily life of its 19th-century inhabitants. The **Art Gallery** has a collection of local seascapes and organizes exhibitions of the work of Bulgarian and international artists.

Artifacts related to sea trade in ancient times fill the **Marine Museum**, in a 15th-century hammam off the road to the seafront. Exhibits here include stone anchors, amphorae, coins and bronze figures. Immediately behind is the **History Museum**, which documents Kavarna's more recent past.

Just outside the town is the seafront district of Chirakman. Once the site of ancient Bizone, it is now Kavarna's resort zone, with restaurants, hotels and a small beach.

Statuette, Marine Museum, Kavarna

🏛 **Ethnographic Museum**
ul. Sava Ganchev 16. **Tel** (0570) 85017. ⬜ 8am–noon, 1–5pm Mon–Fri. 🎫 📷

🏛 **Art Gallery**
ul. Aheloi 1. **Tel** (0570) 84236. ⬜ 9am–noon, 1–5pm Mon–Fri. 🎫

🏛 **History Museum**
ul. Chernomorska 1. **Tel** (0570) 82150. ⬜ 8am–noon, 1–5pm Mon–Fri. 🎫

🏛 **Marine Museum**
ul. Chernomorska 1b. **Tel** (0570) 84288. ⬜ 8am–noon, 1–5pm Mon–Fri. 🎫

Balchik ❻
Балчик

43 km (27 miles) north of Varna. **Map** G2. 🏛 12,500. 🚪 ul. Primorska 6a. 🚌 Ⓜ 🚐

Because it has only a small beach, Balchik does not attract crowds of visitors, so it remains pleasantly quiet throughout

the summer. In Greek times, when it was a busy port and wine producer, Balchik was known as Dionisopolis, in honour of the god of wine. Like Kavarna, it was part of Romania between 1913 and 1940.

Balchik's small **National Revival Complex** is set in pretty gardens next to the Church of Sveti Nikolai (1866). Its centrepiece is a re-creation of the town's first Bulgarian school, established in 1848. The small collection at the **History Museum** documents Balchik's past. Just opposite is a large half-timbered old house. This is the **Ethnographic Museum**, with costumes and exhibits relating to local trades. The **Art Gallery** has an absorbing collection of 20th-century paintings and sculptures related to Balchik. They include vivid modernist depictions of the town by Svetlin Rusev (b. 1933).

Environs
About 2 km (over 1 mile) outside Balchik is the delightful seafront **Palace of Queen Marie**. It was built in 1924 by King Ferdinand of Romania as a retreat for his British-born wife Marie, one of Queen Victoria's grand-daughters. The palace gardens contain Europe's second-largest collection of cacti.

🏛 **National Revival Complex**
ul. Hristo Botev 4. **Tel** (0579) 72177. ⬜ by request at History Museum.

🏛 **Ethnographic Museum**
ul. Vitosha 3. **Tel** (0579) 72177. ⬜ 9am–6pm Mon–Sat. 🎫

🏛 **History Museum**
pl. Nezavisimost 1. **Tel** (0579) 72177. ⬜ 7:30am–6pm Mon–Sat. 🎫

🏛 **Art Gallery**
ul. Otets Paisii 4. **Tel** (0579) 74130. ⬜ 9am–noon, 1–5pm Mon–Fri. 🎫

♟ **Palace of Queen Marie**
2km (over 1 mile) west of Balchik **Tel** (0579) 72058. ⬜ summer: 8:30am–7:30pm daily. 🎫 🔲 📷

Sun and relaxation on Albena's long sandy beach

Albena ❼
Албена

34 km (21 miles) N of Varna.
Map G2. 🚌 Ⓜ 🚗
www.beachbulgaria.com

Like Golden Sands and Sunny Beach, Albena's superb beach has received the Blue Flag award for its cleanliness. It is 5 km (3 miles) long and up to 500 m (550 yds) wide, and with shallow water for some distance offshore, it is perfect for water sports *(see p253)*.

Although Albena is a major resort, its hotels are spread over extensive parkland, giving it a spacious feel. It was built in the 1970s, with a tasteful planning ethic that resulted in buildings melding with the natural environment. Largely because of this (and its cleanliness) Albena has a calmer atmosphere than its neighbour Golden Sands. Besides water sports, Albena has a horse-riding centre, and offers driving safaris to Cape Emona, 150 km (90 miles) to the south.

Environs
Just outside the dusty village of Obrochishte, about 15 km (8 miles) inland from Albena, is the 16th-century **Ak Yazula Baba Tekke**. This pentagonal monastery contains the grave of Ak Yazula Baba, a 14th-century holy man who followed the dervish path of poverty and austerity and who was venerated by local Muslims. As it is also the alleged burial place of St Athanius and Knyaz Boris I, Bulgaria's first Christian ruler, the site is popular with Christians too.

Golden Sands ❽
Златни пясъци

18 km (11 miles) N of Varna.
Map G2. 🚌 Ⓜ 🚗
www.beachbulgaria.com

Bulgaria's second-largest coastal resort after Sunny Beach, Golden Sands (Zlatni Pyasâtsi) amply lives up to its name. Wooded hills, part of the Golden Sands Nature Park, slope down towards the sea and an almost continuous line of newly built hotels. In season, parasols in uniform grid patterns dominate the crowded beach and a full range of water sports is on offer.

Golden Sands' downside is that, as at Sunny Beach, rampant development has continued unchecked for years and the infrastructure has failed to keep pace. Without noise restrictions, loud music emanates from many nightclubs in the heart of the hotel zone, making this a paradise for some and a hell for others.

Sveti Konstantin ❾
Свети Константин

9 km (5 miles) N of Varna. **Map** G2.
🚌 Ⓜ 🚗

A far smaller coastal resort than its northern neighbours, Sveti Konstantin appeals more to families in search of easily accessible facilities. The seafront has several short beaches and rocky coves backed by a woodland of oak, beech and cypress. This gives the resort a tranquil atmosphere. Several of the health complexes along the seafront have hot mineral baths and saunas, and offer therapeutic massages.

In the heart of the resort is the tiny **Monastery of SS Konstantin and Elena**. It was founded in the 17th century but was destroyed during the Russo-Turkish War of 1828–9. Two brothers from Veliko Tûrnovo *(see pp156–7)* rebuilt the monastery and, after the Liberation of 1878, it became a fashionable spot for

Environs
About 7 km (4 miles) inland from Golden Sands is **Aladzha Monastery**. The hermits who settled here in the 6th century cut dozens of cells and chambers into the limestone cliff, and evidence of Stone Age dwellers has also been discovered here. The caves are now linked by sturdy metal steps, but the monks reached them by scrambling up and down perilous ledges using the footholds that are still visible in the cliff face.

The beach at Golden Sands, one of Bulgaria's most popular resorts

Luxury health resort pool at the coastal resort of Sveti Konstantin

weekend breaks. From 1946 its popularity led to the location being developed as Bulgaria's first beach resort, and it became the prototype for Sveti Konstantin's larger neighbour, Golden Sands.

🏛 **Monastery of SS Konstantin and Elena**
Tel (052) 362 076. ⏰ 9am–6pm daily. **www**.mitropolia-varna.org

Massive tree-like pillars of the 50-million-year-old Stone Forest

Stone Forest ❿
Побитите камъни

18 km (11 miles) W of Varna, on the road to Devnya.

As its name suggests, the Stone Forest (pobiti kamûni) is a cluster of weirdly tree-like stone columns. Spread over a barren landscape, they stand in seven groups of more than 300 each. Some are as much as 6 m (20 ft) high and up to 9 m (30 ft) in circumference.

The stones are believed to be 50 million years old, and their origins have long been the subject of scientific speculation. From the numerous theories advanced by experts, it is generally agreed that they formed when separate layers of chalk merged through a layer of sand. Some scientists, however, still support the theory that they are the fossilized trees of an ancient forest.

Kamchiya Nature Reserve ⓫
резерват "Камчия"

25 km (16 miles) S of Varna. **Map** F3.

Just before it reaches the sea, the Kamchiya, eastern Bulgaria's longest river, flows through the nature reserve that takes its name. Established in 1951, the reserve is internationally recognized as a site of ornithological importance. Its densely forested marshland, known as the Longoza, is home to an abundance of rare species, including pelicans and kingfishers. Regular boat trips take tourists up and down the river.

Just outside the reserve is a long sandy beach that has so far escaped development into a resort. It is therefore almost deserted, even at the height of summer, and this may explain its popularity with nudists.

Obzor ⓬
Обзор

62 km (39 miles) S of Varna.
Map F3. 🚶 *1,970.* 🚌 🚗 ⛽
www.beachbulgaria.com

Named Heliopolis (City of the Sun) by the Greeks and later occupied by the Romans, the small town of Obzor is now a thriving, if somewhat brash, coastal resort. Broken columns from the Roman Temple of Jupiter are scattered throughout the town's leafy park, which is surrounded by open-air restaurants and cafés.

Obzor's main attraction is its great beach, in the outskirts to the north. However, as developers are rapidly expanding it, this part of Obzor currently resembles a huge building site.

Sunny Beach ⓭
Слънчев бряг

35 km (22 miles) N of Burgas.
Map F3. 🚌 🏖 🚗 Ⓜ 🚕
www.beachbulgaria.com

Established in the 1960s, Sunny Beach (Slûnchev bryag) was one of Bulgaria's first coastal resorts. It is now the country's largest, and it continues to expand in all directions. Palatial hotels, apartment blocks and Socialist-era leisure complexes stretch out behind a beautiful beach 8 km (5 miles) long.

Sunny Beach, which has Blue Flag status, is particularly popular with families and with visitors on package holidays. Besides a wide range of water sports, the resort also has a multitude of shops, bars, restaurants and nightclubs.

The Kamchiya River estuary, part of the pristine Kamchiya Nature Reserve

The mysterious rock formations of the Stone Forest, near Varna ▷

Nesebûr

Несебър

Set on a rocky peninsula, Nesebûr's beautiful old town is densely packed with historic houses and churches. The site was first settled by Thracians, who founded a town known as Mesembria. It was later taken by Greeks and then by Romans, to whom it capitulated rather than suffer destruction. In the 9th century, when Mesembria was renamed Nesebûr, the town became part of the First Bulgarian Kingdom, but it was in the 13th to 14th centuries, as a powerful city-state, that it reached its commercial and cultural zenith. Today, as a well publicized World Heritage Site, Nesebûr is popular with visitors. Because of this it tends to become very crowded in the summer season.

Bagpiper of Nesebûr

Aerial view of Nesebûr, a town whose origins go back to Thracian times

🏛 Archaeological Museum

ul. Mesembriya 2a. **Tel** (0554) 46019.
🕐 9am–6pm Mon–Fri, 9:30am–1pm, 1:30–6pm Sat–Sun. 🎫 🚻 📷

The collections laid out here provide a fascinating insight into Nesebûr's long history. The displays begin with stone anchors and decorated pottery from the Thracian period (2nd–1st millennium BC), and coins minted in Mesembria in the 5th century BC, which indicate its independence and importance after it became a Greek colony in the 6th century BC. Other exhibits from this period include delicate gold jewellery from Mesembria's necropolis and architectural elements carved with swastikas symbolizing the sun. Red glazed pottery, marble grave-stones and reliefs of Hercules and Thracian horsemen are among exhibits representing the town's Roman period.

Nesebûr's prosperity during the Middle Ages is illustrated by a display of gold coins and gold jewellery, and some fine decorative architectural elements. The collections end with an outstanding array of icons from Nesebûr's churches, some dating back to the 13th century.

🏠 Church of Christ Pantokrator

ul. Mesembriya. 🕐 9am–11pm daily. 📷

This attractive church near the centre of the old town is typical of the churches built during Nesebûr's resurgence in the 13th and 14th centuries. The building's façade features a row of blind arches built with alternating courses of stone and brick, and with decorative motifs in the form of turquoise inlay and red brick swastika motifs. Inside is an art gallery selling works by local artists.

🏠 New Metropolitan Church

ul. Ribarska. 🕐 9am–1pm, 2–6pm.
📷 🚻 📷

Popularly known as the Church of Sveti Stefan, the New Metropolitan Church was founded in the 11th century. It supplanted the Old Metropolitan Church in the 15th century and was enlarged in the 16th.

While the exterior is quite unremarkable, the interior is breathtaking. It is densely covered in 16th- to 18th-century frescoes depicting scenes from the life of the Virgin. Other notable features of the interior are the 16th-century painted iconostasis, the ornate bishop's throne, and an elaborately carved 18th-century wooden pulpit.

🏠 Church of St John Aliturgetos

ul. Ribarska. 🚻

This ruined church is set in an isolated spot overlooking the Black Sea, its east window framing stunning sea views. It was built in the 14th century and was reduced to ruins by an earthquake in 1913. Concrete pillars now support what remains of the roof. Built in stone and brick, the church has blind arches decorated with motifs, such as stars, squares and swastikas, which symbolize the sun and the continuity of life.

Façade of the Church of Christ Pantokrator, with Byzantine-style arches

Ruins of the Old Metropolitan Church, still the centrepiece of old Nesebûr

🏛 Ethnographic Museum

ul. Mesembriya. 🕙10am–1pm, 2–6pm Mon–Sat. 🎟

Occupying Muskoyanin House, the Ethnographic Museum recreates domestic life as it was lived in this fine 18th-century residence. There is also a display of traditional local costumes worn for various seasonal rituals. They include a selection of *lazarki* outfits worn by young girls to celebrate the arrival of spring.

⛪ Old Metropolitan Church

ul. Mitropolska.

Although it is in ruins, the Old Metropolitan Church (Starata Mitropoliya) is still the focal point of Nesebûr's

old town. The church, the oldest and largest in Nesebûr, was founded in the 5th century. It originally formed part of the bishop's palace, but was destroyed by Venetians in the 13th century. Only part of its walls survive. A two-tiered brick and stone arcade culminates in a large central apse that is now a popular meeting point and the venue for plays and concerts.

⛪ Church of Sveta Paraskeva

ul. Hemus. 🕙10am–10pm daily. 🎟

The Byzantine style of this 13th-century church is very similar to that of the Church of Christ Pantokrator. Green ceramics set between layers of red brick and stone decorate the façade's blind arches. The church now houses a private art gallery that sells seascapes painted by local artists.

⛪ Church of Sveti Spas

ul. Aheloi. 🕙 10am–5pm Mon–Fri, 10am–1:30pm Sat–Sun. 🎟 🎟

Like many others built during the Ottoman period, the 17th-century Church of Sveti Spas (Church of the Saviour) is set below street level. The exterior is plain, but within are colourful frescoes, most of

which show scenes from the lives of Christ and the Virgin. A curiosity of the frescoes is that some have been marked with graffiti of sailing boats. They were created by sailors praying for safety at sea. The floor also houses a Byzantine princess's gravestone.

Early 17th-century frescoes in the Church of Sveti Spas

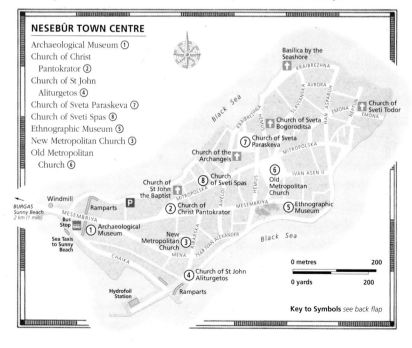

NESEBÛR TOWN CENTRE

Archaeological Museum ①
Church of Christ Pantokrator ②
Church of St John Aliturgetos ④
Church of Sveta Paraskeva ⑦
Church of Sveti Spas ⑧
Ethnographic Museum ⑤
New Metropolitan Church ③
Old Metropolitan Church ⑥

Basilica by the Seashore
KRAIBREZHNA

Church of Sveti Todor

Black Sea

Church of Sveta Bogoroditsa

Church of Sveta Paraskeva ⑦

Church of the Archangels

Old Metropolitan Church ⑥

IVAN ASEN II

MITROPOLSKA

Church of St John the Baptist

Church of Sveti Spas ⑧

Ethnographic Museum ⑤

Windmill

Ramparts

BURGAS Sunny Beach 2 km (1 mile)

Bus Stop

Sea Taxis to Sunny Beach

Archaeological Museum ①

Church of Christ Pantokrator ②

New Metropolitan Church ③

MESEMBRIYA

CHAIKA

Hydrofoil Station

Ramparts

Church of St John Aliturgetos ④

Black Sea

0 metres 200
0 yards 200

Key to Symbols see back flap

Pomorie 🟟
Поморие

20 km (12 miles) N of Burgas. **Map** F3. 🚶 *13,650.* 🚌 🚐 🚗 ⛴ *daily.*

Today, as in ancient times, Pomorie is known for its salt pans and its dry white wine, *Pomoriiski dimyat.* Largely destroyed by fire in 1906, this coastal town was rebuilt in the 1950s, which explains the rather unsightly concrete buildings that line its streets. One survivor of the fire is the Church of the Transfiguration (1763), with 17th-century icons.

Next to Lake Pomorie, just outside the town, a working salt pan at the **Salt Museum** accompanies an exhibition about the trade in "white gold" that brought the town prosperity. The lake itself is a magnet for birdwatchers, who come to spot storks and pelicans on their migration route across the Black Sea.

🏛 **Salt Museum**
Tel (0596) 25344. 🕐 10am–6pm Mon–Sat. 📷 ♿
www.saltmuseum.org

Salt pans at the Salt Museum on the outskirts of Pomorie

Burgas 🟟
Бургас

160 km (100 miles) S of Varna. **Map** F3. 🚶 *193,000.* ✈ ✕ 🚉 🚌 🚐 🚗 ⛴ *daily.* **www.**bourgas.net

Although it tends to be overlooked as Varna's (*see pp198–9*) ugly sister, Burgas is in fact a pleasant city, whose pedestrianized centre has benefited from recent refurbishment. In the early 1800s, Burgas was depopulated after attacks by *kurzdhali* bandits, but by the mid-19th century it had recovered to enjoy an economic boom based on craftsmanship and the export of grain.

Burgas has several fine churches and interesting museums. The **Ethnographic Museum**, in a 19th-century house, contains a collection of local traditional costume, including women's aprons whose distinctive and colourful designs were unique to their villages. Also on display are some intimidating *kukeri* costumes (*see p102*), complete with bells and wooden swords. Nearby is the bulky **Church of SS Kiril i Metodii** , designed by Ricardo Toskanini, the Italian architect who strongly influenced Burgas's architecture in the early 20th century. At the **Natural History Museum** visitors can see a glittering array of Bulgarian minerals and giant Brazilian crystals, as well as butterflies, insects, crustaceans and stuffed mammals.

On the corner of ulitsa Mitropolit and ulitsa Lermontov, the little Armenian Church (variable opening hours) is a striking sight. Its attractive exterior belies its dour interior. Built in 1853, it serves Burgas's small Armenian community. Close by is

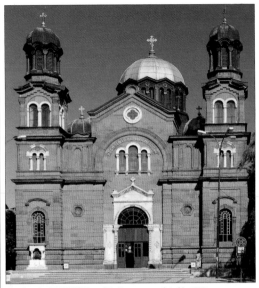

The Church of SS Kiril i Metodii in Burgas, completed in 1905

the **Archaeological Museum**. Its small but captivating display begins with axe heads, stone anchors and knives dating back ten thousand years. Bronze Age pottery is followed by various items from the period of Greek colonization. The most striking exhibits are a gold necklace and earrings found at the cremation site of a Thracian priestess. Burgas's **Art Gallery**, in a former synagogue, offers the opportunity to see some fine 18th- and 19th-century icons, as well as works by modern Bulgarian painters and local artists.

Just outside the town centre, at the far end of bulevard Bogoridi, are the attractive Sea Gardens. They were laid out in 1910, with open-air cafés and restaurants that command sea views. Some intriguing Eastern-bloc sculptures of the 1970s are dotted about between flowerbeds.

Environs
Just outside Burgas, on the road to Sozopol, is **Lake Poda**, a haven for rare birds and plants. Managed by the Bulgarian Society for the Preservation of Birds, the lake and its environs are of international importance as a habitat for breeding colonies of spoonbills, ibises and herons.

🏛 Ethnographic Museum
ul. Slavianska 69. *Tel (056) 842
587.* ☐ *10am–7pm Mon–Sat.* 📷
📷 📷 www.bourgas.net

⛪ Church of SS Kiril i Metodii
pl. Sveti Kiril i Metodii. ☐ *Variable.*
📷 *8am, 9am Sun.* 📷

🏛 Natural History Museum
ul. Fotinov 30. *Tel (056) 843 239.*
☐ *10am–7pm Mon–Sat.* 📷 📷
www.bourgas.net

🏛 Archaeological Museum
ul. Bogoridi 21. *Tel (056) 843 541.*
☐ *10am–6pm Mon–Sat.* 📷 📷 📷
www.bourgas.net

🏛 Art Gallery
ul. Mitropolit Simeon 24.
☐ *9am–6pm Mon–Fri.* 📷 📷 📷
www.bourgas.net/ArtGallery

Sozopol ⑰
Созопол

32 km (20 miles) S of Burgas. **Map**
F3. 🚶 4,350. 🚌 🚍 🚗 🚢 *daily.*
🎭 *Apollonia Arts Festival (first 10 days
in Sep).* www.beachbulgaria.com

With sandy bays to the north
and south, Sozopol's historic
old town stands on a peninsula jutting out into the Black
Sea. The cobbled streets of
this picturesque fishing port
are densely lined with attractive old houses.

Ancient artifacts discovered
in the harbour area suggest
that the site has been inhabited since the 5th millennium
BC. Thracians settled on the
peninsula in the 2nd millennium BC, but it was from the
early 7th century BC, when it
became the Greek colony of
Apollonia Pontica, that this
fishing port rose to power
and prosperity. Romans conquered and destroyed the
town in 72 BC, and in AD 330
Apollonia was absorbed into
the Byzantine Empire. It was
then renamed Sozopolis
("Saved Town"), in reference
to its adoption of Christianity.

During the Middle Ages,
Sozopol was one of the First
Bulgarian Kingdom's major
ports, and, despite coming
under Ottoman rule in 1453,
it remained an important
centre of shipbuilding, commerce and fishing until it was
overtaken by Burgas in the
mid-19th century.

Wooden houses along a street in
Sozopol's old town

The collections in the **Archaeological Museum** document
Sozopol's long history.
Amphorae of various shapes
predominate, but there are
also some superb Greek
pottery vessels decorated with
scenes that celebrate Dionysus, god of wine and pleasure.
Upstairs there is a fascinating
display of figurines from
Apollonia's necropolis, which
was in use from the 4th to the
3rd centuries BC. Simple
stone anchors of the 2nd–1st
millennium BC attest to early
trading relations between the
Thracians of Sozopol and the
eastern Mediterranean.

Remains of Sozopol's fortifications, built from the 4th to
14th centuries AD, form part
of the **South Fortress Wall and
Tower Museum**. Most of the
town's medieval churches
were destroyed in the Ottoman
period, but later examples
remain. Among them are the
15th-century Church of Sveta
Bogoroditsa, with elaborate
wooden iconostases, and the

Church of Sveti Georgi (1836),
which has colourful icons.
The small Church of Sveti
Zosim, dedicated to the Orthodox patron saint of seafarers,
has icons by Dimitar of Sozopol, an artist of the National
Revival period. At the end of
the peninsula is Sozopol's **Art
Gallery**, with seascapes by
local artists. Sozopol also
hosts the Apollonia Arts Festival *(see p35)*, one of Bulgaria's foremost cultural events.

🏛 Archaeological Museum
pl. Han Krum 3. *Tel (0550) 22226.*
☐ *8am–6pm daily.* 📷 📷

**⛪ South Fortress Wall and
Tower Museum**
ul. Milet. *Tel (0550) 220267.*
☐ *9:30am–9:30pm daily.* 📷 📷

🏛 Art Gallery
ul. Kiril i Metodii 78. *Tel (0550)
22202.* ☐ *9am–7pm Mon–Sat.* 📷

Ropotamo Nature
Reserve ⑱
резерват "Ропотамо"

18 km (11 miles) S of Sozopol.
Map F4. 🚌 🚍 🚗 ☐ *9am–
9pm daily.* 📷 ♿ 🏨 🛒 📷

The wide estuary of the
Ropotamo River forms part of
the Ropotamo Nature Reserve,
set up in 1940 to protect
extensive marshland and the
largest expanse of sand dunes
in Bulgaria. Covering 1,000 ha
(2,470 acres), the reserve is
home to over 200 species of
birds and a variety of rare
plants and flowers, including
the endemic sand lily. Regular
boat trips carry tourists along
the river, where its famous
water lilies flower spectacu-
larly from June to October.

The estuary of the Ropotamo River, part of Ropotamo Nature Reserve

Primorsko ⓳
Приморско

55 km (34 miles) S of Burgas.
Map F4. 🏘 2,430. 🚌 🚏 🚗
🚢 daily.

This bustling town is set on a
peninsula between two
estuaries. With 10 km (6 miles)
of sandy beaches to the north
and south, it has long been a
popular spot for holidaymakers.
In high season the streets in the
town centre are uncomfortably
cluttered with souvenir stalls
and the beaches are densely
covered with parasols. But
those who venture slightly
further will find quiet creeks,
pristine dunes and rocky pools,
with the forested Strandzha
Mountains in the background.

Lozenets ⓴
Лозенец

60 km (37 miles) S of Burgas.
Map E4. 🏘 470. 🚌 🚏 🚗

Until quite recently, Lozenets
was a quiet coastal backwater,
but it has now become one of
the Black Sea's most fashionable resorts. While wealthier
visitors frequent the resort's
small number of smart bars,
restaurants and clubs on the
main street, elsewhere simple
garden restaurants cater to
humbler holidaymakers.
    The extensive beaches just
north of Lozenets attract
windsurfers and kitesurfers.
Several watersports schools
also operate here during the
summer season.

**Windsurfing in warm summer
waters at the resort of Lozenets**

Tsarevo ㉑
Царево

70 km (43 miles) S of Burgas.
Map F4. 🏘 5,900. 🚌 🚏 🚗
🛈 in the bus station. 🚢 daily.

Founded in the 7th century
BC as a Greek colony,
Tsarevo is now a well
established beach resort, with
a small harbour that bustles
with fishing boats. On the
promontory south of Tsarevo,
well away from the noise and
bustle of the town in high
season, is the **Church of
Uspenie Bogorodichno** (1810).
It contains an impressive
collection of 19th-century
icons and from its pretty
garden there are beautiful
views of Tsarevo and its
coastline. A long beach
stretches away north of the
town, but unfortunately much
of it is being developed.

🔒 **Church of Uspenie
Bogorodichno**
Vesiliko quarter. 🕐 8am–9pm
daily. ✝ 8am, 9am Sun.

Church of Uspenie Bogorodichno, on a promontory south of Tsarevo

Ahtopol ㉒
Ахтопол

85 km (53 miles) S of Burgas.
Map G4. 🏘 1,200. 🚌 🚏 🚗
🚢 daily.

Set on a rocky peninsula at
the foot of the Strandzha
Mountains, Ahtopol is another
popular coastal resort, with a
large sandy beach on its
northern side. In summer,
the town centre becomes
very crowded with Bulgarian
holidaymakers as well as
foreign visitors.
    However, Ahtopol's old
town offers greater tranquillity.
The streets of this picturesque
district are lined with wooden
houses shaded by fig trees.
The **Chapel of the Ascension**,
built in 1796, contains brightly
painted antique icons.

🔒 **Chapel of the Ascension**
ul. Briz. 🕐 8am–noon, 3:30–
8:30pm daily. ♿

**Beach at Sinemorets, at the southern
end of Bulgaria's Black Sea coastline**

Sinemorets ㉓
Синеморец

90 km (56 miles) S of Burgas.
Map G4. 🏘 260. 🚌 🚏 🚗

As it fell within Bulgaria's postwar border zone, Sinemorets
was inaccessible during the
Communist period. After
1989, the first visitors to come
here found just a tiny village
with pristine beaches. For a
time, Sinemorets was the haven
of young Bulgarians, who
camped along the coast. But
the village has now been
discovered by the tourism
industry and is suffering the
same fate as coastal towns
further north. Hotels and
apartment blocks are springing up along the coastline,
but there are still unspoiled
beaches south of the village.

Strandzha Nature Park Tour ㉔

Locked into Bulgaria's border zone until 1989, Strandzha's vast oak and beech forests escaped the ravages of logging. The park was created in 1995 and covers 1,160 sq km (450 sq miles) between the central Strandzha Mountains and the Black Sea. The five reserves within the park provide a secure habitat for endangered animals such as golden eagles, grey-headed woodpeckers, wolves, pine martens and otters. Rare plants include the Strandzha whortleberry, Caucasus primrose and cherry laurel.

TIPS FOR DRIVERS

Road map F4.
Length of tour: approximately 55 km (34 miles).
Stopping-off places: There are guesthouses, restaurants, bars and cafés in Brushlyan. Also if there's time it's worth considering a detour to Gramatikovo.

Silkossia Reserve ②
Bulgaria's oldest reserve, this is one of the few places in the country where the delightful Strandzha rhododendron flourishes. Its pinkish-mauve violet flowers blossom in May.

Bûlgari ①
This tiny hilltop village is renowned for its annual fire-dancing ceremony, which takes place on 3 and 4 June, the feast day of St Konstantin and St Elena.

TSAREVO

BURGAS
Veleka 98
Zabernovo
907
Kondolovo ①
②
Petrova Niva
Kosti
H a s e k i y a t a
Gramatikovo
Stoilovo
⑤
98
9
Aydere
Veleka
Bratanova Cave
9
9
③
④
KIRKLARELI
Gradishte 710 m

Dense beech and oak forests
dominate the park. Strandzha's border zone location has protected its nature from destructive human activity.

Malko Tûrnovo ③
Interesting archaeological finds from the region, as well as items from the more recent past, fill the village's History Museum, in a National Revival building.

0 kilometres 5
0 miles 5

KEY

— Tour route
— Main road
— Other road
- - Trail
▬ International border
△ Peak
⋒ Cave

Brushlyan ⑤
With attractive 18th-century wooden houses and a 17th-century walled and sunken church, the small village of Brushlyan is an architectural reserve. Its church school and picturesque peasant dwellings are of particular interest.

Mishkova Niva ④
A Thracian burial ground and a Roman necropolis were discovered here. Of the park's many archaeological sites, this is one of the easiest to reach. Visits can be arranged through the History Museum in Malko Tûrnovo.

TRAVELLERS'
NEEDS

WHERE TO STAY

From luxurious hotels in major towns and cities to atmospheric monasteries in isolated locations, Bulgaria offers an ever-increasing choice of accommodation options.

Hotel sign in Cyrillic script

In recent years there has been a boom in the construction of new hotels, especially those in the four-star category and above. Both the Black Sea resorts and winter sports centres now offer accommodation ranging from convenient self-catering apartments to luxurious spa hotels. In rural areas, basic but comfortable accommodation, with traditional hospitality, is offered in private houses, and by the country's growing number of bed-and-breakfast establishments, often in historic houses.

HOTELS

There is a profusion of hotels in Sofia, on the Black Sea coast and in mountain skiing areas. By contrast, in parts of northern and central Bulgaria, where the tourist industry is less well developed, the choice of accommodation is much more limited.

Bulgarian hotels are supposedly graded according to the international five-star system. Even so, the number of stars allocated to particular establishments can sometimes seem a little too generous. As a general rule, a four-star hotel in Bulgaria is roughly equal to a three-star hotel elsewhere.

Rooms in most recently built hotels with a three-star rating or above have bathrooms with baths or shower cubicles. In some slightly older hotels, however, rooms still have old-style Bulgarian bathrooms with an open, uncurtained shower and a drain in the middle of the floor.

Room in the five-star Grand Hotel, in central Sofia (see p219)

In Sofia, in ski resorts and in coastal resorts, most hotels in the four-star category and above have a gym and a sauna and in many cases a swimming pool.

Nearly all Bulgarian hotels have satellite or cable television broadcasting programmes in the major European languages, although they may make an extra charge for access to premium film channels.

SPA RESORTS

Several areas of Bulgaria are renowned for their natural mineral springs. Traditionally, accommodation in these areas was provided by sanatoria, which were built primarily for patients being treated by the Bulgarian health service, but which also catered for visitors. Today, the growing popularity of spa and wellness tourism has led to an increasing number of well-equipped four- and five-star spa hotels being built in these areas.

Bulgaria's main spa centres are Sandanski and Kyustendil, south of Sofia, Velingrad and Devin, in the Rhodope Mountains, and Albena and Golden Sands, on the Black Sea coast. All have hotels with swimming pools filled either with warm water from mineral springs or with sea water, depending on their location. The hotels also have wellness centres with saunas and steam baths, and offer reinvigorating thalassotherapy or spa therapies, and various beauty treatments.

Aquapark seen from a hotel balcony at Sunny Beach, on the Black Sea

◁ Parasols set out on the sandy beach at Varna

APARTMENTS

Self-catering apartments are an increasingly common feature on the Black Sea coast and in inland skiing resorts. Many form part of apartment hotels. These generally offer two-bedroom, family-size apartments or studios, but also provide the usual hotel facilities, such as a reception desk, chambermaids and, in many cases, a breakfast room.

PRIVATE ACCOMMODATION

In mountain and seaside areas, many Bulgarian families rent private rooms *(chastni kvartiri)* to visitors during the summer season. Compared to those of hotels, prices for rooms in private houses are very low and the hosts are usually extremely hospitable. However, bear in mind that you will be sharing your hosts' bathroom and that in most cases breakfast is not included in the price. Accommodation in private houses is organized by the tourist offices and travel agencies in each area. It can be booked on arrival in the relevant location.

BED AND BREAKFAST

Family-run bed-and-breakfast establishments (B&Bs) are an increasingly common feature of rural or mountain regions. Although most B&Bs are in modern family houses, some, such as those in historic

Campsite at Oazis Beach, on the Black Sea coast

mountain villages like Koprivshtitsa, Kovachevitsa and Zheravna, are in beautiful restored 19th-century houses, and frequently have rooms furnished with sheepskin rugs and hand-woven textiles.

HOSTELS, CAMPSITES AND MONASTERIES

Sofia is well supplied with informal, backpacker-friendly hostels. These commonly have one or more dormitory rooms with bunk beds, as well as a small communal area, and approachable English-speaking staff. In some of Sofia's hostels, there are also self-contained double rooms and breakfast is included in the price.

Outside Sofia hostel accommodation is rare, although you will find friendly hostel-type establishments in Plovdiv, Veliko Tûrnovo and Varna.

Spending a few nights at a campsite *(kûmping)* is another inexpensive, albeit increasingly elusive, option.

There were once many campsites outside Bulgaria's most scenic towns and along the Black Sea coast. However, since many of them have now been sold off to property developers, their number has fallen dramatically in recent years. The continued existence of those that remain is far from certain. Camping anywhere but in a designated campsite is illegal in Bulgaria.

Basic accommodation is also available at some of Bulgaria's larger monasteries, such as Rila and Troyan. To book a room, it's best to contact the monasteries directly.

RESERVATIONS

As most hotels are geared to taking block bookings from package-holiday companies, it is inadvisable to arrive in Bulgaria without a hotel reservation, particularly in summer. Most hotels accept advance bookings from independent travellers by phone, fax or e-mail. An increasing number of central-booking internet sites, such as **Discover Bulgaria**, **Booking. com** and **Inn 26**, offer a wide choice of accommodation throughout Bulgaria.

DIRECTORY

HOTEL BOOKING WEBSITES

Discover Bulgaria
www.discover-bulgaria.com

Booking.com
www.booking.com

Inn 26
www.inn26.com

Modern hotel in a traditional-style house, with large swimming pool

Choosing a Hotel

The hotels listed below have been selected across a wide range of price categories for their facilities, good value, character or location. Some also have a restaurant. They are listed by region, starting with Sofia. The other hotels are listed alphabetically by area. For a list of restaurants, see *pp234–45*. For map references see *pp93–7*.

SOFIA

Art Hostel.   €

ul. Angel Kunchev 21a **Tel** *(02) 987 0545* **Rooms** *8*   **City Map 3 B3**

This hostel, in a very central apartment, has eight simply furnished rooms with wooden floorboards and high ceilings. There is a communal kitchen and a shared bathroom in the hallway. On the ground floor there are art exhibitions. Breakfast is served in a café round the corner. **www.art-hostel.com**

Ganesha   €€

ul. Al. fon Humbolt 26 **Tel** *(02) 971 3815* **Rooms** *20*

Pleasant medium-sized establishment located 2 km (just over a mile) east of the city centre, in a lively area of residential streets and shops. Rooms are of varying shapes and sizes – so have a look first – but all have a small TV and an en-suite shower and toilet. Optional breakfast costs a couple of extra euros. **www.hotelganesha-bg.com**

Niky   €€

ul. Neofit Rilski 16 **Tel** *(02) 952 3058* **Fax** *(02) 951 6091* **Rooms** *23*

Bright, clean and friendly hotel in the heart of the city. There are a few cosy en-suite doubles, but most rooms are apartment-style, with a lounge space, TV, small kitchenette and spacious bathroom. The ground floor grill-restaurant has an attractive garden, and is a popular dining-out venue for local people in summer. **www.hotel-niky.com**

Red Bed and Breakfast   €€

ul. Lyuben Karavelov 15 **Tel & Fax** *(02) 988 8188* **Rooms** *6*   **City Map 4 E4**

Friendly and informal B&B in a central location, housed in the upper storeys of the Red House Cultural Centre *(see p77)*. Rooms can be simply furnished or plushly decorated, with TV and antique wardrobe. Toilets and bathrooms are located in the hallway. Breakfast is delivered to your room at the time of your choice. **www.redbandb.com**

Rotasar   €€

ul. Costa Lulchev 15a 1 **Tel** *(02) 971 4571* **Rooms** *18*

Friendly, intimate hotel 2 km (just over a mile) east of the city centre, offering a mixture of double rooms and studio apartments, each with homely furnishings. TV, en-suite bathroom and internet connection are included. Unusual paintings and prints add atmosphere. Optional breakfast costs a few euros extra. **www.rotasar.com**

The Rooms   €€

ul. Pop Bogomil 10 **Tel** *(02) 983 3508* **Rooms** *5*   **City Map 2 D1**

Not quite a hostel, this is more an informal and youthful B&B offering a mixture of single and double rooms. Located in a converted 19th-century apartment building in a quiet residential street, it features high ceilings and a sprinkling of antique furnishings. Some bathrooms are en suite, others are shared. **theroomshostel@yahoo.com**

Bulgari   €€€

ul. Pirotska 50 **Tel** *(02) 831 0060* **Fax** *(02) 983 3229* **Rooms** *12*

Small and friendly hotel in one of Sofia's oldest shopping areas, just round the corner from the Zhenski Pazar market. Rooms are low-ceilinged and simply furnished, but all have a small TV, desk space and WiFi internet connection. Some bathrooms have a bath, others have a Bulgarian-style open shower. **www.bulgarihotel.net**

Latinka   €€€

ul. Latinka 28a **Tel** *(02) 870 0848* **Rooms** *26*

Comfortable mid-sized hotel with a friendly intimate atmosphere, located in a residential area 3 km (2 miles) southeast of the centre. Strolling into the centre through the nearby Borisova Gradina Park makes for a great introduction to the city. Room facilities include TV and internet connection. There is also a restaurant. **www.hotel-latinka-sofia.com**

Scotty's Boutique Hotel   €€€

ul. Ekzarh Yosif 11 **Tel** *(02) 983 6777* **Fax** *(02) 983 3229* **Rooms** *16*   **City Map 1 B3**

In a historic district containing Sofia's main mosque, synagogue and market hall, Scotty's occupies the upper floors of a 19th-century apartment block. Rooms are decorated in contemporary minimalist style and have a TV, minibar and spacious bathrooms. No breakfast available but there are plenty of cafés nearby.

Key to Symbols *see back cover flap*

Apartment House Dunav

ul. Dunav 38 **Tel** *(02) 983 3002* **Fax** *(02) 983 3804* **Rooms** *14*   **City Map 2 E2**

In an old-fashioned residential street, Dunav is suitable for both short or long stays. It has self-catering units, ranging in size from 2-person studio to 2-room family apartment. Each apartment feature wooden floors, pastel colours and neat modern bathrooms. Breakfast can be delivered to your room on request. **www.dunavapartmenthouse.com**

Diter

ul. Han Asparuh 65 **Tel & Fax** *(02) 989 8998* **Rooms** *21*   **City Map 3 C3**

Friendly establishment in a lovingly restored 19th-century mansion in a quiet cobbled street. Rooms feature warm colour schemes, TV, minibar, internet connection and plenty of desk space. Powerful bathroom showers are perfect for an aquatic massage. An atmospheric basement breakfast room adds to the charm. **www.diterhotel.com**

Light

ul. Veslets 37 **Tel** *(02) 917 9090* **Fax** *(02) 917 9010* **Rooms** *31*   **City Map 1 C2**

Stylish contemporary hotel in a tranquil 19th-century street, handily placed just northeast of the central sights. Rooms are plush and cosy, although there is a touch of modern minimalism about the lobby and communal areas. There is a small gym and sauna on site. **www.hotels.light.bg**

Sofia Plaza

bul. Hristo Botev 154 **Tel** *(02) 813 7979* **Fax** *(02) 813 7912* **Rooms** *50*

A medium-sized, friendly place within easy reach of Sofia's train and bus stations, the Sofia Plaza has pastel-coloured rooms with TV, minibar, internet connection and small desk. Also available are family rooms sleeping 4–5 people and including a kitchenette. Other facilities include sauna, solarium, massage and gym. **www.hotelsofiaplaza.com**

Apartment House Sofia

ul. Golo burdo 2–4 **Tel** *(02) 960 2888* **Rooms** *28*

An apartment hotel in the district of Lozenets, 3 km (2 miles) south of the centre, offering everything from studio flats to 2-bedroom family apartments. All feature laminated floors, stylish, modern furnishings and fully-equipped kitchenette. Apartments are cleaned daily. Rates reduce the longer you stay. **www.aphouse-sofia.com**

Art 'Otel

ul. William Gladstone 44 **Tel** *(02) 980 6000* **Fax** *(02) 981 1909* **Rooms** *22*   **City Map 3 B2**

Four-star comforts in a cobbled side street a short walk from Sofia's main shopping drag, bulevard Vitosha. Rooms feature plush carpets, stylish furnishings and internet connection. Some bathrooms have a full-size bathtub, others come with shower-cabin only. On-site sauna available to guests. **www.artotel.biz**

Barcelo Festa

bul. Bulgariya 83 **Tel** *(02) 818 9618* **Fax** *(02) 818 9628* **Rooms** *120*

Classy establishment on the southern fringes of the city. Rooms have a contemporary design, and expansive views of either central Sofia to the north, or Mount Vitosha to the south. Pay a little more and you can have a flat-screen TV, and space aplenty. Gym, sauna and steam-bath are at guests' disposal. **www.barcelosofiafesta.com**

Central Park Hotel

bul. Vitosha 106 **Tel** *(02) 805 8888* **Fax** *(02) 805 8787* **Rooms** *77*   **City Map 3 A4**

Swanky modern 4-star hotel on Sofia's main shopping street, right opposite the National Palace of Culture. Rooms have plush carpets, smart bathrooms and plenty of desk space. Most come with views of nearby parks and key city-centre buildings. The restaurant serves classy international food in a formal environment. **www.centralparkhotel.bg**

Grand Hotel Sofia

ul. Gurko 1 **Tel** *(02) 811 0800* **Fax** *(02) 811 0801* **Rooms** *122*   **City Map 1 C5, 3 C1**

International 5-star comforts in a central location, bordering the City Garden. This modern building has spacious rooms, stylish furnishings and eager, attentive staff. The health centre offers a gym, solarium and beauty treatments. There is a restaurant, an elegant café and a jazzy piano bar in the basement. **www.grandhotelsofia.bg**

Hilton

bul. Bulgaria 1 **Tel** *(02) 933 5000* **Fax** *(02) 933 5111* **Rooms** *245*

High standards of comfort and service in a large, modern hotel, just south of the centre but still within walking distance of the sights. Rooms, in pastel colours, have coffee- and tea-making facilities and spacious bathrooms. Other features include a fine restaurant, swimming pool and good fitness facilities. **www.sofia.hilton.com**

Kempinski Zografski

bul. James Bouchier 100 **Tel** *(02) 969 2222* **Fax** *(02) 969 2223* **Rooms** *420*

Four km (just over 2 miles) south of the centre, the Kempinski Zografski has on-site shopping facilities, fitness rooms, swimming pool and beauty salons. Rooms are equipped to modern 5-star standard, and service is superbly professional. The hotel has five restaurants, a casino, a Viennese-style café and two bars. **www.kempinski.bg**

Oborishte Residence

ul. Oborishte 63 **Tel** *(02) 814 4888* **Fax** *(02) 846 8244* **Rooms** *9*

A cosy and intimate hotel in a leafy, upmarket residential area on the eastern fringes of the city centre. Most of the accommodation is in the form of 2-room apartments. Wood floors, bold colours and contemporary design flourishes help to create a stylish but homely atmosphere. **www.residence-oborishte.com**

Radisson SAS

pl. Narodno sûbranie 4 **Tel** *(02) 933 4334* **Fax** *(02) 933 4335* **Rooms** *136*   **City Map 2 E5, 4 E1**

This is one of Sofia's best hotels in terms of both comfort and location, with rooms offering views of the National Assembly and the Alexandûr Nevski Memorial Church. Rooms are large with good bathrooms. There is a panoramic top-floor restaurant, and a lively pub on the ground floor. **www.sofia.radissonsas.com**

Sheraton Sofia Hotel Balkan

pl. Sveta Nedelya 5 **Tel** *(02) 981 65 41* **Fax** *(02) 980 6464* **Rooms** *188*   **City Map 1 B4**

A central location and an air of chandeliered opulence make the Sheraton a popular choice for those in need of 5-star comforts. All rooms have plush furnishings and bathtubs, while the executive-class rooms on the upper floors feature flat-screen TVs, tea- and coffee-making facilities and antique furniture. **www.luxurycollection.com/sofia**

SkyWay

bul. Simeonovsko shose 166a **Tel** *(02) 819 2100* **Fax** *(02) 819 2199* **Rooms** *85*

This hotel is located in the relative seclusion of Simeonovo, a suburb on the lower slopes of Mount Vitosha. The larger-than-average rooms have a TV, minibar, desk space and warm colour schemes. Facilities include an outdoor swimming pool, a gym and a barbecue. Central Sofia is a 20-minute taxi ride away. **www.skywayhotel.com**

SOUTHERN BULGARIA

BACHKOVO Dzhamura

ul. Osvobozhdenya 74 **Tel** *(03327) 320* **Rooms** *15*   **Map C4**

Situated opposite Bachkovo Monastery across the river and far enough from the busy main road to ensure a peaceful stay, the Dzhamura occupies a prettily restored old house with walls of smooth round river stones. The rooms are spacious and cosily furnished, and most have balconies overlooking the river. The hotel's restaurant is renowned.

BACHKOVO Bachkovo Monastery

Bachkovo Monastery **Tel** *(03327) 277* **Rooms** *10*   **Map C4**

A stay here is as close to monastic life as most of us will get. Some of the monks' cells have been refurbished to a reasonable standard, and converted into guest rooms with simple wooden furniture and en-suite bathrooms. Guests are guaranteed an early night as the monastery gates close at 9pm.

BANSKO Alpin

ul. Neofit Rilski 6 **Tel** *(07443) 8075* **Rooms** *10*   **Map B4**

The Alpin is hidden away down a cobbled back street in Bansko's old town, not too far from the centre. Its clean rooms have pine furniture and stripped wooden floors. Efficient staff provide friendly and helpful service, and food is available from the hotel's small *mehana* (traditional tavern). **www.alpin.bansko.bg**

BANSKO Bansko Hotel Sofia

ul. Radon Tonev 16 **Tel** *(07443) 8502* **Fax** *07443 8362* **Rooms** *18*   **Map B4**

The hotel has the façade of an old Bansko house and a modern, cosy interior. Located on a quiet street just minutes from the town centre, it offers high standards and large rooms for a reasonable price. The small restaurant has a covered winter garden and guests have use of a sauna, steam bath and Jacuzzi. **www.banskohotelsofia.bg**

BANSKO Strazhite

ul. Glazne 7 **Tel** *(0749) 88040* **Fax** *(0749) 88046* **Rooms** *160*   **Map B4**

The Strazhite is a central, modern hotel popular with tour groups. Such traditional motifs as animal skins, rough timber and an open fire are blended with smart leather furniture and large windows. Unfortunately its great views of the Pirin Mountains are under threat from neighbouring developments, but it is still a hotel worth considering.

BANSKO Kempinski Hotel Grand Arena

ul. Pirin 96 **Tel** *(0749) 88888* **Fax** *(0749) 88565* **Rooms** *159*   **Map B4**

Sympathetically styled to match local houses, this huge 5-star hotel complex stands next to the ski-lift base station. It is as luxurious as Bansko gets and guests pay handsomely for the pleasure. Rooms are spacious, with fantastic mountain views. Facilities include indoor and outdoor pools, a spa centre and tennis courts. **www.kempinski-bansko.com**

BLAGOEVGRAD Kristo

Varosha Quarter **Tel** *(073) 880 444* **Fax** *(073) 880 555* **Rooms** *40*   **Map B4**

This charming hotel complex offers excellent value for money in the town's pretty Varosha Quarter. The style is modern traditional with wrought iron and wood furnishings. Most of the spacious, comfortable rooms have lovely views of the town and the church below. There is also a fitness centre and sauna. **www.hotelkristo.net**

BOROVETS Alpin

Tel *(07503) 2201* **Fax** *(07503) 2203* **Rooms** *8, plus 8 chalets*   **Map B4**

Centrally located at the foot of the slopes and close to the ski-lift stations, this small establishment offers a cosier alternative to the massive package-oriented hotels. Rooms are comfortably furnished and guests can use the steam room and Jacuzzi. Accommodation is also available in the Alpin's holiday village of 8 chalets. **www.alpin-hotel.bg**

Key to Price Guide *see p218* **Key to Symbols** *see back cover flap*

BOROVETS Rila

Tel (07503) 2441 **Fax** (07503) 2531 **Rooms** 522   **Map B4**

Bulgaria's largest ski hotel is situated right at the heart of Borovets, next to the slopes and ski-lift stations. It provides excellent 4-star standards and caters mainly for tour groups. Rooms have wonderful mountain views and facilities include a sauna, Jacuzzi, steam baths, fitness centre and ski school. **www.borovets-bg.com**

DEVIN Manolov

ul. Osvobozhdenie 50 **Tel & Fax** (03041) 2269 **Rooms** 8   **Map C4**

Devin's only budget hotel, the well-established Manolov has a good central location and provides clean, spacious and simply furnished rooms. Although the décor is outdated and staff somewhat lethargic, it offers good value for money. Breakfast is not included, but the ground-floor café serves food.

DEVIN Ismena

ul. Guritza 41 **Tel** (03041) 4872 **Fax** (03041) 3917 **Rooms** 18 **Apartments** 4   **Map C4**

Set in the hills above Devin, the traditional-style Ismena is by far its classiest hotel. It is tastefully furnished to a high standard throughout and most of the rooms have fantastic views. There is also a spa centre, a hot pool filled with Devin's famous mineral water, and a restaurant *(see p237)*. **www.ismena-hotel.com**

DOLEN Dzhalovata Kushta

Tel (0898) 433 368 **Rooms** 6   **Map B4**

One of most atmospheric accommodation options in this small village, the Dzhalovata Kushta is an old timber house located close to the church. The rooms feature wood panelling and original fireplaces, and colourful woollen rugs cover the floors and beds. Bathroom facilities are shared and the friendly owners can arrange meals.

GOTSE DELCHEV Malamovata Kushta

ul. Hristo Botev 25 **Tel** (0751) 61230 **Fax** (0751) 61232 **Rooms** 10   **Map B5**

This is a centrally located, family-run hotel in traditional Bulgarian style. The furnishings are dated, but the rooms are large and feature wood-panelled ceilings and pine furniture. Staff are efficient and helpful, and the hotel's rustic restaurant is a good place to sample local dishes. **www.goce.net/maiz**

HASKOVO Central

ul. Varna 1 **Tel** (038) 660 333 **Rooms** 7   **Map D4**

The hotel's imaginatively styled and spacious rooms with sloping ceilings and arched windows make a refreshing change from the perfunctory layout of many Bulgarian hotels. Very centrally located, it has a pleasant café offering refreshments on a lower floor. Advance reservations recommended. **www.geocities.com/hotel_central_haskovo**

HASKOVO Haskovo

ul. Vasil Drumev 20 **Tel** (038) 602 525 **Fax** (038) 602 553 **Rooms** 19   **Map D4**

The Haskovo's exceptionally polite service combined with standards worthy of more than three stars for the price of less make it excellent value. Conveniently located close to the centre, the hotel offers clean, comfortably furnished rooms with good views of the town. There is also a restaurant. **www.hotel-haskovo.com**

KOVACHEVITSA Zhuglevi Kushta

Tel (07527) 416 **Rooms** 6   **Map B4**

Run by the family responsible for the restoration of many of Kovachevitsa's old houses, this guest house offers simply furnished rooms with wooden floors, ceilings and furniture. Thick woollen rugs and blankets create a snug atmosphere. Bathroom facilities are shared and most rooms have great views of the valley and mountains.

KÛRDZHALI Rezidentsia Hotel

Tel (0361) 65558 **Fax** (0361) 65558 **Rooms** 12   **Map D5**

Positioned on a hillside overlooking Kurdzhali and the Rhodope Mountains beyond, the Rezidentsia Hotel takes full advantage of its fantastic location. Although the interior is somewhat dated, all the rooms have balconies, large windows and glorious views. There is also an excellent restaurant.

KYÛSTENDIL Strimon Spa Club

ul. Tsar Simeon I 24 **Tel** (078) 559 000 **Fax** (078) 551 355 **Rooms** 75   **Map A4**

This wonderful 5-star spa hotel has recently been refurbished to a superb standard. Its plush rooms look out onto quiet wooded gardens, and guests can enjoy a wide range of spa therapies utilizing Kyûstendil's 73° C (163° F) mineral water. A romantic option is the heart-shaped Cleopatra's Bath, filled with milk. **www.strimon-spaclub.com**

LESHTEN Leshten

Tel (0888) 544 651 **Rooms** 25   **Map B4**

The 18th- and 19th-century buildings of this remarkable village have been lovingly restored and 15 of them now offer atmospheric accommodation with heating, en-suite bathrooms and cable television. All have great views of the valley and mountains beyond. A honeymoon cottage is a quirky mud hut with luxury furnishings. **leshten@yahoo.com**

MADZHAROVO Nature Information Centre

Madzharovo Nature Reserve **Tel** (03720) 345 or (0887) 389 121 **Rooms** 3   **Map D5**

Most visitors to Madzharovo come for the wildlife, especially the birds. As this place is run by the wardens of the Nature Reserve, it is the perfect spot for keen birdwatchers to stay. The accommodation is clean and comfortable and staff can arrange meals if required. Rooms need to be booked well in advance. **www.bspb.org**

MELNIK Despot Slav

Tel (07437) 248 **Fax** (07437) 271 **Rooms** 24   **Map B5**

Named after Melnik's legendary 13th-century ruler, the hotel is newly built in the town's old style. Plenty of wrought iron work combined with wood panelling, stripped floors, exposed stone walls and open fires creates a comfortable atmosphere. The rooms are spacious and staff provide excellent service. There is a restaurant (see p238).

MELNIK Litova Kushta

Tel (07437) 313 **Rooms** 12   **Map B5**

This rather upmarket hotel is built over one of Melnik's oldest wine cellars cut deep into the rock. The large rooms are smartly furnished and have traditional wooden ceilings, panelling and floors. Hand-painted borders and coving provide a stylish touch. Horse-riding can be arranged from here. **www.litovakushta.com**

MELNIK Lumparova Kushta

Tel (07437) 218 **Rooms** 6   **Map B5**

Probably Melnik's most elegant hotel, the Lumparova Kushta has a capacious reception and dining area (see p238) that leads up to a series of imaginatively decorated rooms. All have high ceilings, stripped wood floors, numerous windows and lovely views. The coving in each room is hand-painted with vines and grapes.

MOGILITSA Babachev Guest House

Tel (03036) 330 **Rooms** 3   **Map C5**

This tiny guesthouse offers the only accommodation in the vicinity. Situated on a grassy hillside overlooking the valley, it is a wonderfully tranquil place to relax. The three rooms share a common bathroom and a small mehana (traditional tavern) provides meals for guests.

PAMPOROVO Malina Cottages

Pamporovo ski resort **Tel** (03095) 8388 **Fax** (03095) 8485 **Rooms** 60, **Apartments** 5   **Map C5**

Surrounded by forest, these 30 triangular wooden chalets are an imaginative alternative to Pamporovo's large hotels. Each has two double rooms, a shared bathroom and kitchen facilities. Though a little cramped, the chalets have their own living rooms and are positioned well apart. **www.marialuisa.bol.bg/malina.html**

PAMPOROVO Orlovetz

Pamporovo ski resort **Tel** (03095) 9000 **Fax** (03095) 8511 **Rooms** 98   **Map C5**

This swanky new 5-star hotel is perched on a thickly forested hillside with fabulous views. The modern interior features plenty of glass to reveal the beauty of the surrounding mountains, and all the rooms have large windows and balconies facing the valley. The luxurious spa centre has a steam room and sauna.

PERNIK Struma

pl. Krakra 1 **Tel** (076) 600 545 **Fax** (076) 601 012 **Rooms** 65   **Map B3**

The centrally located Struma occupies a stern-looking Socialist-era concrete tower block. If you want to stay in Pernik, this is the only hotel (though visitors to the Kukeri festival may want to consider finding accommodation in Sofia). The hotel is currently undergoing refurbishment and guests should ask for a newly decorated room.

PLOVDIV PBI Hostel

ul. Naiden Gerov 13 **Tel** (032) 638 467 **Fax** (032) 638 467 **Rooms** 3   **Map C4**

Offering good-value accommodation in central Plovdiv, the hostel occupies a spacious converted apartment with 18 mixed-dormitory beds and one double room. Tea, coffee and internet access are free, but the establishment is let down by the shower and kitchen facilities being squeezed into a single room.

PLOVDIV Elit

ul. Raiko Daskalov 53 **Tel** (032) 624 537 **Rooms** 7   **Map C4**

Squeezed between tall buildings on one of Plovdiv's main streets, this small hotel is a central option that offers good value for money. Its clean rooms are light and adequately furnished, and staff provide a friendly, helpful service. Breakfast is not included, but there are plenty of cafés and snack bars nearby. **www.hotel-elit.hit.bgbg**

PLOVDIV Bulgaria

ul. Patriarch Evtemii 13 **Tel** (032) 633 599 **Fax** (032) 633 403 **Rooms** 59   **Map C4**

Once an ageing concrete relic of the Socialist regime, the Bulgaria has been refurbished to a superb standard and now offers comfortable, modern rooms in an enviably central location. Much of the ochre-shaded décor features wood panelling, marble and Art Deco metalwork. **www.hotelbulgaria.net**

PLOVDIV Novotel

ul. Zlatyu Boyadzhiev 2 **Tel** (032) 934 444 **Fax** (032) 934 346 **Rooms** 330   **Map C4**

Overlooking the Maritza River, and a few steps from the International Exhibition Centre, this is Plovdiv's largest and most expensive hotel. Facilities include WiFi, a fitness centre and indoor pool, but the eye-catching modern design throughout is the real attraction. Its restaurant, Evridika, is the town's most stylish. **www.icep.bg**

PLOVDIV OLD TOWN Hikers Hostel

ul. Saborna 53 **Tel** (0896) 764 854 **Rooms** 3   **Map C4**

Conveniently located on the Old Town's main street, the hostel is a wonderfully cosy spot. It occupies a small old house that has been tastefully decorated and offers great views of modern Plovdiv. Two mixed dormitories and a small double room can accommodate 16 guests. Internet and tea and coffee are free. **www.hikers-hostel.org**

Key to Price Guide see p218 **Key to Symbols** see back cover flap

PLOVDIV OLD TOWN Residence

ul. Knyaz Tseretelev 11 **Tel** *(032) 632 389* **Fax** *(032) 620 789* **Rooms** *9*   **Map C4**

The hotel's solid marble staircase gives an indication of what to expect. The rooms have sumptuous furnishings, soft drapes, antique-style beds and marble-tiled bathrooms. As with its restaurant (Petr I), the décor may be too close to kitsch for some, but high standards of service and great views make up for it. **residence@abv.bg**

PLOVDIV OLD TOWN Hebros

ul. Konstantin Stoilov 51a **Tel** *(032) 260 180* **Fax** *(032) 260 252* **Rooms** *10*   **Map C4**

This atmospheric hotel consists of two adjacent 19th-century houses that have been lavishly renovated. Furnished with antiques throughout, the hotel features low wooden ceilings and subdued lighting, with an enchanting ambience. Facilities include WiFi and the hotel has an award-winning restaurant *(see p239).* **www.hebros-hotel.com**

RILA MONASTERY Zodiac

Tel *(088) 216 527* **Rooms** *11*   **Map B4**

Though there are several bungalow sites around the monastery, the Zodiac is the only one to offer a reasonable standard of accommodation. The bungalows, whose internal space is adequate, surround a tidy lawn opposite the restaurant *(see p239).* Each has two beds, shared bathroom facilities and satellite television.

RILA MONASTERY Tsarev vruh

Tel & Fax *(07054) 2280* **Rooms** *54*   **Map B4**

Surrounded by forest on the hillside a little beyond the monastery, the Tsarev vruh is a large whitewashed hotel complex offering a good standard of accommodation. The rooms have simple pine furniture. Some have balconies and most have lovely views of the surrounding valley. There is also a restaurant *(see p239).*

SAMOKOV Relax

ul. Rilski skior 8 **Tel** *(0722) 24284* **Rooms** *4*   **Map B4**

Samokov's proximity to the popular ski resort of Borovets has long stifled its hotel industry. The Relax, one of the town's few new hotels, provides good value for money. Its rooms have stripped wooden floors, modern furniture and smart bathrooms. There is also a simple restaurant and café. **www.relaxhotel-bg.com**

SANDANSKI Sandanski

ul. Makedonia **Tel** *(0746) 31165* **Fax** *(0746) 31271* **Rooms** *300*   **Map B5**

An enormous Socialist-era spa hotel shaped like a flat-topped pyramid, the Sandanski offers a comprehensive range of spa treatments. Its facilities and rooms have been refurbished to high standards in recent years and guests can choose from health programmes designed to treat a variety of ailments. **www.interhotelsandanski.com**

SHIROKA LÛKA Kalina

ul. Kapitan Petko Voivoda 63 **Tel** *(03030) 675* **Rooms** *10*   **Map C4**

Furnished in Rhodopean style, with wood panelling and plenty of thick woollen rugs, the Kalina offers clean, quiet rooms with wonderful mountain views. The cosy basement tavern features a roaring fire in winter, nightly bagpipe performances and Bulgarian folk music. Located just off the town's central square. **www.shirokaluka-kalina.com**

SHIROKA LÛKA Zgorovska Kushta

ul. Kapitan Petko Voivoda 117 **Tel** *(03030) 277* **Rooms** *4*   **Map C4**

Situated across the river from the Church of the Assumption, this small hotel occupies one of Shiroka Luka's lovely old timber- and stone-built houses. The en-suite rooms are simply furnished and share a balcony facing forested hills. Traffic noise from the main road may be an annoyance, especially at busy weekends. **www.zgurovskihause.hit.bg**

SMOLYAN Trite Eli

ul. Srednogorets 1 **Tel** *(0301) 81028* **Fax** *(0301) 63862* **Rooms** *5*   **Map C5**

A pleasant family-run hotel located on a small street close to the Avtogara (bus station). The rooms are spotless and simply furnished, with thick Rhodopean rugs on the beds. Most have shared bathrooms. The owners cook fantastic local dishes using their own fresh produce. **Dreitannen_h@yahoo.com**

SMOLYAN Luxor

bul. Bûlgaryia 51 **Tel** *(0301) 63317* **Fax** *(0301) 64572* **Rooms** *19*   **Map C5**

Smolyan's newest hotel has a modern mirror-glass façade and an attractive, stylish interior. Its spacious rooms are smartly furnished and have great mountain views, and all have WiFi. Various room options include a pair of large maisonettes suitable for families. Facilities include a sauna. **www.luxor-bg.com**

TRIGRAD Silivriak Hotel

Tel *(03040) 220* **Rooms** *8*   **Map C5**

Perched on the hillside high above Trigrad, the Silivriak Hotel enjoys sweeping views of the valley and surrounding mountains. It is run by a friendly family, and the rooms are clean and adequately furnished. Downstairs a small *mehana* (traditional tavern) with a cosy open fire provides the guests with much-appreciated sustenance.

VELINGRAD Olymp

ul. Tsar Samuil **Tel** *(0359) 56100* **Fax** *(0359) 51239* **Rooms** *190*   **Map B4**

The 4-star Olymp is a major spa hotel on a forested hillside overlooking Velingrad. Thanks to this location, the restaurant, sunbathing terrace and most of the rooms have splendid views. The décor is mildly Grecian and perhaps not quite as stylish as the 5-star Dvoretsa *(see p224),* but service and standards are high. **www.olymp.velingrad.com**

VELINGRAD Dvoretsa
 €€€
ul. Tosho Staikov 8 **Tel** *(0359) 56200* **Fax** *(0359) 51098* **Rooms** *115*   **Map B4**

The vast 5-star Dvoretsa is tucked away in a neatly wooded park. It offers superb standards of accommodation and service and a broad range of spa treatments. Facilities include sauna, steam room, fitness centre, tennis courts and a hot outdoor pool bordered by an ornamental grotto. **www.dvoretsa.com**

ZLATOGRAD Pachilovska Kushta
€
Ethnographic Museum Complex **Tel** *(03071) 4166* **Rooms** *8*   **Map D5**

The Pachilovska Kushta is a 19th-century National Revival house in the centre of the Ethnographic Museum Complex. It has been turned into an atmospheric guesthouse with luxurious rooms that have antique wooden furniture, wood-panelled ceilings and stripped floors. TVs, plush bathrooms and central heating are modern improvements.

CENTRAL BULGARIA

BOZHENTSI Bozhentsi Village
€
Tel *(067) 193 363* **Fax** *(066) 804 462* **Rooms** *30*   **Map C3**

The tourist information centre at the entrance to Bozhentsi offers a variety of rooms in beautifully restored houses throughout the village. Prices vary according to size and location of rooms, but standards are consistent and all the rooms are cosily furnished. Breakfast is not included. **www.bojentsi.com**

DRYANOVO Dryanovo Monastery
€
4 km (just over 2 miles) south of Dryanovo **Tel** *(0676) 5253* **Rooms** *16*   **Map D3**

In an idyllic location below forests and steep cliffs, this monastery offers accommodation in its residential wing. The rooms, once occupied by monks who lived simply, have been refurbished to meet reasonable standards of comfort. Guests can eat in the small ground-floor restaurant.

ELENA Central
€
ul. Stoyan Mihaelovski 4 **Tel** *(06151) 2348* **Fax** *(06151) 2179* **Rooms** *22*   **Map D3**

Elena's several hotels are strung out along the main street. All offer similar middle-range standards but the Central is probably the most comfortable and it has the town's only (outdoor) pool. Rooms are simply and unimaginatively furnished but guests can use the fitness equipment and sauna. **hotel_central@elena.vali.bg**

GABROVO Gabrovo
€€
bul. Hemus 4 **Tel** *(066) 801 705* **Fax** *(066) 801 725* **Rooms** *23*   **Map D3**

Of the town's two accommodation options (the other is the Socialist-era Balkan), this is the better choice. The Gabrovo Hotel, 4 km (just over 2 miles) south of the town centre, is a modern, family-run establishment with clean, spacious rooms, a garden and a small restaurant for guests. **hotel_gabrovo@mbox.contact.bg**

GLOZHENE MONASTERY LittleSpring Guest House
€
ul. Zdrav 13, Malŭk Izvor **Tel** *(06990) 272* **Rooms** *6*   **Map C3**

Situated in the village of Maluk Izvor, the LittleSpring Guest House is the closest accommodation to the monastery. Cosy, rustic rooms are heated by wood-burning stoves and the upper-floor terrace has lovely views of the valley. The affable English owner is a mountain-biking enthusiast who arranges tours of the region. **maxtbreeds@yahoo.com**

HISAR Hisar Spa Complex
€€
ul. Gurko 1 **Tel** *(0337) 62781* **Fax** *(0337) 62784* **Rooms** *106*   **Map C3**

Once written off as a dilapidated Socialist-era relic, the Hisar Spa Complex has undergone a major refurbishment. Smartly dressed staff provide excellent service and rooms are clean and comfortable. There is a restaurant *(see p240)*, indoor and outdoor pools, and spa treatments that utilize Hisar's warm mineral springs. **www.hotelhissar.com**

KARLOVO Almond
€€
Bademlika Quarter **Tel** *(0335) 91555* **Fax** *(0335) 91554* **Rooms** *9*   **Map C3**

High in the hills above Karlovo, this is a splendid small hotel built on the site of an almond orchard. Gleaming marble floors and staircases combined with plush furniture create an elegant environment where guests can relax and enjoy wonderful views of the Rose Valley. The rooms are stylishly furnished and have Jacuzzis. **www.almondbg.com**

KAZANLŬK Teres
€
ul. Lyubomir Kabakchiev 16 **Tel** *(0431) 64272* **Rooms** *11*   **Map D3**

Located on the edge of the town, next to the Ethnographic Complex, the Teres is a new hotel with a National Revival façade. Staff provide good service and can arrange tours of the owners' rose-oil factory. The rooms are adequately furnished but suffer from unimaginative décor. The hotel has a restaurant *(see p240)*. **www.hotelteres.com**

KOPRIVSHTITSA Bashtina Kushta
€
bul. Hadzhi Nencho Palaveev 32 **Tel** *(07184) 3033* **Rooms** *14*   **Map C3**

Although it has a traditional façade, this is one of the few hotels in Koprivshtitsa with a modern interior. The rooms have spotless tiled floors and contemporary furniture and décor. Architectural traditions have no place here, but the hotel compensates by offering an excellent range of local dishes in its restaurant. **www.fhhotel.info**

Key to Price Guide *see p218* **Key to Symbols** *see back cover flap*

KOPRIVSHTITSA Kalina

bul. Hadzhi Nencho Palaveev 35 **Tel** *(07184) 2032* **Rooms** *6*

Map C3

An attractive ochre-painted replica of a 19th-century mansion, the Kalina is surrounded by pretty walled gardens. The rooms are clean and comfortable, with pine furniture, period fittings and traditional rugs. The hospitable owners are friendly and helpful, and will provide meals if required. **Hotelkalina@fog-bg.net**

KOPRIVSHTITSA Tryanova Kûshta

ul. Geremilov 5 **Tel** *(07184) 3057* **Rooms** *3*, **Apartments** *1*

Map C3

Built in 1895, the Tryanova Kushta is a delightfully authentic wooden house in a tranquil spot on Koprivshtitsa's western hillside. Its three atmospheric rooms are decorated in red, blue and pink and have pine beds and colourful rugs. The downstairs apartment has the original low wooden ceilings that were designed to conserve heat in winter.

KOTEL Chukarite

Izvorite Park **Tel** *(0453) 2475* **Rooms** *14*

Map E3

Tucked away in the Chukarite district above Kotel, the hotel occupies a peaceful spot. Rooms are simply furnished and have improvements such as double glazing and air conditioning but the bathrooms and internal décor await refurbishment. The downstairs restaurant has a roaring fire and serves typical national cuisine. **tvkotel@mail.bg**

LOVECH Oasis

ul. Ivan Drasov 17 **Tel** *(068) 600 612* **Fax** *(068) 626 239* **Rooms** *22*

Map C2

In a quiet spot adjacent to the Varosha Quarter and overlooking the Ossam River, the Oasis is a homely hotel in the traditional style. Staff are polite and helpful and the rooms are comfortably furnished with pine beds and shaggy woollen rugs. Guests can dine in the hotel's cosy *mehana* (traditional tavern). **kristina_19@abv.bg**

LOVECH Presidium Palace

ul. Turgovska 51 **Tel** *(068) 600 170* **Fax** *(068) 600 171* **Rooms** *48*

Map C2

Lovech's smartest hotel, the Presidium Palace has a modern design with plenty of glass, palm trees and boutiques. Its central location, high standards and modern facilities make it the obvious choice for business travellers. Rooms are stylish, with modern bathrooms. There is a sauna, fitness centre and restaurant *(see p241)*. **www.presidium.com**

RIBARITSA Evergreen Palace

Tel *(06902) 2066* **Fax** *(06902) 2042* **Rooms** *15*

Map C3

A wonderfully luxurious riverside hotel set in dense forest. The design is modern and stylish, the rooms spacious and comfortable, and service excellent. Facilities include tennis courts, swimming pools, a sauna and a fitness centre and restaurant *(see p241)*. Horse-riding can be arranged at the neighbouring stables. **www.evergreen-palace.com**

SLIVEN Sliven

bul. Hadzhi Dimitûr 2 **Tel** *(044) 624 056* **Rooms** *88*

Map E3

This 17-storey Socialist-era hotel is currently central Sliven's best accommodation option. The building is undergoing renovation and now offers a choice of smartly refurbished rooms or cheaper rooms with dated furnishings. There is a restaurant and the great views of the Blue Rocks above the town are an added attraction. **www.hotel.sliven.net**

STARA ZAGORA Forum

ul. Hadzhi Dimitûr Asenov 94 **Tel & Fax** *(042) 631 616* **Rooms** *16*

Map D3

A classy establishment in a restored building with a boldly painted façade, the Forum is one of the town's top hotels. Its spacious rooms have contemporary furnishings, smart bathrooms and access to wireless internet. Facilities include a multimedia conference centre and massage room. Staff are polite and efficient. **www.hotelforum.bg**

TETEVEN Vit

ul. Mihael Koichev 2 **Tel** *(0678) 2034* **Rooms** *11*

Map C3

The Vit's hillside position in the suburbs of Teteven provides its rooms with pleasant views of the forested crags that loom over the town. Among the attractions here are polite staff, good standards and a decent restaurant *(see p241)*. The small outdoor pool is a bonus, but it's a little too close to the main street.

TROYAN Troyan Plaza

ul. Slaveikov 54 **Tel** *(0670) 64399* **Fax** *(0670) 64299* **Rooms** *60*

Map C3

Impressive new 4-star hotel close to the centre of Troyan. The façade is a combination of glass and metal with stone and timber cladding. The rooms have plush furnishings and staff provide a good standard of service. Facilities include a spa centre, fitness equipment, solarium, swimming pool and restaurant *(see p241)*. **www.troyanplaza.com**

TRYAVNA Zograf

ul. Slaveikov 1 **Tel** *(0677) 4970* **Rooms** *19*

Map D3

Next to the stone bridge in the heart of Tryavna's old town, the Zograf occupies a National Revival building adorned with tasteful works of art. The clean, comfortable rooms have contemporary furniture and laminate floors. There is also a snug *mehana (see p241)* and a paved courtyard with seating overlooking the river. **zograf@unicsbg.net**

TRYAVNA Ralitsa

ul. Kaleto 16a **Tel** *(0677) 2262* **Fax** *(0677) 2402* **Rooms** *76*

Map D3

High in the wooded hills above Tryavna, this large hotel complex has superb views of the town and surrounding countryside. Though slightly dated, it offers a good range of facilities and rooms are furnished to a reasonable standard. Guests have use of fitness equipment, sauna and swimming pool. **www.tryavna.bg/ralitsa**

VELIKO TŬRNOVO Hikers Hostel

ul. Reservoarska 91 **Tel** *(0889) 691 661* **Rooms** *4*   **Map D3**

High in the Varosha quarter, the relaxed Hikers Hostel offers mixed dormitories and one double room. Quirky wooden furniture fills the comfortable communal area, and an outdoor summer terrace commands great views of Tsarevets. Tea, coffee, kitchen facilities, internet access and a pick-up service are included. **www.hikers-hostel.org**

VELIKO TŬRNOVO Comfort

ul. Panoyot Tipografov 5 **Tel** *(062) 628 728* **Fax** *(062) 623 525* **Rooms** *7* **Map D3**

This cosy hotel in the Varosha quarter features wood panelling and parquet floors, and commands tremendous views of Tsarevets. All the rooms have large windows and some have balconies as well. The owners maintain spotless standards and provide friendly and helpful service. Internet access is available. **hotel_komfortvt@abv.bg**

VELIKO TŬRNOVO Yantra

ul. Opalchenska 2 **Tel** *(062) 600 607* **Fax** *(062) 606 569* **Rooms** *71* **Map D3**

A new, high-class hotel facing the centre of town, with stunning views of Tsarevets to the rear. Accommodation is spacious and richly furnished; guests pay a little extra for rooms overlooking Tsarevets. Facilities include a spa centre, fitness equipment, business centre, casino, wireless internet and restaurant *(see p242)*. **office@yantrabg.com**

YAMBOL Tundzha

ul. Buzludzha 13 **Tel** *(046) 662 771* **Fax** *(046) 641 295* **Rooms** *82* **Map E3**

The Tundzha occupies a Socialist-era block that towers over the town centre. The lobby has been refurbished in Grecian style with an odd assortment of statues and columns. The hotel is being renovated,and those rooms that have not yet been modernized retain their 1970s décor but are slightly cheaper. **www.hotel-tundzha.domino.bg**

ZHERAVNA Eko

Tel *(04585) 389* **Rooms** *6*   **Map E3**

A tremendously atmospheric hotel situated in a restored 18th-century house. Built almost entirely of wood, the six rooms provide wonderfully snug accommodation and share a first-floor balcony overlooking pretty walled gardens. Guests can dine in a small downstairs *mehana* (tavern) with stone walls and an open fire. **www.ekohotel-jeravna.hit.bg**

NORTHERN BULGARIA

BELOGRADCHIK Madona

ul. Hristo Botev 26 **Tel** *(0936) 5546* **Rooms** *6*   **Map A2**

This small, friendly B&B on a quiet residential street has small but comfortable rooms with TV. Bathrooms are a little cramped and feature Bulgarian-style open showers. For breakfast you will be offered a choice of *mekitsi* (deep-fried dough balls served with jam or cheese) or *banichki* (cheese pastries). **www.madonahotel.belogradchik.info**

CHIPROVTSI Torlatsite

ul. Pavleto 31 **Tel** *(0887) 892 790, (0885) 358 592* **Rooms** *4* **Map A2**

A centrally located B&B in a house decorated in traditional style. The rooms have TV and en-suite bathrooms. The B&B is run by a carpet-making family. Weaving demonstrations are available to interested guests and a small range of kilims is offered for sale. Local specialities are served in the downstairs restaurant. **www.torlacite.com**

DOBRICH Rezidentzia

ul. Batovska 20 **Tel** *(058) 604 246* **Rooms** *15*   **Map F2**

Located southeast of the centre, in the grounds of a former government residence once used by top communist leaders. The rooms have laminated floors, TV and minibar and the bathrooms feature Bulgarian-style open showers. The restaurant has a pleasant outdoor terrace and guests can use the swimming pool. **www.rezidentzia.domino.bg**

DOBRICH Sport Palas

bul. 25 Septemvri 1a **Tel** *(058) 603 622* **Fax** *(058) 601 077* **Rooms** *45* **Map F2**

The neat rooms in this park-side hotel are plainly decorated in muted browns and greys, and each has a small TV and simple bathroom. Fitness facilities include up-to-date exercise machines and a sauna, and there is a restaurant *(see p242)*. The hotel is next to one of Dobrich's most popular open-air swimming pools. **http://sportpalas.tur-sport.com**

DOBRICH Hotel Complex Bulgaria

pl. Svoboda 8 **Tel** *(058) 600 226* **Fax** *(058) 601 007* **Rooms** *170* **Map F2**

This modern, 10-storey building in the centre of town will suit people who like to have everything under one roof. As well as three bars and two restaurants (one of which has panoramic views), the hotel also offers a casino, sauna, solarium and indoor pool. Rooms are plain but comfortable, with TV and minibar. **www.bulgaria-dobrich.com**

ISPERIH Alen Mak

ul. Vasil Levski 79 **Tel** *(08331) 2359* **Rooms** *15*   **Map E2**

Situated on Isperih's pedestrianized main street, the Alen Mak is a simple but comfortable hotel suitable for visitors on a brief stopover to visit the Thracian tombs at Sveshtari. Rooms, decorated in creamy colours, include a small TV and en-suite bathrooms with Bulgarian-style open shower. The downstairs restaurant can get lively at weekends.

Key to Price Guide *see p218* **Key to Symbols** *see back cover flap*

IVANOVO Polomie Lodge

ul. Pirin 1 **Tel** *(0889) 478 531*   **Rooms** *3*   €€   **Map E2**

A top-class B&B in a beautifully decorated modern house, just off the main street. Rooms have wooden floors and wood-panelled walls and ceilings. The shared bathrooms have state-of-the-art massage showers. Groups or a family can rent the whole house on a self-catering basis.**kath@polomie.eu www.polomie.eu**

RUSE Anna Palace

ul. Knyazheska 4 **Tel** *(082) 825 005* **Fax** *(082 825 522* **Rooms** *30*   €€€   **Map D2**

The Anna Palace occupies one of central Ruse's most elegant mansions, built for a Greek industrialist in 1888. Rooms are decorated in pastel colours, and have solid reproduction furniture and spacious bathrooms. The hotel's six apartments have antique furniture and ceramic stoves. There is also a restaurant. **www.annapalace.com**

RUSE Luliaka

Zapaden park **Tel** *(082) 821 161*   **Rooms** *11*   €€€   **Map D2**

Located 6 km (4 miles) west of central Ruse, just off the main road to Sofia, the Luliaka is a tastefully restored three-storey building set in an attractive riverside park. Rooms are either doubles or studio apartments with small river-facing balconies. There is also a sauna, a gym, two outdoor pools and a smart restaurant. **www.luliaka.com**

RUSE Bistra i Galina

ul. Han Asparuh 8 **Tel** *(082) 823 344*   **Rooms** *40*   €€€€   **Map D2**

A bold, modern building on a residential street near the centre of Ruse, the Bistra i Galina offers spacious, fully-equipped rooms decorated in soothing shades of pink and peach. Staff are friendly and professional, and the hotel has the added attraction of a small indoor pool with a Jacuzzi-style section **www.bghotel.bg**

RUSE Danube Plaza

pl. Svoboda 5 **Tel** *(082) 822 929*   **Rooms** *75*   €€€€   **Map D2**

Ideally located right on the main square, this hotel has a mix of plainly decorated rooms with simple shower-equipped bathrooms, and slightly plusher 3-star rooms with deeper carpets and modern bathroom fittings. The hotel's garden restaurant with live music is a popular attraction in summer. **www.danubeplaza.com**

SHUMEN Kyoshkove

Park Kyoshkove **Tel** *(054) 801 301* **Fax** *(054) 802 102* **Rooms** *18*   €€   **Map E2**

Situated in leafy Park Kyoshkove, 2 km (just over 1 mile) east of Shumen, and within striking distance of the Shumen fortress, this hotel has neat, simply furnished rooms with TV, minibar and internet connection. From the balcony you can almost touch the pine trees. Breakfast is served in the ground-floor terraced restaurant. **www.kyoshkove.com**

SHUMEN Shumen

pl. Oborishte **Tel** *(054) 879 143* **Fax** *(054) 800 003* **Rooms** *200*   €€   **Map E2**

This six-storey 1980s hotel makes a conveniently central sightseeing base. Rooms are neat and well-presented, with TV and minibar. As well as all the facilities associated with a large city-centre hotel, the Shumen has a 24-hour lobby bar, a nightclub with floor show, and a top-floor restaurant with panoramic views. **www.hotelsh.ro-ni.net**

SILISTRA Drustar

ul. Kapitan Mamarchev 10 **Tel** *(086) 812 200*   **Rooms** *44*   €€€   **Map F1**

A smart modern five-storey building with fortress-like towers, a reference to the medieval fortress that once stood on this spot. The rooms feature deep-pile carpets and designer furniture, and many have views of the nearby Danube. Additional facilities include a formal restaurant and a basement bar-nightclub. **www.hoteldrustar.com**

SREBURNA Pelican Lake Guesthouse

ul. Petko Simov 16 **Tel** *(085) 15322*   **Rooms** *2*   €   **Map F1**

Mere steps away from the bird-filled Sreburna Nature Reserve, this friendly B&B is in a beautifully renovated house, . Guests can use the kitchen, and lunchtime and evening meals (with a strong vegetarian slant) are available at a small extra cost. The owners, who are keen birdwatchers, can organize tours of the reserve. **www.srebarnabirding.com**

SVISHTOV Hotel Voenen Klub

ul. Aleko Konstantinov 2 **Tel** *(0631) 64274*   **Rooms** *15*   €   **Map D2**

Right on Svishtov's main street, the former Bulgarian Army Club now houses a smart, medium-sized hotel offering bright rooms with laminated floors, modern fittings and en-suite bathrooms with Bulgarian-style open showers. There is a formal restaurant on the ground floor, and a relaxing café on the floor above, with views of the main square.

VIDIN Hotel Anna Kristina

ul. Baba Vida 2 **Tel** *(094) 606 037*   **Rooms** *21*   €   **Map A1**

Modern comforts await visitors to this lovingly restored mansion beside Vidin's riverside gardens. Rooms have TV, a minibar and smart modern bathrooms. The garden café-bar and small outdoor pool add a resort-like atmosphere in summer. There is also a restaurant. **www.annakristinahotel.com**

VIDIN Old Town Hotel

ul. Knyaz Boris I, 2 **Tel** *(094) 600 023*   **Rooms** *8*   €€€   **Map A1**

A welcoming, family-run hotel located in a renovated 19th-century building, just off the city's main square and within easy strolling distance of Vidin's extensive riverside gardens. The rooms have TV, minibar and small but neat bathrooms. **oldtown_vd@abv.bg**

VRATSA Motel Chaika

€€

Vratsata Gorge **Tel** *(092) 621 369* **Rooms** *32*   **Map B2**

In a chalet-style building 2 km (just over 1 mile) west of central Vratsa, at the entrance to the dramatic Vratsa gorge, the Chaika offers comfortable rooms with modern furnishings, TV and minibar. An excellent base for hiking in the gorge and surrounding hills, the Chaika also has one of the best restaurants in the area. **chaika_hotel@avb.bg**

BLACK SEA COAST

ALBENA Laguna Beach

€€€

Albena Resort **Tel** *(0579) 62959* **Fax** *(0579) 62030* **Rooms** *190*   **Map G2**

One of Albena's many 4-star hotels, the Laguna Beach has established a reputation for good service. It is situated right on the beach and has a stepped design typical of this resort. The excellent facilities include a huge pool, childcare and entertainment, and a cinema. **www.albena.bg**

ALBENA Ralitsa
€€€€

Albena Resort **Tel** *(0579) 62391* **Fax** *(0579) 62269* **Rooms** *285*   **Map G2**

The Ralitsa is situated in Albena's wooded park about a ten-minute walk from the beach. It's a huge hotel with high standards and almost every conceivable facility. Plenty of children's activities are available and there are tennis and basketball courts, three pools and two restaurants. Prices are all-inclusive. **www.albena.bg**

BALCHIK White House
€€

ul. Geo Milev 18 **Tel & Fax** *(0579) 73951* **Rooms** *16*   **Map G2**

A modern hotel located next to Balchik's marina, the well-established White House is efficiently run and offers comfortable standards. Rooms have contemporary furniture and stripped pine floors; some have balconies with sea views. Its smart seafront restaurant *(see p243)* is one of the town's best. **www.bgglobe.net/white_house.html**

BURGAS Bulgaria

€€€€

ul. Alexandrovska 21 **Tel** *(056) 842 820* **Fax** *(056) 841 291* **Rooms** *203*   **Map F3**

Burgas's most imposing landmark is the16-floor concrete Bulgaria hotel. It was built in 1976 to accommodate high-ranking bureaucrats and foreign diplomats, and its recent refurbishment has returned it to the high standards of its heyday. As you'd expect, the rooms have fantastic views of Burgas and the coast. **www.bulgaria-hotel.com**

GOLDEN SANDS Kamchia
€€

Tel *(052) 355 511* **Rooms** *121*   **Map G2**

One of the resort's older hotels, the Kamchia has recently undergone a thorough refurbishment. Now comfortable and with consistently good service, the hotel offers excellent value for money as it is situated just 150 m (500 ft) from the sea. The rooms are a little narrow but have balconies with pleasant views. **www.goldensands.bg**

GOLDEN SANDS Berlin Golden Beach

€€€€

Tel *(052) 384 151* **Rooms** *276*   **Map G2**

A huge luxury complex right on the beach, the Berlin Golden Beach is a well-managed hotel offering high standards of service. All the rooms have fantastic sea views. Its attractive range of facilities includes mineral-water pools, children's entertainment and tennis courts. **www.lti-berlin.net**

KAVARNA Venera
€

ul. Chaika 6 **Tel** *(0570) 84878* **Fax** *(0570) 82254* **Rooms** *15*   **Map G2**

The family-run Venera sits on a hillside above the Chirakman resort area of Kavarna. The spacious, simply furnished rooms have spotlessly clean tiled floors and balconies with wonderful sea views. The hotel's small restaurant has a covered terrace looking out to sea. **kastroi@abv.bg**

LOZENETS Friends

€€

ul. Ribarska 43 **Tel** *(0888) 606 575* **Rooms** *25*   **Map F4**

One of Lozenets' new hotspots, the relaxing Friends Hotel is set amid leafy gardens next to its fashionable sushi restaurant *(see p244)*. The rooms are comfortably furnished and have balconies overlooking the garden. Guests have use of a Jacuzzi, and the nearest beach is just minutes away. **www.friendshotel.org**

NESEBŮR White House
€€

ul. Tsar Simeon 2 **Tel** *(0554) 424 888* **Rooms** *10*   **Map F3**

Situated in the heart of Nesebur's old town, the White House offers comfortable accommodation, with luxurious features such as leather sofas, for a reasonable price. The rooftop terrace has sea views, and guests have use of a fitness centre and internet café. **www.white-house-13.8k.com**

NESEBŮR Sveti Stephan
€€€

ul. Ribarska 11 **Tel** *(0554) 43604* **Rooms** *18*   **Map F3**

Located opposite the New Metropolitan Church originally known as Sveti Stefan, this is a modern hotel whose façade mimics the style of Nesebur's 19th-century National Revival buildings. Excellent service is combined with comfortably furnished rooms and sea views. There is also a fitness centre, sauna, Jacuzzi and solarium.

Key to Price Guide *see p218* **Key to Symbols** *see back cover flap*

OBZOR Helios Beach

ul. Chernomorska 44 **Tel** *(0554) 32175* **Fax** *(0554) 32265* **Rooms** *191* **Map F3**

Obzor has a magnificent sandy beach along which monolithic hotel complexes are mushrooming at a startling pace. The tree-shaded Helios Beach is the most attractive of these as it consists of several unobtrusive concrete buildings set at a slanting angle to the beach. Service is excellent and prices all-inclusive. **heliosbeach@relax-plus.com**

PRIMORSKO Flamingo

ul. Mart 8 **Tel** *(0550) 33031* **Fax** *(0550) 32272* **Rooms** *38* **Map F4**

Rising out of the trees on the eastern side of the Primorsko peninsula, the Flamingo is a modest hotel with good standards and service. It faces the sea and many of the rooms have balconies with lovely views. Its small restaurant has a fountain and a pleasant summer terrace.

RUSSALKA HOLIDAY VILLAGE

Above Kavarna **Tel** *(02) 962 4215* **Fax** *(02) 962 4705* **Bungalows** *500* **Map G2**

Far smaller and quieter than the resorts further south, Russalka Holiday Village is ideal for families. It's in an isolated spot with rocky coves and beaches. Staff can arrange a variety of activities for guests of all ages, and facilities include a fitness centre, tennis courts, diving tuition and a nightclub. Price are all-inclusive. **www.russalka-holidays.com**

SINEMORETS Casa Domingo

ul. Ribarska **Tel** *(0550) 66093* **Fax** *(0550) 66095* **Rooms** *44* **Map G4**

In contrast to the busy main street and overdevelopment of Sinemorets, the Casa Domingo is an oasis of tranquillity. The hotel is a single-storey affair whose comfortable rooms are grouped around a central courtyard and pool. Polite staff can arrange a variety of activities for guests including boat trips and canoeing. **www.casadomingo.info**

SOZOPOL Orion

ul. Vihren 28 **Tel** *(0550) 23193* **Fax** *(0550) 22037* **Rooms** *16* **Map F3**

Set high on a hill in the new town, and facing the Sozopol and Burgas bays to the northwest, the Orion is one of the few hotels on the Bulgarian coast that offers romantic views of sunsets over the sea. The hotel is family-run, with clean rooms, and it has an excellent restaurant with outdoor terrace. **www.hotel-orion.net**

SOZOPOL Rusalka

ul. Milet 36 **Tel** *(0550) 23047* **Rooms** *12* **Map F3**

Plenty of houses in Sozopol's old town offer private rooms, but the Rusalka is one of only a handful of hotels here. Set on the edge of the peninsula, it faces south and all the rooms have balconies with breathtaking sea views. Standards of comfort, cleanliness and service are high. There is also a restaurant *(see p245)*. **www.rusalka.sozopol.com**

SUNNY BEACH Neptun Beach

Tel *(0554) 26605* **Rooms** *376* **Map F3**

Sunny Beach is full of large hotels catering for visitors on package holidays. Their standards vary enormously, but the Neptun Beach has a reputation for consistently good service. It offers spacious rooms with superb sea views and many amenities, including children's entertainment, outdoor Jacuzzi, and karaoke bar. **www.neptunbeach.com**

SVETI KONSTANTIN Piero

Koraten Complex **Tel** *(052) 362 424* **Rooms** *6* **Map G2**

Hidden down a side street to the southwest of Sveti Konstantin, the Piero is a tranquil family-run hotel with a quiet garden. Its clean, spacious rooms have tiled floors and simple furnishings, and its small restaurant provides meals for guests. The beach is only five minutes' walk away.

TSAREVO Vesiliko Complex

ul. Vesiliko 136 **Tel** *(0590) 54022* **Fax** *(0590) 53022* **Rooms** *22* **Map F4**

A thoughtfully designed complex of single-storey buildings with rooms and apartments, the Vesiliko has an idyllic setting in Tsarevo's old quarter. Many rooms have outdoor terraces with sea views. Standards are high in relation to the surprisingly low prices. Facilities include an indoor pool and wireless internet. **www.wasiliko.bginvent.net**

TYULENOVO Delfina

Next to the harbour **Tel** *(057) 432 221* **Rooms** *10* **Map G2**

The Delfina is a modern hotel that overlooks Tyulenovo's tiny harbour. The rooms are clean and adequately furnished, and have balconies with excellent sea views. The hotel also has a restaurant *(see p245)* As the Delfina tends to fill up with groups in the high season, it is advisable to reserve in advance. **mihaylov_sinove@abv.bg**

VARNA Panorama

bul. Primorski 31 **Tel** *(052) 687 300* **Fax** *(052) 626 033* **Rooms** *57* **Map F2**

The gleaming, leather-furnished lobby of this plush new hotel is an indication of its high class. Rooms have neutral décor, with comfortable furniture, and balconies with lovely sea views. Facilities include wireless internet, a fitness centre and a sauna. One disadvantage, however, is that it is right next to the busy bulevard Primorski. **www.panoramabg.com**

VARNA Grand Hotel Musala Palace

ul. Musala 3 **Tel** *(052) 664 100* **Fax** *(052) 664 196* **Rooms** *24* **Map F2**

A central 5-star hotel housed in a 19th-century building refurbished to staggeringly high standards, with prices to match. Thick carpets, Art Nouveau décor, impeccably liveried staff and rooms with original works of art and flat-screen TVs are among the extravagant features here. The restaurant *(see p245)* is equally fine. **www.musalapalace.bg**

WHERE TO EAT

A s new restaurants continue to open almost everywhere in Bulgaria, the range of eating options throughout the country is also increasing. Styles of restaurant vary greatly, from folksy eateries offering the best of traditional Bulgarian cooking, to elegant establishments specializing in modern European cuisine. In the middle range are restaurants serving national and international food.

Restaurant sign in Nesebûr

The most common types of restaurant, and the most authentically Bulgarian, are *mehani* (taverns) and *kruchmi* (inns), which serve traditional Bulgarian dishes, often accompanied by local wines. Bulgaria also has top-quality gourmet restaurants, notably in Sofia and on the Black Sea coast. While inexpensive Chinese restaurants can be found in large cities, other types of exotic cuisine are largely unknown outside Sofia.

Beachside tables outside a restaurant in Sozopol, on the Black Sea

CHOOSING A RESTAURANT

The most widespread type of restaurant in Bulgaria is the *mehana*, or tavern, an informal establishment serving a range of Bulgarian dishes and regional specialities. Most *mehani* also have a long list of Bulgarian wines *(see pp28–9)* and a full range of other alcoholic drinks. *Mehani* are usually homely places, often with brightly coloured tablecloths and a decor of folkloric objects, such as traditional pottery laid out on shelves and old agricultural implements hung on the walls. In popular tourist areas, *mehani* often have live musical entertainment in the form of regional folk-singing evenings.

A *kruchma* (inn) is similar to a *mehana* in its informal, folksy style. Traditionally the *kruchma* was where the men of the village gathered to drink and play cards. Today,

however, the word *kruchma* is often appropriated by smart regional restaurants so as to convey a sense of welcoming rustic authenticity. At a *mehana* or *kruchma* you can spend a whole evening lingering over a full meal, but it is also perfectly acceptable simply to sit at the bar and enjoy a drink while nibbling at a snack or salad.

Any establishment calling itself a restaurant *(restorant)* is likely to offer a mixture of Bulgarian and international food. Service in a restaurant is usually slightly more formal than in a *mehana* or *kruchma*, and the decor often follows international rather than local styles. In Sofia and the major Black Sea resorts an increasing number of restaurants specialize in French, Italian or Japanese cuisine. While they are inexpensive, many of these restaurants have high culinary standards.

As almost everywhere else in the world, every Bulgarian city has at least one Chinese restaurant *(Kitaiski restorant)*. Most offer a familiar range of Chinese food, frequently served in large portions and at very reasonable prices.

Pizzerias are springing up almost everywhere in Bulgaria. However, the pizzas that they serve are usually made with locally produced ingredients,

The Melita café, on ulitsa Graf Ignatiev, in Sofia

Interior of the Checkpoint Charly restaurant in Sofia (see p235)

traditional hors-d'oeuvres are various combinations of cheese, eggs and vegetables baked in earthenware pots, a wide range of vegetables fried in breadcrumbs, and cubed vegetables grilled on a kebab skewer. Common Bulgarian hors-d'oeuvres include *chushka byurek* (a large pepper stuffed with cheese and fried in batter or breadcrumbs) and aubergine *(patladzhan)* fried and served with yoghurt.

Vegetarians should be wary of vegetable soups and stews. Many of these apparently meat-free dishes are made with meat stock.

THE BILL AND TIPPING

Like the menu, the bill *(smetkata)* is usually written in Cyrillic. If you are confused about the names of dishes you ordered or about the amount you have been charged, refer back to the original menu.

Credit cards are only accepted in smarter restaurants in Sofia and other major towns and cities. Restaurant bills rarely include service, and it is customary to leave a tip of about 10 per cent.

SMOKING

Smoking is still widespread in Bulgaria. Restaurants are legally obliged to provide a certain number of tables for non-smokers. In practice, these tables are often placed in close proximity to those set aside for smokers, so that cigarette smoke can be difficult to avoid.

and are unfortunately not the equal of the authentic Italian- or American-style pizzas that are available in other countries.

WHEN TO EAT

Mehani and restaurants are usually open from 11am until 11pm or midnight. Little distinction is made between lunch *(obyad)* and dinner *(vecherya)* and the same menu of dishes is usually offered all through the day.

RESERVATIONS

Bulgaria's best restaurants generally attract a large clientele, so it is a good idea to reserve a table, especially at weekends. As restaurant staff may not always have a good command of English, or any other European language, it is often best to make your reservation by calling at the restaurant in person rather than booking by phone.

READING THE MENU

Both in *mehani* and restaurants, menus are written in Cyrillic script *(see pp286–8).* In Sofia and in tourist resorts, menus in English are often available. However, as translations are rarely perfect, some thought and imagination may be required to make out precisely what is on offer. Most menus are divided into sections, typically covering snacks, salads, hors d'oeuvres, main dishes and desserts. Vegetarian dishes are listed as *yastiya bez meso* ("meatless dishes") or as *postno yadene* ("fasting food").

VEGETARIANS

There is only a handful of dedicated vegetarian restaurants in Bulgaria, and most of these are in Sofia. Mainstream *mehani* and restaurants rarely include meat-free options in their list of main courses, but there are always plenty of salads and hors d'oeuvres that are suitable for vegetarians. Combining two or three of these makes a healthy and filling meal.

Bulgarian salads are particularly noted for the fresh vegetables that make up most of their ingredients. Among

Sign for O!Shipka restaurant

Live music at the Hadzhidraganovite kushti restaurant in Sofia (see p234)

The Flavours of Bulgaria

Bulgarian food is similar in many ways to that of the Greece and Turkey: filo pastries *(byurek)*; tomato, cucumber and white cheese salad *(shopska salata)*; moussaka *(musaka)* and stuffed vine leaves *(sarmi)* are among the shared dishes. But there are important differences too, not least the use of sunflower instead of olive oil for cooking and flavouring. Away from the Black Sea, there is less emphasis on fish dishes and a stronger reliance on vegetables and fruit. A salad or a selection of *meze* often begin a meal, both traditionally accompanied by a glass of *rakiya,* the local brandy.

Bunch of fresh dill

Farmer from Dobarsko, showing off the tomato crop

THE MOUNTAINS

Geography plays the biggest role in regional variations of Bulgarian cuisine. Livestock farming in the lower mountain ranges – most notably in the Rhodopes, Stara Planina, Strandzha, Rila and Pirin – is a tradition that goes back thousands of years. The omnipresent *kiselo mlyako* (sour yoghurt made with ewes', cows' or buffalo milk) is usually eaten plain, but it also forms the base for *tarator* soup and the drink *ayryan.* Bulgarian *sirene* cheese will be a familiar sight and taste for most visitors, since it is very similar to Greek *feta.* However, it is inadvisable to compare them in front of a Bulgarian – unless it's to say that the Bulgarian version is better. *Sirene* turns up in a huge number of dishes, from filo pastry *banitsa* to *shopska salata.* The hard, yellow cheese *kashkaval* is not as widely used, but it is an essential part of any *meze.* Also key to any group of *meze* dishes are examples of Bulgaria's huge range of sausages and cured meats. Spicy sausages such as *sudzhuk, banski staretz* and *strandzhansko dyado,* and the air-cured ham *elenski but,* seasoned with herbs,

Tarama Kyopolou Cured ham Sarmi Country bread
Sudzhuk salami

Sirene cheese
Kashkaval cheese

Selection of the many dishes that make up a Bulgarian *meze*

BULGARIAN DISHES AND SPECIALITIES

Kidney beans

Many of the traditional dishes of Bulgaria feature yoghurt, cheese, spices and herbs. *Chubritsa* is a herb similar to oregano and appears dried and crumbled onto soups, stews and even bread. Dill-scented *tarator* soup is wonderfully cooling on a hot summer day. Many dishes are meatless, such as the "monastery-style" bean soup of white kidney beans and vegetables, believed to have originated with one of the country's many religious orders. Bulgarians love stuffed vegetable dishes, peppers being a favourite. Usually baked, in summer peppers are filled with *sirene* cheese and egg and deep-fried. Carp, from the rivers such as the Danube, is the traditional dish for the important feast day of St Nicholas and, at Christmas and New Year, *banitsa* will have lucky charms hidden among its filo leaves.

Tarator, *the national dish, is a creamy, chilled soup made with yoghurt, dill, walnuts and sunflower oil.*

Bulgarian fruit and vegetables, piled high on a Sofia market stall

THE COAST

The dwindling fish stocks of the Black Sea are slowly on the mend and it is possible once more to enjoy excellent grilled bonito and stewed or fried scad when they arrive at the end of summer. Sprats, served fried or marinated, are available throughout the year. Mussels are plentiful and good, but must come from pollution-free sources. Bulgarian fish soup, *ribena chorba*, is seasoned with thyme, and may be made with fresh or saltwater fish.

all stem from the need to preserve meat to last through the long and bitter mountain winters. Hearty stews are a mountain tradition too, with *kavarma* and pork ribs with kidney beans among the tastiest and most popular.

THE PLAINS

The best of Bulgaria's fruit and vegetables are grown on the plains to the south and north of the Stara Planina range, usually without fertilizers. Berries, orchard fruits, melons and grapes (for the table as well as for wine) are among the many superb fruits. The peppers, tomatoes, cucumbers, onions, aubergines (eggplant), courgettes (zucchini) and potatoes are arguably the best in Europe and certainly among the cheapest. They feature prominently in a wide range of stews that go by the generic name of *gyuvetch*. Many salad dishes, such as *shopska* and *ovcharska* (shepherd's salad), originated on the plains and are at their very best here because of the freshness of the produce.

Fields of sunflowers in the countryside around Bozhentsi

ON THE MENU

Banitsa Savoury filo pastry pie filled with *sirene* and egg, vegetables or minced meat.

Kavarma Veal pork, chicken or lamb, stewed with onions and good local red wine.

Kyopolou Aubergine, pepper and tomato dip with garlic, parsley and red wine vinegar.

Kyufteta Spiced roasted, fried or grilled meatballs.

Shkembe chorba Soup made of veal tripe flavoured with garlic, said to be an infallible cure for a hangover.

Sirene po shopski Layers of cheese, peppers and tomato topped with an egg and baked in a small pot.

Tarama Creamy dip made from salted fish roe blended with chopped onion, soaked bread and sunflower oil.

Shopska salad *is a delicious mix of chopped tomatoes, cucumbers, peppers, onions and grated white cheese.*

Sweet peppers *are filled with a variety of stuffings, from rice or cheese and egg to meat, and baked or fried.*

Baklava, *filo pastry layered with walnuts and cinnamon and doused in syrup, is also eaten in Greece and Turkey.*

Choosing a Restaurant

The restaurants in this guide have been selected across a wide range of price categories for their good value, exceptional food and interesting location. This chart lists the restaurants by region, in chapter order. Map references for the Sofia restaurants correspond with the Sofia Street Finder *(see pp93–7).*

PRICE DETAILS
The following price ranges are for a three-course meal for one, including a half-bottle of house wine, tax and service.
€ Under 10 euros
€€ 10–20 euros
€€€ 20–30 euros
€€€€ Over 30 euros

SOFIA

Dani's €
ul. Angel Kunchev 18a **Tel** *(02) 987 4548*   **City Map 3 B2**

A deli-style café-restaurant on a quiet downtown corner, furnished with a couple of narrow tables flanked by tall wooden stools. On the menu is an inventive range of sandwiches, salads, soups and pastas, many of which are perfect for vegetarians. Dani's is also famous for its refreshing home-made lemonade.

Jimmy's sladoledena kushta €
ul. Angel Kunchev 11 **Tel** *(02) 980 3099*   **City Map 3 B3**

This renowned café-cum-sweet shop serves supremely palatable ice creams (to eat in or take away), as well as scrumptious pancakes and gateaux. It is also a good place to indulge in a decent cup of coffee or one of the house's luxuriant hot chocolate drinks.

Before & After   €€
ul. Hristo Belchev 12 **Tel** *(02) 981 6088*   **City Map 3 B2**

A delightful city-centre café-restaurant with an Art Nouveau theme. This is an excellent place in which to indulge in a coffee-and-cakes sightseeing break, but it also offers a large choice of full meals, including some mouth-watering pan-fried fish. It is often used as a venue for tango evenings, and photographs of dancers cover the walls.

Chevermeto   €€
bul. Cherni vruh 31 **Tel** *(02) 963 0308*

Colourful kilims (small woven carpets), sheepskin rugs and other traditional textiles decorate this folklore-themed restaurant in the basement of the Hemus hotel. On the menu, Bulgarian stews and grills predominate, alongside the *cheverme* (spit-roast lamb) from which the establishment gets its name. Live folk music and dancing every evening.

Hadzhidraganovite kushti   €€
ul. Kozlodui 75 **Tel** *(02) 931 3148*

An attractive folk-themed restaurant midway between the city centre and the train station. A huge menu of authentic Bulgarian dishes (including plenty of delicious salads and starters that vegetarians can choose from) is accompanied by a long list of Bulgarian wines and spirits. Folk musicians in national costume circulate from room to room.

Halbite   €€
ul. Neofit Rilski 72 **Tel** *(02) 980 4147*   **City Map 4 C3**

Hidden away at the end of a narrow passageway, Halbite provides a broad selection of traditional Bulgarian grilled meats and vegetarian dishes. Bare wood floors and wooden tables help to create an earthy and intimate atmosphere. Appropriately for a place whose name means "tankards", there's a large choice of beers at the bar .

Olive's   €€
ul. Graf Ignatiev 12 **Tel** *(02) 986 0902*   **City Map 3 B2**

This roomy, central café-restaurant offers a little bit of everything: pizzas, burgers, pastas and salads are perfect for a quick lunch, while more substantial steaks or fish dishes are well suited to a more relaxed evening meal. With friendly, jean-clad staff and vintage adverts adorning the walls, the emphasis is on enjoyment rather than formal dining.

Pastorant   €€
ul. Tsar Asen 16 **Tel** *(02) 981 4482*   **City Map 3 A2**

A friendly and informal pasta restaurant in a residential street just minutes away from bulevard Vitosha. Mixing modern design with folksy textiles and wooden tables, the décor is pleasantly relaxing. Fresh pasta with authentic sauces form the backbone of the menu, and there are always a couple of freshly made cakes or puddings for dessert.

Pod Lipite €€
ul. Elin Pelin 1 **Tel** *(02) 866 5053*

Just over the road from Borisova Gradina Park, "Under the Limes" recreates the atmosphere of a 19th-century country tavern with wood-beamed interior and delicious home cooking. The emphasis is on grilled and oven-baked meats, although there is a healthy choice of vegetarian dishes on the starter menu. Reservations necessary.

Key to Symbols *see back cover flap*

Pri Latsi

 €€

ul. Oborishte 18 **Tel** *(02) 846 8687*

A Hungarian-run restaurant located in a small and welcoming split-level space decorated with folksy textiles and ceramics, Pri Latsi's speciality is spicy paprika-rich goulash (several varieties are on the menu) served with home-made noodles or dumplings. For dessert, the *shamloi galushki* (syrup-covered balls of deep-fried dough) are irresistible.

Vagabond

 €€

ul. Svetoslav Terter 5 **Tel** *(02) 944 1465*

Just east of Orlov Most (Orlov Bridge), Vagabond has the homely and intimate feel of a domestic dining room. The menu has a genuinely international flavour although it is the Russian-influenced dishes that stand out. Vodka with *selyodka* (marinated herring) makes an ideal starter, and the home-made *pelmeni* (meat-filled dumplings) are outstanding.

Boyansko Hanche

 €€€

pl. Sborishte **Tel** *(02) 856 3016*

Conveniently situated round the corner from Boyana Church, this folk-style restaurant offers the full range of Bulgarian cuisine and a sprinkling of international steak and chicken dishes in a modern building decked out in traditional textiles. Live performances of traditional song and dance every evening.

Bulgari

€€€

bul. Knyaz Dondukov 71 **Tel** *(02) 843 5419*   **City Map 2 F3**

The Bulgari, in a 19th-century town house just northeast of Sofia's main sightseeing area, offers elegant dining in a room decorated with black-and-white photographs of old Sofia. The national repertoire of grilled meats, roast lamb and oven-baked stews predominates, although the modern European dishes are also excellent.

Egur Egur

€€€

ul. Sheinovo 18 **Tel** *(02) 946 1765*   **City Map 4 E2**

This classy Armenian restaurant serves delicious skewer-grilled meats, exotic sweet-and-sour stews, and intriguing vegetarian dishes featuring aubergines, courgettes, mushrooms and peppers. The interior is elegantly furnished and the service attentive. There is second Egur Egur at ul. Dobrudzha 10.

Gioia

€€€

ul. Lavele 11 **Tel** *(02) 986 0854*   **City Map 1 A4**

For quality Italian food in an intimate setting, there is no better place in Sofia. The menu features innumerable varieties of fresh pasta. Main courses include veal cutlets and some highly recommended fish dishes. The wine list is as Italian as the food, and the espresso coffee is as dark and strong as you would expect.

L'Etranger

€€€

ul. Tsar Simeon 78 **Tel** *(02) 983 1417*   **City Map 1 C2**

Located in an anonymous side street just off bustling bulevard Knyaginya Mariya Luiza, this intimate, family-run French bistro is worth seeking out. Whether you're here for a quick lunch or a multi-course meal, the food is excellent, authentic and none too expensive. Delicious desserts and a carefully chosen list of French wines add to the experience.

Mahaloto

€€€

bul. Vasil Levski 51 **Tel** *(0887) 617 972*   **City Map 4 D4**

A welcoming city-centre restaurant in a red-brick cellar, offering a classy mixture of Bulgarian and international cuisine, backed up by a strong list of quality wines. Stand-out dishes include the trout with walnuts, and the chicken breast with cream and mushroom sauce. In summer head for the quiet, tree-shaded terrace behind the building.

Manastirska Magernitsa

€€€

ul. Han Asparuh 67 **Tel** *(02) 980 3883*   **City Map 3 C3**

Plushly decorated city-centre villa featuring flowery wallpaper and near-antique furnishings. Its name means "monastery refectory" so it is no surprise to discover that many of the dishes on offer were researched from the cook books of Bulgaria's monasteries. Lentil, bean and pepper-based recipes feature strongly, alongside expertly grilled meat dishes.

Pri Yafata

€€€

ul. Solunska 28 **Tel** *(02) 980 1727*   **City Map 3 A2**

One of central Sofia's most enjoyable folk-themed restaurants, Pri Yafata boasts a colourful collection of embroidered tablecloths, striped rugs and old muskets hanging from the walls. A huge range of Bulgarian specialities is augmented by quality wines from every region of the country, and a large list of potent, fruit flavoured *rakiyas*.

Sushi Bar

€€€

ul. Denkoglu 18 **Tel** *(02) 981 8442*   **City Map 3 A1**

Smart but by no means over-formal, Sushi Bar is just round the corner from Sofia's main shopping street and makes the perfect place for a quick lunch or a more leisurely Oriental meal. The huge menu of expertly prepared sushi is available in small helpings of two or three pieces, or in set menus featuring various types of sushi on one plate.

Checkpoint Charly

 €€€€

ul. Ivan Vazov 12 **Tel** *(02) 988 0370*   **City Map 4 D2**

In this stylish eatery minimalist décor is melded with ironic communist-era decorations, including place mats designed to resemble the propaganda-filled newspapers of the socialist years. Quality international cuisine from steak to roast duck, and high-class live jazz at weekends – when you will need to reserve in order to get a table.

Chepishev
ul. Ivanitsa Danchev 27 **Tel** (02) 959 1010

This upmarket restaurant in the mountainside suburb of Boyana is perfect for a special night out. Served up by attentive staff, the Bulgarian and modern European dishes are prepared to gourmet standards. There is an impressive list of international wines, although it is the huge selection of whiskies that really make the place famous.

Otvud aleya zad shkafa
ul. Budapeshta 31 **Tel** (02) 983 5545   *City Map 2 D2*

Housed in a beautifully restored Art Nouveau building in a quiet street northeast of the centre, "Beyond the alley behind the cupboard" is one of Sofia's most atmospheric and charming restaurants. The menu features a mixture of Bulgarian and modern European dishes – all are excellently prepared.

Talisman
ul. Dimitur Hadzhikostov 14 **Tel** (02) 963 4924

One of Sofia's more elegant dining venues, the Talisman features classy crockery and cut glassware in a stylishly old-fashioned, wood-panelled dining room. A small but well-chosen range of European dishes forms the backbone of the menu. Service is impeccable, and the wine list is one of the city's best.

Uno Enoteca
bul. Vasil Levski 45 **Tel** (02) 981 4372   *City Map 4 D4*

Modern European cuisine with a strong Mediterranean flavour, backed up by a wide-ranging list of vintage wines from both Bulgaria and abroad. Combining exceptional standards of service with old-fashioned elegance, this is one of the best places in the city for formal, special-occasion dining.

Vishnite
ul. Hristo Smirnenski 45 **Tel** (02) 963 4984 or (0890) 866 730

Hidden away in the residential district of Lozenets, 3 km (2 miles) southeast of the centre, Vishnite is delightfully intimate and makes for a cosy venue for fine dining. The menu features several classic European dishes (usually including one fish dish), backed up by a small but well-chosen selection of wines. Only four tables, so be sure to make a reservation.

SOUTHERN BULGARIA

BACHKOVO Dzhamura (Dzhamura Hotel)
ul. Osvobozhdenya 74 **Tel** (03327) 230   *Map C4*

The large restaurant has both a cosy interior warmed by a large open fire and a spacious open terrace overlooking the river. It's a good place to relax after the bustle of monastery tourism and, though vegetarians are catered for, this is a carnivorous eatery where grilled meat and fish dominate the menu.

BACHKOVO Vodopada
Main car park **Tel** (0896) 021 053   *Map C4*

Outdoor tables surround the gushing waterfall that gives the restaurant its name. Located next to the monastery's access road, guests have a good view of bustling tourists and pay the restaurant's inflated prices for the privilege. The food, however, is very good and comes in large portions; *kyopole* (aubergine and garlic paste) is particularly tasty.

BANKSO Mexana Hadzhi Rushovi
ul. Pirin 33 **Tel** (0878) 805 532   *Map B4*

This intimate *mehana* (tavern) is concealed behind traditional stone walls and a hefty wooden door and the interior features the usual bare walls hung with animal skins. The specialities are dishes such as Bansko black pudding (*kurvavitsa*), Bansko-style aubergines (*patlazhan po Banski*), and yoghurt with locally picked forest fruits.

BANSKO Come Prima
ul. Pirin 96 **Tel** (0749) 88888   *Map B4*

Bansko's most exclusive restaurant is a sophisticated affair on the ground floor of the Kempinski Hotel (see p220). Numerous waiting staff provide faultless service and chefs prepare meals in an open show kitchen. The brief menu is supplemented by daily-changing specials and includes grilled octopus and homemade pasta with duck confit.

BLAGOEVGRAD 12te Stola
ul. Stefan Cholakov 3 **Tel** (0888) 994 599   *Map B4*

Situated in a lovely restored National Revival house next door to the Church of the Annunciation, the 12te Stola has wooden tables in an outdoor courtyard as well as indoor seating. Stripped wood floors and exposed beams throughout create a pleasant environment. The menu offers typical Bulgarian dishes prepared to a good standard.

BLAGOEVGRAD Planeta Italia
ul. Raiko Daskalov 2 **Tel** (073) 887 587   *Map B4*

One of the many cafés and restaurants in streets leading off ploshtad Makedonia, Planeta Italia offers an alternative that lies somewhere between Bulgarian and Italian cuisine. Drinks come with a complimentary appetizer and service is efficient. A good range of thin-crust pizzas is offered, but the pasta is over-cooked and the sauces lack flavour.

Key to Price Guide *see p234* **Key to Symbols** *see back cover flap*

BOROVETS Hunters
Tel *(0750) 32509*   **Map B4**

The friendly restaurant owner, who is also a ski instructor and mountain guide, spent time as a chef in Turkey, which accounts for the menu's eclectic mix. Turkish bread and kebabs are offered alongside Bulgarian cuisine, English and Swedish breakfasts, and fried trout. The walls are decorated with tea towels donated by English guests.

BOROVETS Bulgarian Dish
Tel *(0750) 32243*   **Map B4**

Situated right at the bottom of the slopes next to the Alpin hotel *(see p220)*, this restaurant lives up to its name by serving up plenty of local cuisine. The cosy interior has wooden beams, exposed stone, and a blazing fire to defrost chilly skiers. Bean soup and a variety of grilled meats feature on the menu.

DEVIN Elit
ul. Undola 2 **Tel** *(03041) 2240*   **Map C4**

The restaurant's outdoor tables, just off the main square, give diners the opportunity to watch local people calmly promenading in the tree-shaded centre. This is a modern place that offers traditional local dishes as well as mussels, squid and freshly caught mackerel, trout and carp.

DEVIN Ismena (Ismena Hotel)
ul. Guritza, 41 **Tel** *(03041) 4872*   **Map C4**

At this restaurant, in the Ismena hotel *(see p221)*, diners can choose between the smartly furnished interior and the outdoor terrace, with superb mountain views. This is a good place to try local dishes, such as *klin* (a pastry cooked with rice and eggs) or *marudnik* (a thick pancake with cheese). There is plenty of grilled, roasted and fried meat, too.

GOTSE DELCHEV Malamovata Kushta
ul. Hristo Botev 25 **Tel** *(0751) 61230*   **Map B5**

Located opposite the History Museum, this traditional-style Bulgarian restaurant is decorated with hunting trophies, rifles, and antique oddments. Its tables are covered with Bulgaria's ubiquitous red-and-white tablecloths. Meat is cooked on an open fire, and dishes include *bob kurvavitsa* (beans with black pudding) and chicken pancakes.

HASKOVO Gurkova Kushta
ul. Gurko 6 **Tel** *(038) 668 356*   **Map D4**

Just up the road from the Church of Sveta Bogoroditsa, this is an atmospheric eatery with a pleasantly shaded courtyard in the grounds of a renovated 19th-century house. Plenty of grilled meat options are complemented by a wide range of Bulgarian dishes.

HASKOVO Haskovo
ul. Vasil Drumev 20 **Tel** *(038) 602 538*   **Map D4**

At the Haskovo, one of the town's classier restaurants, pastel drapery, carpets and comfortable seating provide a pleasant dining environment. The wide range of international cuisine is supplemented by some classic Bulgarian offal dishes, including lamb intestines, lungs and liver fried in butter. A live band entertains diners most nights.

KOVACHEVITSA Zhuglevi Kushta
Tel *(07527) 416*   **Map B4**

With a domed clay oven set deep into the stone wall and used for baking bread and roasting meat, this tavern has a great atmosphere. Its traditional Bulgarian dishes are prepared with local produce and the fruit juices made from wild berries are delicious. The pleasantly shaded summer garden has a children's play area.

KÛRDZHALI Arpezos
ul. Republikanska 46 **Tel** *(0361) 60237*   **Map D5**

Though the Arpezos Hotel is showing signs of age, its restaurant has managed to maintain high standards. Excellent service accompanies an imaginative menu featuring the Rhodopean specialities of *kachamak* (meat stew) and *patatnik* (spicy potato pancake) as well as fresh carp caught in Lake Kurdzhali. *Mousaka* and *baklava* add a Turkish flavour.

KYUSTENDIL Strimon (Strimon Spa Club)
ul. Tsar Simeon I 24 **Tel** *(078) 559 000*   **Map A4**

A chic restaurant where diners are waited on by an army of uniformed staff. Plush furnishings and comfortable chairs put visitors in the mood for some high-class cuisine. Ravioli with walnut pesto, duck with onion, and chicken in wine sauce are unlikely to disappoint. The neighbouring winery is a snug place to try some of Bulgaria's finest wines.

LESHTEN Leshten mehana
Tel *(0888) 544 651*   **Map B4**

The *mehana*, in the centre of the village in a restored old house, has a lovely garden with tables under the shade of a large old tree. It serves Bulgarian dishes prepared with fresh local produce. *Chushki byurek* (stuffed peppers) and *kavarma* (meat stew) are among the delicious offerings, and the home-made wine is well worth a try.

MELNIK Sveta Varvara
Tel *(07437) 388*   **Map D5**

Taking its name from the ruined church nearby, the Sveta Varvara has a great location on a hillside just below Kordupulov House. Its long vine-shaded terrace is reasonably peaceful and overlooks the dry valley below. The brief menu covers Bulgarian standards such as *kavarma* (meat stew) and an assortment of grilled meat options.

MELNIK Despot Slav

Tel (07437) 248

Map B5

An elegant blend of stylish wrought-iron furniture and traditionally exposed wood and stone set the scene at this restaurant, in the hotel of the same name *(see p222)*. The usual vegetarian dishes are available, but the emphasis is on meat. Hunter's rabbit pie, spiced chicken, duck and pork are among the tantalizing options.

MELNIK Lumparova Kushta

Tel (07437) 218

Map B5

An excellent hotel restaurant *(see p222)* with a high wooden ceiling, stone walls and a large double fireplace. All the food is prepared with local ingredients and cooked to order. The stuffed rabbit, Thracian *mousaka* with aubergine, and baked spinach with rice are delicious. The homemade *banitsa* (flaky pastry with cheese) is not to be missed.

MELNIK Mencheva Kushta

Tel (07437) 339

Map B5

Tables and chairs are squeezed into the various rooms of this atmospheric old house. Bare stone walls are cluttered with antique knick-knacks and there's even space for a small fish pond. The menu begins with a selection of over 30 *rakiyas* (fruit brandies) and offers traditional dishes such as nettle soup and *otshtipez* (minced meat with cheese).

PAMPOROVO Chanove

Tel (03095) 8212

Map C5

Close to the main ski lifts in the centre of Pamporovo, the Chanove is an old-style place with plenty of exposed timber, hunting trophies and a roaring open fire. Bulgarian dishes include such favourites as goose lungs with honey and apples, chicken hearts, tripe rolls, and delicious *bob churba* (bean soup).

PAMPOROVO White House

Tel (03095) 8554

Map C5

Like the Chanove restaurant *(see above)* on the other side of the street, the White House is a rustic-themed eatery with exposed wooden beams, cow bells and a few stuffed animals. The blazing central fire is a welcome feature of this pleasant spot, which offers hearty traditional dishes as well as pasta and pizzas.

PERNIK Leo

pl. Krakra **Tel** (0897) 886 856

Map B3

The Leo is an aspiring upmarket restaurant with smart modern décor, comfortable chairs and two floors of tables surrounding a central dance floor. Bulgarian cuisine is accompanied by such relatively adventurous dishes as chicken with avocado, pork with basil, and duck with orange sauce. Closed on Sundays.

PLOVDIV Devatnaysti Vek

ul. Tsar Koloyan 1a **Tel** (032) 653 882

Map C4

The walls of this romanticized version of a 19th-century Bulgarian tavern are hung with antique rifles and other oddments. Traditional tablecloths and brown-glazed crockery complete the picture. The standard Bulgarian dishes include *manastirski keremida*, an appetizing mixture of tongue, intestines and mushrooms baked with cheese.

PLOVDIV Gusto

ul. Otets Paisi 26 **Tel** (032) 623 711

Map C4

This Italian restaurant lacks an Italian chef, but the dishes are reasonably original, and certainly offer an appealing alternative to traditional Bulgarian food. Spinach meatballs, avocado salad, pizzas, pasta, and lasagne feature on the menu, and the excellent wine list has a helpful description of each bottle.

PLOVDIV Pri Lino

bul. 6 Septemvri 135 **Tel** (032) 631 751

Map C4

An 18th-century mosque has been converted to accommodate this atmospheric restaurant. The smartly furnished dining area occupies the old prayer hall and the interior of the domed ceiling is painted with bold murals depicting the raucous antics of comical characters. The brief menu offers a selection of Italian dishes accompanied by pasta.

PLOVDIV OLD TOWN Kambanata

ul. Saborna 2b **Tel** (032) 260 665

Map C4

More affordable and less showy than many others in Plovdiv's old town, the Kambanata is a straightforward affair with an open terrace overlooking the main street and a basement dining area under the Church of Sveta Bogoroditsa. The menu offers a range of Bulgarian dishes including veal cutlet, chicken steak and smoked pork.

PLOVDIV OLD TOWN Konyushite na Tsarya

ul. Saborna (beyond Zlatyu Boyadzhiev House) **Tel** (0898) 542 787

Map C4

"The King's Stables", tucked away in hilly gardens off the main street, is a lovely spot to escape the crowds. The outdoor restaurant occupies a series of shaded terraces next to some of Plovdiv's ancient Roman walls. Bulgarian dishes fill up much of the brief menu, which unusually offers a vegetarian beef steak. Open in summer only.

PLOVDIV OLD TOWN Art Café Philippopolis

ul. Saborna 29 **Tel** (032) 624 851

Map C4

More of a café than a restaurant, the Philippopolis features an outdoor terrace scattered with cast iron furniture and with sweeping views of modern Plovdiv. Delicious mains include pancakes layered with vegetables and beef marinated with ginger, while apple strudel and walnut pie are among the tempting desserts.

Key to Price Guide *see p234* **Key to Symbols** *see back cover flap*

PLOVDIV OLD TOWN Janet
 €€

ul. 4 Yanuari 3 **Tel** *(032) 626 044* **Map C4**

Housed in a lovely National Revival mansion built for a wealthy merchant in 1868, the restaurant features smartly furnished dining rooms and a pleasant tree-shaded courtyard. Specials include rabbit with garlic and sausage, Rhodopean veal fillet and grilled octopus. Attentive waiting staff offer a high standard of service.

PLOVDIV OLD TOWN Puldin
€€

ul. Knyaz Tseretelev 3 **Tel** *(032) 631 720* **Map C4**

This capacious restaurant has two dining rooms and a large courtyard with rustic seating. The Ritual Hall has high ceilings, tall windows and smart furniture. The Bulgarian-style tavern downstairs is bedecked with traditional rugs, tablecloths and crockery. A special feature on both menus is the excellent Trakian Grill of spiced meat balls, chicken and lamb.

PLOVDIV OLD TOWN Hebros
€€€

ul. Konstantin Stoilov 51 **Tel** *(032) 260 180* **Map C4**

Voted Bulgaria's best restaurant for two years running and still in the top ten, the Hebros is an unmistakably high-class affair. The brief menu is supplemented by daily-changing specials, each with their own recommended wine. The delights include foie gras with apples, rabbit with plums, and pear and fig confit.

PLOVDIV OLD TOWN Petr I
€€€

ul. Knyaz Tseretelev 11 **Tel** *(032) 632 389* **Map C4**

An expensive Russian restaurant whose sumptuous decoration borders on kitsch, Petr I is nonetheless a delightful experience and has splendid city views from its terrace. Liveried waiting staff provide suitably aloof service and a nightly floor show of colourfully costumed dancers entertains diners. The Russian-themed menu includes a page of vodkas.

RILA MONASTERY Tsarev vruh (Tsarev vruh Hotel)
 €

Tel *(07054) 2280* **Map B4**

Rustic wooden tables are spread out over the peaceful garden of the Tsarev vruh hotel *(see p223)*, just above the Rilska River. This is a quiet alternative to the crowded restaurants closer to the monastery. The menu follows the theme of Bulgarian cuisine, with grilled meats predominating. The fresh local trout is recommended.

RILA MONASTERY Zodiac
 €

Tel *(0888) 216 527* **Map B4**

The menu is simple Bulgarian fare and the location is great. Outdoor tables separated by latticework screens and covered with individual canopies are set out on a well-kept lawn. From this idyllic spot diners have views of forested hills and the towering Rila Mountains beyond. The restaurant is part of the Zodiac hotel *(see p223)*.

RILA MONASTERY Drushliavitsa
€€

Tel *(0888) 278 756* **Map B4**

A stream runs under the Drushliavitsa's outdoor terrace, right beside the monastery walls. Hearty Bulgarian dishes include an excellent *shkembe churba* (tripe soup) and an equally good *bob churba* (bean soup). Freshly caught trout and beef steak are also on the menu. The restaurant is usually busy and has surprisingly good service.

SAMOKOV Starata Kushta
 €

ul. Zahari Zograf 13 **Tel** *(0885) 882 828* **Map B4**

The Starata Kushta occupies an atmospheric 19th-century house opposite the Metropolitan Church. The restaurant's four rooms have traditional tablecloths, cushions and period oddments that create an intimate and relaxed environment. The cuisine is predictably Bulgarian and features plenty of salads and grilled meat.

SANDANSKI Tropikana
 €

ul. Makedonia **Tel** *(0898) 726 578* **Map B5**

The Tropikana occupies a tranquil spot opposite the Sandanski hotel *(see p223)*. The menu features Bulgarian dishes that take some getting used to – such as fried chicken hearts and deep-fried calf brain. More appealing alternatives are *bob po vodenicharski* (beans with bacon) and *trakisko vreteno*, a local dish of minced meat and onion.

SHIROKA LÛKA Mehana Pri Slavchev (Kalina Hotel)
 €

ul. Kapitan Petko Voivoda 63 **Tel** *(03030) 675* **Map B5**

A cosy, traditional-style tavern in the Kalina hotel *(see p223)*. Delicious local dishes include *patatnik* (potato pancake), Rhodope rice pudding, *sudjik* (flat sausage), *tikvichka banitsa* (pumpkin pastry) and roast lamb cooked on the roaring open fire. Folk musicians in traditional dress entertain guests every night.

SMOLYAN Otmura
 €

bul. Bulgaria 35 **Tel** *(0301) 63868* **Map C5**

Steps from bulevard Bulgaria lead down to this small restaurant. Although it is not a high-class affair, the Otmura has a reputation for great food, and its outdoor terrace is a lovely place to enjoy mountainous scenery around Smolyan. The Rhodopean *patatnik* (spicy potato pancake) is delicious.

SMOLYAN Riben Dar
 €

ul. Snezhanka 16 **Tel** *(0301) 63220* **Map C5**

Tucked away in a residential area in the hills immediately above town, the Riben Dar is tricky to locate, but for those in search of fish the effort is well worth it. The homely restaurant serves up over 100 dishes ranging from locally caught trout to Black Sea and Mediterranean fish.

VELINGRAD Omar (Rich Hotel) €
bul. Saedinenie 500 **Tel** *(0359) 57803*   **Map B4**

The Omar's pictorial menu gives diners a fairly good idea of what will end up on their plates. Situated in a walled courtyard next to the hotel's outdoor pool, this traditional-style eatery has rustic furniture and an open fire for grilling meat. One of the delicious options is *Tatarsko kyufte* (a meatball stuffed with cheese).

CENTRAL BULGARIA

ARBANASI Payak Mehana €€
Tel *(062) 606 810*   **Map D3**

Just off the main square, the Payak is a traditional-style *mehana* (tavern) in one of Arbanasi's restored old houses. Thick stone walls surround the outdoor seating in its pleasant garden. The interior features typical Bulgarian décor and a blazing fire in winter. Specials include Bandit's Shashlik – a kebab with half a kilo (over 1lb) of meat.

ETÛRA COMPLEX Stranopriemnitsa €€
Tel *(066) 801 831*   **Map D3**

Part of the Stranopriemnitsa hotel, near the eastern entrance to the complex, this restaurant is a traditional Bulgarian affair with ubiquitous red-and-white table-cloths, cart wheels and waiting staff in national costume. Service is brisk and diners can choose from a good selection of local dishes.

GABROVO Pizza Tempo €
ul. Pencho Slaveykov 1 **Tel** *(066) 806 920*   **Map C3**

A stylish Italian-themed restaurant with deliberately faded décor and a rustic open kitchen where chefs can be observed tossing balls of dough. The pizzas are thin-crust and tasty enough. Pasta dishes are also available, as are various mixtures baked in small ceramic troughs.

HISAR Panorama (Hisar Spa Complex) €€
ul. Gurko 1 **Tel** *(0337) 62781*   **Map C3**

With great views from its terrace on the fifth floor of the Hisar Spa Complex *(see p224)*, the modern Panorama restaurant is a relaxing place to dine. As well as typical Bulgarian dishes such as *Teteven bob* (beans) and Rhodopi veal fillet, it has an Arabic menu with dishes including spiced chicken and vegetables, and veal with garlic and spices.

KARLOVO Mehana Vodopad €
ul. Vodopad 41 **Tel** *(0335) 93127*   **Map C3**

Named after the nearby Suchurum waterfall *(vodopad)* in the leafy park just above Karlovo, this is a traditional-style *mehana* whose many outdoor tables make it popular with local people for summer dining. The interior walls are decorated with local costumes, typically Bulgarian tablecloths and a variety of rural knick-knacks.

KAZANLÛK Teres (Teres Hotel) €
ul. Lyubomir Kabakchiev 16 **Tel** *(0431) 64272*   **Map D3**

A good place to stop for refreshments before visiting the nearby Kazanlûk Tomb or the neighbouring Ethnographic Complex, the Teres offers well-prepared Bulgarian cuisine, pizzas and fish. Its pleasant garden has outdoor seating and the smartly dressed staff are polite and efficient. The restaurant is part of the Teres hotel *(see p224)*.

KOPRIVSHTITSA 20 April Tavern €
pl. 20 April **Tel** *(07184) 2157 or (0889) 368 220*   **Map C3**

A traditional-style *mehana* (tavern) on the town's main square named after the date of the April Rising of 1876. It has a terrace for outdoor dining in summer and a blazing fire to warm guests in winter. The Bulgarian cuisine served here includes aubergine in tomato sauce, chicken kebab and yoghurt with forest fruits.

KOPRIVSHTITSA Dyado Liben €
bul. Hadzhi Nencho Palaveev 47 **Tel** *(07184) 2109*   **Map C3**

Housed in one of Koprivshtitsa's 19th-century mansions, the Dyado Liben is a wonderfully atmospheric restaurant. Tables fill the wood-panelled salon and symmetrical rooms upstairs, while outdoor seating fills the cobbled courtyard. The brief menu encompasses Bulgarian and Serbian cuisine, with an emphasis on grilled meat.

KOPRIVSHTITSA Purvata Pushka (Sveti Georgi Hotel) €€
ul. Tomangelova 18 **Tel** *(07184) 2393*   **Map C3**

Concealed behind stone walls near the post office, the Pervata Pushka (The First Rifle) is part of the Sveti Georgi Hotel. The courtyard has plenty of outdoor seating, and steps lead down into a cosy *mehana* with a blazing fire and fluffy woollen seat covers. Beans cooked in a ceramic pot, grilled meat and lamb fillet are among the offerings.

LOVECH Pri Voivodite Mehana €
ul. Marin Pop Lukanov, Varosha Quarter **Tel** *(0888) 837 513*   **Map C2**

Behind stone walls in the old Varosha quarter, this 19th-century traditional *mehana* surrounds a courtyard with outdoor seating. Red-and-white tablecloths, traditional crockery, cart wheels and millstones provide the backdrop for diners, who come to enjoy the excellent local food. Try the bean soup, lamb stew and *perlenka* (grilled flatbread filled with cheese).

Key to Price Guide *see p234* **Key to Symbols** *see back cover flap*

LOVECH Apollo (Presidium Palace Hotel) €€

*ul. Turgovska 51 **Tel** (068) 600 170*

Map C2

The refreshing modern design of this upmarket restaurant features stylish furniture, and a pleasant outdoor terrace. The brief but imaginative menu offers trout, tiger shrimps, pepper steak and various other dishes accompanied by an excellent range of wines. The restaurant is part of the Presidium Palace hotel, in the centre of Lovech *(see p225)*.

RIBARITSA Express €

*ul. Georgi Benkovski 121a **Tel** (0888) 805 532*

Map C3

Although the food is unexceptional and standards basic, the train carriage that houses this small restaurant is a welcome novelty. Located in central Ribaritsa, just off the main road, the Express has outdoor tables with great views of the countryside. There is also tree-shaded seating beside an adjacent stream.

RIBARITSA Evergreen Palace  €€

***Tel** (06902) 2066*

Map C3

Fresh trout, goose liver and duck with apple sauce are among the delicious offerings of this restaurant, part of the Evergreen Palace hotel *(see p225)*. Plush furnishings and subdued lighting create an appealing ambience, and a huge full-length window provides fantastic views of the mountains. There is also a good range of Bulgarian wines.

STARA ZAGORA Forum (Hotel Forum) €€

*ul. Hadzhi Dimitûr 94 **Tel** (042) 623 221*

Map D3

This upmarket restaurant in the Hotel Forum *(see p225)* offers a high standard of Bulgarian and international food. While the main dining area is furnished in contemporary style, the traditional-style *mehana* downstairs has exposed stone walls and an open fire. Diners can choose from an excellent range of wines.

TETEVEN Maxim €

*ul. Emil Markov 27 **Tel** (0678) 5552*

Map C3

This churchlike, medieval-style restaurant occupies the roomy basement of the new Maxim complex. Stained-glass windows, suits of armour and heraldic shields attempt to carry the theme, but the brightly painted walls and gleaming tiled floor undo the effort. Bulgarian cuisine is supplemented by international specials such as the American breakfast.

TETEVEN Teteven Mehana  €

*ul. Simeon Kumanov 46 **Tel** (0678) 5096*

Map C3

Located above the town centre, opposite the Church of Sveta Nedelya, the Teteven Mehana is a great traditional tavern in the vaulted ground-floor rooms of an old house. Its bare stone walls, Teteven rugs, wooden furniture and typical Bulgarian tablecloths make for plenty of atmosphere. The menu offers local and national dishes.

TETEVEN Vit €€

*ul. Mihael Koichev 2 **Tel** (0678) 2034*

Map C3

Part of the newly constructed Vit hotel *(see p225)*, this smartly furnished restaurant has a central fireplace and a menu that features local dishes, fish, and a good range of wines. There is live music – predominantly a mixture of 1980s covers and Bulgarian folk – most nights.

TROYAN Troyan Mehana (Troyan Plaza Hotel) €€

*ul. Slaveykov 54 **Tel** (0670) 64399*

Map C3

Part of the brand-new 4-star Troyan Plaza Hotel complex *(see p225)*, this is a fun interpretation of a traditional Bulgarian tavern. Imaginative touches include rustic furniture in a giant wooden barrel, a table made from a well, and a full-size covered wagon with seating inside. A wide range of Bulgarian dishes is available.

TRYAVNA Pizza Domino €

*ul. Angel Kunchev 36 **Tel** (0677) 2322*

Map D3

A central eatery with outdoor seating on a wooden terrace and a fashionable interior hung with modern art. Typically for Bulgaria, the pizzas are thin-crust with sloppy toppings, but are edible nonetheless. Other options include pasta, an endless list of salads, freshly made bread and baked potatoes.

TRYAVNA Starata Loza €€

*ul. Slaveykov 44 **Tel** (0677) 4501*

Map D3

Opened in 1990, the "Old Vine" claims to be Tryavna's first private restaurant. Its well-established reputation attracts a constant stream of diners, who can sit on the vine-shaded terrace or inside the traditional style *mehana*. Bulgarian delicacies include stewed calf's tongue, rolled tripe and fried brains.

TRYAVNA Zograf Mehana €€

*ul. Slaveykov 1 **Tel** (0677) 4970*

Map D3

An old-style tavern in the basement of the Zograf Hotel *(see p225)*. The open fire, wooden furniture and decorative bric-à-brac create a snug environment where diners can choose from a good range of Bulgarian food. Trout stuffed with bacon and cheese, Cossack pork and hunter's rabbit are among the options on offer.

VELIKO TÛRNOVO Klub na Architekta €

*ul. Velcho Dzhamdzhiyata 14 **Tel** (062) 621 451*

Map D3

Reached by a flight of steps leading down off ulitsa Nikola Pikolo, this traditional-style tavern is built onto the steep hillside above the Yantra River. Spring water trickling from the bare rock walls of its cave-like interior, candlelight and hefty wooden tables create a snug environment that's popular with local people.

VELIKO TÛRNOVO Pizza Tempo
ul. Ivailo 4 **Tel** *(062) 606 920*

Map D3

Exposed brick walls, tiled floors and wooden beams create a comfortable rustic environment for this bustling pizza restaurant. Besides a good range of pizzas, pasta and Bulgarian dishes are also on the menu. This is an enormously popular eatery, and evening tables require advance reservations.

VELIKO TÛRNOVO Vinarnata
ul. Stefan Stambolov 79 **Tel** *(062) 603 252*

Map D3

The Vinarnata has a conveniently central location, and impressive views down onto the Yantra River from the rear. The witty menu provides an amusing overview of the selection of dishes on offer, which cover a vast range of salads, Bulgarian dishes and grilled meat.

VELIKO TÛRNOVO Yantra
ul. Opalchenska 2 **Tel** *(062) 600 607*

Map D3

One of the town's best, this capacious restaurant is part of the Yantra hotel *(see p226)*. Offering an excellent choice of Bulgarian and international cuisine, it serves diners in three rooms furnished in contemporary style. The large windows overlooking the citadel of Tsarevets make this a great spot from which to enjoy its sound and light show.

YAMBOL Pizza Bezisten Yug
Tel *(046) 664 366*

Map E3

Part of the restored 15th-century Bezisten Bazaar on Yambol's main square, this simple restaurant is popular with local people, and offers a reasonable range of thin-crust pizzas and Bulgarian dishes. Its arched ceiling and colourful interior murals create a pleasant dining environment.

ZHERAVNA Staryat Mehana
Tel *(04585) 200*

Map E3

A traditional Bulgarian *mehana* in a restored 19th-century house. Typically for Zheravna, it features wooden panelling, ceilings and floors. An open fire heats the interior in winter and a pretty walled garden has summer seating. Excellent *bob churba* (bean soup) and *chuski byurek* (peppers stuffed with cheese) are among the offerings.

NORTHERN BULGARIA

BELOGRADCHIK Madona
ul. Hristo Botev 26 **Tel** *(0936) 5546*

Map A2

A family-run *mehana* with views of Belogradchik's famous rocks. Among the excellent local specialities that stand out are *churba od kopriva*, a nettle soup flavoured with cheese, peppers and carrots, and *grohchano*, diced pork served with fried onions and raw garlic. Try to leave room for the *panirani yabulki sus med* (apple fritters with honey).

BERKOVITSA Krusteva kushta
ul. Sheinovo 5 **Tel** *(0953) 88099*

Map B2

This 19th-century-style house on a central street has a wooden-beamed interior and a walled garden courtyard. On the menu is a Bulgarian repertoire of salads and meat dishes, well prepared and attentively served. Local culinary curiosities include an exceedingly tasty *kebap po berkovski* (diced pork, onions and herbs served in an earthenware jug).

CHIPROVTSI Gostopriemnitsa Kipro
ul. Balkanska 46 **Tel** *(09554) 2974*

Map A2

Wooden tables and benches fill this homely *mehana*, where a broad range of Bulgarian grilled meat dishes and excellent fresh salads are served. Regional specialities worth trying include red peppers stuffed with paprika-flavoured beans, and *kachamak*, a polenta-style porridge flavoured with butter and salty white cheese.

DOBRICH Sport Palas
bul. 25 Septemvri 1a **Tel** *(058) 603 622*

Map F2

Popular with discerning local people, this restaurant offers traditional Bulgarian cooking with a modern European twist. Service is attentive, and there is a good choice of local wines and *rakiyas*. The restaurant, in the Sport Palas hotel *(see p226)*, is next to one of Dobrich's most popular open-air swimming pools, so a pre-meal dip is part of the attraction.

ISPERIH Restorant Parka
ul. Tsar Osvoboditel **Tel** *(0896) 696 125*

Map E2

If you have been visiting the Thracian tombs at Sveshtari, 7 km (4 miles) to the southeast, this is a convenient place to eat. Set in the leafy surrounds of the town park, the unpretentious restaurant is a reliable source of traditional Bulgarian grills. The local speciality, *Ludogorski kebap* (pork and vegetables baked in a clay pot with an egg), is worth trying.

MONTANA Chardatsite
pl. Zheravitsa 1

Map B2

Occupying the first floor of the high-rise Zhitomir hotel, the Chardatsite provides sweeping views of Montana's main square. The emphasis is on grilled meats, and the Serbian-style *veshalitse* (fillets of pork or veal stuffed with cheese, peppers and ham) are particularly good. Live Bulgarian folk-pop bands raise the temperature at weekends.

Key to Price Guide *see p234* **Key to Symbols** *see back cover flap*

PLEVEN Bulgarski koren
ul. Naicho Tsanov 4 **Tel** *(064) 29090* **Map C2**

Traditional Bulgarian food in a National Revival-style house just northwest of the centre. With a walled garden shaded by trees and a pretty stream, it is the perfect place to sit outside on warm summer evenings. The *gyuveche* dishes (meat and vegetables baked in a clay pot) are excellent, and there is a good selection of local red and white wines.

RUSE Mehana Chiflika
ul. Otets Paisii 2 **Tel** *(082) 828 222* **Map D2**

A roomy restaurant decorated with agricultural implements, and hung with corn cobs. This is a great place in which to sample traditional Bulgarian cuisine, with familiar salads and grilled meats augmented by an excellent *bob* (paprika-laced beans baked in an earthenware pot) and spicy *nadenichki* (thin sausages). Good-value lunchtime menus.

SHUMEN Popsheytanova kushta
ul. Tsar Osvoboditel 158 **Tel** *(054) 802 222* **Map E2**

In a modern building enlivened by folkloric design touches, this restaurant is known for its charcoal-grilled meats, with a wider range of cuts (including rabbit and lamb) than you'll find elsewhere. Try the sizzling meat and vegetable dishes served on a *sache* (hot metal plate). *Kanapsko meze* (baked tongue, brain and tripe covered in cheese) is a local speciality.

SILISTRA Nikulden
ul. Pristanishtna 2 **Tel** *(086) 822 214* **Map F1**

This riverside pavilion, with wood-panelled walls and a profusion of house plants, is renowned for its selection of local Danube-caught fish. Succulent fillets of *som* (catfish), *sharan* (carp) and other catches-of-the-day are served grilled or pan-fried in batter according to choice. A glass of the local *kaisieva rakiya* (apricot brandy) makes the perfect aperitif.

SVISHTOV Bay Ganyu
ul. Dragan Tsankov 12 **Tel** *(0631) 23403* **Map D2**

Hidden away in a residential street a few steps away from Svishtov's main square, the Bay Ganyu offers traditional Bulgarian cooking in a cosy dining room decorated with textiles and folksy crockery. The grilled Danube fish dishes are always worth trying, and there is an extensive variety of salads and vegetable-based starters. Open evenings only.

SVISHTOV Svishtov
ul. Dimitûr Shishmanov 10 **Tel** *(0631) 64366* **Map D2**

In the same building as the Archaeological Exhibition, the Svishtov has stone floors, wooden beams and pillars, and bric-à-brac on the walls. The freshly made salads are rich in tomatoes and red peppers. Main courses feature familiar Bulgarian grills alongside roast-meat dishes such as *dzholan* (pork calves) and locally caught pan-fried fish.

VIDIN Anna Kristina
ul. Baba Vida 2 **Tel** *(094) 606 037* **Map A1**

A smart hotel restaurant *(see p227)* with outdoor seating in shaded gazebo-type constructions. Charcoal-grilled cuts of pork and beef form the backbone of the menu, with *shashlik*-style skewered kebabs featuring as something of a speciality. A bottle of Gumza, the local red wine, makes an ideal accompaniment.

VIDIN Hotel Bononia
ul. Bdin 2 **Tel** *(094) 606 031* **Map A1**

This rather staid hotel restaurant is greatly enhanced by the summer garden, which looks towards the city's riverside park. It is a reliable place to try traditional Bulgarian salads and pot-baked dishes, and there is a satisfying range of Serbian-influenced grilled dishes such as *pleskavice* (burger-style patties) and *cevapcici* (minced-meat rissoles).

VRATSA Chaika
Vratsata Gorge **Tel** *(092) 622 367* **Map B2**

Located 2 km (just over a mile) west of Vratsa at the entrance to Vratsata Gorge, the Chaika serves traditional Bulgarian grilled dishes to a high standard, as well as offering international-style steaks and pan-fried freshwater fish. The home-baked bread buns are delicious. A large outdoor dining area adjoins an attractive artificial lake.

BLACK SEA COAST

BALCHIK Roma
ul. Primorska **Tel** *(0579) 77045* **Map G2**

A cavernous restaurant whose resident band plays covers and requests every night. Food is standard Bulgarian cuisine along with a reasonable range of fresh fish, and the bar serves a colourful array of potent cocktails. Plenty of disco lights and a large dance floor make this one of Balchik's liveliest spots.

BALCHIK White House
ul. Geo Milev 18 **Tel** *(0579) 73951* **Map G2**

The smartly uniformed waiting staff at one of Balchik's best restaurants, part of the White House hotel *(see p228)*, provide impeccable service and high-quality food at reasonable prices. The pleasantly shaded terrace overlooks the sea and the marina. A comprehensive wine list is accompanied by an equally good range of *rakiya* (fruit brandy).

BURGAS Vodenitsata €
Morska Gradina (Sea Gardens), northern end **Tel** *(0897) 988 334*   **Map F3**

One of several outdoor eateries in Burgas's peaceful Sea Gardens, the Vodenitsata (Watermill) is a bustling place where diners may have to queue for a seat on balmy summer evenings. Some tables have sea views and service is usually efficient. Fresh fish dishes, pizza, and Bulgarian cuisine are on the menu.

DURANKULAK Zlatna Ribka €
Near Durankulak village.   **Map G2**

Situated at the northern end of Lake Durankulak and accessed by a dirt track from the main road, the "Golden Fish" is a hugely popular restaurant despite its isolated location. It serves freshly caught fish from the lake and has seating in the garden at the water's edge.

GOLDEN SANDS Taj Mahal €€
Next to Admiral Hotel **Tel** *(0886) 600 030*   **Map G2**

This atmospheric Indian restaurant, surrounded by lush green lawns, offers great cuisine cooked by Indian chefs. The deliciously spiced food is served in generous portions by waiting staff in saris and traditional dress. Comfortable sofas scattered with colourful cushions surround the smart dining tables.

KAMEN BRIAG Trite Kestena €
Village centre   **Map G2**

Kamen Briag's oldest restaurant, in the heart of the village, has slowly expanded over the years and now occupies a large courtyard with extra seating in two wooden towers. Vines and plum trees provide shade in the sweltering summer heat. Food comprises fresh fish, Bulgarian dishes, and good range of salads of vegetables grown in the back garden.

KAVARNA Midena Ferma Dulboka €€
Midway between Kavarna and Bulgarevo **Tel** *(0899) 911 377*   **Map G2**

Occupying a spectacular spot below steep cliffs and right at the water's edge, this legendary restaurant serves over 50 dishes, from mussel *mousaka* to a dessert of mussels stuffed with apple, made with fresh produce from its offshore mussel farm. A new neighbouring restaurant, confusingly named Dulboka, offers similar fare on a wooden terrace.

LOZENETS Starata Kushta €
ul. Georgi Kondolov 2 **Tel** *(0550) 57257*   **Map F4**

"The Old House" is hugely popular with visitors and, despite its capacity for over 200 diners, evening tables must be booked in advance. It follows the traditional Bulgarian theme of rustic wooden tables, red-and-white tablecloths, and cart wheels and offers such favourites as *shkembe churba* (tripe soup) and an wide range of grilled meats.

LOZENETS Friends €€
ul. Ribarska 45 **Tel** *(0888) 606 575*   **Map F4**

This cool restaurant with stylish white wooden furniture has recently emerged in newly fashionable Lozenets. The main attraction is the well prepared sushi, which diners can choose from a pictorial menu. It also offers a wide range of fish dishes and plenty of traditional meat dishes too. The restaurant is part of the Friends hotel (*see p228*).

NESEBÛR Plakamoto €
ul. Ivan Alexander 8 **Tel** *(0554) 45544*   **Map F3**

Hidden away to the south of the old town, this idyllic restaurant is housed in a restored 19th-century building next to the sea. The large outdoor terrace shaded by fig trees has great views and diners can choose from fish dishes including Black Sea mussels and conger eel as well as a good range of Bulgarian dishes.

NESEBÛR Kapitanska Sreshta €€
ul. Mena 22 **Tel** *(0554) 42124*   **Map F3**

Nesebur's medieval stone walls provide a fitting backdrop to this atmospheric restaurant. It occupies a lovely old house and has a wide, shaded terrace overlooking the harbour. The menu covers a broad range of fish dishes including conger eel, shark and swordfish. Diners pay a little extra for its established reputation.

POMORIE Kotvata €
bul. Yavorov 2   **Map F3**

Just along the seafront from the Interhotel Pomorie, the Kotvata (Anchor) is a pleasant outdoor restaurant. Diners have superb views right out to sea and can look down on colourful wooden fishing boats moored on the beach. The menu offers a good choice of fish and a great selection of desserts.

SHABLA Bai Pesho €
Tel *(0888) 221 771*   **Map G2**

This simple yet atmospheric eatery is right on the seafront of Shabla village, with a large open terrace facing the sea. Local people travel from miles around to taste Bai Pesho's legendary fish soup. Located near Shabla lighthouse, the village is not to be confused with the inland town of Shabla about 5 km (3 miles) away.

SINEMORETS Casa Domingo €€
ul. Ribarska **Tel** *(0550) 66093*   **Map G4**

Despite the many unsightly new establishments springing up all over Sinemorets, the Casa Domingo remains a bastion of good taste and style. Vine-shaded outdoor seating surrounds a pool at the centre of its enclosed courtyard, where diners can sample a variety of seafood dishes or traditional Bulgarian cuisine.

Key to Price Guide *see p234* **Key to Symbols** *see back cover flap*

SOZOPOL Chez Les Artistes

ul. Kiril i Metodii 72

Map F3 €

Deriving its name from the neighbouring art gallery rather than its own artistic merits, this restaurant is located towards the end of the old town peninsula. Outdoor tables occupy a leafy garden from where diners can enjoy wonderful sea views. The menu offers a good range of Black Sea fish dishes alongside traditional Bulgarian cuisine.

SOZOPOL Rusalka

ul. Milet 36 **Tel** *(0550) 23047*

Map F3 €

The Rusalka is one of several restaurants on the south of the old town peninsula. Waves crash against rocks directly below and diners have views of the main beach, jammed with umbrellas and sunbathers in summer. The menu features a variety of seafood as well as pizza and pasta. The restaurant is part of the Rusalka hotel *(see p229)*.

SUNNY BEACH Kasablanka

Next to Europa Hotel **Tel** *(0888) 709 980*

Map F3 €

An open-air beach restaurant right next to the sea, Kasablanka seats over 200 diners and offers a reasonable range of Bulgarian and international cuisine. Wooden tables, quirky columns, billowing drapes and a straw roof add to its desert-island charm. The well-stocked bar has a bewildering array of cocktails.

SUNNY BEACH Piccadilly

Opposite Hotel Maritsa **Tel** *(0887) 314 152*

Map F3 €€

A lively place popular with British tourists, the Piccadilly has a resident band to entertain diners every night. The multilingual staff provide friendly and efficient service. The menu has a good range of seafood, grilled meat, steaks, and English and Bulgarian cuisine, and even offers "pig on a spit".

SUNNY BEACH Hanska Shatra

Tel *(0554) 22811*

Map F3 €€€

A massive concrete replica of a "Khan's Tent" lit by neon lights on a hilltop north of Sunny Beach. This themed restaurant is cheesy but fun nonetheless. Diners can choose from a range of Bulgarian and international cuisine, and are entertained with endless floorshows featuring costumed dancers. The outdoor terrace has great views of the coast.

TAUKLIMAN (Russalka Holiday Village)

Tel *(0570) 82009*

Map G2 €

Part of the Russalka Holiday Village complex *(see p229)*, the stylish Taukliman is one of the best restaurants in the region. Billowing drapes and upholstered chairs create an intimate atmosphere and the outdoor terrace has sweeping sea views. Fish dominate the brief menu and delicious dishes include mussel cocktail and fried shark.

TSAREVO Morska Zvezda

ul. Vasiliko 15 **Tel** *(0550) 52583*

Map F4 €

Owned by a local fisherman, this is a wonderfully simple outdoor eatery with plastic furniture and a straw roof. It has a well-established reputation as one of the best fish restaurants in the area. The roughly printed menu lists over 30 seafood dishes cooked from the owner's daily catch.

TYULENOVO Delfina

Next to the harbour **Tel** *(057) 432 221*

Map G2 €

Tyulenovo's only restaurant occupies the ground floor of the Delfina hotel *(see p229)*. Outdoor tables in the pleasant tree-shaded garden have views of the tiny harbour and sea beyond. Bulgarian dishes and locally caught fish are on the menu. Service is inefficient, but impatient diners have nowhere else to go.

VARNA Panorama

bul. Slivnitsa 33 **Tel** *(052) 612 235*

Map F2 €

The Panorama restaurant is worth visiting just to take in the breathtaking views from its vantage point on the 15th floor of the Cherno More Hotel. From here the entire city is visible, with miles of coastline to the north and south. The menu covers a wide range of Bulgarian cuisine; the trout stuffed with vegetables and walnuts is recommended.

VARNA Pri Monahinite

ul. Primorski 47 **Tel** *(052) 611 830*

Map F2 €€

The Pri Monahinite (At the Nun's) is one of Varna's most atmospheric and imaginative restaurants. The vast menu covers dishes from almost every region of Bulgaria with delightfully poetic names such as "Salad of Young Nedelya's Worries". The only disappointment is that the outdoor terrace borders a busy main road.

VARNA Tambuku

On the seafront, close to the Aquarium **Tel** *(052) 610 864*

Map F2 €€

In a great spot right next to the sea, this open-air fish restaurant evokes a vaguely desert island theme through its use of rough wood furniture and proximity to the beach. Numerous small aquariums provide additional décor. Baked salmon with whisky and broccoli sauce is among the specials and there is also a sushi menu.

VARNA Musala Palace (Grand Hotel Musala Palace)

ul. Musala 3 **Tel** *(052) 664 100*

Map F2 €€€€

Varna's classiest restaurant, in the Grand Hotel Musala Palace *(see p229)*, is a wonderfully refined affair, with velvet upholstery, silver cutlery and impeccable waiting staff. The award-winning chef prepares a brief choice of European dishes that include roast duckling, venison and fresh Black Sea turbot. Daily specials supplement the menu.

SHOPPING IN BULGARIA

Bright modern malls and shops selling clothes by major international labels are an increasingly common feature of Bulgaria's town and city centres. By contrast, and quite untouched by international retail culture, Bulgaria also has a wealth of shops, open-air markets and stalls selling everything from Bulgarian-made soaps to *rakiya*, Bulgarian brandy. In every town centre there is a market, with stalls stacked with fruit,

Traditional glazed bowl from Troyan

vegetables and flowers, and street kiosks with meticulously arranged trays of dried fruit, nuts and sweets. Bulgaria's rich handicrafts tradition includes the distinctive pottery from Troyan, weaving and embroidery, woodcarving and metalwork. In coastal resorts and other areas frequented by visitors, streets and promenades are lined with souvenir stalls offering dolls in traditional costume, replicas of antique icons and local craft items.

OPENING HOURS

In major towns and cities and in holiday resorts, shops are open from 10am to 8pm Monday to Saturday, and often stay open later during the summer season. In Sofia and in towns along the Black Sea coast, shops also open on Sundays, closing at various times between 2pm and 6pm.

Food shops and supermarkets in major towns and cities are open from 7am to 10pm Monday to Saturday, and from 7am to 6pm on Sunday. In smaller towns, shops may close much earlier, and may also close at lunchtime.

MARKETS

Every town in the country has an open-air market, where fresh fruit and vegetables, all sorts of Bulgarian cheeses and sausages are sold. While markets in cities follow regular shop hours, those in

smaller towns may be open only in the morning, or on certain days of the week.

Several of Bulgaria's most picturesque outdoor markets sell not only fresh produce, clothing and household goods but also handicrafts. The liveliest of these markets are the daily **Zhenski pazar** in Sofia, the daily market in Varna, and the Sunday morning market in Bansko.

The daily **Bric-à-brac market** in front of the Aleksandŭr Nevski Memorial Church in Sofia is the best place to go for antiques, old postcards, and Communist-era medals and militaria.

PAYMENT METHODS

Cash is still the most common means of paying for goods in Bulgaria. Cheques are rarely accepted, and credit cards can only be used in the more prestigious shops in Sofia and other major cities.

It is not customary to haggle, except when you are shopping for bric-à-brac or craft items in the more informal markets, where prices are not marked.

Window of a clothes shop on bulevard Vitosha in Sofia

CRAFTS AND SOUVENIRS

High-quality craft items predominate on Bulgaria's souvenir stalls, with ceramics, embroidery and traditional textiles among the most popular items. Pottery from the central Bulgarian town of Troyan, decorated with flowing patterns in bright colours, is one of the most typically Bulgarian souvenirs. While Troyan plates and jugs are available throughout the country, the widest choice of the finest-quality pieces can be found at the **Arts and Crafts Exhibition** in Oreshak, near Troyan Monastery.

Stall with fresh fruit and vegetables at Rimska Stena market, Sofia

Traditional Bulgarian textiles include vividly patterned kilims hand-woven on vertical looms by the womenfolk of highland villages such as Kotel and Chiprovtsi. Other hand-woven items include fleecy rugs *(guberi)* from villages in the Rhodope Mountains, and tufted goat-hair rugs *(kozyatsi)* from highland villages all over Bulgaria. Brightly coloured blouses, delicately embroidered with folk motifs, are usually also of a high quality.

Bulgaria is a major producer of attar of roses, an essential oil extracted from the damask rose, which is used all over the world as an ingredient of perfumes and beauty products. Locally made soaps, skin creams and eau de cologne made from Bulgarian attar of roses are available in high-street pharmacies and supermarkets throughout the country. Other craft items that the visitor might consider buying include traditional copper pots and coffee sets, and hand-painted copies of Orthodox icons.

Souvenirs are sold on market stalls and in small shops in tourist resorts throughout the country. Specialist outlets selling the best-quality handicrafts include **Traditzia** and the **Ethnographic Museum Shop** in Sofia. Shops in the Stariya Dobrich quarter in Dobrich, and the Samovodska charshiya in Veliko Tûrnovo, are good places to pick up good-quality items made by local craft workshops.

BOOKS AND CDS

Bulgarian bookshops offer a wide range of books on the subject of Bulgaria's scenic beauty, historic sights and cultural heritage. Many are lavishly illustrated and have text in English. Bookshops are also good places to go to buy road maps and town plans.

The liveliest place to browse for books is the open-air book market on ploshtad Slaveykov in Sofia *(see p82)*. Here, a multitude of

Embroidered blouses and other traditional clothes for sale in Bansko

stalls are loaded with books old and new. Books, as well as stationery, CDs and DVDs, can also be found in multi-media stores, which are increasingly common in larger towns and cities.

As might be expected in a country with such rich musical traditions, CDs of Bulgarian folk music are widely available on souvenir stalls, at museum shops and in music stores. However, as there are many low-quality recordings on the market, it is advisable to choose albums released by reputable labels such as Kuker and Gega, which specialize in traditional Bulgarian music. Although high-street multimedia stores carry a wide selection of traditional folk music recordings, the best places to go for advice on what to buy are specialist shops like **Dyukyan Meloman** in Sofia.

WINE AND RAKIYA

Most food shops and super-markets carry a wide selection of Bulgarian wines. While Bulgarian Merlots and Cabernet Sauvignons are on a par with red wines from else-where in Europe, domestic varieties, such as Melnik from the southwest *(see pp116–17)* and Mavrud from the Asenovgrad region, have a much more distinctive character. Bulgarian wines of the highest quality are those produced by leading

Bottle of Bulgarian *rakiya*

wineries such as Todoroff and Damyanitza. These excellent wines are available in stores throughout the country.

Bottles of *rakiya* (grape or plum brandy) also make very good gifts. Look for bottles marked *otlezhala* (meaning "matured"), as these are likely to be of superior quality.

DIRECTORY

MARKETS

Zhenski pazar
ul. Stefan Stambolov, Sofia.
Map 1 A2. 8am–3pm daily.

Bric-à-brac
pl. Aleksandûr Nevski, Sofia.
Map 2 E4. 8am–dusk daily.

Clothes and handicrafts
ul. Tsar Simeon, Bansko.
8am–2pm Sun.

Clothes and handicrafts
pl. Mitropolit Simeon, Varna.
8am–3pm, daily.

CRAFTS SHOPS

Traditzia
bul. Vasil Levski 36, Sofia.
Map 3 C4. Tel *(02) 981 7765.*
www.traditzia.bg

Ethnographic Museum Shop
pl. Aleksandûr Batenberg 1, Sofia.
Map 1 C4.

Arts and Crafts Exhibition
Oreshak, near Troyan Monastery.

CD SHOPS

Dyukyan Meloman
ul. 6 Septemvri 7a, Sofia.
Map 4 D1. Tel *(02) 988 5862.*

ENTERTAINMENT IN BULGARIA

Bulgaria's classical music, ballet and theatre season runs from the beginning of October to the end of June. During this time, the country's fine orchestras, opera and ballet companies perform at venues in Sofia and other major towns, and theatre companies stage productions of classic and contemporary plays.

Aleko Konstantinov Satirical Theatre sign

Through the summer months, a succession of arts festivals take place in the towns of the Black Sea coast, with stimulating programmes of music, drama and dance. Bulgaria's vigorous folk culture also offers the opportunity to see and hear traditional Bulgarian dancing and music at one of several major summer folk festivals.

CLASSICAL MUSIC, OPERA AND DANCE

Bulgaria has a fine tradition of classical music. The quality is high, and tickets for concerts are very reasonably priced. The Bulgarian Philharmonic Orchestra, which performs weekly at the Bulgarian Hall (Zala Bulgariya) in Sofia, is the country's most prestigious orchestra. However, the provinces aren't forgotten and Plovdiv, Varna and Burgas also maintain good symphony orchestras. Many of Bulgaria's best orchestras and soloists perform at Varna Summer International Festival in July, a month-long orchestral, choral and chamber music event.

The leading opera and ballet companies in the country operate under the aegis of the **Bulgarian National Opera and Ballet** in Sofia. Close ties with Russian ballet schools have produced some excellent dancers and international companies often visit Sofia on tour. However, several regional cities do maintain pretty good opera companies. The **Plovdiv Operatic and Philharmonic Society, Stara Zagora Opera** and **Varna Opera and Philharmonic Society** are among the best. Plovdiv is definitely the best place to go for open-air opera. In summer, the town's Roman theatre is the venue for performances of Verdi's *Aïda* and other classics.

Poster at the National Theatre in Sofia

THEATRE

Every sizeable town and city in Bulgaria has at least one theatre, where a varied programme of classic and modern drama is staged. Sofia, where there are between about 10 and 12 different plays to choose from on any evening during the season, offers the widest choice of productions.

For visitors from other countries, the main disadvantage is that almost all performances are in Bulgarian, with simultaneous translations very rarely provided. However, leading theatres, such as the **Ivan Vazov National Theatre** in Sofia, perform many classic plays (such as the works of Shakespeare), which English-speaking visitors may know well enough to allow them to follow the plot and enjoy the performance.

Bulgaria also has several imaginative and daring theatre directors, whose work is visually stunning, even if you cannot follow the dialogue. The **Sfumato Theatre Workshop** in Sofia has an international reputation for putting on contemporary and avant-garde plays. The main festival for challenging modern drama is Scene at the Crossroads (Stsena na krustoput), which takes place in Plovdiv in mid-September and in which international and Bulgarian actors take part. Excellent modern drama also forms part of Sozopol's Arts Festival, in early September.

Performance by members of the Bulgarian National Opera and Ballet, Sofia

CINEMA

New Hollywood blockbusters and other international films reach Bulgaria a month or two after being premièred elsewhere. They are screened in their original language, with subtitles in Bulgarian.

Modern multiplexes with comfortable seats and high-quality sound are common in Sofia. Outside the capital, cinemas tend to be old-fashioned and badly ventilated. Both in Sofia and elsewhere, cinema tickets are inexpensive.

FOLK MUSIC AND DANCE

Performances of traditional folk music and dancing are a regular feature of folk-style restaurants in Sofia and in holiday resorts.

Authentic folk festivals are an important feature of the Bulgarian calendar. The leading folk festival is that held in Koprivshtitsa. The main event is the International Folk Festival, at which folk dancers and musicians from all over Bulgaria perform. This takes place every five years (the next in summer 2010) on a meadow outside the village. The Folklore Days festival, a smaller gathering featuring local folk singers and dancers, is held in central Koprivshtitsa in mid-August each year.

Other major events include Pirin pee ("Pirin Sings"), a celebration of Bulgarian-Macedonian music held at Predel, west of Bansko; and Rozhenskia Subor ("Rozhen Gathering"), a festival of Rhodopean music held on a mountainside near Smolyan.

The Arena Multiplex in Sofia

Pre-Christian rites are other occasions when traditional Bulgarian music is played. The *kukeri* rites *(see p102)* involve masked mummers dancing wildly to strident musical accompaniment.

Chervilo Club-Bar in Sofia, one of many nightclubs in the capital

ROCK, JAZZ AND NIGHTCLUBS

Local bands playing popular rock and jazz standards are a frequent feature of bars and clubs in cities and holiday resorts. Big names in rock and pop perform at the National Palace of Culture in Sofia.

Club culture is highly developed in Bulgaria, with local and international house and techno DJs spinning discs to large and appreciative audiences in Sofia and in coastal resorts during the season.

International jazz musicians gather for two important annual events: the Varna International Jazz Festival in early August, and the Bansko Jazz Festival in mid-August.

DIRECTORY

CLASSICAL MUSIC, OPERA AND BALLET

Bulgarian National Opera and Ballet, Sofia
Tel (02) 987 1366.
www.operasofia.com

Plovdiv Opera and Philharmonic Society
Tel (032) 625 553.
www.ofd-plovdiv.org

Stara Zagora Opera
Tel (042) 622 265.
www.operastzagora.com

Varna Opera and Philharmonic Society
Tel (052) 613 002.
www.operavarna.bg

THEATRES

Ivan Vazov National Theatre, Sofia
Tel (02) 811 9219.
www.nationaltheatre.bg

Sfumato Theatre Workshop, Sofia
Tel (02) 944 0127.
www.sfumato.info

ARTS FESTIVALS

Apollonia, Sozopol
www.apollonia.bg

Folk dancers at the Apollonia Arts Festival, Sozopol

OUTDOOR ACTIVITIES

With the beaches of the Black Sea coast, which stretches for 354 km (220 miles) along the country's eastern border, and spectacular mountains in the interior, Bulgaria offers almost endless possibilities for active holidays. On the coast, well-organized beach resorts offer a great range of water sports, from windsurfing to kiteboarding, while the waters of nearby bays and rocky coves are perfect for learning scuba diving. The mountain resorts offer excellent skiing and snowboarding in winter, and in summer they become bases for hiking and mountain-biking. Other sports include rafting and kayaking on fast-flowing rivers, rock climbing and caving, and horse-riding. Bulgaria also has wide tracts of unspoilt countryside that is rich in flora and fauna. With wetlands and other pristine habitats attracting native as well as migratory birds, Bulgaria also offers unrivalled birdwatching.

HIKING

With four major mountain chains and several smaller ranges, Bulgaria offers a great variety of hiking trails that traverse stunningly beautiful scenery. It is easy to get away from it all as the country is roughly the size of England but the population is only around the 8 million mark.

The Rila and Pirin ranges south of Sofia are the easiest to explore, with winter-sports resorts such as Borovets and Bansko becoming convenient hiking bases in spring and summer. The pine-cloaked Rila massif culminates in Mount Musala, which at 2,925m (9,600 ft) is the highest peak in the Balkans. However, it is the breathtakingly beautiful Seven Lakes locality, in the western part of the range, that attracts most day-trip hikers.

The neighbouring Pirin range has a spectacular array of jagged limestone peaks, with 45 summits over 2,590m (8,500ft) high. The cable car

Chapel in the rock, Rusenski Lom National Park

from Bansko and chairlift from Dobrinishte make the Pirin one of the most accessible areas of mountain wilderness in Bulgaria, with gushing streams, mountain lakes and panoramic views awaiting those who make the trip. In both the Rila and Pirin ranges, paths are well marked and a network of mountain huts

provides stopping places for walkers. The Rhodope Mountains, which dominate southern Bulgaria, feature coniferous forests and fragrant meadows, and are dotted with rustic villages and areas of karst landscape with such spectacular features as Trigrad Gorge and the Yagodina Cave.

The Balkan range runs the length of northern Bulgaria from east to west: along its main ridge runs the longest marked hiking route in Bulgaria. Walking the entire trail, which forms part of the trans-European E3 hiking route, will take about 20 days. Those who only have enough time to walk a short stretch of the Balkan Range should aim for the prettiest area, the Central Balkan National Park, south of the town of Troyan. Limestone cliffs, highland meadows and beech forests characterize the Iskur Gorge, north of Sofia, and the nearby Vrachanski National Park.

Near the Danube port of Ruse, the canyons of the Rusenski Lom National Park are famous for their medieval rock-hewn monasteries and pretty wild flowers.

Reliable, up-to-date hiking maps are available for all the most popular hiking areas in Bulgaria. Although they are sporadically available from newspaper kiosks and tourist agencies in mountain resorts,

Hikers at a pass high in the Pirin Mountains, in southwestern Bulgaria

it is best to buy them before you head for the mountains, from specialist shops in Sofia such as the **Stenata** sports shop or at the office of **Zig Zag Holidays**. Zig Zag and **trekkingbulgaria.com** can organise guided or self-guided holidays.

MOUNTAIN BIKING

The vast network of gravel tracks and forestry roads that threads through Bulgaria's wooded mountains provides great potential for mountain biking. The sport is relatively undeveloped here, and few mountain biking routes are marked. So you're likely to have the mountain to yourselves. However, there are several signed trails around Velingrad and Momchilovtsi, in the Rhodope Mountains, and around Teteven and Troyan, in the Central Balkan range. Bansko in summer is also a good area for mountain biking; try **Mountain Tracks** in town or just rent a bike from a hotel (do check it out first though). The Velingrad-based agency **BikeArea** publishes mountain-biking maps of the vicinity and also organizes guided mountain-biking tours. Many places offer bikes for rent at reasonable prices.

HORSE RIDING

A wide variety of horseback riding holidays is available in Bulgaria, ranging from in-vigorating gallops along Black Sea beaches to one-day or one-week treks through some

The ski resort of Borovets, in the northern Rila Mountains

stunning inland mountain scenery. Travelling on horse enables the visitor to cover a lot of ground and yet see the countryside close-up and at a comfortable pace. Stables offering excursions for all abilities are based at Albena, on the northern Black Sea coast, Ribaritsa and Uzana in the central Balkans, Trigrad in the Rhodopes and Beli Iskur in the Rila Mountains. Equine holiday specialists such as **Arkantours** and **Horseriding Bulgaria** can provide more details and arrange bookings.

WINTER SPORTS

Skiing is a major aspect of Bulgaria's leisure industry but to date the country has really struggled to dispel its image as solely a budget or even downmarket option. This was brought on by a combination of poor ski facilities and bad food and accommodation. However, this is all changing

and after substantial investment the resort of Bansko now has a very modern ski-lift system, snowmaking facilities, good food and and lively après ski. With good pistes for skiers of all abilities, Bansko even has some exhilarating descents for advanced skiers. In addition, you can even go heli-skiing here for a fraction of the price you would pay elsewhere in Europe or North America. For novices or inexperienced skiers, the resorts of Borovets and Pamporovo, with their excellent ski schools and nursery slopes in or near the centre of the resort, are also recommended. For those staying in Sofia, Mt Vitosha, just outside the capital, makes an ideal destination for a weekend excursion.

All of these resorts have ski schools with instructors who speak good English. Most UK ski operators, such as **Inghams Travel**, offer ski holidays in Bulgaria but there are also plenty of Bulgarian companies such as **Bulgariaski** offering the same type of holidays, often at better prices.

Snowshoeing, which requires no previous experience, is an increasingly popular winter sport in Bulgaria thanks largely to the many mountain ranges available. It involves hiking across high-altitude snowfields in specially designed footwear, and provides memorable winter-landscape views. General outdoor trekking and adventure companies such as **Zig Zag Holidays** and **trekkingbulgaria.com** will be able to arrange trips.

Group of mountain bikers on a country road in the Rila Mountains

Kayaker on Lake Pancharevo

RAFTING AND KAYAKING

Wild rivers such as the Struma, in southwestern Bulgaria, the Iskur in the northwest, and the Rusenski Lom in the northeast, provide excellent opportunities for rafting. The sport is usually practicable only in the spring and early summer, when the rivers are at their fullest and fastest, thanks to meltwaters from the mountains above. This is when you will find the best whitewater action.

Those who would rather enjoy more gentle touring can try Lake Batak, in the western Rhodopes, the Kurdzhali reservoir in the eastern Rhodopes, or consider a leisurely kayak tour down the Danube. Specialist Bulgarian tour operators **Zig Zag Holidays** can also organize short kayaking tours like these.

BIRDWATCHING

Bulgaria is home to an amazing variety of wild birds, with over 400 species that are either indigenous or passing through on seasonal migrations.

The best places for birdwatching are the Rhodope Mountains, the shores of the Black Sea and the coastal wetlands around Durankulak, Shabla and Burgas. The latter are important stopping places on the Via Pontica, the north–south migration route that thousands of birds take each autumn and spring on their flights to and from Asia.

Cormorant, one of Bulgaria's sea birds

Slightly inland, the reedy edges of Lake Sreburna, beside the Danube, is the nesting ground or overwintering place for over 180 species of birds. In the eastern Rhodope Mountains, the rocky, arid landscape of the Arda Gorge, near Madzharovo, provides the perfect habitat for three different species of vulture and numerous birds of prey. In the western Rhodope Mountains, the Trigrad gorge is inhabited by several rare species of bird, including the wallcreeper.

Information on birdwatching in Bulgaria is available from the **Bulgarian Society for the Protection of Birds**.

ROCK CLIMBING

With a significant proportion of the countryside classified as mountain, Bulgaria has many opportunities for mountain climbers of all levels.

Bulgaria's prime rock climbing site is the Vratsata gorge just outside Vratsa, where sheer limestone cliffs provide some challenging ascents. There's excellent free climbing opportunities of varying lengths. Gara Lakatnik on the Iskur gorge is a popular extreme sport destination

Other destinations such as the Rila and Pirin Mountains offer varied walking and climbing opportunities with peaks up to 2,900 m (9,500 ft).

Cavern inside the spectacular Magura Cave, near Belogradchik

CAVING

Bulgaria also offers plenty of opportunities for cavers. Caves that are open to visitors include Ledenika Cave, near Vratsa; Magura Cave, near Belogradchik; and the Trigrad and Yagodin caves in the western Rhodope Mountains. Many tour operators offer short "caving trips" accompanied by trained speleologists, but most of the above caves are lit and can be explored without special equipment. Agencies that specialize in adventure holidays – such as **Odysseia-In**, among others – can arrange caving trips to other caves, notably Temnata Dupka, in the Iskur Gorge, Duhlata Cave on Mount Vitosha, and Orlova Chuka in the Rusenski Lom.

Colony of water birds at Lake Pomorie, near Varna

Windsurfers off a beach at Lozenets, on the southern part of the Black Sea coast

WINDSURFING AND KITEBOARDING

Bulgaria is a good place for beginners to learn how to windsurf, although the gentle afternoon breezes may not meet the expectations of more experienced windsurfers. All the main resorts such as Sunny Beach, Golden Sands, Albena, Lozenets and Sozopol have windsurfing schools.

Kiteboarding, which involves being towed at high speeds by a giant parachute-like kite, can be enjoyed at Lozenets, Sunny Beach and Golden Sands.

DIVING

Diving is increasingly popular in Bulgaria, and there are diving schools and centres in nearly all of the Black Sea resorts. **Deep Blue** has diving centres in Sofia, Golden Sands and Sunny Beach. The best areas for underwater exploration are the northern Black Sea coast around Kamen Briag and Tyulenovo, where divers can explore varied rock formations, submerged caves, colourful shoals of fish and exotic sea anemones. There are also several WWII shipwrecks north of Varna at Cape Shabla. However, the visibility is not especially good in the Black Sea and divers used to the rich underwater life of coral reefs may be slightly disappointed.

PARAGLIDING

Bulgaria is an excellent place to learn how to paraglide as the cost is lower than in other European destinations. There's also plenty of hilly terrain to launch from and rocks and plateaux to create thermals. The best time of the year to try this sport is from March to October. **Super Sky Paragliding** is a Sofia-based outfit that can organize lessons and tours in any of the main venues such as Sopot in the central Balkan range, and the southeastern shoulder of Mount Vitosha, near Bistritsa.

DIRECTORY

BIRDWATCHING

Bulgarian Society for the Protection of Birds
www.bspb.org

CAVING

Odysseia-In
www.odysseia-in.com

DIVING

Deep Blue
www.diving-bg.com

HIKING AND ADVENTURE TOURISM

Stenata
l. Bratya Miladinovi 5, Sofia.
www.stenata.com

trekkingbulgaria.com
bul. Cherni Vrah 25, Sofia.
www.trekkingbulgaria.com

Zig Zag Holidays
bul. Aleksandur Stamboliiski 20-V, Sofia. **Tel** (02) 980 5102.
www.zigzagbg.com

HORSERIDING

Arkantours
www.arkantours.com

Horseriding Bulgaria
www.horseridingbulgaria.com

MOUNTAIN BIKING

BikeArea
www.bikearea.org

Mountain Tracks
ul. Pirin, Bansko.
Tel (0888) 788 859.

PARAGLIDING

Super Sky Paragliding
Tel (02) 776 244.
www.supersky.hit.bg

Paragliding behind a speedboat, a popular sport on the Black Sea coast

SURVIVAL GUIDE

PRACTICAL INFORMATION

With fine cities, a beautiful coast-line and stunning mountain scenery, Bulgaria is an attractive destination all year round. On the Black Sea coast, the main holiday season runs from May to September, peaking in July and August, when temperatures are at their highest and the beaches fill with holiday-makers. The skiing season runs from late December to mid-March. Hiking in

Plaque with information for visitors at the entrance to a convent

the country's spectacular mountains can be enjoyed from April through to October, while Bulgaria's historic cities, with their great churches, cathedrals, museums and art galleries, are rewarding places to visit at any time of year. Although travelling in Bulgaria may not be as quick and easy as in other European countries, there are no serious obstacles, and Bulgarians are helpful and courteous towards foreign visitors.

PASSPORTS AND VISAS

To enter Bulgaria, citizens of European Union countries do not need a visa but must have a full (not a visitor's) passport. Citizens of Australia, Canada, New Zealand and the USA do not need a visa for a stay of up to 90 days. Nationals of other countries should check current regulations with the Bulgarian Embassy or Consulate in their home country.

CUSTOMS

Visitors entering Bulgaria from elsewhere in the European Union may bring with them a quantity of goods appropriate to the length of their stay. Visitors entering Bulgaria from a non-EU country can bring in, duty free, 200 cigarettes, 1 litre of spirits, 2 litres of wine and 60 ml. of perfume.

Works of art, antiques and rare coins cannot be taken out of the country without a permit from the Ministry of Culture.

Sofia Airport, Bulgaria's main domestic and international air transport hub

TOURIST INFORMATION

The availability of tourist information in Bulgaria differs greatly from one region to the next. A useful source is the National Information and Publicity Centre in Sofia, which is run by the Bulgarian Tourism Authority (*see p259*) and provides information on the whole country.

There is also a scattering of privately run regional information centres, mostly in

areas of the country that are popular with hikers and skiers, and in towns, such as Bansko and Koprivshtitsa, that attract visitors on account of their historic and cultural interest. Tourist information centres in such places sell maps of their area and give advice on accommodation in the locality. Surprisingly, on account of its popularity as a holiday destination, there are very few tourist information centres on the Black Sea coast.

For details of local attractions and tourist excursions, and advice on local restaurants, ask at the reception desk of your hotel, or go to a privately run travel agency in the nearest town or city.

OPENING HOURS

Museum opening times are far from uniform. In popular tourist spots, museums are generally open from 9am to 5pm Tuesday to Sunday, and sometimes close at lunchtime. Many museums in these

Tourist information center, with leaflets and postcards, in Koprivshtitsa

◁ Fishing boats in the harbour at Nesebûr

A beach-side bar in one of Bulgaria's popular Black Sea resorts

tourist areas frequently stay open longer in the evening during the summer season. Museums in smaller provincial towns are more likely to be open from 9am to 5pm Monday to Friday, with no weekend opening.

Churches and monasteries are open every day, and do not close for lunch. In small or remote villages, however, churches tend only to be open for religious services. A good time to visit is around 5pm, when evening services are commonly held, although visitors should, of course, be considerate and take care not to disturb worshippers.

Payphone for the use of wheelchair users

DISABLED TRAVELLERS

Bulgaria unfortunately lags behind most other European countries in terms of access to public buildings and facilities for disabled people. Pavements everywhere are uneven and unramped, and few public buildings, shops and visitor attractions are adapted for wheelchair users.

Many museums are in older buildings without lifts, and access to archaeological sites is also very difficult.

By contrast, hotels in well-established spa resorts such as Velingrad, Hisarya, Sandanski and Pomorie are likely to have facilities for wheelchair-users. In other parts of

Bulgaria, only the newer and more upmarket hotels have facilities for disabled people. Although most of Sofia's five-star hotels are easily wheelchair-accessible, there is no guarantee that the hotel rooms themselves have been adapted for disabled guests. It is therefore advisable to phone ahead, to check on accessibility and inform the establishment of your particular needs.

GAY & LESBIAN VISITORS

Although Bulgarian society is traditionally patriarchal and conservative, attitudes to gays and lesbians are slowly becoming more relaxed. Today, several openly gay men are prominent in the entertainment and media industries. Sofia has a handful of dedicated gay and lesbian bars and clubs, and a large number of mixed clubs where people of any sexual orientation are welcome.

ELECTRICAL EQUIPMENT

The main electricity supply in Bulgaria is 220/240V, and standard European two-pin plugs are used. To use their own electrical devices in Bulgaria, visitors from the UK will need to buy an adaptor before they travel. However, most rooms in hotels with a four-star rating or above are equipped with hair dryers.

TIME

Bulgaria is in the Eastern European time zone, so that it is two hours ahead of the UK and seven hours ahead of east-coast USA.

In Bulgaria, as in most other European countries, clocks go back one hour in October and forward one hour at the beginning of April.

BODY LANGUAGE

Confusingly, Bulgarians shake their heads when they mean "yes" and nod when they mean "no". Younger Bulgarians, especially those who work in the tourist industry, may reverse these gestures in order to ease understanding. The best way for visitors to ensure that they are not mis-understood is to pronounce a clear yes (da) or no (ne) and not to rely on gestures.

Visitors at a wine-tasting in one of Bulgaria's wine-producing regions

Richly decorated interior of the Church of the Archangels at Arbanasi

RELIGION

Bulgaria is a religiously active country, with most of its population adhering to one of two faiths. While just over 82 per cent of Bulgarians are Christians of the Bulgarian Orthodox denomination, about 12 per cent are Muslims. There is also a small number of Jews.

Most Bulgarian Orthodox churches are beautifully decorated, with icons, frescoes and carved wooden furnishings. In city-centre churches, religious services are held daily, with the Sunday morning service the most important of the week. A timetable giving times of services is usually posted near the entrance of each church. In larger towns and cities, churches are busy throughout the day, with local people coming in to light candles beside the altar or pray to a particular saint.

Bulgaria also has several important Orthodox monasteries. Many are set in beautiful highland areas that offer the perfect conditions for peace and contemplation. Monasteries are also important places of pilgrimage for Bulgarians, and most are open every day throughout the year, welcoming both sightseers and worshippers.

In the calendar of the Orthodox Church, Easter usually falls a week or two later than in the Catholic and Protestant calendars. It is the most joyful religious holiday of the year, and at midnight on Easter Saturday churches are filled with worshippers.

Although Muslim communities are distributed throughout Bulgaria, they are particularly concentrated in the Rhodope Mountains, around Kurdzhali and Haskovo in the southeastern part of the country, and around Shumen and Razgrad in the northeast. Each of the towns in these regions has at least one mosque, and from the top of the minaret the muezzin calls the faithful to prayer five times a day. Friday prayers, for which Muslims assemble on Friday afternoons, is the most important service of the week.

When visiting a church or mosque, visitors should show respect and consideration, and observe certain customs. To avoid the risk of causing offence, visitors should be appropriately dressed. Women with bare arms and low-cut tops, and men with bare legs are likely to be frowned upon. When visiting a mosque, visitors are asked to remove their shoes and women should cover their head, arms and legs. As you walk around a mosque, take care not to pass in front of anyone kneeling in prayer: this is considered to be an act of basic courtesy.

PHOTOGRAPHY

Photography is not allowed in churches unless special permission has been given by the priest. Elsewhere, attitudes to photography are generally quite relaxed. At museums and archaeological sites, the use of cameras is allowed on payment of an extra fee. When photographing people, however, always ask their permission first.

Public transport tickets for sale at a street stall in Sofia

ADMISSION CHARGES

All museums and archaeological and historic sites make a charge for admission, as do those churches and mosques that have the status of tourist attractions as well as places of prayer. Most museums offer a guided tour (beseda) for an extra charge. These tours are usually in Bulgarian only, but it is sometimes possible to arrange a tour in other languages by contacting the museum in advance.

Orthodox monks at one of Bulgaria's monasteries

PUBLIC TOILETS

There are public toilets at main bus and train stations and privately run toilets in central Sofia and in resorts along the Black Sea coast. All museums and restaurants have toilets, as do most cafés, but if you want to use a café toilet you will be expected to stay for at least a cup of coffee.

A charge of 20–50 lv is made for using public and private toilets, with an extra charge for toilet paper. While state-run public toilets are generally badly maintained, those that are privately run are considerably cleaner.

ADDRESSES AND STREET NAMES

The most common terms used in Bulgarian addresses are ulitsa (street; abbreviated to ul.); ploshtad (square; abbreviated to pl.); and bulevard (boulevard; abbreviated to bul.). In addresses a building's street number always comes after the street name, so that "5 Freedom Square", for example, is written as "pl. Svoboda 5".

WOMEN TRAVELLERS

Women travelling alone or together should exercise normal caution. Bulgaria is a relatively safe country, with no particular areas that should be considered dangerous to visit.

Sign for a public toilet

However, as in most other countries, all towns and cities in Bulgaria have insalubrious, badly lit areas, especially in districts outside the centre. Women should avoid walking alone in these areas after dark.

In remote rural areas, where foreign visitors are still a novelty, lone women are likely to become the object of unwanted attention. Hitch-hiking, and travelling on overnight trains in a couchette compartment rather than a sleeper car, are inadvisable.

Fresh-fish stall with signage in Cyrillic script

LANGUAGE

Bulgarian is a Slavonic language related to Russian, Serbian and Croatian, and more distantly to Czech and Polish. Most young Bulgarians speak a few words of English and certain other European languages. Bulgarians of the older generation are more likely to have Russian, which they studied at school, as their second language.

Many museums and art galleries have labels and information panels in Bulgarian only. But most restaurants, especially in holiday resorts, provide menus in English.

Bulgaria was the first country to adopt the Cyrillic alphabet, which was developed in the 9th century by the disciples of St Cyril and St Methodius. Cyrillic, rather than Roman, is still the dominant script in Bulgaria, and names of restaurants, cafés, museums and galleries are generally written in this script. Signs on main roads are usually in both Cyrillic and Roman script. In rural areas, road signs are usually in Cyrillic.

DIRECTORY

EMBASSIES AND CONSULATES

Canada
ul. Moskovska 9, Sofia. **Map** 2 D4.
Tel (02) 969 9710.
consular@canada-bg.org

Ireland
ul. Bacho Kiro 26–28, Sofia.
Map 1 C3. **Tel** (02) 985 3425.
info@embassyofireland.bg

South Africa
ul. Bacho Kiro 26, Sofia.
Map 1 C3. **Tel** (02) 981 6682.
saembsof@techno-link.com

United Kingdom
ul. Moskovska 9, Sofia. **Map** 2 D4.
Tel (02) 933 9222.
britembinf@mail.orbitel.bg

United States
ul. Kozyak 16, Sofia.
Tel (02) 937 5100.
sofia@usembassy.bg

TOURISM ORGANIZATIONS

Bulgarian Tourism Authority
pl. Sveta Nedelya 1, Sofia.
Map 1 B4. **Tel** (02) 987 9778.
www.bulgariatravel.org

USEFUL WEBSITES

www.discover-bulgaria.com
www.inyourpocket.com
www.abvg.net

Foreign visitors at a stall in a flea market in Sofia

Personal Security and Health

Green-cross sign for a pharmacy

Although Bulgaria has a low crime rate, petty theft can be a problem in major towns and cities and in tourist spots. The best way to avoid becoming a victim of petty crime is to take basic precautions. In crowded areas such as shopping malls, markets and train or bus stations, take extra care of your bags and beware of pickpockets. At all times, keep documents, money and credit cards hidden from view, and keep valuables in the safe of your hotel room. When you park your car, never leave anything in view. Basic medical advice is available at pharmacies but, as hospitals are underfunded, make sure you have adequate medical insurance for private care.

Motorcycle traffic policeman on duty in a city centre

Drivers of vehicles with non-Bulgarian number plates receive a disproportionate amount of attention from traffic police. Foreign drivers are quite often flagged down at checkpoints on main highways, and subjected to spot fines for minor infringements that Bulgarian drivers routinely get away with. However, unless you are offered an official receipt, you are not legally obliged to pay these fines.

BEACHES

During the holiday season, life-guards are employed on the beaches of major resorts. These beaches are regularly swept for litter and on almost all of them visitors can expect facilities such as showers. Sun loungers and parasols can be rented for a fee.

Outside the main resorts, many town beaches on the Black Sea charge a small access fee. The funds are supposed to finance the employment of life-guards and litter collectors, but this is not always put into practice.

Some of Bulgaria's most beautiful beaches, particularly along the southern part of the Black Sea coast, are wonderfully wild and uncommercialized, but are without any facilities.

Beach at a popular resort on the Black Sea, with sun loungers and parasols

PERSONAL BELONGINGS

Before you leave home, it is wise to check that you are adequately insured against the loss or theft of luggage and valuable possessions.

Take photocopies of your passport and other important documents. If your passport is lost or stolen, photocopies will help your embassy or consulate to issue a new one. Also make a note of your credit card numbers and the emergency telephone number of the issuing bank, so that you can cancel them immediately if they are lost or stolen. Keep this information secure.

When you park your car, always lock it and make sure any items of value are out of sight. Cameras or camcorders should be carried on a strap or inside a case. Never leave your clothes and other belongings unattended on a beach, even if you are swimming just a few metres away.

Any incidence of theft should be reported immediately to the police. The loss or theft of a passport should be reported without delay to your country's embassy or consulate in Sofia (see p259).

POLICE

Bulgarian police are usually courteous in their dealings with visitors from other countries, but they may not have a good command of English or any other foreign language. If you have to report the loss or theft of property, bear in mind that Bulgarian police are slow in filling out reports, so be prepared to be patient.

Police car in typical white and blue livery

On beaches, exposure to strong sun can be a hazard from May to early October. Young children are especially vulnerable to sunburn. Sunhats, sunglasses, and a high protection factor suncream are essential. Also remember to carry bottled water with you to prevent dehydration, which can lead to heat exhaustion. During the middle of the day, it is best to stay under a parasol or go indoors, so as avoid exposure to the sun when its rays are at their strongest.

MEDICAL CARE

Bulgaria is free from most dangerous contagious diseases, so that visitors need no immunizations. The tap water is also safe to drink. Citizens of countries of the European Union are entitled to use the Bulgarian national health service free of charge. Citizens of other countries must pay for treatment. All foreign visitors, whether or not they are from another EU country, must pay for any but the most basic medicines. You should be able to claim some reimbursement from your insurance company if you keep the receipts.

Bulgarian state-run hospitals often lack the most effective medicines and the most up-to-date facilities. Because of this, it is probably best to seek treatment in a private clinic if you fall ill. Again, you will be able to claim reimbursement if your insurance policy covers this eventuality. Your hotel is

Pharmacy shop with distinctive blue and white signage and snake motif

likely to be able to recommend a reliable private doctor or a reputable private clinic.

Visitors to Bulgaria who are on package holidays should seek the advice of their local tour company representative.

PHARMACIES

Bulgarian pharmacies are easily recognized by the word *apteka*, usually in white against a blue background, and the sign of the coiled Aesculapian snake. Most pharmacies keep normal shop hours *(see p246)*. Every major town and city has a duty pharmacy, with an emergency counter that is open 24 hours a day. All pharmacies post details of the nearest duty pharmacy in their window. Pharmacies are a good source of advice for minor medical problems, although it may be difficult to find one with English-speaking staff. Although most Bulgarian pharmacies carry a selection

of international-brand drugs, they may not stock the particular drug or remedy drugs that you are accustomed to using. If you need special prescription drugs, it is best to bring an adequate supply with you. Every Bulgarian town and city has at least one herbal pharmacy *(Bilkova apteka)* offering natural remedies, very often made from locally sourced herbs and plants. The staff in such pharmacies have a good knowledge of herbal medicine and can offer advice on remedies, but are unlikely to speak English. However, you should be able to communicate adequately using a smile, a phrasebook and basic sign language.

FIRE

Bulgaria's hot, dry summers create prime conditions for forest fires, which can spread with alarming speed. During excursions to forests, visitors should take extreme care to extinguish camp fires, and to dispose of cigarette butts and used matches carefully.

DIRECTORY

EMERGENCY SERVICES

Police

Tel 166

Ambulance

Tel 150

Fire

Tel 160

Fire crew and fire engines at the ready at a station in Sofia

Banking and Local Currency

Postbank, a leading Bulgarian bank

Bulgarian towns and cities are well provided with banks, and automatic cash machines can be found outside most major high-street branches. Credit cards are increasingly commonly accepted in larger hotels, the smarter restaurants and luxury shops, but they are not widely used elsewhere. Almost all other transactions, from paying for a stay in a hostel to buying souvenirs, are customarily made in cash.

BANKS, EXCHANGE AND CASH DISPENSERS

Bank opening hours are 9am to 4pm Monday to Friday. A bank (*banka*) will change all major foreign currencies, basing its rate on the official exchange rates released by the Bulgarian National Bank each morning. Transactions in banks are slow and require a lot of form filling.

If you are changing cash, it can be quicker to go to an exchange bureau (*obmenno byuro*). Exchange bureaux usually have longer opening hours than banks and can be found on high streets in most towns, cities and resorts.

When using an exchange bureau, always check rates carefully: most bureaux offer the same exchange rates as the major banks, but some of those in busy tourist resorts offer disadvantageous deals. Many hotel reception desks also change money, but they rarely offer competitive rates.

Automatic cash machine, with logos of major debit and credit cards

The easiest way to obtain Bulgarian currency is to use an automatic cash machine. These machines are now ubiquitous in Bulgaria's town centres, and they have instructions in English. Most ATMs accept Visa, MasterCard, Maestro and American Express. However, bear in mind that most banks and credit card companies in your home country make a small charge for each withdrawal you make abroad.

TRAVELLER'S CHEQUES AND CREDIT CARDS

Banks in Sofia and large resorts cash traveller's cheques by issuers such as American Express, Thomas Cook and major banks. Cashing traveller's cheques can be a lengthy process as it tends to involve a good deal of bureaucracy. Outside tourist areas, traveller's cheques are not widely accepted.

Credit cards can be used at the more upmarket hotels (with a three-star rating or above), in smart restaurants, and for car hire.

CURRENCY

The currency of Bulgaria is the *lev* (plural: *leva*), which is divided into 100 *stotinki*. As Bulgaria is now a member of the European Union, it may at some time adopt the euro.

As *leva* are not widely available outside Bulgaria, you will need to change or withdraw currency when you arrive in the country. In 1999, after extraordinary inflation, the value of the *lev* was adjusted. Thus 1,000 *leva* became 1 *lev*. Banknotes issued before 1999 are now worthless.

DIRECTORY

BULGARIAN BANKS

ING Bank
ul. Emil Bersinski 12
Sofia 1408.
Tel (02) 917 64 00.

Postbank
bul. Tsar Osvoboditel 14
Sofia 1048.
Tel (02) 8166 000.

LOST CARDS AND TRAVELLER'S CHEQUES

American Express
Tel (44) 20 7365 4846
(Lost cards UK & US)

MasterCard
Tel 1 636 722 7111
(Lost cards UK & US)

Visa
Tel 00 800 0010 888 557 4446
(Cards UK & US)
Tel (44) 20 7937 8091
(Traveller's Cheques UK & US)

Exchange bureau in a tourist location, with signage in English

Banknotes

Banknotes are issued in denominations of 2, 5, 10, 20, 50 and 100 leva. The text on the notes is in Cyrillic, but their value is clearly displayed. Each is illustrated with the portrait of a historical figure who played an important role in the history or culture of the nation.

2 leva banknote

5 leva banknote

10 leva banknote

20 leva banknote

50 leva banknote

100 leva banknote

1 lev coin

50 stotinki coin

20 stotinki coin

10 stotinki coin

5 stotinki coin

Coins

Coins are issued in denominations of 1, 2, 5, 10, 20 and 50 stotinki, and 1 lev. Coins of 1 to 5 stotinki are copper-coloured, and those of 10 to 50 stotinki are silver-coloured. The 1 lev coin has a portrait of St John of Rila, patron saint of Bulgaria, on its reverse.

2 stotinki coin

1 stotinka coin

Communications

Post office sign, with date of its foundation

Bulgaria has national telephone and postal systems, both of which are reasonably efficient, although the postal service is a little slower than in some Western European countries. Bulgarians have enthusiastically embraced the internet, so that even in smaller towns visitors will have no trouble finding an internet café. Foreign newspapers, by contrast, are more difficult to find. Even so, at least one good-quality English-language newspaper, aimed specifically at visitors, is available. Cable and satellite channels dominate Bulgarian television.

Mobile phone-user in a city centre

USING THE TELEPHONE

The main telephone network in Bulgaria is operated by BTK (Bulgarian Telecommunications Company). There are BTK centres in most large towns and cities. They are usually open from 8am to 6pm daily, but those in large towns and cities may be open 24 hours. To make a call from a BTK centre, obtain a token from the counter and use one of the booths.

Bulfon, Mobika and BTK also run the public telephones that you will find on street corners, in hotel lobbies, and other public areas. These

Sign for BTK, Bulgaria's telephone company

telephones are card-operated, with phonecards, or with credit cards for long-distance calls. Phonecards (*fonokarti*) can be bought in post offices and at newspaper kiosks. Buy a couple of different cards to widen the choice of phones available.

Most hotel rooms are equipped with telephones. But calls made from them are much more expensive than from a public telephone.

International calls can be made from all public telephones. To make an international call, dial 00, followed by the country code, the area code (omitting the initial zero), then the number.

Useful country codes are: 44 for the UK, 1 for the USA and Canada, 353 for Ireland, 61 for Australia, 64 for New Zealand, and 27 for South Africa.

The country code for Bulgaria is 359. Area codes in Bulgaria include 02 for Sofia, 056 for Burgas, 032 for Plovdiv, and 052 for Varna.

Bulgaria's mobile telephone network covers the whole country, although reception may be patchy in sparsely populated mountain valleys. Mobile phone usage is widespread in Bulgaria, and visitors who bring their own phone are unlikely to experience any problems.

Bear in mind that, in order to make and receive calls on your mobile phone while abroad, your roaming facility will have to be activated before you leave home. While abroad you will then be charged for both incoming and outgoing calls and text messages. For full details of call charges, contact your mobile phone operator before leaving home.

One way of avoiding high call charges is to buy a pre-paid SIM card from a Bulgarian mobile phone operator such as Mtel, Globul or Vivatel, and insert it into your phone so that you can make calls to Bulgarian numbers, at Bulgarian prices, during your stay. However, some mobile phones will automatically lock if you insert another network's SIM card into them, so check with your original operator before attempting this.

USING A CARD-OPERATED TELEPHONE

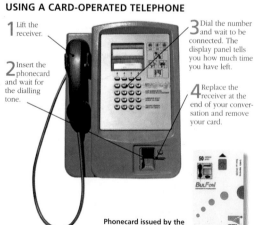

1 Lift the receiver.

2 Insert the phonecard and wait for the dialling tone.

3 Dial the number and wait to be connected. The display panel tells you how much time you have left.

4 Replace the receiver at the end of your conversation and remove your card.

Phonecard issued by the telephone operator Bulfon

POSTAL SERVICES

Post offices *(poshta)* are open 8am to 5pm Monday to Friday, and 8am to 1pm on Saturday. Post offices in large towns and cities may stay open until 7pm or 8pm Monday to Friday. Post offices have separate counters for buying stamps *(marki)*, sending letters *(pisma)* and despatching parcels *(koleti)*, so check that you are in the right queue. Postage stamps can also be bought at most shops that sell postcards.

By standard post, letters and postcards sent to destinations in Europe take about seven days to arrive. Post to North America takes about two weeks. For quicker delivery use the express service *(bûrza)* or airmail *(vûzdushna)*.

Post office in Smolyan, with post boxes outside

TELEVISION AND RADIO

Bulgaria's principal television channels are Kanal 1, which is state-run, and BTV and Nova TV, which are both independently run. All three

Yellow postbox with horn logo and "poshta" in Cyrillic and Roman script

channels broadcast a mixture of domestically made programmes, imported dramas and live sport. Most bars, restaurants and hotels have televisions tuned to international cable channels. Larger hotels offer foreign-language channels, including CNN and BBC World.

Bulgaria's main English newspaper

The BBC World Service and Radio France Internationale are available on VHF in Sofia. Outside Sofia, however, it is difficult to tune in to foreign-language transmissions.

PRESS

Apart from tabloids, sold mostly in coastal resorts, and the *Financial Times* and *Herald Tribune*, sold in cities, few English-language newspapers are available in Bulgaria. The principal English-language newspaper produced in Bulgaria is *The Sofia Echo*, a weekly publication that is particularly strong on business news.

It also carries Sofia theatre and cinema listings for the coming week. *The Sofia Echo* is usually available at newspaper kiosks in Sofia, in resorts on the Black Sea coast and in ski resorts. It can be difficult to find elsewhere. *Vagabond*, a colourful English-language monthly magazine, with lifestyle articles and travel features, is available from news kiosks in the larger towns and cities.

The best of the locally produced publications aimed at foreign visitors are the lively listings-based booklets *Sofia in Your Pocket* and *Bansko in Your Pocket*. Updated seasonally, these handy guides are distributed free of charge, and can be picked up at tourist offices, and in most hotels, restaurants and bars in Sofia and Bansko respectively.

The Sofia-based web magazine **Novinite** (The News), which is updated daily, is a good source of news in English.

INTERNET

There are internet cafés in all major holiday resorts, and in towns and cities. They are usually open from 10am to 9pm. BTK centres also offer internet access.

Many hotels provide free internet access to guests, in the form of one or two computer terminals in the lobby. For those who travel with their laptops, an increasing number of hotels offer either wireless internet or plug-in internet connections in their rooms.

Newspaper kiosk, with a wide selection of papers and magazines

TRAVEL INFORMATION

Logo of
Sofia Airport

Bulgaria is well connected with the rest of Europe by air, and this is the quickest and most economical way of reaching the country. Because of a lack of fast, modern roads and railways in southeastern Europe, travelling to Bulgaria by car, bus or train is somewhat arduous, and impractical for visitors with limited time. Bulgaria itself is served by a network of train and bus routes, to major towns and cities and most rural areas too. For complete independence, however, hiring a car may be the most attractive option.

ARRIVING BY AIR

Sofia, the capital of Bulgaria, is well served by direct flights from most European countries. **Bulgaria Air**, the national carrier, has daily scheduled flights to Sofia from London Gatwick, Amsterdam, Paris and other European capitals. Flight times from the UK are about three hours.

    British Airways provides scheduled flights to Sofia from London Heathrow. The low-cost airlines **easyJet**, **Wizzair** and **Sky Europe** offer flights to Sofia and Burgas from the UK and from central Europe. Other low-cost carriers, such as Ryanair, may start to provide services between the UK and Bulgaria at some time in the future; see www.flycheaper.com for the latest airlines and routes.

    Direct flights to Bulgaria from North America and other non-European countries are rare. Most intercontinental routes involve a direct flight to a European hub such as London, Amsterdam or Frankfurt, and a connecting flight to Bulgaria.

Plane of the Bulgaria Air fleet at Sofia Airport

INTERNATIONAL AIRPORTS

Bulgaria's largest airport serves the capital, Sofia. The airport has convenient transport connections with the city centre, which is about 10 km (6 miles) to the west. Bus no. 84, from Terminal 1, and bus no. 284 from Terminal 2, depart for the city centre every 10–20 minutes. Taxis are also easy to find, and the fare inexpensive.

Much of western and central Bulgaria is easily accessible from Sofia. Although it is not such a convenient entry point if you are heading for the Black Sea coast, there are connecting domestic flights to Varna, on the Black Sea. Alternatively, you can make the connection by car, bus or train, a journey time of 6–7 hours.

    Other airports used by international traffic include Plovdiv, Burgas and Varna. These airports were originally built to handle package-holiday flights and are consequently less well provided with duty-free shops and cafés than Sofia Airport.

AIR FARES

As with most destinations, air fares for flights to Bulgaria vary according to the time of year. They are generally highest during the summer months, although prices also rise significantly during the

The main entrance to Sofia Airport

A hall at Sofia Airport, Bulgaria's main air transport hub

DIRECTORY

AIRLINES

British Airways
Tel (02) 954 7000 in Bulgaria
0870 850 9850 in the UK.
www.ba.com

Bulgaria Air
Tel (02) 402 0400 in Bulgaria
020 7637 7637 in the UK.
www.air.bg

easyJet
www.easyJet.com

Hemus Air
Tel (02) 981 8330 in Bulgaria.
www.hemusair.bg

Sky Europe
Tel (02) 489 4899 in Bulgaria
0905 722 2747 in the UK.
www.skyeurope.com

Wizzair
Tel (02) 960 3888 in Bulgaria
+36 1 470 9488 outside Bulgaria.
www.wizzair.com

AIRPORTS

Sofia
Tel (02) 937 2211.
www.sofia-airport.bg

Varna
www.varna-airport.bg

INTERNATIONAL RAIL TRAVEL

The Man in Seat 61
www.seat61.com

Rail Europe
Tel 0870–837 1371 from the UK
1–877 257 2887 from the US.
www.raileurope.com

Trainseurope
Tel 0871 700 7722.
www.trainseurope.co.uk

skiing season, which runs from mid-December to mid-March. Flights during the Christmas and Easter periods are often fully booked well in advance.

Tickets for flights on low-cost airlines obviously offer excellent value, but to make the most of the lowest fares available travellers should book well in advance, preferably over the internet. However, travellers should bear in mind that additional costs, such as taxes and buying food and drinks, can whittle down the initial difference in price between tickets offered by regular carriers and low-cost airlines.

In summer, charter flights from the UK serve airports such as Varna and Burgas. Seats on these flights are often only available as part of a package deal. See your travel agent for advice.

DOMESTIC FLIGHTS

The only domestic flights in Bulgaria are the daily flights provided by **Hemus Air** between Sofia and Varna, on the Black Sea. Tickets are inexpensive and the flight time is less than one hour.

TRAINS

Travelling to Bulgaria by train is most suitable for those who enjoy rail travel and who are willing to spend at least two days reaching their destination. There are various routes, all of them offering rewarding journeys with much fine scenery and the chance to stop off in some interesting cities. However, the total cost of

travelling to Bulgaria by train is likely to be higher than by air. It may also be difficult to buy a through ticket from western Europe to Bulgaria. Travellers may find is easier to buy one ticket to Budapest, for example, and another for onward travel from there. From continental Europe, the principal routes to Bulgaria are Salzburg to Sofia

Electric train on a local route

via Zagreb and Belgrade, and Budapest to Sofia via Belgrade or Bucharest. Sleeping cars are available on certain stretches.

Approaching Bulgaria from the south, there are direct trains to Sofia from Istanbul, in Turkey, with a journey time of 12–13 hours, and from Thessaloniki, Greece (7 hours).

The best source of information in English on train travel to Bulgaria is **The Man in Seat 61**, a website run by rail travel enthusiasts.

КАТ. НОМЕР	НАПРАВЛЕНИЕ	ПРЕЗ	ЧАС	КОЛ. ЗАК.
Б 8815	БУРГАС - Bursas	Пловдив	13:40	4и
Б 6691	КЮСТЕНДИЛ		14:00	1
П 20111	Г. ОРЯХОВИЦА		14:15	10
П 10113	ПЛОВДИВ - Plovdiv		14:15	1г
П 50223	ДУПНИЦА - Dupnica		14:27	2г
П 10210	ДРАГОМАН		14:35	6г
П 50205	ПЕРНИК - Pernik		15:10	
Б 4613	РУСЕ - Ruse	Г. Оряховица	15:20	

ЗАМИНАВАЩИ DEPARTURE

Electronic departure board at Sofia's main railway station

Travelling by train, bus and taxi

Sign for a taxi rank

Bulgaria's rail network links all major towns and main cities, and a few smaller destinations as well. On some routes, particularly through the mountains, train travel offers the opportunity to enjoy some spectacular scenery.

Signs on a platform at Sofia's Central Train Station

However, the country's railway system is in need of modernization and journey times are slow. An alternative option for travel on intercity routes is to take one of Bulgaria's fast, clean, modern buses. Much of rural Bulgaria is reached by older, local buses, although more remote villages may only be served by one or two a day. For a tailor-made journey, another option is to negotiate a long-distance trip with a taxi driver.

TRAVELLING BY TRAIN

The country's rail network is operated by **Bulgarian State Railways** (Bulgarska durzhavna zheleznitsa, or BDZh). There are three categories of train: the Accelerated Fast Train (Uskoren burz vlak, or UBV), which stops only at principal towns along a route, is the fastest. UBVs run between Sofia and major provincial towns such as Plovdiv, Varna and Burgas. Most UBVs have modern, comfortable carriages and a buffet car.

Inter-city routes are also served by Fast Trains (Burz vlak, or BV), which make more stops than UBVs. They have slightly older carriages, and do not always have a buffet car.

Slowest are the Passenger Trains (Putnicheski vlak, or PV), which stop at every station. Although some of these trains are modern, many are old and uncomfortable. On all classes of train, the toilets are often abominably badly maintained.

Main entrance to Sofia's Central Train Station

Train tickets can be purchased at station ticket offices. Both first-class *(purva klasa)* and second-class *(vtora klasa)* tickets are available for journeys on UBV and BV trains. On PV trains only second-class seating is available. If you are travelling long distances, first-class tickets are a good buy: by Western European standards they are not expensive, and will give you slightly more comfortable seats and more legroom. Reservations *(zapazeni mesta)*

are advisable if you are travelling between Sofia and the Black Sea coast in summer, particularly at weekends.

If you are travelling by overnight train between Sofia and the Black Sea, it is advisable to book a place in a sleeping car *(spalen vagon)*, as the regular carriages are uncomfortable and you may be at risk from petty thieves. Reservations for Sofia–Black Sea coast routes should be made a few days in advance.

In Sofia, advance tickets of all kinds can be purchased from two city-centre bureaux; **Rila Agency**, for international tickets, and the **Transport Service Centre**, for domestic services. BDZh does not offer any kind of rail pass. However, EuroDomino, InterRail and City Star passes are valid for travel on Bulgarian railways.

TRAVELLING BY BUS

Bus services in Bulgaria are operated by several national and regional bus companies. Virtually every town and village in the country is accessible by bus, although the smaller, more remote villages may be served by only one or two buses a day.

Inter-city bus routes linking Sofia with the country's larg-

Train on one of Bulgaria's scenic mountain routes

est towns and cities (notably Plovdiv, Varna, Burgas, Pleven and Ruse) depart several times a day. Buses on these routes are usually modern, with comfortable seats and air conditioning, and there are regular stops for refreshments and the use of toilets. By contrast, buses on provincial routes are likely to be old, with uncomfortable seats.

Some provincial routes are served by minibuses rather than full-size buses. Minibuses are generally faster than buses, but cramped seating makes them uncomfortable.

Bus tickets can be bought from ticket counters at bus stations, but not on the buses themselves. On inter-city routes, advance reservations are advisable if you are travelling on a Friday or Sunday evening, or at any time during major public holiday periods such as Christmas or Easter. Advance reservations are also recommended if you are travelling between Sofia and the Black Sea coast in July and August. Tickets and information on bus travel throughout Bulgaria is available from **Sofia Central Bus Station**.

Private agent selling tickets for journeys on intercity buses

TIMETABLES AND INFORMATION

Thanks to the internet, planning your trip around Bulgaria is vastly simpler than it used to be. Sofia's Central Bus Station

Modern intercity bus at Sofia's newly built Central Bus Station

has clear arrival and departure times as well as prices, all in English. The privately run **Etap Bus Company** also has clear timetables in English on its website. However, while bus and train stations in large towns and cities often have information counters (marked *"informatsiya"*), the staff here seldom speak any other language than Bulgarian.

Bus and train stations usually also have a timetable *(razpisanie)* prominently displayed in the ticket hall, but this will invariably be in Cyrillic. Departures *(zaminavane)* and arrivals *(pristigane)* are listed in two different sections of the timetable. At smaller bus stations, timetables may be incomplete and ticket windows closed without explanation. In such cases your best option is to ask local people whether a particular service is running.

TAXIS

Taxi drivers in Bulgaria most usually take passengers on short journeys within towns and cities, or to and from airports. However, taxi drivers will often agree to undertake

Private bus operator's intercity timetable

longer trips if these are arranged in advance. Metered fares are relatively low, generally ranging from 1 to 2 Lv per km (roughly 2 to 4 Lv per mile). For a long journey, you may prefer to agree on a set fare with the driver in advance. This can be roughly calculated by multiplying the rate per kilometre (displayed on the vehicle's window) by the distance to be travelled.

For more information on travel by taxi, *see p273*. As always don't be tempted to get into a taxi that isn't yellow, even if the driver insists he is an official taxi.

DIRECTORY

BUS INFORMATION

Etap Bus Company
www.etapgroup.com

Sofia Central Bus Station
bul. Knyaginya Mariya Luiza.
www.centralnaavtogara.bg

TRAIN INFORMATION

Bulgarian State Railways
www.bdz.bg

INTERNATIONAL RAIL TICKETS

Rila Agency
ul. Gurko 5, Sofia.
Tel (02) 987 0777.

DOMESTIC RAIL TICKETS

Transport Service Centre
National Palace of Culture (NDK), Sofia.
Tel (02) 865 7186.

Licensed taxi in Sofia

Travelling by car

Exploring Bulgaria by car is an attractive option, as it gives greater freedom and allows you to explore remoter areas of the country that may not be well served by public transport. However, visitors should bear in mind that fast highways are relatively few, and that the condition of other roads often leaves much to be desired. It is best to avoid driving in major cities such as Sofia and Varna, as traffic flow is badly organized and time-consuming jams all too frequent. Road signs on main intercity trunk roads are usually shown in both Cyrillic and Roman script. On minor roads and in rural areas, however, they may be in Cyrillic only.

Sign for an international car- and van-hire agency

international car hire companies before you leave home. Another option, if you want to reach a remote spot not well served by public transport, for example, is to hire a car with driver. You can do this through a car hire company, or by asking a taxi driver for a day rate *(see p269)*.

ROADS

Although some of Bulgaria's highways are well maintained, most of the country's roads are in bad condition, so that travel by road tends to be slow. Many roads have uneven surfaces, ruts and potholes. In mountain areas road surfaces may also be degraded by rock falls and extreme weather conditions, such as heavy rain and ice. Added to this, and alarmingly for oncoming traffic, drivers often suddenly veer from one side of the road to the other so as to avoid these hazards. In rural areas, motorists should also be prepared to encounter slow-moving horse- or donkey-carts.

In winter, especially after heavy rainfall, or when there is snow and ice, rural roads can be slippery and dangerous, and along remote stretches help will not be readily to hand should you find yourself in difficulties. If you are thinking of venturing into the mountains in winter, it is advisable to carry snow chains.

Road signs on major routes are often in both Cyrillic and Roman script but on minor roads they may be in Cyrillic only. Navigation will be much easier with the aid of a reliable map *(see opposite)*.

Desk of a car rental company at one of Bulgaria's airports

CAR HIRE

By Western European standards, hiring a car in Bulgaria is inexpensive. Many international car-hire companies have offices at airports and in stations, and in central Sofia and other major towns and cities. Most Bulgarian travel agents can arrange car hire through one of the well-known international companies. Car

hire desks can also be found in the lobbies of some of the larger resort hotels. Some of the small local car-hire companies offer extremely cheap deals on hatchbacks and other small cars, although the vehicles themselves may not be in the best condition.

To hire a car in Bulgaria you must be over 21 and must show a valid passport and valid driving licence (which you must have held for a minimum of two years). You will also be asked to show your credit card or to pay a cash deposit, and you may require a valid international insurance policy. If you know you will need to hire a car during your stay in Bulgaria, it may be easier, but not necessarily cheaper, to arrange this with one of the main

Stack of road signs in a town

Petrol station on a road in the outskirts of a town

The road to Rila Monastery, one of the better maintained stretches in Bulgaria

FUEL

Petrol *(benzin)* is cheaper in Bulgaria than in Western Europe. The most likely places to find filling stations *(benzinostantsiya)* are on the outskirts of towns and along main highways. In rural areas they can be hard to find, so fill up if you are about to venture off the beaten track. Another hazard, particularly at stations in out-of-the-way places, is dirty or adulterated petrol. To be safe, stick to stations run by Shell, BP or OMV.

VIGNETTES

To drive on public highways, but not on other roads, in Bulgaria drivers must display a windscreen sticker, or vignette *(vinetka)*. Vignettes can be purchased at border checkpoints or at OMV or Shell petrol stations. They cost 10 Leva (€5) for one week, 25 Leva (€12) for one month, or 135 Leva (€69) for one year. Highways for which drivers need a vignette are clearly signed.

Prices for vignettes at a petrol station

RULES OF THE ROAD

Speed limits on Bulgarian roads are 120 km/hr (75 mph) on main highways, 90 km/hr (56 mph) on minor roads, and 50 km/hr (31 mph) in urban areas. Seat belts are compulsory for front-seat passengers. Driving with more than 0.5 mg of alcohol in the bloodstream is strictly forbidden, and punishable by a heavy fine. Using a mobile phone while driving is only permissible with a hands-free set.

Sign for a tolled highway

You may often notice local drivers flaunting these rules. However, foreign drivers should not emulate them, as the Bulgarian police rarely show lenience towards non-Bulgarians.

Highway police are authorized to levy on-the-spot fines for speeding and other traffic offences. If you are stopped and fined, be sure to see an official receipt before paying.

MAPS

Up-to-date road maps of Bulgaria are widely available from petrol stations and bookstores throughout the country. They are usually available in Cyrillic and in Roman-script versions. Detailed area maps are much harder to find. However, in popular mountain areas, you will find local hiking maps on which minor roads are marked.

Maps of Sofia, Plovdiv and Varna, which are updated annually, can be purchased from local newspaper kiosks and bookstores, but maps of other urban areas appear more sporadically and sell out fast.

ASSISTANCE

For information on all aspects of driving in Bulgaria and assistance in case of breakdown, contact the **Union of Bulgarian Motorists**. The organization has 55 regional centres, and its website, in English and Bulgarian, offers information on everything from caravanning to traffic regulations. Through the union you can also arrange any extra insurance that you may need once in Bulgaria.

DIRECTORY

CAR HIRE

Avis
Tel (02) 826 1100.
www.avis.bg

Budget
Tel (02) 937 3388.
www.budget.bg

Europcar
Tel (02) 931 6000.
www.europcar.bg

Holiday Autos
www.holidayautos.co.uk

DRIVING INFORMATION

Union of Bulgarian Motorists
pl. Positano, Sofia.
Tel (02) 980 3308.
www.uab.org

Getting around Sofia

Sign at entrance to Serdika metro station

Public transport in Sofia consists of an extensive network of trams, buses and trolleybuses, with a unified ticketing system, and a fleet of privately run minibuses. The city also has a modern, if still limited, metro line. Another convenient way of getting around Sofia is to hail one of the capital's inexpensive yellow taxis. As in many other capital cities, however, public transport in Sofia is hampered by traffic congestion, particularly during the morning and early evening rush hours, when trams and buses are reduced to a crawl. Lengthy cross-town journeys may also involve changing from one form of public transport to another. Sightseeing trips around the city, as well as day excursions to places further afield, are provided by private tour operators.

Escalator at a station on Sofia's only metro line

Train at one of the stations on Sofia's modern but short metro line

METRO

Sofia's clean, modern metro *(metropoliten)* so far consists of a single underground line. This starts from Triaditsa station, in the western part of the city centre, runs beneath ploshtad Sveta Nedelya and terminates in the western residential suburb of Lyulin. The route mainly serves commuters and, as there are few tourist sights along the way, the metro is of limited use to visitors. Plans are, however, being made to extend it eastwards through the city centre.

Metro services generally run from 5am to 11:30pm daily. Tickets *(bileti)* for a single journey of any length cost 0.70 Lv and can be bought from the ticket counter in each station.

TRAM, BUS AND TROLLEYBUS

Trams *(tramvai)*, buses *(avtobusi)* and trolleybuses *(troleybusi)* provide adequate if at times slow transport all over central Sofia and out to the suburbs. Like the metro, services run from 5am to 11:30pm daily. Information on routes is not always easy to find. Service numbers and route diagrams are displayed at some tram and bus stops, although details of destinations are invariably written in Cyrillic. The best option is to buy an up-to-date map of the city, which will have public transport routes marked on it.

A unified ticketing system applies to travel on trams, buses and trolleybuses (but not for the metro, for which a separate ticket must be bought, nor for minibuses, where you pay the driver). Tickets *(bileti)* can be purchased from kiosks near major bus and tram stops. They are also available at most newspaper kiosks throughout the city. Single tickets cost 0.70 Lv. A strip *(talon)* of 10 tickets costs 6 Lv. Note that the tickets in

Tram on one of the routes in Sofia's extensive public transport network

a strip are numbered 1 to 10 and should be used in sequence: for example, tickets 1 to 9 will not be considered valid unless you have ticket number 10 in your possession. When you board a tram, bus or trolleybus, remember to punch your ticket by inserting it in the small machine near the vehicle's door. Ticket inspectors are a regular presence on public transport, and failure to punch a ticket is likely to result in an on-the-spot fine. Travellers on buses, trams and trolleybuses are also officially required to buy an extra ticket for any large piece of luggage. This rule is, however, only really enforced on routes to and from the airport. Within the city it is widely ignored.

If you intend to make extensive use of public transport in Sofia, a pass can be a convenient option. A one-day pass (karta za edin den) costs 3 Lv and a five-day pass (karta za pet dena) 12 Lv. Both are readily available at kiosks.

Orange "bendy" bus, with separate entry and exit doors, in Sofia

Trolleybus at a stop in Sofia

TOUR BUSES

Private tour companies have buses with routes taking in the city's major sights and attractions. Companies like **Alma Tours** offer full-day and half-day excursions around the city, and arrange

trips to other interesting locations within easy reach of the capital – although this can be done on public transport.

MINIBUSES

Sofia's trams, buses and trolleybuses are augmented by a fleet of privately owned minibuses (marshrutki). These operate specific express routes through the city, from 5am to 11:30pm daily. Although minibuses halt at many of the stops used by buses and trolleybuses, they can also be hailed along their routes and will stop en route to allow passengers to alight if asked.

Minibuses are often faster than trams and buses, but can frequently feel crowded and stuffy. The fare (1.50 Lv) is paid directly to the driver, and passengers must tender the exact coins.

TAXIS

Several private companies run fleets of taxis in Sofia. All licensed taxis are yellow, and have a sticker displayed in the windscreen or side window indicating their rates in Bulgarian leva (Lv).

Taxi fares are quite low by Western European standards. They

Sign for taxi rank in central Sofia

range from 1 Lv per kilometre (about 2 Lv per mile) during the day and rise by about 50 per cent at night. It is customary to tip the driver 10 per cent of the fare.

There are taxi ranks at most major intersections in Sofia. Taxis can also be hailed as they cruise the streets of the city centre. A small green light inside the windscreen indicates that the taxi is available, and small red light indicates that it is taken.

Taxis can also be ordered by telephone but it is usually easier to ask the reception staff at your hotel to make the call.

Unlicensed taxis tend to congregate at locations such as airports and main railway stations, where disoriented foreign travellers may be easy to swindle. Never be tempted to get into a "taxi" that isn't yellow, no matter what the driver says. This advice should be followed throughout Bulgaria.

DIRECTORY

TOUR BUSES

Alma Tours
bul. A. Stambolyiski 27, Sofia.
Map 1 A4. **Tel** (02) 986 5691

TAXIS

OK Supertrans
Tel (02) 973 2121

Radio CB Taxi
Tel (02) 91263

Sofiataxi
Tel (02) 974 4747

Yellow licensed taxi from one of Sofia's privately run fleets

General Index

Acknowledgments

HACHETTE LIVRE POLSKA would like to thank the following staff at Dorling Kindersley:

Publisher
Douglas Amrine

List Managers
Vivien Antwi, Christine Stroyan,

Managing Art Editor
Jane Ewart

Senior Editor
Hugh Thompson

Designers
Kate Leonard, Karen Constanti

Map Co-ordinator
Casper Morris

DTP Manager
Natasha Lu, Jamie McNeill

Additional Picture Research
Rachel Barber, Ellen Root

Production Controller
Linda Dare

DORLING KINDERSLEY would like to thank all those whose contributions and assistance have made the preparation of this book possible:

Main Contributors
Jonathan Bousfield, Matt Willis

Factchecker
Petya Milkova

Proofreader
Stewart J Wild

Indexer
Hilary Bird

Additional Photography
Ian O'Leary, Frank Greenaway,
Kim Taylor, Jerry Young

Additional Illustrations
Gary Cross, Chapel Design and Marketing Ltd.,

Cartography
Base mapping supplied by Cartographia Ltd.,
Budapest 2006.

Special Assistance
The Publishers would like to thank the staff at shops, museums, hotels, restaurants and other organizations in Bulgaria for their invaluable help. Particular thanks go to: Jolanta Antczak at BE&W; Ilian Dimitrov at PhotoTresor (AZ Press OOD); Desislava Haytova at Bulgaria Photos Net; Beata Ibrahim at Corbis; Carlo Irek at 4Corners Images; Tim Kantoch at Photolibrary Group; Nevena Nikolova at Unofficial Info site of the Museum Town Koprivshtitza; Csilla Pataky at Cartographia Ltd., Budapest; Boryana Punchewa, Director of the Bulgarian Institute of Culture in Warsaw; Milena Trapcheva at Sofia Photo Agency (Novinite Ltd).

Photography Permissions
The Publishers would like to thank all those who gave permission to photograph at musuems, palaces, churches, restaurants, hotels, shops and other sights too numerous to list individually. Particular thanks go to: Iliya Chernev, Executive Secretary of the International Bagpipe Festival in Shiroka Laka; Grazyna Chroszcz at Fotodesigner; Emil Iliev, General Manager of the International Jazz Festival in Bansko; ImagesFromBulgaria.com; Katya Ivanova at Strandja Nature Park Directorate; Yassen Jekoff, photographer; Bisjera Josifova at National Art Gallery in Sofia; Martin Mitov, photographer; Ivan Pajkinski, Director of the Museum of History, Vratza; Rumiana Pashaliyska Director of the National Museum of Literature in Sofia; Peter Petrov, photographer; Ana Rousseva, International Relations Officer at Apollonia Art Foundation; Diana Terzieva at Central Balkan National Park Directorate; Maria Vassileva, Chief Curator at Sofia Art Gallery; Kosu Zareb, Director of the Historical Museum in Kazanlak.

Picture Credits
t=top; tc=top centre; tr=top right; tl=top left; cla=centre left above; ca=centre above; cra=centre right above; cl=centre left; c=centre; cr=centre right; clb=centre left below; cb=centre below; crb=centre right below; bl=bottom left; bc=bottom centre; br=bottom right; b=bottom.

The Publishers are grateful to the following individuals, companies and picture libraries for permission to reproduce their photographs:

4CORNERS IMAGES: SIME/Schmid Reinhard 254–5.

AKG IMAGES: 22cla; Erich Lessing 28tl, 84tr; Ullslein Bild – Archiv 22tr.
ALAMY IMAGES: A+P 23tl; Vladimir Alexeev 26tr; David Ball 108cl; Bulgaria Alan King 22-3; Cephas/Mick Rock 18b; Craft Alan King 20bl; Ilian Religion 48cl ilian studio 20clb; Image Register 044 24br; Isifa Image Service s.r.o/Kubes 110bl; Melvyn Longhurst 22dlb, 48cr, 48br, 232tl; Nikreates 25 crb, 34ca, 49cra, 58-9, 62bc, 78-9, 81b, 104tl, 119crb, 120tc, 121tr,

128cla, 128clb, 128br, 138bl, 139br, 142br, 145b, 256bl, 264tr, 264bl; Nicholas Pitt 15b; Rolf Richardson 24bl; Robert Harding Picture Library 16t; /Peter Scholey 17tr; /Adam Woolfitt 21tl; rochaphoto 108bc; World Pictures 19br; Gregory Wrona 19tc, 27tr.
APOLLONIA ARTS FESTIVAL: 36bl.
ARDEA: Emil Enchev 27cra, 27bc; John Mason 26cb; Johan De Meester 27bl; Duncan Usher 26bl, 26clb; M. Watson 27crb; Wardene Weisser 27cb.
AZ PRESS OOD: 30tr; 30cla; 30clb; 30b; 31t; 31c; 32bl; 34bl; 37bc; 42fbr; 44fbr; 53tc; 54-5; 61br; 74c; 74bl; 86tl; 87br; 99b; 102tc; 102bl; 104cla; 105tl; 105cr; 105br; 122cl; 123cr; 128tr; 129cra; 129crb; 130clb; 138cr; 143cra; 143bl; 166b; 189b; 208cla; 248b; 251tr; 267c; Vladimir Alexeev 110tr, 110tl; Jivko Aratov 20-1, 25bl; Rosen Dimitrov 20cb, 20br, 21crb, 21br, 25ca, 48bl; Renard Dudlei 21tr; Mihail Mihailov 108tr; Angel Nenov 111br; Yavor Popov 20tl, 25br, 40c; Dimo Rogev 21cra, 41b, 49br; Nikolai V. Vassilev 20tr.

BANSKO 21 CENTURY FOUNDATION: 35br.
BGIMAGES.ORG: 13br, 59c.
BORINA PUBLISHING HOUSE: 175cla, 175cra, 175crb.
THE BRIDGEMAN ART LIBRARY: K. Savitsky Art Museum, Penzia Russia *The Defence of the Eagle Aerie on the Shipka in 1887* (1893) Andrei Nikolaevich Popev 49bl.
BULGARIA PHOTOS NET/ET HS-CORP: Elena Haytova 37tr, 131tr, 134c.
BULGARIANWINES.COM: Festa Wines 28tr, 29br.

CEPHAS PICTURE LIBRARY: Mick Rock 28br, 29tr.
ILIYA CHERNEV: 127tr.
CORBIS: Paul Almasy 23cra; Bettmann 51tr, 51bl; 52clb, 52bc, 67bl, 115br; Darrell Gulin 213tr; Hulton-Deutsch Collection 47br, 50crb, 50br; Yevgeny Khaldei 51fbr; NATO/CNP 53crb; Jose F. Poblete 49tl; RF/Comstock Select 67t; Sygma/Anderson Thorne 53bc; Adam Woolfitt 35tl; zefa/Stefan Schuetz 31br.

EUROPEAN HERITAGE WINES: 29bc.

GETTY IMAGES: AFP/Dimitar Dilkoff 18tr; AFP/Tcvetan Tomchev 15c.
GRAND HOTEL SOFIA: 216cr.
G.E.P. CHROSZCZ: 150tl.
GULIVER PHOTOS LTD: 27cla.

HEMISPHERES IMAGES: Bertrand Gardel 24tr; Christian Guy 10cl, 14, 16bl, 17bl, 22bl, 214-5.
STOYAN HRISTOV: 150cla.

IMAGESFROMBULGARIA.COM: 75bl.

YASSEN JEKOFF: 213tl.
JUPITER IMAGES: Chris Sanders 24cra.

LITOV'S HOUSE: 117bl.
LONELY PLANET IMAGES: Paul Greenway 25tr.

PETER MACHKOVSKI: 150b, 151tl.
MARTIN MITOV: 118cra.
MARY EVANS PICTURE LIBRARY: 8-9, 9c, 50tl, 52tr, 55c, 128bl, 215c, 255c.
NANKO MINKOV: 150tr, 151cl, 151b.

NOVINITE LTD: 34br, 36tr, 67br, 90bl, 260tr, 261br, 272cl.

PESHEV.ORG: from "The Man who Stopped Hitler" By Gabriele Nissim 67cr.
PETER PETROV: 34tc, 183cla, 183bl, 230cl.
PHOTOLIBRARY: 2-3; Anthony Blake Photo Libarary 29tl.
PHOTOSHOT/NHPA: Jordi Bass Casas 27c.
PHOTOSHOT WORLD PICTURES: 27cl.

REUTERS: Stoyan Nenov 22br.
SOFIA PHOTO AGENCY 34br, 36tr, 67br, 90bl, 260tr, 261br, 272cl.
SOFIA SYNAGOGUE: 67cl.
SLAVEYKOV MUSEUM: 82cr.
STANDART NEWS: 143br.
SUPERSTOCK: Wojtek Buss 23crb.

ZAGREUS WINERY: 29crb.

JACKET: Front – DK IMAGES: Dorota Jarymowicz clb; PHOTOLIBRARY: Rosine Mazin main image. Back – 4CORNERS IMAGES: SIME/Schmid Reinhard clb; DK IMAGES: Dorota Jarymowiczowie tl, cla; Piotr Ostrowski & Mirek Osip bl; Spine – DK IMAGES: Piotr Ostrowski & Mirek Osip b; PHOTOLIBRARY: Rosine Mazin t.
All other images © Dorling Kindersley.
For further information see: www.dkimages.com

SPECIAL EDITIONS OF DK TRAVEL GUIDES

DK Travel Guides can be purchased in bulk quantities at discounted prices for use in promotions or as premiums. We are also able to offer special editions and personalized jackets, corporate imprints, and excerpts from all of our books, tailored specifically to meet your own needs.

To find out more, please contact:
(in the United States) **SpecialSales@dk.com**
(in the UK) **Sarah.Burgess@dk.com**
(in Canada) DK Special Sales at **general@tourmaline.ca**
(in Australia) **business.development@pearson.com.au**

Phrase Book

In the Phrase Book, the English is given in the left-hand column, with the Bulgarian in the middle column. The right-hand column provides a transliteration. The exception is in the Menu Decoder section, where the Bulgarian is given in the left-hand column and the English translation in the right-hand column, for ease of use. Because of the existence of genders in Bulgarian, in a few cases both masculine and feminine forms of a phrase are given. The Phrase Book gives a phonetic guide to the pronunciation of words and phrases used in everyday situations, such as when eating out or shopping.

GUIDELINES FOR PRONUNCIATION

The Bulgarian Cyrillic alphabet has 30 letters. The right-hand column of the alphabet, below, demonstrates how Cyrillic letters are pronounced by comparing them to sounds in English words. However, some letters vary in how they are pronounced according to their position in a word. Several consonants have no equivalent in English.

THE CYRILLIC ALPHABET

А а	a	alimony
Б б	b	bed
В в	v	vet
Г г	g	get
Д д	d	debt
Е е	e	egg
Ж ж	zh	leisure (but a little harder)
З з	z	zither
И и	i	see
Й й	y	boy (see note 1)
К к	k	king
Л л	l	loot
М м	m	match
Н н	n	never
О о	o	rob
П п	p	pea
Р р	r	rat (rolling, as in Italian)
С с	s	stop
Т т	t	toffee
У у	u	boot
Ф ф	f	fellow
Х х	h	hello
Ц ц	ts	lets
Ч ч	ch	chair
Ш ш	sh	shove
Щ щ	sht	smashed (with a slight roll)
Ъ ъ	a or u	(see note 2)
ь		soft sign (no sound, but see note 3)
Ю ю	yu	youth
Я я	ya	yak

Notes

1) Й This letter has no distinct sound of its own. It usually softens the preceding vowel.
2) Ъ It is pronounced like a in across or u in cut.
3) The soft sign (ь, marked in the pronunciation guide as ') softens the preceding consonant and adds a slight y sound: for instance, n' would sound like ny in 'canyon'.

In Emergency

Help!	Помощ!	Pomosht!
Stop!	Спрете!	Sprete!
Look out!	Внимавайте!	Vnimavayte!
Call a doctor	Извикайте лекар	Izvikayte lekar!
Call an ambulance!	Извикайте	Izvikayte lineyka!
	линейка!	
Call the police!	Обадете се	Obadete se
	на полицията!	na politziyata!
Call the	Извикайте	Izvikayte fire
department!	пожарната!	pozharnata!
Where is the	Къде е най-близкият	Kade e nay
nearest telephone?	телефон?	blizkiyat telefon?
Where is the	Къде е най-близката	Kade e nay
nearest hospital?	болница?	blizkata bolnitza?

Communications Essentials

Yes/No	Да/Не	Da/Ne
Please (offering)	Заповядайте	Zapovyadayte
Please (asking)	Моля	Molya
Thank you	Благодаря	Blagodarya
No, thank you	Не, благодаря	Ne, blagodarya
Excuse me, please	Извинете	Izvinete
Hello	Здравейте	Zdraveyte
Good morning	Добро утро	Dobro utro
Good day/hello	Добър ден	Dobar den
(useful general greeting when meeting anyone)		
Good night	Лека нощ	Leka nosht
Goodbye	Довиждане	Dovizhdane
morning	утро	utro
afternoon	следобед	sledobed
evening	вечер	vecher
yesterday	вчера	vchera
today	днес	dnes
tomorrow	утре	utre
here	тук	tuk
there	там	tam
What?	Какво?	Kakvo?
When?	Кога?	Koga?
Why?	Защо?	Zashto?
Where?	Къде?	Kade?

Useful Phrases

How are you?	Как сте?	Kak ste?
Very well, thank you (only I am very well)	Благодаря, добре съм	Blagodarya, dobre sam
Pleased to meet you	Приятно ми е	Priyatno mi e
See you soon!	До скоро	Do skoro
Excellent!	Чудесно!	Chudesno!
Is there ... here?	Има ли ... тук?	Ima li ... tuk?
Where can I get ...?	Къде мога да намеря ...?	Kade moga da namerya...?
How do you get to?	Как се стига до ...?	Kak se stiga do...?
How far is ...?	Колко далеч е ...?	Kolko dalech e...?
Do you speak English?	Говорите ли английски,	Govorite li angliski
I can't speak Bulgarian	Не говоря български	Ne govorya balgarski
I don't understand	Не разбирам	Ne razbiram
Can you help me? (Could you help me?)	Бихте ли ми помогнали?	Bihte li mi pomognali?
Please speak slowly	Моля, говорете бавно	Molya, govorete bavno
Sorry!	Извинете!	Izvinete!
Do you have...?	Имате ли ...?	Imate li ...?

Useful Words

big	голям	golyam
small	малък	malak
hot	горещ	goresht
cold	студен	studen
good	добър	dobar
bad	лош	losh
enough	достатъчно	dostatachno
well	добре	dobre
open	отворен	otvoren
closed	затворен	zatvoren
left	ляво	lyavo
right	дясно	dyasno
straight on	направо	napravo
near	близо	blizo
far	далеч	dalech
up	горе	gore
down	долу	dolu
early	рано	rano
late	късно	kasno
entrance	вход	chod
exit	изход	iz-hod
toilet WC	тоалетна	toaletna
free/unoccupied	свободна	svobodna
free/no charge	безплатна	bezplatna

Making a Telephone Call

Can I call abroad from here?	Мога ли да се обадя в чужбина от тук?	Moga li da se obadya v chuzhbina ot tuk?
I would like to call collect	Искам да се обадя за сметка на търсения абонат	Iskam da se obadya za smetka na tarseniya abonat
Local call	градски разговор	gradski razgovor
I'll ring back later	Ще се обадя отново по-късно	Shte se obadya otnovo po kasno
Could I leave a message for him/her?	Бихте ли му/й предали ..?	Bichte li mu/i predali ...
Hold on!	Не затваряйте!	Ne zatvaryayte!
Could you speak up a little, please?	Моля, бихте ли говорили по-високо?	Molya bihte li goborili po visoko?

Shopping

How much is this?	Колко струва това?	Kolko struva tova?
I would like ...	Бих искал/ искала	Bih iskal (for a man)/ iskala (for a woman)
Do you have ...?	Имате ли ...?	Imate li ...?
I'm just looking	Само гледам	Samo gledam
Do you take credit cards?	Мога ли до платя с кредитна карта?	Moga li da platya s kreditna karta?
What time do you open?	В колко часа отваряте?	V kolko chasa otvaryate?
What time do you close?	В колко часа затваряте?	V kolko chasa zatvaryate?
this one	този	tozi
that one	онзи	onzi
expensive	скъп	skup
cheap	евтин	evtin
size	размер	razmer
white	бял	byal
black	черен	cheren
red	червен	cherven
yellow	жълт	zhalt
green	зелен	zelen
blue	син	sin
brown	кафяв	kafyav

Types of Shop

antique dealer	антикварен магазин	antikvaren magazin
baker's	хлебарница	hlebarnitza
bank	банка	banka
bar	бар	bar
bookshop	книжарница	knizharnitza
café	кафене	kafene
cake shop	сладкарница	sladkarnitza
chemist	аптека	apteka
department store	универсален магазин	universalen magazin
florist	цветарски магазин	tzvetarski magazin
greengrocer	плод-зеленчук	plod zelenchuk
market	пазар	pazar
newspapers kiosk (and magazines)	будка за вестници (и списания)	budka za vestnitzi (i spisaniya)
post office	поща	poshta
shoe shop	магазин за обувки	magazin za obuvki
souvenir shop	магазин за сувенири	magazin za suveniri
supermarket	супермаркет	supermarket
travel agent	пътническа агенция	patnicheska aghentziya

Staying in a Hotel

Have you any vacancies?	Имате ли свободни стаи?	Imate li svobodni stai?
Double room with double bed	двойна стая с двойно легло	dvoyna staya s dvoyno leglo
twin room	двойна стая с две легла	dvoyna staya s dve legla
single room	единична стая	edinichna staya
non-smoking	за непушачи	za nepushachi
room with a bath/shower	стая с вана/душ	staya s vana/dush
porter	портиер-пиколо	portier pikolo
key	ключ	klyuch
I have a reservation	Имам резервация	Imam rezervatziya

Sightseeing

Bus	автобус	avtobus
Tram	трамвай	tramvye
trolley bus	тролейбус	troleybus
train	влак	vlak
underground	метро	metro
bus stop	автобусна спирка	avtobusna spirka
tram stop	трамвайна спирка	tramviner spirka
art gallery	картинна галерия	kartinna galeria
palace	дворец	dvoretz
cathedral	катедрала	katedrala
church	църква	tzarkva
monastery	манастир	manastir
garden	градина	gradina
library	библиотека	biblioteka
museum	музей	muzey
tourist information	туристическа информация	turisticheska informatziya
closed for public holiday	затварено поради официален празник	zatvoreno poradi ofitzialen praznik

Eating Out

A table for ... please	Моля, маса за ...	Molya masa za ...
I want to reserve a table	Искам да резервирам маса	Iskam da rezerviram masa
The bill, please	Моля, сметката	Molya smetkata
I am a vegetarian	Аз съм вегетарианец/ вегетарианка	Az sam veghetarianetz/ veghetarianka
I'd like ...	Искам ...	Iskam ...
waiter/waitress	сервитьор/ сервитьорка	servityor/ servityorka
menu	меню	menyu
wine list	селекция от вина	selektziya ot vina
chef's special	специалитет на готвача	spetzialitet na gotvacha
tip	бакшиш	bakshish
glass	чаша	chasha
bottle	бутилка	butilka

knife	нож	nozh
fork	вилица	vilitza
spoon	лъжица	lazhitza
breakfast	закуска	zakuska
barbecue	барбекю	barbekyu
lunch	обяд	obyad
dinner	вечеря	vecherya
main courses	основни ястия	osnovni yastiya
starters	предястия,	predyastiya,
	ордьоври	ordyovri
vegetables	зеленчуци	zelenchutzi
desserts	десерти	desserti
rare	алангле	alangle
well done	добре опечен	dobre opechen

Menu Decoder

apple	ябълка	yabalka
mineral water	минерална вода	mineralna voda
beans	фасул/боб	fasul/bob
banana	банан	banan
cherries	череши	chereshi
lamb	агнешко	agneshko
peppers	чушки	chushki
chicken	пилешко	pileshko
chocolate	шоколад	shokolad
sugar	захар	zahar
vinegar	оцет	otzet
ice cream	сладолед	sladoled
white wine	бяло вино	byalo vino
garlic	чесън	chessan
boiled	варен	varen
mushrooms	гъби	gabi
goulash	гулаш	gulash
fruit	плодове	plodove
fruit juice	плодов сок	plodov sok
onions	лук	luk
fish	риба	riba
meat	месо	meso
coffee	кафе	kafe
bread	хляб	hlyab
potatoes	картофи	kartofi
sausage	наденица	nadenitza
bacon	бекон	bekon
soup	супа	supa
liver	дроб	drob
beef	телешко	teleshko
mustard	горчица	gorchitza
orange	портокал	portokal
oil	олио	olio
tomatoes	домати	domati
steamed	задушен на пара	zadushen na para
pie	пай	pay
(in Bulgarian this refers to sweet pies only)		
pork	свинско	svinsko
fried in batter	паниран	paniran
rice	ориз	oriz
steak	бифтек	biftek
grilled	на скара	na skara
cheese	кашкавал	kashkaval
feta/white cheese	сирене	sirene
salad	салата	salata
salt	сол	sol
ham	шунка	shunka
beer	бира	bira
fried/roasted	пържен/печен	parzhen/pechen
fried potatoes/chips	пържени картофи	parzheni kartofi
cake, pastry	торта/паста	torta/pasta
sandwich	сандвич	sandvich

sauce	сос	sos
tea	чай	chai
milk	мляко	mlyako
cream	сметана	smetana
seafood	ястия от риба,	yastiya ot riba
	раци, миди	ratzi midi
egg	яйце	yaytze
stuffed	пълнен	palnen
red wine	червено вино	cherveno vino
roll	кифла	kifla
dumplings	кнедли	knedli
watermelon	диня	dinya
melon	пъпеш	papesh
meatballs	кюфтета	kyufteta

Numbers

0	нула	nula
1	едно	edno
2	две	dve
3	три	tri
4	четири	chetiri
5	пет	pet
6	шест	shest
7	седем	sedem
8	осем	osem
9	девет	devet
10	десет	deset
11	единадесет	edinayset
12	дванадесет	dvanayset
13	тринадесет	trinayset
14	четиринадесет	chetirinayset
15	петнадесет	petnayset
16	шестнадесет	shestnayset
17	седемнадесет	sedemnayset
18	осемнадесет	osemnayset
19	деветнадесет	devetnayset
20	двадесет	dvayset
21	двадесет и едно	dvayset i edno
22	двадесет и две	dvayset i dve
30	тридесет	triyset
31	тридесет и едно	triyset i edno
32	тридесет и две	triyset i dve
40	четиридесет	chetirset
50	петдесет	petdeset
60	шестдесет	shestdeset
70	седемдесет	sedemdeset
80	осемдесет	osemdeset
90	деветдесет	devetdeset
100	сто	sto
110	сто и десет	sto i deset
200	двеста	dvesta
300	триста	trista
1000	хиляда	hilyada
10,000	десет хиляди	deset hilyadi
1,000,000	един милион	edin milion

Time

one minute	една минута	edna minuta
hour	час	chas
half an hour	половин час	polovin chas
Sunday	неделя	nedelya
Monday	понеделник	ponedelnik
Tuesday	вторник	vtornik
Wednesday	сряда	sryada
Thursday	четвъртък	chetvartak
Friday	петък	petak
Saturday	събота	sabota